RULES FOR CATEGORICAL SYLLOGISMS

Rule 1: *The middle term must be distributed at least once.*
Fallacy: Undistributed middle.

Rule 2: *If a term is distributed in the conclusion, then it must be distributed in the premise.*
Fallacy: Illicit major; illicit minor.

Rule 3: *Two negative premises are not allowed.*
Fallacy: Exclusive premises.

Rule 4: *One negative premise is allowed if and only if the conclusion is negative.*
Fallacy: Drawing an affirmative conclusion from a negative premise; drawing a negative conclusion from affirmative premises.

Rule 5: *If both premises are universal, the conclusion cannot be particular.*
Fallacy: Existential fallacy.

(NOTE: If only Rule 5 is broken, the syllogism is conditionally valid, that is, valid on the assumption that certain terms denote actually existing things.)

TRUTH TABLES FOR THE PROPOSITIONAL CONNECTIVES

$\sim p$		$p \cdot q$			$p \vee q$			$p \supset q$			$p \equiv q$		
F	T	T	T	T	T	T	T	T	T	T	T	T	T
T	F	T	F	F	T	T	F	T	F	F	T	F	F
		F	F	T	F	T	T	F	T	T	F	F	T
		F	F	F	F	F	F	F	T	F	F	T	F

RULES FOR THE PROBABILITY CALCULUS

1. $P(A \text{ or not } A) = 1$
2. $P(A \text{ and not } A) = 0$
3. $P(A \text{ and } B) = P(A) \times P(B)$ (when A and B are independent)
4. $P(A \text{ and } B) = P(A) \times P(B \text{ given } A)$
5. $P(A \text{ or } B) = P(A) + P(B)$ (when A and B are mutually exclusive)
6. $P(A \text{ or } B) = P(A) + P(B) - P(A \text{ and } B)$
7. $P(A) = 1 - P(\text{not } A)$

A CONCISE INTRODUCTION TO LOGIC

PATRICK J. HURLEY
University of San Diego

Wadsworth Publishing Company
Belmont, California

A division of Wadsworth, Inc.

To: MARY
HEIDI
JOHN
STEPHEN
MAGGIE
EMERY

Philosophy Editor: Kenneth King
Signing Representative: Aline Faben
Production: Del Mar Associates
Designer: Richard Carter
Copy Editor: Jackie Estrada
Cover Designer: Adriane Bosworth
Compositor: Computer Typesetting Services, Inc.

Printed in the United States of America

1 2 3 4 5 6 7 8 9 10—86 85 84 83 82

Library of Congress Cataloging in Publication Data

Hurley, Patrick J., 1942–
    A concise introduction to logic.

    Includes index.
    1. Logic.   I. Title.
BC108.H83   160   81-21938
ISBN 0-534-01120-9   AACR2

PREFACE

One of the aims of studying logic is to develop the skills needed to construct sound arguments of one's own and to evaluate the arguments of others. Additional aims include the cultivation of habits of correct reasoning and the development of a sensitivity for the clear and accurate use of language. Accomplishing these objectives requires that the student thoroughly understand the central concepts of the subject and be able to apply them in actual situations. To facilitate achievement of these goals, this text clearly and simply presents the central concepts of logic. Examples are used extensively, and key terms are introduced in boldface type and defined in the Glossary/Index. Furthermore, to insure that the student acquires sufficient practice in applying the basic principles, the text includes over 1600 exercise problems and questions selected to illustrate the main points and guard against the most typical mistakes. Answers to selected exercises are given in the back of the book.

Ways of Using the Text

Depending on the instructor's individual preferences, this text can be approached in many different ways. The most straightforward approach, of course, is simply to begin with Chapter 1 and continue through, covering as much material as the time allows. In the course of a semester, the first six or seven chapters can be covered in this way. Many instructors may want to skip Chapter 2, however. Doing so will pose no problems in treating subsequent chapters and will allow a more extensive coverage of the more formal topics later on.

For those who wish to place special emphasis on modern formal logic, Chapters 6 and 7 (propositional logic) can be taken up immediately after Chapter 1. Before proceeding to predicate logic in Chapter 8, however, some of the topics in Chapter 4 (categorical propositions) should be covered: specifically, the material dealing with quantifiers, subject and predicate terms, the modern square of opposition, Venn diagrams for propositions, and translation techniques. Covering these topics will insure an intuitive foundation for the symbolic techniques in Chapter 8.

For those who wish a brief treatment of informal fallacies, the last section of Chapter 3 can be skipped. The first three sections of this chapter provide a standard treatment of this material. On the other hand, those who wish a more extensive treatment of informal fallacies than that offered in Chapter 3 can proceed directly to Section 9.3 (statistical reasoning), which can be regarded as a natural extension of the material in Chapter 3. Of course, Chapter 3, like Chapter 2, can be skipped altogether or returned to after a treatment of the more formal topics.

In general, the material in each chapter is arranged so that certain later sections can be skipped without affecting subsequent chapters. For example, those wishing a brief treatment of natural deduction in both propositional and predicate logic may want to skip the last three sections of Chapter 7 and the last three (or even four) sections of Chapter 8. In Chapter 8 the material essential to the topic is presented in the first two sections. The more complex procedures involved in translating relational predicates and overlapping quantifiers are put off until the end, and the restrictions on universal generalization needed for conditional proof and overlapping quantifiers are developed only as needed.

Analogously, in Chapter 5 the material essential to categorical syllogisms is handled in the first two sections, and any or all of the later sections can be skipped if so desired. Those wishing to treat Chapters 7 and 8 will certainly want to cover most of Chapter 6, but the portion of Section 6.4 dealing with the refutation of dilemmas can easily be skipped, as can the section dealing with indirect truth tables (assuming one also skips Section 8.5). The material in the four sections of Chapter 9 (induction) depends only slightly on earlier chapters, so these sections can be treated in any order one chooses.

Acknowledgments

Most of the manuscript was typed by Ann Field, secretary in the College of Arts and Sciences at USD. Without her dedication to the project, the book would have taken months longer to finish. Others who helped with the typing, and to whom I am also indebted, are Susan von Niederhäusern, Peter J. Bailey, and Monica Wagner. I also want to thank Robert Corbeil, professor of biology at USD, who generously lent the services of his word processor.

My first contact with Wadsworth Publishing Company was through Aline Faben. Her enthusiasm for the book is what prompted me to send Wadsworth the manuscript. Ken King, philosophy editor at Wadsworth, saw the book through to its completion, and for his constant attention and support I am most grateful. It has been a pleasure working with Jackie Estrada, the copy editor; and the frequent phone calls to Nancy Sjöberg, the production supervisor, have been a delight.

I want to thank Donald Cress, Northern Illinois University, DeKalb; George Gale, University of Missouri, Kansas City; Paul Roth, University of Missouri, Saint Louis; and Robert Burch, Texas A & M University, for their extensive comments. Thanks for reviews of the book also go to John R. Bosworth, Oklahoma State University; William F. Cooper, Baylor University; Evan Fales, University of Iowa; Glen Kessler, University of Virginia; John Mize, Long Beach City College; Larry D. Mayhew, Western Kentucky University; R. Puligandla, University of Toledo; Daniel Rothbart, George Mason University; Lynne Spellman, University of Arkansas; and John Sweigart, James Madison University. Any errors or oversights that may remain after their input are my own doing. In addition, Robert Burch has produced a fine study guide to accompany this text, and I am confident many students will find it useful as a supplementary source of exercises and a review for examinations.

Finally, I am indebted to the University of San Diego for providing sabbatical released time and grant funds to help cover typing costs. In addition, I want to thank the many students who have offered constructive criticism and provided examples for some of the exercises.

CONTENTS

1
BASIC CONCEPTS

1.1 ARGUMENTS, PREMISES, AND CONCLUSIONS

Logic may be defined as the science that evaluates arguments. All of us encounter arguments in our day-to-day experience. We read them in books and newspapers, hear them on television, and formulate them when communicating with friends and associates. The aim of logic is to develop a system of methods and principles that we may use as criteria for evaluating the arguments of others and as guides in constructing arguments of our own. Among the benefits to be expected from the study of logic is an increase in confidence that we are making sense when we criticize the arguments of others and when we advance arguments of our own.

Argument, as it is used in logic, means a group of statements, one of which (the conclusion) is intended to follow from the other or others (the premises). All arguments may be placed in one of two basic groups: those in which the conclusion really does follow from the premises, and those in which it does not, even though it is intended to. The former are said to be good arguments, the latter bad arguments. The purpose of logic, as the science that evaluates arguments, is thus to develop methods and techniques that allow us to distinguish good arguments from bad.

As is apparent from the above definition, the term "argument" has a very specific meaning in logic. It does not mean, for example, a mere verbal fight, as one might have with one's parent, spouse, or friend. Let us examine the features of this definition in greater detail. First of all, an argument is a group of statements. A **statement** is a sentence that is either true or false; in other words, typically a declarative sentence. The following sentences are statements:

> Hydrogen is combustible.
> World War II began in 1939.
> Some ducks are fish.
> Abraham Lincoln was assassinated.

Many sentences, of course, cannot be said to be either true or false. Questions, proposals, suggestions, commands, and exclamations usually cannot, and so are not usually classified as statements. The following sentences are not statements:

> What is the atomic weight of carbon? (question)
> Let's go to the park today. (proposal)
> We suggest that you travel by bus. (suggestion)
> Turn to the left at the next corner. (command)
> Right on! (exclamation)

The statements that make up an argument are divided into one or more premises and one and only one conclusion. The **premises** are the statements that set forth the evidence, and the **conclusion** is the statement that is intended to follow from the evidence. Here is an example of an argument:

> All cats are animals.
> Felix is a cat.
> Therefore, Felix is an animal.

The first two statements are the premises; the third is the conclusion. In this argument the conclusion really does follow from the premises, and so the argument is a good one. But consider this argument:

> Some cats are white Persians.
> Felix is a cat.
> Therefore, Felix is a white Persian.

In this argument the conclusion does not in fact follow from the premises, even though it appears that it is intended to, and so the argument is not a good one.

One of the most important tasks in the analysis of arguments is being able to distinguish premises from conclusion. If what is thought to be a conclusion is really a premise, and vice versa, the subsequent analysis cannot possibly be correct. Frequently, arguments contain certain indi-

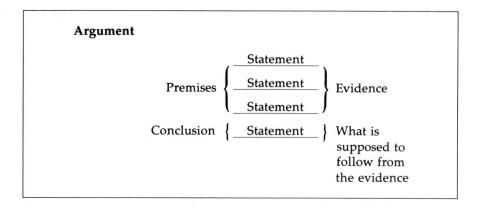

Argument

Premises { Statement / Statement / Statement } Evidence

Conclusion { Statement } What is supposed to follow from the evidence

cator words that provide clues in identifying premises and conclusion. Some typical **conclusion indicators** are:

therefore	hence	whence
wherefore	thus	so
accordingly	consequently	it follows that
we may conclude	we may infer	implies that
entails that	it must be that	

Whenever a statement follows one of these indicators, it can usually be identified as the conclusion. By process of elimination the other statements in the argument are the premises. Example:

This pen is out of ink. Consequently, it will not write.

The conclusion of this argument is "It will not write," and the premise is "This pen is out of ink."

If an argument does not contain a conclusion indicator, it may contain a premise indicator. Some typical **premise indicators** are:

since	in that	seeing that
as indicated by	may be inferred from	for the reason that
because	as	inasmuch as
for		

Any statement following one of these indicators can usually be identified as a premise. Example:

This locket is worth a lot of money, since it is made of platinum.

The premise of this argument is "It is made of platinum," and the conclusion is "This locket is worth a lot of money."

One premise indicator not included in the above list is "for this reason." This indicator is special in that it comes immediately *after* the premise that it indicates. "For this reason" means for the reason (premise) that was just given. In other words, the premise is the statement that occurs immediately *before* "for this reason." One should be careful not to confuse "for this reason" with "for the reason that."

Sometimes a single indicator can be used to identify more than one premise. Consider the following argument:

Jenkins is taller than Smith, for Jenkins is taller than
Williams, and Williams is taller than Smith.

The premise indicator "for" goes with both "Jenkins is taller than Williams" and "Williams is taller than Smith"; so these are the premises. By process of elimination, "Jenkins is taller than Smith" is the conclusion.

Sometimes an argument contains no indicators. When this occurs, the reader/listener must ask himself or herself such questions as: What is the arguer leading up to? What is he or she trying to prove? What seems to be the main point of the passage? What does the arguer want us to believe? The answers to these questions should point to the conclusion. Example:

The space program deserves increased expenditures in the
years ahead. Not only does the national defense depend upon
it, but the program will more than pay for itself in terms of
technological spinoffs. Furthermore, at current funding levels
the program cannot fulfill its anticipated potential.

The main point of this argument is that the space program deserves increased expenditures in the years ahead. All the other statements provide support for this statement. Accordingly, the argument is analyzed as follows:

P_1: The national defense is dependent upon the space program.

P_2: The space program will more than pay for itself in terms of technological spinoffs.

P_3: At current funding levels the space program cannot fulfill its anticipated potential.

C: The space program deserves increased expenditures in the years ahead.

When restructuring arguments such as this, one should remain as close as possible to the original version, while at the same time attending to the requirement that premises and conclusion be complete sentences that are meaningful in the order in which they are listed.

Passages that contain arguments sometimes contain statements that are neither premises nor conclusion. Only statements that are actually intended to support the conclusion should be included in the list of premises. If a statement is irrelevant to the conclusion or, for example, simply makes a passing comment, it should not be included within the context of the argument. Example:

> Socialized medicine is not recommended because it would result in a reduction in the overall quality of medical care available to the average citizen. In addition, it might very well bankrupt the federal treasury. This is the whole case against socialized medicine in a nutshell.

The conclusion of this argument is "Socialized medicine is not recommended," and the two statements following the word "because" are the premises. The last statement makes only a passing comment about the argument itself and is therefore neither a premise nor a conclusion.

The reasoning process that lies behind an argument is called an **inference.** In other words, an inference is what goes on in someone's mind when he or she constructs an argument. Because inferences are mental processes, they are both private and nonlinguistic and are therefore incapable of being directly analyzed by logical principles. They may, however, be indirectly analyzed via the arguments in terms of which they are expressed. As we will see in the next section, inferences may be expressed not only through arguments but through conditional statements and explanations as well. For the purposes of testing, however, many such inferences may be reexpressed in the form of arguments.

That which is expressed by a statement is called a **proposition.** In other words, a proposition is the information content of a statement. Because information may be expressed in many different ways, it follows that one and the same proposition may be expressed by different statements. Furthermore, because the information content of a single statement may shift depending on the time and the place in which it is asserted, one and the same statement may express different propositions. The following statements all express the same proposition:

> The sculptor carves the statue.
> The statue is carved by the sculptor.
> Der Bildhauer meisselt die statue.
> Le sculpteur grave le statue.

Conversely, each of the following statements expresses a different proposition, depending on the time and the place in which it is asserted:

The headwaters of this river are in Switzerland.
Tomorrow is the middle of the week.

The first of these statements could express a proposition about the Rhine, Volga, Mississippi, or any other river, depending on the place in which it is asserted, and the second could express a proposition about any one of the days of the week, depending on the time it is asserted.

As these examples illustrate, a legitimate distinction exists between the meanings of "proposition" and "statement." In practice, however, this distinction is frequently ignored and the two terms are used interchangeably. The reason why the distinction is maintained in theory is to provide for the successful analysis of certain types of arguments. Consider the following:

> If Thomas is discovered, he will be arrested. Thomas will be discovered. Therefore, he will be arrested.

This is a good argument; the conclusion follows from the premises. But if it is analyzed exclusively in terms of its component *statements*, there is no way of proving that the conclusion follows from the premises. Because "Thomas is discovered" and "Thomas will be discovered" are not literally the same statement, the two premises cannot be connected together; but if this cannot be done, the conclusion cannot be derived. Since these statements do, however (at least within the context of the argument), express the same *proposition*, if the analysis is conducted in terms of propositions it may readily be established that the conclusion follows logically from the premises.

EXERCISE 1.1

I. Each of the following passages contains a single argument. Using the letters "P" and "C," identify the premises and conclusion of each argument, writing premises first and conclusion last. List the premises in the order in which they make the most sense, and write both premises and conclusion in the form of single declarative sentences. Indicator words may be eliminated once premises and conclusion have been appropriately labeled. The exercises marked with a star are answered in the back of the text.

★1. Catherine most likely will not be going to the concert tonight because her car has a dead battery and she has no other means of transportation.

2. This wine tastes sweet, so it can't be Cabernet.

3. The California condor is threatened with extinction inasmuch as the condor population has been decreasing yearly and fewer than fifty birds are alive at this time.

4. Chicago is either in Illinois or Wisconsin. But it's not in Wisconsin. It follows that Chicago is in Illinois.

★5. No incompetent businessmen are corporate officers. Hence, no shareholders are corporate officers since all shareholders are incompetent businessmen.

6. Since the fire broke out in the bank at 1:36 A.M., and at that time the electricity was shut off in the building, we may conclude that the fire was not caused by an electrical malfunction.

7. Philosophy is a good subject to study, for it constitutes the intellectual foundation of Western civilization.

8. The most serious threat facing the modern world is nuclear war. A nuclear confrontation between the superpowers might eliminate civilization altogether, and the likelihood of such a confrontation is ever increasing as more nations join the nuclear club. Anyone at all familiar with international politics will accept this argument without question.

9. Since the good, according to Plato, is that which furthers a person's real interests, it follows that in any given case when the good is known, men will seek it.
(Avrum Stroll and Richard Popkin, *Philosophy and the Human Spirit*)

★10. Punishment, when speedy and specific, may suppress undesirable behavior, but it cannot teach or encourage desirable alternatives. Therefore, it is crucial to use positive techniques to model and reinforce appropriate behavior that the person can use in place of the unacceptable response that has to be suppressed.
(Walter Mischel and Harriet Mischel, *Essentials of Psychology*)

11. Since the drive for profits underlies the very existence of business organizations, it follows that a most important function of an accounting system is to provide information about the profitability of a business.
(Walter B. Meigs and Robert F. Meigs, *Accounting*)

12. Since private property helps people define themselves, since it frees people from mundane cares of daily subsistence, and since it is finite, no individual should accumulate so much property that others are prevented from accumulating the necessities of life.
(Leon P. Baradat, *Political Ideologies, Their Origins and Impact*)

13. To every existing thing God wills some good. Hence, since to love any thing is nothing else than to will good to that thing, it is manifest that God loves everything that exists.
(Thomas Aquinas, *Summa Theologica*)

14. Women of the working class, especially wage workers, should not have more than two children at most. The average working man can support no more and the average working woman can take care of no more in decent fashion.

(Margaret Sanger, *Family Limitations*)

★15. Every art and every inquiry, and similarly every action and pursuit, is thought to aim at some good; and for this reason the good has rightly been declared to be that at which all things aim.

(Aristotle, *Nicomachean Ethics*)

16. Poverty offers numerous benefits to the nonpoor. Antipoverty programs provide jobs for middle-class professionals in social work, penology and public health. Such workers' future advancement is tied to the continued growth of bureaucracies dependent on the existence of poverty.

(J. John Palen, *Social Problems*)

17. Corn is an annual crop. Butcher's meat, a crop which requires four or five years to grow. As an acre of land, therefore, will produce a much smaller quantity of the one species of food than the other, the inferiority of the quantity must be compensated by the superiority of the price.

(Adam Smith, *The Wealth of Nations*)

18. Neither a borrower nor lender be
For loan oft loses both itself and friend,
And borrowing dulls the edge of husbandry.

(William Shakespeare, *Hamlet* I, 3)

19. All over the world the close of the sixteenth century saw monarchy prevailing and tending towards absolutism. Germany and Italy were patchworks of autocratic princely dominions, Spain was practically autocratic, the throne had never been so powerful in England, and as the seventeenth century drew on, the French monarchy gradually became the grandest and most consolidated power in Europe.

(H. G. Wells, *The Outline of History*)

★20. As the denial or perversion of justice by the sentences of courts, as well as in any other manner, is with reason classed among the just causes of war, it will follow that the federal judiciary ought to have cognizance of all causes in which the citizens of other countries are concerned.

(Alexander Hamilton, *Federalist Papers*, No. 80)

21. The more modern nations detest each other the more meekly they follow each other; for all competition is in its nature only a furious plagiarism.

(G. K. Chesterton, *Charles Dickens*)

22. The proliferation of subcults is most evident in the world of work. Many subcults spring up around occupational specialties. Thus, as the society moves towards greater specialization, it generates more and more subcultural variety.

(Alvin Toffler, *Future Shock*)

23. Since the secondary light [from the moon] does not inherently belong to the moon, and is not received from any star or from the sun, and since in the whole universe there is no other body left but the earth, what must we conclude? What is to be proposed? Surely we must assert that the lunar body (or any other dark and sunless orb) is illuminated by the earth.

(Galileo Galilei, *The Starry Messenger*)

24. How do education and training affect lifetime income? Are they worth their cost? The evidence answers, decidedly yes. Men who never finish eight grades of school earn scarcely $3,800 annually; college graduates do three times as well. Unemployment among school dropouts exceeds that of graduates by a growing margin.

(Paul Samuelson, *Economics*, 7th edition)

★25. To the owner of a commodity, every other commodity is, in regard to his own, a particular equivalent, and consequently his own commodity is the universal equivalent for all the others.

(Karl Marx, *Capital*)

II. Define the following terms:

logic	conclusion indicators
argument	premise indicators
statement	inference
premise	proposition
conclusion	

III. Answer "true" or "false" to the following statements:

1. The purpose of the premise or premises is to set forth the reasons or evidence given in support of the conclusion.

2. Some arguments have more than one conclusion.

3. All arguments must have more than one premise.

4. The words "therefore," "hence," "so," "since," and "thus" are all conclusion indicators.

5. The words "for," "because," "as," and "for the reason that" are all premise indicators.

6. The terms "inference" and "argument" have exactly the same meaning.

7. The terms "proposition" and "statement" have exactly the same meaning.

8. Different statements may express the same proposition.

9. One and the same statement may express different propositions.

10. Any sentence that is either true or false is a statement.

1.2 RECOGNIZING ARGUMENTS

Not all passages contain arguments. Accordingly, since logic deals with arguments, it is important to be able to distinguish passages that contain arguments from those that do not. The key to making this distinction lies in identifying the intention of the author. If the author intends that something be proved, the passage contains an argument; otherwise it does not.

Frequently, an author gives evidence of his or her intention to prove something by using indicator words such as "since," "because," "therefore," "it follows that," and so on. Thus, when indicator words occur in a passage, the reader or listener is usually justified in calling the passage an argument. Care must be exercised, however, to ensure that such words are actually used to indicate that evidence is being presented in support of something the author wants us to believe. As we will see presently, "since," "because," and "thus" are often used for other purposes. Their mere presence in a passage, therefore, is no guarantee that the passage contains an argument.

There are many passages, on the other hand, that contain arguments even though they contain no indicator words. When confronted with such a passage, the reader or listener must examine the relationship between the statements. If one or more statements do in fact provide evidence for another, the reader or listener can usually conclude that the passage contains an argument. Example:

> The water in Spirit Lake is not as pure as it looks. Farmers
> spray the surrounding fields with insecticide, and streams
> carry the runoff from the fields into the lake.

Even though this passage contains no indicator words, an argument exists because the second and third statements (the premises) do in fact support the first (the conclusion).

If no indicators appear in a passage and no single statement is in fact supported by any of the others, a passage may still contain an argument if there is merely the intention that some statement be supported by one or more others. Such a passage would not contain a good argument, but it might contain an argument nevertheless. In the final analysis, therefore, if the content and arrangement of the statements in a passage lead the reader/listener to believe that the author intended one or more of them to support one of the others, regardless of whether they actually do, the reader is justified in calling the passage an argument. Otherwise it is called a nonargument.

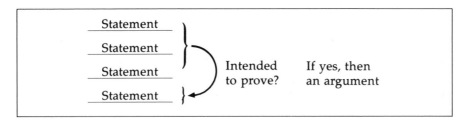

Statement			
Statement	Intended	If yes, then	
Statement	to prove?	an argument	
Statement			

In distinguishing passages that contain arguments from those that do not, it frequently helps to be familiar with some of the typical kinds of nonarguments. They include: descriptive reports, exhortations, warnings, pieces of advice, aphorisms, statements of belief, statements of opinion, illustrations, conditional statements, and explanations. Let us consider these various kinds of nonarguments.

A **descriptive report** usually consists of a number of statements that, taken together, cause a certain picture to appear in the mind of the reader or listener. The intention that some statement provide evidence for another is usually not a factor. Example:

> Five robbers entered the First National Bank when it opened for business on Friday. After emptying the cash boxes they locked the tellers and the operations officer in the vault. A few minutes later the police arrived, and after a brief exchange of gunfire, the robbers were arrested.

Exhortations (such as "You should visit your dentist right away"), **warnings,** and **pieces of advice** are kinds of discourse aimed at modifying someone's behavior, but they rarely involve any effort to *prove* to someone that he or she should do something or act in a certain way. **Aphorisms** (such as "Look before you leap" or "He who hesitates is lost") almost never contain arguments.

Statements of belief (such as "I believe that genetic engineering is worthwhile") and **statements of opinion** (such as "I think that the Russians are not to be trusted") are expressions of what someone happens to think about something at a particular time. They are reports of mental states, and as such they rarely contain any justification that what is believed or opined is in fact true.

The three kinds of phraseology that are liable to cause the most trouble are illustrations, conditional statements, and explanations.

Illustrations

An **illustration** consists of a statement about a certain subject combined with a reference to one or more specific instances intended to exemplify that statement. Example:

> Several metals have a high melting point; the melting point of copper is 1083°C.

The intention is not to *prove* that several metals have a high melting point but merely to illustrate what "high melting point" means.

Illustrations frequently masquerade as arguments because they are often introduced by the word "thus," which is often a conclusion indicator. Example:

> Chemical elements, as well as compounds, can be represented by molecular formulas. Thus, oxygen is represented by "O_2," sodium chloride by "NaCl," and sulfuric acid by "H_2SO_4."

Once again, the intention is not to prove that chemical elements and compounds can be represented by molecular formulas but to provide an illustration of how it is done. Since this type of phraseology is extremely common in ordinary written English, the reader must be attentive to the intention of the author. If the intention is to prove something, the passage contains an argument; if it is merely to show what something means or how something is done, the passage is not an argument.

Conditional Statements

A **conditional statement** is an "if . . . then . . ." statement; for example:

> If it rains, then the valley will flood.

Every conditional statement is made up of two component statements. The component statement immediately following the "if" is called the **antecedent,** and the one following the "then" is called the **consequent.** (Occasionally, the word "then" is left out, and occasionally the order of antecedent and consequent is reversed.) In the above example the antecedent is "it rains," and the consequent is "the valley will flood." This example asserts a causal connection between the rain and the flooding, but not all conditional statements involve causality. For example, the statement "If yellow fever is an infectious disease, then the Dallas Cowboys are a football team" is just as much a conditional statement as the one about the rain.

Conditional statements are not arguments for the following reason. In an argument the premises are asserted to be true (at least hypo-

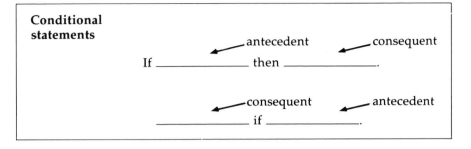

Conditional statements

If _____ antecedent _____ then _____ consequent _____ .

_____ consequent _____ if _____ antecedent _____ .

thetically), and the conclusion, because it is claimed to follow from the premises, is also asserted to be true. In a conditional statement, on the other hand, neither the antecedent nor the consequent is asserted to be true. What is asserted is that *if* the antecedent is true, then the consequent is true. For example, the conditional statement, "If yellow fever is an infectious disease, then the Dallas Cowboys are a footabll team" does not assert that yellow fever *is* an infectious disease. It merely asserts that *if* it is, then the Dallas Cowboys are a football team. Because neither the antecedent nor the consequent is asserted to be true, conditional statements are not arguments.

Some conditional statements are similar to arguments, however, because they express inferences, or reasoning processes, just as arguments do. Consider the following:

> If both Smith and Jones are Americans, then Smith is an American.

> If the electricity was shut off earlier today, then the clock in the kitchen is wrong.

The consequent of these conditional statements is inferentially linked to the antecedent, much in the way that the conclusion of an argument is inferentially linked to the premises. Nevertheless, these conditional statements are not arguments.* An argument expresses an inference in a special way, in terms of one or more premises that present evidence and a conclusion that is claimed to follow from that evidence. Because the antecedent of a conditional statement is not asserted to be true, it presents no evidence; and because it presents no evidence, a conditional statement is not an argument, even though it may express an inference.

---

*In saying this we are temporarily ignoring the possibility of these statements being enthymemes. As we will see in Chapter 5, an enthymeme is an argument in which a premise or conclusion (or both) is implied but not stated. If, to the second example, we add the premise "The electricity was shut off earlier today" and the conclusion "Therefore, the clock in the kitchen is wrong," we have a complete argument. To decide whether a conditional statement is an enthymeme, we must be familiar with the context in which it occurs.

The inferences expressed in conditional statements such as these may, however, be reexpressed in the form of arguments. These examples may be reexpressed as follows:

> Both Smith and Jones are Americans.
> Therefore, Smith is an American.

> The electricity was shut off earlier today.
> Therefore, the clock in the kitchen is wrong.

The relation between conditional statements and arguments is further elaborated by the principle that the inference expressed in any argument may be reexpressed in the form of a conditional statement. This is done by joining the premises together with the conjunction "and" and by letting the resulting chain of premises serve as the antecedent and the conclusion serve as the consequent. The conditional statement that results is called the **corresponding conditional.** For example, the inference expressed in the argument

> All governors are executives.
> No congressmen are executives.
> Therefore, no congressmen are governors.

may be reexpressed in the corresponding conditional

> If all governors are executives and no congressmen are executives, then no congressmen are governors.

Finally, while no single conditional statement is an argument, a conditional statement may serve as either the premise or the conclusion (or both) of an argument, as the following examples illustrate:

> If this tree gets water, then it will grow.
> This tree does get water.
> Therefore, it will grow.

> If it rains, then the daisies will bloom.
> If the daisies bloom, then someone will pick them.
> Therefore, if it rains, then someone will pick the daisies.

The relation between conditional statements and arguments may now be summarized as follows:

1. A single conditional statement is not an argument.
2. A conditional statement may serve as either the premise or the conclusion (or both) of an argument.
3. The inferential content of any argument may be reexpressed in the form of a conditional statement.

4. The inferential content of a conditional statement may be reexpressed in the form of an argument.

The first two rules are especially pertinent to the recognition of arguments. According to the first rule, if a passage consists of a single conditional statement, it is not an argument. But if it consists of a conditional statement together with some other statement, then, by the second rule, it *may* be an argument, depending on such factors as the presence of indicator words and the relation of the statements to each other.

Explanations

Now that we have seen how arguments differ from conditional statements, let us turn to the question of **explanations.** Here are some examples:

> All the houses in this neighborhood are missing their roofs because a tornado swept through here yesterday.
>
> The sky appears blue from the earth's surface because light rays from the sun are scattered by particles in the atmosphere.
>
> Margaret Harris looks so haggard this morning because she's suffering from a migraine headache.

Every explanation is composed of two distinct components: the **explanandum** and the **explanans.** The explanandum is the statement that describes the event or phenomenon to be explained, and the explanans is the statement or group of statements that purport to do the explaining. In the first example above, the explanandum is the statement "All the houses in this neighborhood are missing their roofs," and the explanans is "a tornado swept through here yesterday."

Explanations are sometimes mistaken for arguments because they frequently contain the indicator word "because." Despite this fact, explanations are not arguments for the following reason. In an explanation the explanans is intended to show *why* something is the case, whereas in an argument the premises are intended to prove *that* something is the case. In the first example above, the fact that the houses in the neighborhood are missing their roofs is apparent to sensory observation. The statement that a tornado swept through yesterday is not intended to prove *that* the houses are missing their roofs (which is obvious) but rather to explain *why* they are missing their roofs. In the second example the fact that the sky appears blue is readily apparent to everyone. The intention of the passage is to explain *why* it appears blue—not to prove *that* it appears blue. Similarly, in the third example, both speaker and listener can presumably see that Margaret Harris looks haggard. The intention of the passage is to explain *why* she looks haggard.

Explanations bear a similarity to arguments in that, like certain conditional statements, they express inferences. But this fact is not sufficient to make them arguments. An argument is a special kind of expression of an inference, one that attempts to prove something on the basis of evidence. Because explanations do not attempt to prove anything, they are not arguments.

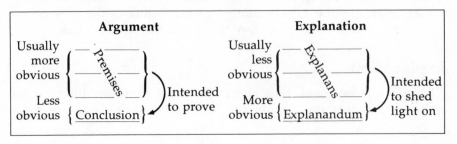

The inferences expressed in many explanations may, however, be reexpressed in the form of arguments. This is particularly true of the explanations found in science. For example, the inference expressed in the blue sky example may be reexpressed in the following argument:

> Light rays from the sun are scattered by particles in the atmosphere. Therefore, the sky appears blue from the earth's surface.

In distinguishing explanations from arguments, first identify the statement that is either the conclusion or the explanandum (this is usually the statement that occurs before the word "because"). Then ask the question: Is the event described in this statement relatively obvious or apparent to sensory observation? If the answer is "yes," then ask: Is the remainder of the passage intended to shed light on this event? If the answer is again "yes," the passage in question is an explanation.

While a basic distinction exists between arguments and explanations, some passages may be interpreted as being either arguments or explanations (or both). Consider the following:

> The patient shows a reduced leukocyte count today because radiation treatments were recently commenced.

The author's intention in this passage may be either to prove *that* the leukocyte (white blood cell) count is down, or to explain *why* it is down, or both. Thus, the passage may be interpreted as being either an argument, an explanation, or both. If the author cannot be questioned about his or her exact intention, we may appeal to a principle of "charity" and interpret such passages as both arguments and explanations.

Our analysis of illustrations and explanations points up the fact that certain indicator words, especially the words "because" and "thus," can have a twofold meaning. Sometimes "because" indicates a premise, sometimes an explanans; and sometimes "thus" indicates an illustration and sometimes a conclusion. Another indicator that readily admits of a double meaning is the word "since," as exemplified by the following passages:

> Since Edison invented the phonograph there have been many technological developments.

> Since Edison invented the phonograph he deserves credit for a major technological development.

In the first passage (which is *not* an argument) "since" means "from the time that." This is the *temporal* meaning of the word. The second passage (which *is* an argument) expresses the *logical* meaning of "since."

EXERCISE 1.2

I. Determine which of the following passages contain arguments. In those that do, identify the conclusion.

★1. The price of gold increased yesterday because of increased tensions in the Middle East.

2. If public education fails to improve the quality of instruction in both primary and secondary schools, then it is likely that it will lose additional students to the private sector in the years ahead.

3. Freedom of the press is the most important of our constitutionally guaranteed freedoms. Without it, our other freedoms would be immediately threatened. Furthermore, it provides the fulcrum for the advancement of new freedoms.

4. An explosion, caused by a leaking gas main, rocked the Plaza Hotel Tuesday morning. All the windows on the first floor were blown into the street, small fires were ignited in several locations, and over twenty persons, most of them hotel residents, were injured.

★5. If Barbara was married on December 31 of last year, she can file a joint tax return for that year. But Barbara was married on December 31 of last year. Thus, she can file a joint tax return for that year.

6. The Swiss Alps contain a number of very high peaks. Thus, the Weisshorn, Matterhorn, and Nadelhorn are all over 14,000 feet.

7. It is strongly recommended that you have your house inspected for termite damage at the earliest possible opportunity.

8. I think that the Conrad Corporation's acquisition of Datamark will result in increased earnings for both companies.

9. Since Julius Caesar conquered Gaul, there have been numerous geopolitical changes in Western Europe.

★10. Shut the cage door, you fool! The lions are escaping into the streets!

11. If this chewing gum contains sugar, then it's fattening. But if it's fattening, then you shouldn't buy any. Thus, if this chewing gum contains sugar, then you shouldn't buy any.

12. It is impossible to send Johnny to camp and at the same time to enroll Eileen in Madame Le Farge's ballet school. Camp costs over $200, tuition in the ballet school is $500, and we have less than $600 available at this time.

13. Several members of the Omega Club have substantial holdings in real estate. One member, Tracy Hawkins, owns over 100 condominiums.

14. If two equal molecules are formed of the same substance and have the same temperature, each of them receives from the other as much heat as it gives up. Their mutual action may thus be regarded as null, since the result of this action can bring about no change in the state of the molecules.

(Joseph Fourier, *Analytical Theory of Heat*)

★15. I believe that the testing of the student's achievements in order to see if he meets some criterion held by the teacher, is directly contrary to the implications of therapy for significant learning.

(Carl R. Rogers, *On Becoming a Person*)

16. Young people at universities study to achieve knowledge and not to learn a trade. We must all learn how to support ourselves, but we must also learn how to live. We need a lot of engineers in the modern world, but we do not want a world of modern engineers.

(Winston Churchill, *A Churchill Reader*, ed. Colin R. Coote)

17. No business concern wants to sell on credit to a customer who will prove unable or unwilling to pay his or her account. Consequently, most business organizations include a credit department which must reach a decision on the credit worthiness of each prospective customer.

(Walter B. Meigs and Robert F. Meigs, *Accounting*)

18. Behavior evoked by brain stimulation is sensitive to environmental changes, even in animals. Gibbons attacked their cage mates in a Yale laboratory when their brains were stimulated. The same animals, moved to Bermuda and placed in a large corral, did not behave aggressively at all in response to the same stimulation.

(Walter Mischel and Harriet Mischel, *Essentials of Psychology*)

19. Since the days of the Viet Nam War and the Federal programs of Johnson's Great Society, the American economy has been plagued

simultaneously by inflation and unemployment, for which no satis-factory solution has been found.

(Thomas R. Dye et al., *Governing the American Democracy*)

★20. Dachshunds are ideal dogs for small children, as they are already stretched and pulled to such a length that the child cannot do much harm one way or the other.

(Robert Benchley, quoted in *Cold Noses and Warm Hearts*)

21. The price of raw hides is a good deal lower at present than it was a few years ago, owing probably to the taking off the duty upon seal-skins, and to the allowing, for a limited time, the importation of raw hides from Ireland.

(Adam Smith, *The Wealth of Nations*)

22. The coarsest type of humor is the *practical joke:* pulling away the chair from the dignitary's lowered bottom. The victim is perceived first as a person of consequence, then suddenly as an inert body subject to the laws of physics: authority is debunked by gravity, mind by matter; man is degraded to a mechanism.

(Arthur Koestler, *Janus: A Summing Up*)

23. If we place a solid homogeneous mass, having the form of a sphere or cube, in a medium maintained at a constant temperature, and if it remains immersed for a very long time, it will acquire at all points a temperature differing very little from that of the fluid.

(Joseph Fourier, *Analytical Theory of Heat*)

24. Silver, mercury, and all the other metals except iron and zinc, are insoluble in diluted sulfuric acid, because they have not sufficient affinity with oxygen to draw it off from its combination either with the sulfur, the sulfurous acid, or the hydrogen.

(Antoine Lavoisier, *Elements of Chemistry*)

★25. Words are slippery customers. The full meaning of a word does not appear until it is placed in its context. . . . And even then the meaning will depend upon the listener, upon the speaker, upon their entire experience of the language, upon their knowledge of one another, and upon the whole situation.

(C. Cherry, *On Human Communication*)

26. Income measures the amount of money coming into a family in a given year; wealth, on the other hand, is a measure of the amount of money a family has managed to accumulate over a long period of time. While income is a fairly good measure of the year-by-year flow of money, wealth is a much better indicator of how money is passed down from generation to generation.

(J. Victor Baldridge, *Sociology*)

27. A person never becomes truly self-reliant. Even though he deals effectively with things, he is necessarily dependent upon those who have taught him to do so. They have selected the things he is dependent upon and determined the kinds and degrees of dependencies.
(B. F. Skinner, *Beyond Freedom and Dignity*)

28. There is no doubt that some businessmen conspire to shorten the useful life of their products in order to guarantee replacement sales. There is, similarly, no doubt that many of the annual model changes with which American (and other) consumers are increasingly familiar are not technologically substantive.
(Alvin Toffler, *Future Shock*)

29. We must resign ourselves to the fact that snow blindness is inherent in the human condition; if it were not so, then everything we know today about the theory of numbers, or analytical geometry, would have been discovered within a few generations after Euclid.
(Arthur Koestler, *The Act of Creation*)

★30. Almost all living things act to free themselves from harmful contacts. . . . A person sneezes and frees his respiratory passages from irritating substances. He vomits and frees his stomach from indigestible or poisonous food. He pulls back his hand and frees it from a sharp or hot object.
(B. F. Skinner, *Beyond Freedom and Dignity*)

II. Define the following terms:

conditional statement	explanation
antecedent	explanandum
consequent	explanans
corresponding conditional	

III. Answer "true" or "false" to the following statements:

1. If a passage contains "thus" or "because," then it necessarily contains an argument.

2. A single conditional statement may be an argument.

3. The inferential content of any argument may be reexpressed in the form of a conditional statement.

4. The conclusion or premise of an argument may be a conditional statement.

5. All explanations are arguments.

6. Statements of belief are usually arguments.

7. Illustrations are usually arguments.

8. In an explanation, the explanandum is frequently relatively obvious or apparent to sensory observation.

9. Some conditional statements express inferences.

10. The word "since" always indicates a premise.

IV. Page through a book, magazine, or newspaper and find two arguments, one with indicator words, the other without. Copy the arguments as written, giving the appropriate reference. Then identify the premises and conclusion of each.

1.3 DEDUCTION AND INDUCTION

Arguments (and their corresponding inferential processes) can be divided into two groups: deductive and inductive. A **deductive argument** is an argument in which the conclusion is intended to follow *necessarily* from the premises, whereas an **inductive argument** is one in which the conclusion is intended to follow only *probably* from the premises. Thus, the distinction between inductive and deductive arguments, as does the distinction between arguments and nonarguments, goes back to the intention of the author. If the author intends his or her conclusion to follow necessarily, or with absolute certainty, the argument is deductive. But if he or she intends the conclusion to follow only probably, the argument is inductive.

Inductive and deductive arguments may be distinguished from each other by means of (a) the occurrence of special indicator words, and (b) the nature of the actual relationship between premises and conclusion. If, in drawing a conclusion, the author uses such words as "probable," "improbable," "plausible," "implausible," "likely," "unlikely," or "reasonable to conclude," the argument is usually inductive. If, on the other hand, he or she uses such words as "necessarily," "certainly," "absolutely," or "definitely," the argument is usually deductive. (The phrase "must happen that" is not a reliable indicator. "Must" can imply either probability or necessity.)

When none of these indicator words occurs in an argument, one must turn to the nature of the relationship between premises and conclusion. If the conclusion does in fact follow necessarily from the premises, one

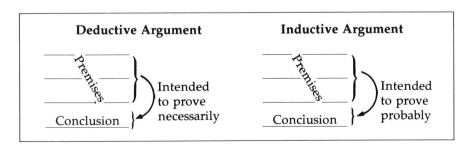

may usually assume that the arguer intended it so and conclude that the argument is deductive. When the conclusion does not in fact follow necessarily from the premises, the general procedure the arguer uses may indicate his or her intention to argue deductively. For example, arguments whose conclusions rest upon some arithmetic or geometric computation or measurement are usually deductive.

Sometimes the format the arguer uses provides a clue to the deductive nature of his or her argument. One kind of argument recognizable in terms of format, which is typically deductive, is a categorical syllogism. Here is an example:

> All professors are academicians.
> No academicians are headhunters.
> Therefore, no professors are headhunters.

Categorical syllogisms will be treated in greater depth in Chapter 5. For now we will simply say that a categorical syllogism is an argument composed of exactly two premises and one conclusion, each of which begins with one of the words "all," "no," or "some." Whenever an argument appears in this format, one can usually assume that the arguer's intention is to argue deductively.

In the absence of indicator words, inductive arguments may usually be recognized by the obvious intention of the arguer that the content of the conclusion in some way go beyond the content of the premises. The premises of such an argument typically deal with some subject that is relatively familiar, and the conclusion then moves beyond this to a subject that is less familiar or that little is known about. Such an argument may take any of several forms: predictions about the future, arguments from analogy, inductive generalizations, arguments based on signs, and causal inferences, to name just a few.

In a **prediction,** the premises deal with some known event in the present or past, and the conclusion moves beyond this event to some event in the relative future. For example, someone might argue that because certain meteorological phenomena have been observed to develop over a certain region of Southern California, a storm will occur there in six hours. Or again, one might argue that because certain fluctuations occurred in the prime interest rate on Friday, the value of the dollar will decrease against foreign currencies on Monday. Nearly everyone realizes that the future cannot be known with certainty; thus, whenever an argument makes a prediction about the future, one can usually assume that the author's intention is to argue probabilistically—that is, inductively.

An **argument from analogy** is an argument that depends on the existence of an analogy, or similarity, between two things or states of affairs. Because of the existence of this analogy, a certain condition that affects the better-known thing or situation is concluded to affect the similar, lesser-known thing or situation. For example, someone might argue that because the oil being pumped from a certain well in Texas has a high sulfur content, the oil being pumped from nearby wells also has a high sulfur content. The argument depends on the existence of a similarity, or analogy, between the oil in the tested well and the oil in the untested wells. The certitude attending such an inference is obviously probabilistic at best.

An **inductive generalization** is an argument that proceeds from the knowledge of a selected sample to some claim about the whole group. Because the members of the sample have a certain characteristic, it is argued that all the members of the group have that same characteristic. For example, one might argue that because three oranges selected from a certain crate were especially tasty and juicy, all the oranges from that crate are especially tasty and juicy. Or again, one might argue that because six out of a total of nine members sampled from a certain labor union intend to vote for Johnson for union president, two-thirds of the entire membership intend to vote for Johnson. These examples illustrate the use of statistics in inductive argumentation.

An **argument based on signs** is an argument that proceeds from the knowledge of a certain sign to a knowledge of the thing or situation that the sign symbolizes. For example, when driving on an unfamiliar highway one might see a sign indicating that the road makes several sharp turns one mile ahead. Based on this information, one might argue that the road does indeed make several sharp turns one mile ahead. Because the sign might be misplaced or in error about the turns, the conclusion is only probable.

A **causal inference** underlies arguments that proceed from knowledge of a cause to knowledge of the effect, or, conversely, from knowledge of an effect to knowledge of a cause. For example, from the knowledge that a bottle of wine had been accidentally left in the freezer overnight, someone might conclude that it had frozen (cause to effect). Conversely, after tasting a piece of chicken and finding it dry and crunchy, one might conclude that it had been overcooked (effect to cause). Because specific instances of cause and effect can never be known with absolute certainty, one may usually assume, in the absence of deductive indicator words, that such arguments are inductive.

Arguments from effect to cause are sometimes confused with arguments based on signs because an effect can sometimes be interpreted as a "sign" of the cause. For example, a symptom is sometimes viewed as a sign of a disease. This mistake can be avoided if one remembers that a sign, in the proper sense of the term, is not usually produced *by* the thing it signifies. An effect, on the other hand, is always produced by its correlative cause.

Another mistake that is sometimes made is to confuse arguments in geometry, which are always deductive, with arguments from analogy or inductive generalizations. For example, an argument that concludes that a triangle has a certain attribute (such as a right angle) because another triangle, with which it is congruent, also has that attribute, might be mistaken for an argument from analogy. Similarly, an argument that concludes that all triangles have a certain attribute (such as angles totaling two right angles) because any particular triangle has that attribute, might be mistaken for an inductive generalization. Arguments such as these, however, are always deductive because the conclusion follows necessarily and with complete certainty from the premises.

Two final points need to be made about the distinction between inductive and deductive arguments. First, there is a tradition extending back to the time of Aristotle which holds that inductive arguments are those that proceed from the particular to the general, while deductive arguments are those that proceed from the general to the particular. (A **particular statement** is one that makes a claim about one or more particular members of a class, while a **general statement** makes a claim about *all* the members of a class.) It is true, of course, that many inductive and deductive arguments do work in this way; but this fact should not be used as a criterion for distinguishing induction from deduction. As a matter of fact, there are deductive arguments that proceed from the general to the general, from the particular to the particular, and from the particular to the general, as well as from the general to the particular; and there are inductive arguments that do the same. For example, here is a deductive argument that proceeds from the particular to the general:

> One is a prime number.
> Three is a prime number.
> Five is a prime number.
> Seven is a prime number.
> Therefore, all odd numbers between zero and eight are prime numbers.

And here is one that proceeds from the particular to the particular:

> Gabriel is a wolf.
> Gabriel has a tail.
> Therefore, Gabriel's tail is the tail of a wolf.

Here is an inductive argument that proceeds from the general to the particular:

> All emeralds previously found have been green.
> Therefore, the next emerald to be found will be green.

The other varieties are easy to construct. The point is that the criterion for distinguishing inductive from deductive arguments arises, in general, not from the kinds of statements in the argument but from the intention of the author. If the intention is that the conclusion follow necessarily, the argument is deductive; but if the intention is that it follow only probably, the argument is inductive.

The second point is that frequently, when arguments are phrased in ordinary language, their authors intend merely that the conclusion *follow* from the premises, without intending specifically *how* it should follow—whether necessarily or probabilistically. Under these circumstances it may, of course, be difficult to determine whether the argument in question is deductive or inductive. If we pursue this line of thought further, we are led to the suggestion that the distinction between induction and deduction may involve an element of artificiality. Much of logic is, of course, an artificial construct used for the purpose of identifying (and, perhaps, introducing) some intelligible structure in (or into) the way people use language. If the inductive-deductive distinction is such an artificial construct, the fact nevertheless remains that it is a highly useful distinction for the general purpose of language analysis. If some arguments should appear along the way that cannot be immediately assigned to either the inductive or the deductive variety, their occurrence merely illustrates the fact that no analytical tool can ever be expected to fit every possible set of circumstances.

EXERCISE 1.3

I. Determine whether the following arguments are inductive or deductive. If inductive, attempt to determine whether the argument is a prediction, argument from analogy, generalization, argument based on signs, or causal inference.

★1. Because triangle A is congruent with triangle B, and triangle A is isosceles, it follows that triangle B is isosceles.

2. The sign on the candy machine reads "Out of Order." The candy machine must be broken.

3. The annual rainfall in Central City has been over 15 inches every year for the past 30 years. Therefore, the annual rainfall next year will probably be over 15 inches.

4. All guitar players are musicians, and some guitar players are not astronauts. It follows that some musicians are not astronauts.

★5. The prime rib, beef stroganoff, and lobster thermidor at the Pioneer House are all excellent. The likely conclusion is that all the entrees on the menu are excellent.

6. There are eight people in this class. It follows that at least two of them were born on the same day of the week.

7. Barbara's skin has a peculiar yellowish hue, and she complains of loss of energy. Barbara must have hepatitis.

8. Henry is taller than John, and John is taller than Michael. The necessary conclusion is that Henry is taller than Michael.

9. These mushrooms have a very similar appearance to the ones growing in the garden. The mushrooms growing in the garden are edible. The conclusion is therefore warranted that these mushrooms are edible.

★10. Although both front and rear doors were found open after the robbery, there were pry marks around the lock on the rear door and deposits of mud near the threshold. It must be the case that the thief entered through the rear door and left through the front.

11. Because the apparent daily movement which is common to both the planets and the fixed stars is seen to travel from the east to the west, but the far slower single movements of the single planets travel in the opposite direction from west to east, it is therefore certain that these movements cannot depend on the common movement of the world but should be assigned to the planets themselves.
(Johannes Kepler, *Epitomy of Copernican Astronomy*)

12. Reserves of coal in the United States have an energy equivalent 33 times that of oil and natural gas. On a world-wide basis the multiple is about 10. By shifting to a coal-based economy, we could satisfy our energy requirements for at least a century, probably longer.
(William L. Masterson and Emil J. Slowinski, *Principles of Chemistry*)

13. Probably most of human behavior operates on the basis of inference. Most of the time we just do not have the facts on which to base our behavior. Yet to make sense of what we do and to anticipate what we should do in the future, we must make assumptions, draw conclusions.
(F. S. Sathre-Eldon et al., *Let's Talk*)

14. The graphical method for solving a system of equations is an approximation, since reading the point of intersection depends on the accuracy with which the lines are drawn and on the ability to interpret the coordinates of the point.
(Karl J. Smith and Patrick J. Boyle, *Intermediate Algebra for College Students*)

★15. That [the moons of Jupiter] revolve in unequal circles is manifestly deduced from the fact that at the longest elongation from Jupiter it is never possible to see two of these moons in conjunction, whereas in

the vicinity of Jupiter they are found united two, three, and sometimes all four together.

(Galileo Galilei, The Starry Messenger)

16. The pituitary gland is divided into two lobes, the anterior and the
    posterior. The *anterior lobe* produces hormones that stimulate the thy-
    roid gland and the adrenal gland, both of which control other
    behavior. It also produces gonadotrophins, which are involved in sex-
    ual behavior, and growth hormones, which control the body's
    development. Thus, the anterior lobe controls not only specific behav-
    ior, but other glands as well.

(Lester A. Lefton, Psychology)

17. Given present growth rates in underdeveloped countries, the limited
    practice of birth control, and the difficulty of slowing the current
    growth momentum, it can be said with virtual certainty that none of
    the people now reading this book will ever live in a world where the
    population is not growing.

(J. John Palen, Social Problems)

18. The interpretation of the laws is the proper and peculiar province of
    the courts. A constitution is, in fact, and must be regarded by the
    judges, as a fundamental law. It therefore belongs to them to ascertain
    its meaning, as well as the meaning of any particular act proceeding
    from the legislative body.

(Alexander Hamilton, Federalist Papers, No. 78)

19. The Simpson incident had shown me that a dog was kept in the
    stables, and yet, though someone had been in and had fetched out a
    horse, he had not barked enough to arouse the two lads in the loft.
    Obviously the midnight visitor was someone whom the dog knew
    well.

(A. Conan Doyle, Memoirs of Sherlock Holmes)

★20. Eternity is simultaneously whole. But time has a before and an after.
    Therefore time and eternity are not the same thing.

(Thomas Aquinas, Summa Theologica)

21. Since electrons have charges equal in magnitude but opposite in sign
    to those of protons, a neutral atom of atomic number Z will have Z
    electrons outside its nucleus.

(William L. Masterson and Emil J. Slowinski, Principles
of Chemistry)

22. In consequence of the division of labor, the whole of every man's
    attention comes naturally to be directed towards some one very sim-
    ple object. It is naturally to be expected, therefore, that some one or
    other of those who are employed in each particular branch of labor

should soon find out easier and readier methods of performing their own particular work.

(Adam Smith, The Wealth of Nations)

II. Define the following terms:

deductive argument   argument based on signs
inductive argument   causal inference
prediction   particular statement
argument from analogy   general statement
inductive generalization

III. Answer "true" or "false" to the following statements:

1. In an inductive argument, it is intended that the conclusion contain information not contained in the premises.

2. In a deductive argument, the conclusion is not supposed to contain information not contained in the premises.

3. A geometrical proof is an example of an inductive argument.

4. Categorical syllogisms are deductive arguments.

5. An argument from analogy is a deductive argument.

6. An argument based on signs is an inductive argument.

7. A causal inference always proceeds from knowledge of a cause to knowledge of an effect.

8. An argument that predicts what will happen in the future, based upon what has happened in the past, is an inductive argument.

9. Inductive arguments always proceed from the particular to the general.

10. Deductive arguments always proceed from the general to the particular.

IV. Page through a book, magazine, or newspaper and find two arguments, one inductive and the other deductive. Copy the arguments as written, giving the appropriate reference. Then identify the premises and conclusion of each.

1.4 VALIDITY, TRUTH, SOUNDNESS, STRENGTH, COGENCY

Every deductive argument is either valid or invalid. A **valid deductive argument** is an argument in which the conclusion follows necessarily from the premises, or, in other words, an argument such that if the premises are assumed true, then, on the basis of that assumption, it necessarily follows that the conclusion is true. Conversely, an **invalid deductive argument** is one in which the conclusion does not follow necessarily from the premises (even though it is intended to), or, in other words, an argument such that if the premises are assumed true, then, on the basis of that assumption, it does not necessarily follow that the conclusion is true.

The phrase "even though it is intended to" guards against mistaking invalid deductive arguments for inductive arguments. Even though the conclusion of a dedutive argument may not follow necessarily from the premises, the argument remains deductive because of the *intention* that it follow necessarily. With inductive arguments, on the other hand, there is the intention that the conclusion follow probabilistically.

Two immediate consequences follow from these definitions. The first is that there is no middle ground between valid and invalid. There are no arguments that are "almost" valid or "almost" invalid. If the conclusion does follow necessarily, the argument is valid; if not, it is invalid.

The second consequence is that there is only an indirect relation between validity and truth. For an argument to be valid, it is not necessary that either the premises or the conclusion be true, but merely that *if* the premises are *assumed* true, the conclusion be true on the basis of that assumption. Here is an example of a valid argument having false premises and a false conclusion:

> All scientists are accountants.
> Jane Fonda is a scientist.
> Therefore, Jane Fonda is an accountant.

To see that this argument is valid one must ignore the fact that the premises are false and attempt to determine what *would* follow if the premises *were* true. Clearly, if the premises were true, it would necessarily follow that Jane Fonda would be an accountant. Anyone who did not accept this conclusion on the assumption that the premises are true would be guilty of self-contradiction. Thus, this argument is valid.

Just as the occurrence of false premises and a false conclusion does not prevent an argument from being valid, so the occurrence of true premises and a true conclusion does not guarantee validity. Here is an example of an invalid argument having true premises and a true conclusion:

> All actresses are human beings.
> Liv Ullmann is a human being.
> Therefore, Liv Ullmann is an actress.

The question is not whether the premises and conclusion are true but whether the conclusion *follows necessarily* from the premises. In the above argument if one assumes that actresses comprise one part of the class of human beings and that Liv Ullmann occupies another part, then Liv Ullmann would *not* be an actress. In other words, if one assumes that the premises are true, it does not *necessarily* follow that the conclusion is true, and so the argument is invalid.

While it is true, in general, that the truth or falsity of the premises and conclusion tell us nothing about the validity or invalidity of an argument, there is one combination of truth and falsity that is always decisive. Any deductive argument having true premises and a false conclusion is necessarily invalid. This is perhaps the most important fact in all of deductive logic. The entire system of deductive logic would be quite useless if it accepted as valid any inferential process by which a person could start with truth in the premises and arrive at falsity in the conclusion.

A **sound argument** is a deductive argument that is *valid* and has *true premises*. Both conditions must be met for an argument to be sound, and if either is missing the argument is *unsound*. The qualification that the premises must be true means that *all* the premises must be true. Because a valid argument is one in which if the premises are true the conclusion is necessarily true, and because a sound argument does in fact have true premises, it follows that every sound argument, by definition, will have a true conclusion as well. A sound argument, therefore, is what is meant by a "good" deductive argument in the fullest sense of the term.

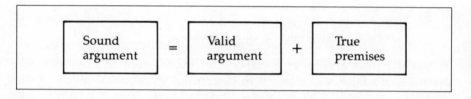

Let us now consider inductive arguments. Inductive arguments are either strong or weak. A **strong inductive argument** is one in which the conclusion follows probably from the premises, or, in other words, an argument such that if the premises are assumed true, then, on the basis of that assumption, the conclusion is probably true. A **weak inductive argument** is one in which the conclusion does not follow probably from the premises (even though it is intended to), or, in other words, an argument such that if the premises are assumed true, then, on the basis of that assumption, the conclusion is not probably true.

Here are two examples of inductive arguments. The first is weak, the second strong:

> This barrel contains one hundred apples.
> Three apples selected at random were found to be ripe.
> Therefore, probably all one hundred apples are ripe.

This barrel contains one hundred apples.
Eighty apples selected at random were found to be ripe.
Therefore, probably all one hundred apples are ripe.

As is evident from these examples, strength and weakness, unlike validity and invalidity, generally admit of degrees. The first argument is not absolutely weak nor the second absolutely strong. Both arguments would be strengthened or weakened by the random selection of a larger or smaller sample. The incorporation of additional premises into an inductive argument will also generally tend to strengthen or weaken it. For example, if the premise "One unripe apple that had been found earlier was removed" were added to the second argument, the argument would presumably be weakened.

As with validity and invalidity, strength and weakness are only indirectly related to truth and falsity. The central question is whether the conclusion would probably be true if the premises are assumed true. Here is an example of a strong inductive argument having a false premise and a probably false conclusion:

> Of the many American presidents in the past, the vast majority have been Federalists. Therefore, probably the next American president will be a Federalist.

In fact, only two of the previous American presidents were Federalists. But if it were assumed that the vast majority were Federalists, the conclusion would probably follow that the next one would be as well.

Conversely, the fact that the premises of an inductive argument are true and the conclusion probably true does not make the argument strong. Here is an example of a weak inductive argument having a true premise and a probably true conclusion:

> During the past 50 years, inflation has consistently reduced the value of the American dollar. Therefore, industrial productivity will probably increase in the years ahead.

Even though the premise is true and the conclusion probably true, the conclusion does not follow probably from the premise—there is no direct connection between inflation and increased industrial productivity.

As with deductive arguments, however, there is one combination of truth and probable falsity that is decisive for inductive arguments. Any inductive argument having true premises and a probably false conclusion is always weak. Inductive logic would be useless if it accepted as strong any inductive argument having true premises and a probably false conclusion.

A **cogent argument** is an inductive argument that is *strong* and has *true premises,* and if either condition is missing the argument is *uncogent.*

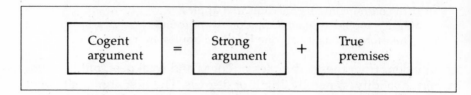

A cogent argument is the inductive analogue of a sound deductive argument and is what is meant by a "good" inductive argument without qualification. Because the conclusion of a cogent argument is genuinely supported by true premises, it follows that the conclusion of every cogent argument is probably true.

One final piece of terminology needs to be introduced. We saw in the first section of this chapter that, from the standpoint of logic, every statement is considered to be either true or false. The attributes of truth and falsity are called **truth values.** The truth value of the statement "The earth is round," for example, is *true,* and the truth value of the statement "The earth is flat" is *false.*

The various alternatives open to statements and arguments may be summarized as follows. Note that in logic one never speaks of an argument as being "true" or "false," and one never speaks of a statement as being "valid," "invalid," "strong," or "weak."

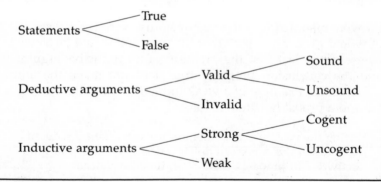

EXERCISE 1.4

I. For each of the following deductive arguments, identify the premises and conclusion as true or false. Then determine whether the argument is valid or invalid. In arguments that have false premises, this decision depends on whether the conclusion *would* necessarily be true if the premises *were* true. Finally, determine whether each argument is sound or unsound.

★1. Since *Moby Dick* was written by Shakespeare, and *Moby Dick* is a science fiction novel, it follows that Shakespeare wrote a science fiction novel.

2. If George Washington was beheaded, then George Washington died. George Washington died. Therefore, George Washington was beheaded.

3. Since some fruits are green, and some fruits are apples, it follows that some fruits are green apples.

4. The United States Congress has more members than there are days in the year. Therefore, at least two members of Congress have the same birthday.

★5. Since World War I occurred before the American Civil War, and the American Civil War occurred after World War II, it follows that World War I occurred before World War II.

6. Since Winston Churchill was English, and Winston Churchill was a famous statesman, we may conclude that at least one Englishman was a famous statesman.

7. Chicago is a city in Canada and Canada is part of the United States. Therefore, Chicago is a city in the United States.

8. Since the Department of Defense Building in Washington, D.C. has the shape of a hexagon, it follows that it has seven sides.

II. The following inductive arguments involve rolling a single standard die. In each case it should be presupposed that the die is indeed a standard one, with six faces marked 1 through 6. Identify the premise of each argument as true or false, and the conclusion as probably true or probably false. Then determine whether each argument is strong or weak. In arguments that have a false premise, this decision depends on whether the conclusion *would* probably be true if the premise *were* true. Finally, determine whether each argument is cogent or uncogent.

★1. A standard die is marked with numbers 1 through 6. Therefore, probably the next roll will turn up a 6.

2. A standard die is marked with numbers 1 through 6. Therefore, probably the next roll will turn up a number less than 6.

3. A standard die is marked with a 1 and five 6s. Therefore, probably the next roll will turn up a 6.

4. Some dice are made of plastic. Therefore, probably the next roll will turn up a number less than 6.

★5. A standard die is marked with a 1 and five 6s. Therefore, probably the next roll will turn up a number less than 6.

6. A standard die is marked with numbers 1 through 6. Therefore, probably the next roll will turn up a number greater than 1.

7. A standard die is marked with numbers 1 through 4 and two 6s. Therefore, probably the next roll will turn up a 4.

8. A standard die is marked with numbers 1 through 4 and two 6s. Therefore, probably the next roll will turn up a number greater than 1.

III. Determine whether the following arguments are inductive or deductive. If inductive, determine whether strong or weak. If deductive, determine whether valid or invalid.

★1. Since Agatha is the mother of Raquel and the sister of Tom, it follows that Tom is the uncle of Raquel.

2. This food is nourishing for horses. Since horses and humans are similar in many ways, this food must be nourishing for humans as well.

3. The label on this bottle depicts a skull and crossbones. The obvious conclusion is that the contents are poisonous.

4. Since Christmas is always on a Thursday, it follows that the day after Christmas is always a Friday.

★5. This figure is a Euclidean triangle. Therefore, the sum of its angles is equal to two right angles.

6. By accident Karen baked her brownies two hours longer than she should have. Therefore, they have probably been ruined.

7. Those palm trees on the beach have all been snapped off at the roots. The damage must have been done by a beaver.

8. Since Phyllis is the cousin of Denise, and Denise is the cousin of Harriet, it follows necessarily that Harriet is the cousin of Phyllis.

9. The picnic scheduled in the park for tomorrow will most likely be cancelled. It's been snowing for six days straight.

★10. Circle A has exactly twice the diameter of circle B. From this we may conclude that circle A has exactly twice the area of circle B.

11. Robert has lost consistently at blackjack every day for the past several days. Therefore, it is very likely that he will win today.

12. Since John loves Nancy and Nancy loves Peter, it follows necessarily that John loves Peter.

13. The Battle of Hastings happened in either 1066 or 1076. But it didn't happen in 1066. Therefore, it happened in 1076.

14. This cash register drawer contains over 100 coins. Three coins selected at random were found to have dates earlier than 1945. Therefore, probably all of the coins in the drawer have dates earlier than 1945.

★15. Harry will never be able to solve that difficult problem in advanced calculus in the limited time allowed. He has never studied anything beyond algebra, and in that he earned only a $C-$.

16. Since $x + y = 10$, and $x = 7$, it follows that $y = 4$.

17. Joe's birthday is exactly one week after Mark's, and Mark's is on May 10. Hence, Joe's is on May 17.

18. Statistics reveal that 86 percent of those who receive flu shots do not get the flu. Jack received a flu shot one month ago. Therefore, he should be immune, even though the flu is going around now.

19. If taxes increase, there will be budgetary cutbacks. If there are budgetary cutbacks, a funding drive will be initiated. Therefore, if taxes increase, a funding drive will be initiated.

★20. Since Michael is a Pisces, it necessarily follows that he was born in March.

IV. Define the following terms:

valid argument	weak argument
invalid argument	cogent argument
sound argument	uncogent argument
unsound argument	truth value
strong argument	

V. Answer "true" or "false" to the following statements:

1. Some arguments, while not completely valid, are almost valid.

2. Inductive arguments admit of varying degrees of strength and weakness.

3. Invalid deductive arguments are basically the same as inductive arguments.

4. If a deductive argument has true premises and a false conclusion, it is necessarily invalid.

5. A valid argument may have a false premise and a false conclusion.

6. A valid argument may have a false premise and a true conclusion.

7. A sound argument may be invalid.

8. A sound argument may have a false conclusion.

9. A strong argument may have false premises and a probably false conclusion.

10. A strong argument may have true premises and a probably false conclusion.

11. A cogent argument may have a probably false conclusion.

12. A cogent argument must be inductively strong.

13. If an argument has true premises and a true conclusion, we know that it is a good argument.

14. A statement may legitimately be spoken of as "valid" or "invalid."

15. An argument may legitimately be spoken of as "true" or "false."

1.5 PROVING INVALIDITY

In the previous section we saw that a valid deductive argument is one in which if the premises are assumed true, the conclusion is necessarily true. Let us analyze this concept of validity a little further. For these purposes the following argument will prove instructive:

> All adlers are bobkins.
> All bobkins are crockers.
> Therefore, all adlers are crockers.

Because the words "adlers," "bobkins," and "crockers" are meaningless, we do not know whether any of the statements in this argument are true or false. Yet, we do know that if we *assume* that the premises are true, the conclusion must *necessarily* be true. That is, if we assume that the adlers, whatever they might be, are included in the bobkins, and the bobkins in the crockers, then we must accept the conclusion that the adlers are included in the crockers. By definition, therefore, the argument is valid.

This fact is important for understanding the nature of validity because it shows that the validity of an argument has nothing to do with its specific subject matter. Even though we know nothing about adlers, bobkins, and crockers, we still know that the argument is valid. Rather, the validity of an argument arises from the *form* or *structure* of the argument. The argument above is valid because of the way in which the terms "adlers," "bobkins," and "crockers" are arranged in the statements. If we represent these terms by their first letters, we obtain the following argument form:

> All A are B.
> All B are C.
> Therefore, all A are C.

This is a valid argument form. Its validity rests purely upon the arrangement of the letters within the statements, and it has nothing to do with what the letters might stand for. In light of this fact, we can substitute any terms we choose in place of A, B, and C, and as long as we are consistent, we will obtain a valid argument. For example, we might substitute "daisies" for A, "flowers" for B, and "plants" for C and obtain a valid argument.

Depending on what words we substitute, the premises and conclusion

A CONCISE INTRODUCTION TO LOGIC

will sometimes turn out to be true and sometimes false. But whatever arrangement of truth and falsity we obtain, it will always be the case that if we *assume* that the premises are true, the conclusion will be true on the basis of that assumption. The following arguments have been produced by substituting various terms in place of the letters in the valid argument form above. All of them, therefore, are valid. Notice the various arrangements of truth and falsity in the premises and conclusion:

All tigers are mammals.
All mammals are animals.   True premises
Therefore, all tigers are animals.   True conclusion

All pigs are fish.
All fish are birds.   False premises
Therefore, all pigs are birds.   False conclusion

All rabbits are fish.
All fish are mammals.   False premises
Therefore, all rabbits are mammals.   True conclusion

The only arrangement of truth and falsity missing here is true premises and false conclusion. Try as we may, we can never produce an argument having true premises and a false conclusion from a valid form. By definition, such an argument would be invalid and would therefore have an invalid form, instead of the valid form from which it was produced.

Let us turn now to the concept of invalidity. Consider the following argument:

All adlers are bobkins.
All crockers are bobkins.
Therefore, all adlers are crockers.

As with the previous argument, we do not know whether the premises and conclusion of this argument are true or false. But if we assume that the premises are true, it is not *necessarily* the case that the conclusion is true. It might be the case, for example, that the adlers make up one part of the bobkins, that the crockers make up another part, and that the adlers and the crockers are completely separate from one another. In this case the premises would be true and the conclusion false. The argument is therefore invalid. If we represent the terms in this argument by their first letters, we obtain the following argument form:

All *A* are *B*.
All *C* are *B*.
Therefore, all *A* are *C*.

This is an invalid form. Accordingly, since invalidity, like validity, has nothing to do with the specific subject matter of an argument, we may substitute any terms we choose in place of the letters and obtain an invalid argument. It is important only that we be consistent in the substitution and that the three terms selected be nonsynonymous. The following arguments were produced in this way and are therefore invalid. Notice the various arrangements of truth and falsity in the premises and conclusion:

All tigers are animals.	
All mammals are animals.	True premises
Therefore, all tigers are mammals.	True conclusion
All cats are animals.	
All dogs are animals.	True premises
Therefore, all cats are dogs.	False conclusion
All pigs are fish.	
All birds are fish.	False premises
Therefore, all pigs are birds.	False conclusion
All rabbits are fish.	
All mammals are fish.	False premises
Therefore, all rabbits are mammals.	True conclusion

These four arguments, like the previous three, are called **substitution instances** of their respective form. If we compare this group of invalid arguments with the group of valid ones we will notice one distinguishing characteristic: The invalid form has a substitution instance in which the premises are true and the conclusion false. This fact provides the basis for an alternate definition of **invalidity:** *An argument is invalid if and only if its form allows for a substitution instance having true premises and a false conclusion.* That this definition correctly characterizes invalid arguments may be seen as follows. If an argument is invalid, it has an invalid form. But if the form is invalid, there is at least one substitution instance having true premises and a false conclusion; otherwise, every substitution instance having true premises would have a true conclusion, and by definition the form would be valid. Conversely, if a substitution instance exists having true premises and a false conclusion, the substitution instance is clearly invalid and thus has an invalid form. But since this form is identical to that of the original argument, the existence of this substitution instance proves the original argument invalid.

This alternate definition of invalidity leads directly to a method for *proving* invalidity. If a deductive argument is known to be invalid in the first place, it may be proven invalid by isolating the form of the argument and then constructing a substitution instance having true premises and a false conclusion. Let us apply this method to the following argument:

Since some employees are not social climbers and all vice-presidents are employees, we may conclude that some vice-presidents are not social climbers.

This argument is invalid because the employees who are not social climbers might not be vice-presidents. Accordingly, we can *prove* the argument invalid by constructing a substitution instance of its form. The form of the argument is as follows:

> Some E are not S.
> All V are E.
> Therefore, some V are not S.

Let us now make the following substitution:

> E = animals
> S = mammals
> V = dogs

The resulting substitution instance is:

> Some animals are not mammals.
> All dogs are animals.
> Therefore, some dogs are not mammals.

The substitution instance has true premises and a false conclusion and is therefore, by definition, invalid. Since it has the same form as the original argument, it constitutes proof that the original argument is invalid.

Not all deductive arguments, of course, are of the same general type as the one above. Consider the following:

> If the government imposes import restrictions, the price of automobiles will rise. Therefore, since the government will not impose import restrictions, it follows that the price of automobiles will not rise.

This argument is invalid because the price of automobiles might rise even though import restrictions are not imposed. It has the following form:

> If G, then P.
> Not G.
> Therefore, not P.

This form differs from the previous one in that its letters stand for complete statements. G, for example, stands for "The government imposes import restrictions." If we make the substitution

G = Abraham Lincoln committed suicide.
P = Abraham Lincoln is dead.

we obtain the following substitution instance:

If Abraham Lincoln committed suicide, then Abraham Lincoln
  is dead.
Abraham Lincoln did not commit suicide.
Therefore, Abraham Lincoln is not dead.

Since the premises are true and the conclusion false, the substitution instance is clearly invalid. Thus, it constitutes proof that the original argument is invalid.

When constructing a substitution instance for an argument having a conditional statement as a premise (such as the one above), it is recommended that the statement substituted in place of the conditional statement express some kind of necessary connection. In the example above, the first premise asserts the necessary connection between suicide and death. There can be no doubt about the truth of such a statement.

Constructing substitution instances to prove arguments invalid requires a little ingenuity because there is no rule that will automatically produce the required term or statement to be substituted. Any term or statement will work, of course, provided that it yields a substitution instance that has premises that are *clearly* true and a conclusion that is *clearly* false. Ideally, the truth value of these statements should be known to the average individual; otherwise, the substitution instance cannot be depended upon to prove anything. If, for example, P in the above argument form had been replaced by the statement "George Wilson is dead," the substitution instance would be useless, because nobody knows whether this statement is true or false.

The method of constructing substitution instances is only useful for proving arguments invalid, because, as we saw earlier, the only arrangement of truth and falsity that proves anything is true premises and false conclusion. If a substitution instance is produced having true premises and a true conclusion, it does *not* prove that the argument is valid. Furthermore, the method is only useful for deductive arguments because the strength and weakness of inductive arguments is only partially dependent on the form of the argument. Accordingly, no method that relates exclusively to the form of an inductive argument can be used to prove the argument weak.

One final comment is needed regarding the form of an argument. It often happens that the form is not explicit and that making it explicit requires an analysis of the meaning of the language. Many of the arguments in Exercise 1.4 were of this sort. Consider the following example:

This figure is a square.
Therefore, this figure has four sides.

The conclusion follows necessarily from the premise because every square, by definition, has four sides. To make the form of the argument explicit, a premise must be added stating this fact:

This figure is a square.
All squares have four sides.
Therefore, this figure has four sides.

The original argument has what may be called a suppressed premise. Sometimes a suppressed premise can cause deception in identifying the form of an argument. Consider the following example:

If Katharine Ross is married to Jack Nicholson,
    then Katharine Ross is Jack Nicholson's wife.
Katharine Ross is not married to Jack Nicholson.
Therefore, Katharine Ross is not Jack Nicholson's wife.

Where M stands for "Katharine Ross is married to Jack Nicholson," and W stands for "Katharine Ross is Jack Nicholson's wife," this argument appears to have the following form:

If M, then W.
Not M.
Therefore, not W.

Since this form is identical to that of the earlier, invalid argument about import restrictions, it might appear that the Katharine Ross argument is invalid. Upon further analysis, however, it may be seen that the conclusion follows necessarily from the second premise by itself and that the argument is therefore valid. Like the argument about the square, this argument hides a premise: "If Katharine Ross is not married to Jack Nicholson, then Katharine Ross is not Jack Nicholson's wife." Since the first premise of the original argument is irrelevant to the question of validity, it may be deleted. Substituting the hidden premise in its place, we have:

If Katharine Ross is not married to Jack Nicholson, then Katharine Ross is not Jack Nicholson's wife.
Katharine Ross is not married to Jack Nicholson.
Therefore, Katharine Ross is not Jack Nicholson's wife.

The form of this argument is:

If not *M,* then not *W.*
Not *M.*
Therefore, not *W.*

This form, which is valid, may be taken to be the real form of the original argument. The notion of the "real form" of an argument is important only in connection with valid arguments. If an argument is valid, the real form is the form according to which the conclusion follows necessarily from the premises.

As these examples illustrate, the statement at the beginning of this section that the validity of an argument is concerned not with the subject matter but rather with the form of an argument needs qualification. When the form of an argument is immediately clear, the subject matter is irrelevant to the question of validity. But when the form is not clear, the subject matter may have to be analyzed to determine what the form is.

EXERCISE 1.5

I. Six of the following eight arguments are invalid. Identify the invalid ones and then use the method of constructing substitution instances to prove each invalid. To do this, isolate the form of each invalid argument, using letters to represent the terms. Then select three new terms to replace the letters, yielding a substitution instance having true premises and a false conclusion. Select these three terms from the following list of five: "cats," "dogs," "mammals," "fish," and "animals."

★1. All candidates running in this election are liberal-minded individuals, for all astute politicians are candidates running in this election and all liberal-minded individuals are astute politicians.

2. No zookeepers are constant complainers, so some constant complainers are underpaid workers, since some underpaid workers are not zookeepers.

3. Some former athletes are not boring individuals, because no talkative cabdrivers are boring individuals and some talkative cabdrivers are former athletes.

4. No basket makers are successful businessmen, and all successful businessmen are wealthy entrepreneurs. Thus, no basket makers are wealthy entrepreneurs.

★5. Some early risers are not violinists, for some early risers are not scotch drinkers and some violinists are not scotch drinkers.

6. All crocodiles are lazy gluttons, so no crocodiles are discontented lizards for no discontented lizards are lazy gluttons.

7. Some red-headed gypsies are wild dancers and no wild dancers are totally stable individuals. Hence no red-headed gypsies are totally stable individuals.

8. Some ladies who lunch on cayenne peppers are easily provoked simpletons, because all easily provoked simpletons are shy and sulky creatures and some shy and sulky creatures are ladies who lunch on cayenne peppers.

II. Use the method of constructing substitution instances to prove each of the following arguments invalid.

★1. If construction costs increase, the price of housing will rise. Therefore, the price of housing will not rise, since construction costs will not increase.

2. If there is a drought, the corn harvest will be skimpy. The corn harvest will be skimpy. Hence, there will be a drought.

3. If the teachers strike, the parents will complain. If the children miss school, the parents will complain. Thus, if the teachers strike, the children will miss school.

4. Some cars are red Chevrolets, since some cars are red and some cars are Chevrolets.

5. All swift runners are fine athletes. Therefore, all runners are athletes.

2
MEANING AND DEFINITION

2.1 THE INTENSION AND EXTENSION OF TERMS

Although the primary aim of logic is the analysis and evaluation of arguments, the interrelated topics of meaning and definition have long occupied a prominent position within the discipline, for a number of reasons. Among them, arguments are composed of statements, statements are made up of words, words have meanings, and meanings are conveyed through definitions. In addition, logic, especially formal logic, is heavily dependent on definitions to attribute highly specific meanings to its technical terminology.

The basic units of any ordinary language are *words*. Logic, however, is mainly concerned not with words in general but with terms. A **term** is any word or arrangement of words that may serve as the subject of a statement. Terms consist of proper names, common names, and descriptive phrases. Here are some examples:

Proper names	Common names	Descriptive phrases
Napoleon	animal	first president of the United States
North Dakota	restitution	
The United States Senate	house	author of *Hamlet*
	activity	books in my library
Edmund Muskie	person	officers in the Swiss Navy
Robinson Crusoe		blue things
		those who study hard

Words that are not terms include verbs, nonsubstantive adjectives, adverbs, prepositions, conjunctions, and all nonsyntactic arrangements of words. The following words are not terms; none can serve as the subject of a statement:

dictatorial	moreover
runs quickly	craves
above and beyond	cabbages into again the forest

The last example is a nonsyntactic arrangement.

At this point it is important to distinguish the *use* of a word from the *mention* of a word. Without this distinction any word can be imagined to serve as the subject of a statement and, therefore, to count as a term. The word "wherever," for example, is not a term, but "wherever" (in quotes) can serve as the subject of a statement, such as " 'Wherever' is an eight-letter word." But in this statement, it is not the word itself that is the subject but rather the *quoted* word. The word is said to be *mentioned*—not *used*. On the other hand, "wherever" is *used* in this statement: "I will follow you wherever you go." In distinguishing terms from nonterms one must be sure that the word or group of words can be *used* as the subject of a statement.

Words are usually considered to be symbols, and the entities they symbolize are usually called **meanings**. Terms, being made up of words, are also symbols, but the meanings they symbolize are of two kinds: intensional and extensional. The **intensional meaning** consists of the qualities or attributes that the term "connotes," and the **extensional meaning** consists of the members of the class that the term "denotes." These two kinds of meaning will provide the basis for the definitional techniques developed in Section 2.3.

The intensional meaning is otherwise known as the **intension** or **connotation**, and the extensional meaning is known as the **extension** or **denotation**. Thus, for example, the intension (or connotation) of the term "cat" consists of the attributes of being furry, of having four legs,

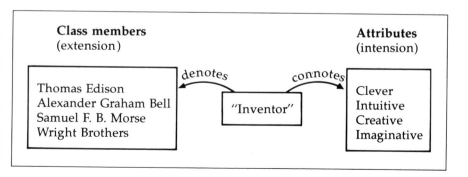

of moving in a certain way, of emitting certain sounds, and so on, and the extension (or denotation) consists of the cats themselves—all the cats in the universe. As this example illustrates, logic uses the terms "connotation" and "denotation" differently from the way they are used in grammar. In grammar, "connotation" refers to the subtle nuances of a word, whereas "denotation" refers to the word's direct and specific meaning.

Because terms symbolize meanings to individual persons, it is inevitable for subjective elements to invade the notion of connotation. For example, to a cat lover, the connotation of the word "cat" might include the attributes of being cuddly and adorable, while to one who hates cats it might include those of being obnoxious and disgusting. Because these subjective elements inevitably lead to confusion when it comes to identifying the connotation of specific terms, logicians typically restrict the meaning of "connotation" to what may be called conventional connotation. The **conventional connotation** of a term consists of the properties or attributes that the term commonly connotes to the members of the community who speak the language in question. Under this interpretation, the connotation of a term remains more or less the same from person to person and from time to time.

The denotation of a term also typically remains the same from person to person, but it may change with the passage of time. The denotation of "presently living cat," for example, is constantly fluctuating as some cats die and others are born. The denotation of the term "cat," on the other hand, is presumably constant because it denotes all cats, past, present, and future.

Sometimes the denotation of a term can change radically with the passage of time. The terms "presently living dinosaur" and "present king of France," for example, at one time denoted actually existing entities, but today all such entities have perished. Accordingly, these terms now have what is called **empty extension**. They are said to denote the empty (or "null") class, the class that has no members. Other terms with empty extension include "unicorn," "leprechaun," "gnome," "elf," and "griffin." While these terms have empty extension, however, they do not have empty intension. "Presently living dinosaur" and "present king of France," as well as "unicorn," "elf," and "griffin," connote a variety of intelligible attributes.

The fact that some terms have empty extension leads us to an important connection between extension and intension; namely, that *intension determines extension*. The intensional meaning of a term serves as the criterion for deciding what the extension consists of. Because we know the attributes connoted by the term "unicorn," for example, we know that the term has empty extension. That is, we know that there are no four-legged mammals having a single straight horn projecting from their forehead. Similarly, the intension of the word "cat" serves as the criterion for determining what is and what is not a member of the class of cats. Because intension determines extension, it follows that there are no terms having empty intension. If a term had empty intension, there would be no criterion for identifying its extension; as a result, the term would have no meaning at all.

It is sometimes alleged that certain terms, such as proper names and serial numbers, have extension without having intension. The term "George," for example, might be said to denote all the people named "George," without connoting anything. Such a view is mistaken, however, because the term "George" clearly connotes the attribute of having the name "George"; if this were not the case, there would be no way of telling what the extension of the term "George" is. We determine whether or not someone is named "George" by asking him "Is your name 'George'?" or, in other words, "Is the attribute of having the name 'George' one of the attributes that you possess?" Similarly, any specific serial number connotes the attribute of manifesting that number in some visible manner.

The distinction between intension and extension may be further illustrated by comparing the way in which these concepts can be used to give order to random sequences of terms. Terms may be put in the order of increasing intension, increasing extension, decreasing intension, and decreasing extension. A series of terms is in the order of **increasing intension** when each term in the series (except the first) connotes more attributes than the one preceding it. In other words, each term in the series (except the first) is *more specific* than the one preceding it. (A term is specific to the degree that it connotes more attributes.) The order of **decreasing intension** is the reverse of that of increasing intension.

A series of terms is in the order of **increasing extension** when each term in the series (except the first) denotes a class having more members than the class denoted by the term preceding it. In other words, the class size gets larger with each successive term. **Decreasing extension** is, of course, the reverse of this order. Examples:

increasing intension:	animal, mammal, feline, tiger
increasing extension:	tiger, feline, mammal, animal
decreasing intension:	tiger, feline, mammal, animal
decreasing extension:	animal, mammal, feline, tiger

These examples illustrate a fact pertaining to most such series: the order of increasing intension is usually the same as that of decreasing extension. Conversely, the order of decreasing intension is usually the same as that of increasing extension. There are some exceptions, however. Consider the following series:

unicorn; unicorn with blue eyes; unicorn with blue eyes and green horn; unicorn with blue eyes, green horn, and a weight of over 400 pounds

Each term in this series has empty extension; so, while the series exhibits the order of increasing intension, it does not exhibit the order of decreasing extension. Here is another, slightly different, example:

living human being; living human being with a genetic code; living human being with a genetic code and a brain; living human being with a genetic code, a brain, and a height of less than 100 feet

In this series none of the terms has empty extension, but each term has exactly the *same* extension as the others. Thus, while the intension increases with each successive term, once again the extension does not decrease.

EXERCISE 2.1

I. The following exercises deal with words and terms.

1. Determine which of the following words or groups of words are terms and which are nonterms.

extortion	Thomas Jefferson
laborious	Empire State Building
cunningly	annoy
practitioner	render satisfactory
seriousness	graceful dancer
forever	wake up
whoever studies	not only
interestingly impassive	tallest man on the squad
scarlet	mountaintop
reinvestment	between
therefore	since

2. Name some of the attributes connoted by the following terms. Express your answer with adjectives or adjectival phrases. Example: The term "elephant" connotes the attributes of being large, having tusks, having a trunk, and so on.

drum	wolf
politician	Mona Lisa
devil	Statue of Liberty
fanatic	riot
carrot	piano

3. Name three items denoted by the terms in the left-hand column below and all items denoted by the terms in the right-hand column.

newspaper	tallest mountain on earth
scientist	prime number less than 10
manufacturer	U.S. Senator from New York
river	language of Switzerland
opera	Scandinavian country

4. Put the following sequences of terms in the order of increasing intension:

   ★a. conifer, Sitka spruce, tree, spruce, plant
   b. Italian sports car, car, vehicle, Maserati, sports car
   c. Doctor of Medicine, person, brain surgeon, professional person,
      surgeon
   d. wallaby, marsupial, mammal, animal, kangaroo
   e. parallelogram, polygon, square, rectangle, quadrilateral

5. Construct a series of four terms that exhibits increasing intension but
nondecreasing extension.

II. Answer "true" or "false" to the following statements:

1. All words have an intensional meaning and an extensional meaning.

2. The intensional meaning of a term consists of the attributes connoted
by the term.

3. The extensional meaning of a term consists of the members of the class
denoted by the term.

4. The extension of a term always remains the same with the passage of
time.

5. Some terms have empty intension.

6. Some terms have empty extension.

7. The intension of a term determines the extension.

8. The intension of a term determines how specific the term is.

9. The order of increasing intension is always the same as that of decreasing extension.

10. "Leprechaun" and "unicorn" have the same extension.

2.2 DEFINITIONS AND THEIR PURPOSES

Over the years philosophers have held various conflicting views about
the purpose of definitions. For Plato, to mention just one, definitions

were intended to explicate the meaning of certain eternal essences or forms, such as justice, piety, and virtue. For most logicians today, however, definitions are intended exclusively to explicate the meaning of *words.* In conformity with this latter position, we may define **definition** as a group of words that assigns a meaning to some word or group of words. Accordingly, every definition consists of two parts: the definiendum and the definiens. The **definiendum** is the word or group of words that is supposed to be defined, and the **definiens** is the word or group of words that does the defining. For example, in the definition " 'Tiger' means a large, striped, ferocious feline indigenous to the jungles of India and Asia," the word "tiger" is the definiendum, and everything after the word "means" is the definiens. The definiens is not itself the meaning of the definiendum; rather, it is the group of words that symbolizes (or that is supposed to symbolize) the *same* meaning as the definiendum. Because we presumably know in advance what the definiens symbolizes, we are led, via the definition, to understand what the definiendum symbolizes. It is in this way that the definition "assigns" a meaning to its definiendum.

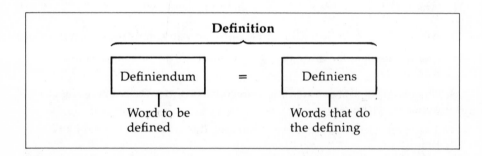

Once it has been decided that definitions explicate the meaning of words, other disagreements emerge among the philosophers. Some argue that since a definition is merely a rule that allows one set of words (the definiens) to be used in place of another set (the definiendum), definitions communicate no information at all about the subject matter of the definiendum. Others take the opposite tack and argue that since definitions result in a clarification of language, they provide a means for the discovery of deeper philosophical truths. It seems, however, that neither of these approaches is able to make good sense of all the various kinds of definitions that are actually employed in ordinary usage. As a result, instead of beginning their analysis of definitions with a set of a priori criteria, many logicians take a pragmatic approach and begin with a survey of the various kinds of definitions that are actually used and of the functions that they actually serve. This is the approach taken here.

Stipulative Definitions

A **stipulative definition** assigns a meaning to a word for the first time. This may involve either coining a new word or giving a new meaning to an old word. The purpose of a stipulative definition is usually to replace a more complex expression with a simpler one.

The need for a stipulative definition is often occasioned by some new phenomenon or development. For example, a few years ago the attempt was made at a certain zoo to crossbreed tigers and lions. Because of the genetic similarity of the two species, the attempt succeeded. Offspring were produced from a male tiger and a female lion and from a male lion and a female tiger. When the offspring were born, it became appropriate to give them names. Of course, the names "offspring of male tiger and female lion" and "offspring of male lion and female tiger" could have been used, but these names were hardly convenient. Instead, the names "tigon" and "liger" were selected. Any two new words would have sufficed equally well for naming the offspring—"topar" and "largine" for example—but "tigon" and "liger" were considered more appropriate, for obvious reasons. "Tigon" was taken to mean the offspring of a male tiger and a female lion, and "liger" the offspring of a male lion and a female tiger. These assignments of meanings were accomplished through stipulative definitions.

Because humankind is continually coming up with new creations, whether it be new food concoctions, new inventions, new modes of behavior, new kinds of apparel, new dances, or whatever, stipulative definitions are continually being used to introduce names for these things. Sometimes these definitions are only implicit and amount to little more than the spontaneous association of a word with some action—as was probably the case when the words "bop," "twist," "jerk," and "chicken" came to be known as dances a few years ago. At other times, they are definitely explicit, as when the word "penicillin" was selected as the name for an antibacterial substance produced by certain *Penicillium* molds, or when the symbol "10^5" was chosen as a simple substitute for "$10 \times 10 \times 10 \times 10 \times 10$."

Because a stipulative definition is a completely arbitrary assignment of a meaning to a word for the first time, there can be no such thing as a "true" or "false" stipulative definition. Furthermore, for the same reason, a stipulative definition cannot provide any new information about the subject matter of the definiendum. The fact that the word "tigon" was selected to replace "offspring of a male tiger and a female lion" tells us nothing new about the nature of the animal in question. One stipulative definition may, however, be more or less convenient or more or less appropriate than another.

Stipulative definitions are misused in verbal disputes when one person covertly uses a word in a peculiar way and then proceeds to assume that everyone else uses that word in the same way. Under these circumstances that person is said to be using the word "stipulatively." In such cases the assumption that other persons use the word in the same way is rarely justified.

Lexical Definitions

A **lexical definition** is used to report the meaning that a word already has in a language. Dictionary definitions are all instances of lexical definitions. Thus, in contrast with a stipulative definition, which assigns a meaning to a word for the first time, a lexical definition may be true or false depending on whether it does or does not report the way a word is actually used. Because words are frequently used in more than one way, lexical definitions have the further purpose of eliminating the ambiguity that would otherwise arise if one of these meanings were to be confused with another.

At this point, it is useful to distinguish ambiguity from vagueness. A word is **vague** if it lacks clarity; that is, if its meaning is blurred or fuzzy around the edges. For example, words such as "love," "happiness," "peace," "excessive," "fresh," "rich," "poor," "normal," "conservative," and "polluted" are vague. We can rarely tell with any degree of precision whether they apply to a given situation. A word is **ambiguous**, on the other hand, when it can be interpreted as having two or more clearly distinct meanings in a given context. Many commonly used words have two or more relatively precise meanings. When, in a given context, it is uncertain which of these meanings is intended, ambiguity results. Some words that are subject to ambiguous usage are "light," "bank," "sound," "right," and "race." "Light" can mean, among other things, light in weight or radiant energy; "bank" can mean a financial institution or the slope bordering a river; and so on.

Because a lexical definition lists the various meanings that a word can have, a person who consults such a definition is better prepared to avoid ambiguous constructions of his or her own and to detect those of others. The undetected ambiguity causes the most trouble. In many cases the problem lies not with the obvious differences in meaning that words such as "light" and "bank" may have but with the subtle shadings of meaning that are more likely to be confused with one another. A good lexical definition will distinguish these various shadings and thereby guard against the possibility that two such meanings will be unconsciously jumbled together into one.

Precising Definitions

The purpose of a **precising definition** is to reduce the vagueness of a word that, in the absence of such a definition, is vague. Once the vagueness has been reduced, one can reach a decision as to the applicability of the word to a specific situation. We have noted 'that the word "poor" is vague. If legislation were ever introduced to give direct financial assistance to the poor, a precising definition would have to be supplied specifying exactly who is poor and who is not. The definition " 'Poor' means having an annual income of less than $4,000 and a net worth of less than $20,000" is an example of a precising definition.

Whenever words are taken from ordinary usage and employed in a highly systematic context such as science, mathematics, medicine, or law, they must always be clarified by means of a precising definition. The terms "force," "energy," "acid," "element," "number," "equality," "contract," and "agent" have all been given precising definitions by specific disciplines.

Sometimes the substance of a court trial may revolve around the precise usage of a term. A recent trial in California addressed the question of whether a man who had driven a bicycle while intoxicated violated the motor vehicle code. The question concerned whether, for these purposes, a bicycle could be considered a "vehicle." The court decided in the negative, and the decision amounted to an incremental extension of an already existent precising definition for the word "vehicle."

Another example involves the practice of surgical transplantation of vital organs. Before a heart transplant can be conducted, the donor must be dead; otherwise the surgeon will be accused of murder. If the donor is dead for too long, however, the success of the transplant will be imperiled. But exactly when is a person considered to be dead? Is it when the heart stops beating, when the person stops breathing, when rigor mortis sets in, or some other time? The question involves the meaning of the term "moment of death." The courts have decided that "moment of death" should be taken to mean the moment the brain stops functioning, as measured by an electroencephalograph. This decision amounts to the acceptance of a precising definition for "moment of death."

A precising definition differs from a stipulative definition in that the latter involves a purely arbitrary assignment of meaning, whereas the assignment of meaning in a precising definition is not at all arbitrary. A great deal of care must be taken to insure that the assignment of meaning in a precising definition is appropriate and legitimate for the context within which the term is to be employed.

Theoretical Definitions

A **theoretical definition** provides a theoretical picture or characterization of the entity or entities denoted by the definiendum. In other words, it provides a way of viewing or conceiving these entities that suggests deductive consequences, further investigation (experimental or otherwise), and whatever else would be entailed by the acceptance of a theory governing these entities. The definition of the term "heat" found in texts dealing with the kinetic theory of heat provides a good example: " 'heat' means the energy associated with the random motion of the molecules of a substance." This definition does more than merely assign a meaning to a word; it provides a way of conceiving the physical phenomenon that is heat. In so doing, it suggests the deductive consequence that as the molecules of a substance speed up, the temperature of the substance increases. In addition, it suggests a number of experiments— experiments investigating the relationship between molecular velocity and the phenomena of radiation, gas pressure, molecular elasticity, and molecular configuration. In short, this definition of "heat" provides the impetus for an entire theory about heat.

Other examples of theoretical definitions are the definition of "light" as a form of electromagnetic radiation, and the definition of "force," "mass," and "acceleration" in Newton's second law of motion as expressed in the equation "$F = MA$." The latter is a kind of contextual definition in which each term is defined in terms of the other two. Both definitions entail numerous deductive consequences about the phenomena involved and suggest numerous avenues of experimental investigation.

Not all theoretical definitions are associated with science. Many terms in philosophy, such as "substance," "form," "cause," "change," "idea," "good," "mind," and "God," have been given theoretical definitions. In fact, most of the major philosophers in history have given these terms their own peculiar theoretical definitions, and this fact accounts in part for the unique character of their respective philosophies. For example, Leibniz's definition of "substance" in terms of what he called "monads" laid the foundation for his metaphysical theory, and John Stuart Mill's definition of "good" as the greatest happiness of the greatest number provided the underpinnings for his utilitarian theory of ethics.

Like stipulative definitions, theoretical definitions are neither true nor false, strictly speaking. They may, however, be more or less interesting or more or less fruitful, depending on the deductive consequences they entail and on the outcome of the experiments they suggest.

Persuasive Definitions

The purpose of a **persuasive definition** is to engender a favorable or unfavorable attitude toward what is denoted by the definiendum. This purpose is accomplished by assigning an emotionally charged or value-laden meaning to a word while making it appear that the word really has (or ought to have) that meaning in the language in which it is used. Thus, persuasive definitions amount to a certain synthesis of stipulative, lexical, and, possibly, theoretical definitions backed by the rhetorical motive to engender a certain attitude. As a result of this synthesis, a persuasive definition masquerades as an honest assignment of meaning to a term while condemning or blessing with approval the subject matter of the definiendum. Here are some examples of opposing pairs of persuasive definitions:

> "Abortion" means the ruthless murdering of innocent human beings.
> "Abortion" means a safe and established surgical procedure whereby a woman is relieved of an unwanted burden.

> "Liberal" means a drippy-eyed do-gooder obsessed with giving away other people's money.
> "Liberal" means a genuine humanitarian committed to the goals of adequate housing and health care and of equal opportunity for all of our citizens.

> "Capitalism" means the economic system in which individuals are afforded the God-given freedom to own property and conduct business as they choose.
> "Capitalism" means the economic system in which humanity is sacrificed to the wanton quest for money, and mutual understanding and respect are replaced by alienation, greed, and selfishness.

> "Taxation" means the procedure by means of which our commonwealth is preserved and sustained.
> "Taxation" means the procedure used by bureaucrats to rip off the people who elected them.

The objective of a persuasive definition is to influence the attitudes of the reader or listener; thus, such definitions may be used with considerable effectiveness in political speeches and editorial columns. While persuasive definitions may, like lexical definitions, be evaluated as either true or false, the primary issue is neither truth or falsity but the effectiveness of such definitions as instruments of persuasion.

EXERCISE 2.2

I. These exercises pertain to kinds of definitions.

1. Invent stipulative definitions for two new words that you wish to introduce into the language for the first time.

2. Construct lexical definitions for "peace" and "pawn." Interpret both words as nouns, and indicate two different meanings for each.

3. Construct precising definitions for "middle-aged" and "alcoholic." Interpret both words as relating to people and specify the purpose for which the definitions are to be used.

4. Construct theoretical definitions for "energy" and "atom."

5. Construct opposing pairs of persuasive definitions for "conservative" and "socialism."

II. Answer "true" or "false" to the following statements:

1. From the standpoint of logic, many definitions are concerned not with words but with things.
2. The definiendum is the word or term that is supposed to be defined.
3. The definiens is the word or group of words that assigns a meaning to the word being defined.
4. A stipulative definition is either true or false.
5. A lexical definition reports the way a word is actually used in a language.
6. One of the purposes of a lexical definition is to guard against the ambiguous use of a word.
7. The meaning given to a word by a precising definition is completely arbitrary.
8. Theoretical definitions are either true or false, just as are lexical definitions.
9. Theoretical definitions provide a theoretical characterization of the entity or entities denoted by the word being defined.
10. The purpose of a persuasive definition is to influence attitudes.

2.3 DEFINITIONAL TECHNIQUES

In the last section we presented a survey of some of the kinds of definitions actually in use and the functions they are intended to serve. In this section we will investigate some of the techniques used to produce these definitions. These techniques may be classified in terms of the two kinds of meaning, intensional and extensional, discussed in Section 2.1.

Extensional (Denotative) Definitions

An **extensional definition** is one that assigns a meaning to a term by indicating the members of the class that the definiendum denotes. There are at least three ways of indicating the members of a class: pointing to them, naming them individually, and naming them in groups. The three kinds of definitions that result are called, respectively, demonstrative or ostensive definition, enumerative definition, and definition by subclass.

Demonstrative (ostensive) definitions are probably the most primitive form of definition. All one need know to understand such a definition is the meaning of pointing. As the following examples illustrate, such definitions may be either partial or complete, depending upon whether all or only some of the members of the class denoted by the definiendum are pointed to:

> "Chair" means this and this and this—as you point to a number of chairs, one after the other.
>
> "Washington Monument" means that—as you point to it.

If you were attempting to teach a foreigner your own native language, and neither of you understood a word of each other's language, demonstrative definition would almost certainly be one of the methods you would use.

Because demonstrative definitions are the most primitive, they are also the most limited. In addition to the limitations affecting all extensional definitions (which will be discussed shortly), there is the obvious limitation that the required objects be available for being pointed at. For example, if one wishes to define the word "sun" and it happens to be nighttime, or the word "dog" and none happen to be in the vicinity, a demonstrative definition cannot be used.

Demonstrative definitions differ from the other kinds of definitions in that the definiens is constituted at least in part by a gesture—the gesture of pointing. Since the definiens in any definition is a group of words, however, a gesture, such as pointing, must count as a word. While this conclusion may appear strange at first, it is supported by the fact that the "words" in many sign languages consist exclusively of gestures.

Enumerative definitions assign a meaning to a term by naming the members of the class the term denotes. Like demonstrative definitions, they may also be either partial or complete. Examples:

> "Actor" means a person such as Gregory Peck, Rod Steiger, or Jack Lemmon.
>
> "Planet" means one of the following: Mercury, Venus, Earth, Mars, Saturn, Jupiter, Neptune, Uranus, or Pluto.

Complete enumerative definitions are usually more satisfying than partial ones because they identify the definiendum with greater assurance. Relatively few classes, however, can be completely enumerated. Many classes, for example the class of real numbers greater than 1 but less than 2, have an infinite number of members. Others, for example the class of stars and the class of persons, while not infinite, have still too many members to enumerate. Therefore, anything approximating a complete enumerative definition of terms denoting these classes is clearly impossible. Then there are others—the class of insects and the class of trees, for example—the vast majority of whose members have no names. For terms that denote these classes, either a demonstrative definition or a definition by subclass is the more appropriate choice.

A **definition by subclass** assigns a meaning to a term by naming subclasses of the class denoted by the term. Such a definition, too, may be either partial or complete, depending on whether the subclasses named, when taken together, include all the members of the class or only some of them. Examples:

> "Tree" means an oak, pine, elm, spruce, maple, and the like.
>
> "Flower" means a rose, lily, daisy, geranium, zinnia, and the like.
>
> "Cetacean" means either a whale, a dolphin, or a porpoise.
>
> "Fictional work" means either a poem, a play, a novel, or a short story.

The first two are partial, the second two complete. As with definitions by enumeration, complete definitions by subclass are more satisfying than partial ones; but because relatively few terms denote classes that admit of a conveniently small number of subclasses, complete definitions by subclass are often difficult, if not impossible, to provide.

Extensional definitions are chiefly used as techniques for producing lexical and stipulative definitions. Lexical definitions are aimed at communicating how a word is actually used, and one of the ways of doing so is by identifying the members of the class that the word denotes. Dictionaries frequently include references to the individual members (or to the subclasses) of the class denoted by the word being defined. Sometimes they even include a kind of demonstrative definition when they provide a picture of the object that the word denotes. Not all lexical definitions have to occur in dictionaries, however. A lexical definition can just as well be spoken, as when one person attempts to explain verbally to another how a word is used in a language. Such attempts, incidentally, often have recourse to all three kinds of extensional definition.

Stipulative definitions are used to assign a meaning to a word for the first time. This task may be accomplished by all three kinds of extensional definition. For example, a biologist engaged in naming and classifying types of fish might assign names to the specific varieties by pointing to their respective tanks (demonstrative definition), and then he might assign a class name to the whole group by referring to the names of the specific varieties (definition by subclass). An astronomer might point via his telescope to a newly discovered comet and announce, "That comet will henceforth be known as 'Henderson's Comet'" (demonstrative definition). The organizer of a children's game might make the stipulation: "John, Mary, and Billy will be called 'Buccaneers,' and Judy, George, and Nancy will be 'Pirates' " (enumerative definition).

Although it is conceivable that extensional definitions could also serve as techniques for theoretical and persuasive definitions (though this would be highly unusual), extensional definitions by themselves cannot properly serve as precising definitions for the following reason. The function of a precising definition is to clarify a vague word, and vagueness is a problem affecting intensional meaning. Because the intension is imprecise, the extension is indefinite. To attempt to render the intension precise by exactly specifying the extension (as with an extensional definition) would be tantamount to having extension determine intension—which cannot be done.

The principle that intension determines extension, whereas the converse is not true, underlies the fact that all extensional definitions suffer serious deficiencies. For example, in the case of the demonstrative definition of the word "chair," if all the chairs pointed to are made of wood, the listener might get the idea that "chair" means "wood," instead of something to sit on. Similarly, he might get the idea that "Washington Monument" means "tall," or "pointed," or any of a number of other things. From the definition of "actor" he might think that "actor" means "famous man"—which would include Albert Einstein and Winston Churchill. From the definition of "tree" the listener might get the idea that "tree" means "firmly planted in the ground," which would also include the pilings of a building. And he might think that "cetacean" means "fast swimmer" instead of "aquatic mammal." In other words, it makes no difference how many individuals or subclasses are named in an extensional definition, there is no assurance that the listener or reader will get the *intensional* meaning. Extensions can *suggest* intensions, but they cannot *determine* them.

Intensional (Connotative) Definitions

An **intensional definition** is one that assigns a meaning to a word by indicating the qualities or attributes that the word connotes. Because at least three strategies may be used to indicate the attributes a word connotes, there are at least three kinds of intensional definitions: synonymous definition, operational definition, and definition by genus and difference.

A **synonymous definition** is one in which the definiens is a single word that connotes the same attributes as the definiendum. In other words, the definiens is a synonym of the word being defined. Examples:

> "Physician" means doctor.
> "Intentional" means willful.

"Voracious" means ravenous.
"Observe" means see.

When a single word can be found that has the same intensional meaning as the word being defined, a synonymous definition is a highly concise way of assigning a meaning. Many words, however, have subtle shades of meaning that are not connoted by any other single word. For example, the word "wisdom" is not exactly synonymous with either "knowledge," "understanding," or "sense"; and "envious" is not exactly synonymous with either "jealous" or "covetous."

An **operational definition** assigns a meaning to a word by specifying certain experimental procedures that determine whether or not the word applies to a certain thing. Examples:

> One substance is "harder than" another if and only if one scratches the other when the two are rubbed together.
>
> A subject has "brain activity" if and only if an electroencephalograph shows oscillations when attached to the subject's head.
>
> A "potential difference" exists between two conductors if and only if a voltmeter shows a reading when connected to the two conductors.
>
> A solution is an "acid" if and only if litmus paper turns red when placed in contact with it.

Each of these definitions prescribes an operation to be performed. The first prescribes that the two substances in question be rubbed together, the second that the electroencephalograph be connected to the patient's head and observed for oscillations, the third that the voltmeter be connected to the two conductors and observed for deflection, and the fourth that the litmus paper be placed in the solution and observed for color change. Unless it specifies such an operation, a definition cannot be an operational definition. For example, the definition "A solution is an 'acid' if and only if it has a pH of less than 7," while good in other respects, is not an operational definition because it prescribes no operation.

Operational definitions were invented for the purpose of tying down relatively abstract concepts to the solid ground of empirical reality. In this they succeed fairly well; yet, from the standpoint of ordinary language usage, they involve certain deficiencies. One of these deficiencies concerns the fact that operational definitions usually convey only *part* of the intensional meaning of a term. Certainly "brain activity" means more than oscillations on an electroencephalograph, just as "acid" means more than blue litmus paper turning red. This deficiency becomes more acute when one attempts to apply operational definitions to terms outside the framework of science. For example, no adequate operational definition could be given for such words as "love," "respect," "freedom," and "dignity."

A **definition by genus and difference** assigns a meaning to a term by identifying a genus term and one or more difference words that, when combined, convey the meaning of the term being defined. Definition by genus and difference is more generally applicable and achieves more adequate results than any of the other kinds of intensional definition. To explain how it works, we must first explain the meanings of the terms "genus," "species," and "specific difference."

In logic, "genus" and "species" have a somewhat different meaning than they have in biology. In logic, "genus" simply means a relatively larger class, and "species" means a relatively smaller subclass of the genus. For example, we may speak of the genus animal and the species mammal, or of the genus mammal and the species feline, or of the genus feline and the species tiger, or of the genus tiger and the species Bengal tiger. In other words, genus and species are merely relative classifications.

The "specific difference," or "difference," for short, is the attribute or attributes that distinguish the various species within a genus. For example, the specific difference that distinguishes tigers from other species in the genus feline would include the attributes of being large, striped, ferocious, and so on. Because the specific difference is what distinguishes the species, when a genus is qualified by a specific difference a species is identified. Definition by genus and difference is based upon this fact. It consists in combining a term denoting a genus with a word or group of words connoting a specific difference so that the combination identifies the meaning of the term denoting the species.

Let us construct a definition by genus and difference for the word "ice." The first step is to identify a genus of which ice is the species. The required genus is water. Next we must identify a specific difference (attribute) that makes ice a special form of water. The required difference is frozen. The completed definition may now be written out:

"Ice" means frozen water.	ice = species
	water = genus
	frozen = difference

A definition by genus and difference is easy to construct. Simply select a term that is more general than the term to be defined, then narrow it down so that it means the same thing as the term being defined. Examples:

Species		**Difference**	**Genus**
"Daughter"	means a	female	offspring.
"Husband"	means a	married	man.

"Doe"	means a	female	deer.
"Fawn"	means a	very young	deer.
"Skyscraper"	means a	very tall	building.

Other examples are more sophisticated:

> "Tent" means a collapsible shelter made of canvas or other material that is stretched and sustained by poles.

"Tent" is the species, "shelter" is the genus, and "collapsible" and "made of canvas . . ." the difference.

Definition by genus and difference is the most effective of the intensional definitions for producing the five kinds of definition discussed in Section 2.2. Stipulative, lexical, precising, theoretical, and persuasive definitions can all be constructed according to the method of genus and difference. Lexical definitions are typically definitions of this type. Operational definition can serve as the method for constructing stipulative, lexical, precising, and persuasive definitions, but because of the limitations we have noted, it typically could not be used to produce a *complete* lexical definition. Other techniques would have to be used in addition. Synonymous definition may be used to produce only lexical definitions. Since, in a synonymous definition, the definiendum must have a meaning before a synonym can be found, this technique cannot be used to produce stipulative definitions, and the fact that the definiens of such a definition contains no more information than the definiendum prohibits its use in constructing precising, theoretical, and persuasive definitions.

EXERCISE 2.3

I. Construct a partial enumerative definition for the following terms by naming three members of the class the term denotes. Then find a nonsynonymous term that these members serve equally well to define.
Example: "Poet" means a person such as Wordsworth, Coleridge, or Shelley. A nonsynonymous term is "Englishman."

★1. skyscraper
2. corporation
3. island
4. composer
5. novel

6. painting
7. prime number
8. mountain
9. language
10. philosopher

II. Construct a complete enumerative definition for the following terms:

1. ocean
2. zodiac sign

3. continent
4. New England state

III. Construct a definition by subclass for the following terms by naming three subclasses of the class the term denotes. Then find a nonsynonymous term that these subclasses serve equally well to define.

★1. animal
 2. fish
 3. vehicle
 4. gemstone
 5. polygon

6. plant
7. dessert
8. insect
9. professional person
10. musical composition

IV. Construct a complete definition by subclass for the following terms:

1. living being
2. quadrilateral

3. regular polyhedron
4. circulating American coin

V. Construct synonymous definitions for the following terms:

★1. intersection
 2. fabric
 3. tendency
 4. nucleus
 5. stratum
 6. abode

7. wedlock
8. cellar
9. summit
10. dais
11. apparel
12. chamber

13. neophyte
14. command
15. facade
16. lawyer
17. dusk
18. error

VI. Construct operational definitions for the following words:

★1. genius
 2. ferromagnetic

3. fluorescent
4. alkaline

VII. Construct definitions by genus and difference for the following terms. In each definition identify the genus term.

★1. drake
 2. biologist
 3. felony
 4. widow
 5. library

6. hammer
7. hurricane
8. prime number
9. oak
10. truck

VIII. Answer "true" or "false" to the following statements:

1. The technique of extensional definition may be used to produce precising definitions.

2. The technique of extensional definition may be used to produce stipulative and lexical definitions.

3. Most extensional definitions convey the precise intensional meaning of a term.

4. An intensional definition conveys the meaning of a term by indicating the members of the class the term denotes.

5. In a synonymous definition the definiens must be a single word.

6. The technique of synonymous definition may be used to construct precising definitions.

7. Operational definitions typically convey the entire intensional meaning of a word.

8. The species is a subclass of the genus.

9. The specific difference is an attribute or set of attributes that identifies a species.

10. Definition by genus and difference may be used to produce stipulative, lexical, precising, theoretical, and persuasive definitions.

2.4 CRITERIA FOR LEXICAL DEFINITIONS

Because the function of a lexical definition is to report the way a word is actually used in a language, lexical definitions are the ones we most frequently encounter and are what most people mean when they speak of the "definition" of a word. Accordingly, it is appropriate that we have a set of rules that we may use in constructing lexical definitions of our own and in evaluating the lexical definitions of others. Since the rules presented here are intended specifically for lexical definitions, it is only natural that many of them do not apply to the other kinds of definition. The unique functions that are served by stipulative, precising, theoretical, and persuasive definitions prescribe different sets of criteria.

> Rule 1: A lexical definition should convey the essential
> meaning of the word being defined.

The word "man" is occasionally defined as "featherless biped." Such a definition fails to convey the essential meaning of "man" as the word is used in ordinary English. It says nothing about the attributes that distinguish man from the other animals, namely, the capacity to reason and to use language on a sophisticated level. A more adequate definition would be " 'man' means the animal that has the capacity to reason and to speak."

If a lexical definition is to be given in terms of an operational definition or in terms of any of the forms of extensional definition, it should usually be supplemented by one of the other forms of intensional definition, preferably definition by genus and difference. As we have noted, from the standpoint of ordinary language usage an operational definition often conveys only part of the intensional meaning of a word, and this part frequently misses the essential meaning altogether. As for extensional definitions, at best they can only *suggest* the essential meaning of a word; they cannot *determine* it precisely. As a result, no adequate lexical definition can consist exclusively of extensional definitions.

Rule 2:   A lexical definition should be neither too broad nor too narrow.

If a definition is too broad, the definiens includes too much; if it is too narrow, the definiens includes too little. If, for example, "bird" were defined as "any warm-blooded animal having wings," the definition would be too broad because it would include bats, and bats are not birds. If, on the other hand, "bird" were defined as "any warm-blooded, feathered animal that can fly," the definition would be too narrow because it would exclude ostriches, which cannot fly.

The only types of lexical definitions that tend to be susceptible to either of these deficiencies are synonymous definitions and definitions by genus and difference. With synonymous definitions, one must be careful that the definiens really is a synonym of the definiendum. For example, the definition " 'king' means ruler" is too broad because many rulers are not kings. "Ruler" is not genuinely synonymous with "king." As for definitions by genus and difference, one must insure that the specific difference narrows the genus in exactly the right way. Both of the above definitions of "bird" are definitions by genus and difference in which the specific difference fails to restrict the genus in exactly the right manner.

Rule 3:   A lexical definition must not be circular.

Sometimes the problem of circularity appears in connection with *pairs* of definitions. The following pair is circular:

"Science" means the activity engaged in by scientists.
"Scientist" means anyone who engages in science.

At other times a definition may be intrinsically circular. Of the following, the first is a synonymous definition, the second a definition by genus and difference:

"Quiet" means quietude.
"Silence" means the state of being silent.

Certain operational definitions also run the risk of circularity:

"Time" means whatever is measured by a clock.

Surely a person would have to know what "time" means before he could understand the purpose of a clock.

Rule 4:   A lexical definition should not be negative when it can be affirmative.

Of the following two definitions, the first is affirmative, the second negative:

"Concord" means harmony.
"Concord" means the absence of discord.

Some words, however, are intrinsically negative. For them, a negative definition is quite appropriate. Examples:

"Bald" means the absence of hair.
"Darkness" means the absence of light.

Rule 5:   A lexical definition should not be expressed in figurative, obscure, vague, or ambiguous language.

A definition is *figurative* if it involves metaphors or tends to paint a picture instead of exposing the essential meaning of a term. Examples:

"Architecture" means frozen music.
"Camel" means a ship of the desert.

A definition is *obscure* if its meaning is hidden. One source of obscurity is overly technical language. Compare these two definitions:

"Bunny" means a mammalian of the family Leporidae of the order Lagomorpha whose young are born furless and blind.

"Bunny" means a rabbit.

The problem lies not with technical language as such but with *needlessly* technical language. Because "bunny" is very much a nontechnical term, no technical definition is needed. On the other hand, some words are intrinsically technical, and for them only a technical definition will suffice. Example:

"Neutrino" means a quasi-massless lepton obeying Fermi-Dirac statistics and having one-half quantum unit of spin.

A definition is *vague* if its meaning is blurred. Example:

"Democracy" means a kind of government where the people are in control.

This definition fails to identify the people who are in control, how they exercise their control, and what they are in control of.

A definition is *ambiguous* if it lends itself to more than one distinct interpretation. Example:

> "Triangle" means a figure composed of three straight lines in which all the angles are equal to 180°.

Does this mean that each angle separately is equal to 180° or that the angles taken together are equal to 180°? Either interpretation is possible given the ambiguous meaning of "all the angles are equal to 180°."

> Rule 6: A lexical definition should avoid affective terminology.

Affective terminology is any kind of word usage that plays upon the emotions of the reader or listener. It includes sarcastic and facetious language and any other kind of language that is liable to influence attitudes. Examples:

> "Communism" means that "brilliant" invention of Karl Marx and other foolish political visionaries in which the national wealth is supposed to be held in common by the people.

> "Theism" means belief in that great Santa Claus in the sky.

The second example also violates Rule 5 because it contains a metaphor.

> Rule 7: A lexical definition should indicate the context to which the definiens pertains.

This rule applies to any definition in which the context of the definiens is important to the meaning of the definiendum. For example, the definition " 'Deuce' means a tie in points toward a game or in games toward a set" is practically meaningless without any reference to tennis. Whenever the definiendum is a word that means different things in different contexts, a reference to the context is important. Examples:

> "Strike" means (in baseball) a pitch at which a batter swings and misses.

> "Strike" means (in bowling) the act of knocking down all the pins with the first ball of a frame.

> "Strike" means (in fishing) a pull on a line made by a fish in taking the bait.

It is not always necessary to make *explicit* reference to the context, but at least the phraseology of the definiens should indicate what the context is.

EXERCISE 2.4

Criticize the following definitions in light of the seven rules for lexical definitions:

★1. A sculpture is a three-dimensional image made of marble.

2. "Elusory" means elusive.

3. "Develop" means to transform by the action of chemicals.

4. A cynic is a person who knows the price of everything and the value of nothing.

(Oscar Wilde)

★5. A slide rule is a device made of wood, plastic, or metal that consists of a sliding piece that moves between two mutually attached stationary pieces.

6. A theist is anyone who is not an atheist or an agnostic.

7. "Intelligence" means whatever is measured by an IQ test.

8. A symphony is a musical piece written for full orchestra.

9. Feminism is a militant movement originated by a group of deviant women for the purpose of undermining the natural distinction between the sexes.

★10. A radio is an electronic device consisting of an antenna, variable-frequency oscillator, and mixer circuitry operating in conjunction with RF, IF, and AF amplification stages, the last of which feeds an AF transducer.

11. Logic is the study of arguments including definitions.

12. A house is a structure made of wood or stone intended for human habitation.

13. Satire is a kind of glass, wherein beholders do generally discover everybody's face but their own.

(Jonathan Swift)

14. A carpenter's square is a square used by a carpenter.

★15. "Safety" means a play in which a player grounds the ball behind his own goal line when the ball was caused to cross the goal line by his own team.

16. Puberty: the time in life in which the two sexes begin first to be acquainted.

(Johnson's Dictionary)

17. "Normal" means an attribute possessed by people who are able to get on in the world.

18. An organic substance is any substance that is not inorganic.

19. Faith is the bird that sings when the dawn is still dark.
                                                      (Rabindranath Tagore)

★20. "Faith" means reason succumbing to insecurity.

21. "Gammon" means, in backgammon, a victory in which one player defeats another before he can remove any of his men from the board.

22. A cello is a stringed musical instrument played with a bow.

23. Tobacco is a plant grown in the southeastern United States that, when enjoyed in the form of cigars and cigarettes, produces a most delightful and satisfying taste and aroma.

24. History is the unfolding of miscalculations.
                                                      (Barbara Tuchman)

★25. "Camera" means a device for taking photographs.

26. "Photograph" means an image produced by the combined action of electromagnetic radiation in the range of 4000 to 7000 Angstroms and certain organic reducing agents such as diaminophenol hydrochloride on silver halide particles affixed to a backing material of high alpha cellulose content.

27. Mackerel: a sea-fish.
                                                      (Johnson's Dictionary)

28. Animal: a living creature corporeal, distinct, on the one side, from pure spirit, on the other, from pure matter.
                                                      (Johnson's Dictionary)

29. "Pen" means an instrument used for writing on paper.

★30. Wine is an alcoholic beverage made from grapes.

3
INFORMAL FALLACIES

3.1 FALLACIES IN GENERAL

A **fallacy** is a certain kind of defect in an argument. One way that an argument can be defective is by having one or more false premises. Another way is by containing a fallacy. Both deductive and inductive arguments may be affected by fallacies; if either kind contains a fallacy, it is either unsound or uncogent, depending on the kind of argument.

Fallacies are usually divided into two groups: formal and informal. A **formal fallacy** is one that may be identified through mere inspection of the form or structure of an argument. Here is an example of a deductive argument that contains a formal fallacy:

> All tigers are animals.
> All mammals are animals.
> Therefore, all tigers are mammals.

This argument has the following form:

> All *A* are *B*.
> All *C* are *B*.
> Therefore, all *A* are *C*.

Through mere inspection of this form, one can see that the argument is invalid. The fact that *A*, *B*, and *C* stand respectively for "tigers," "animals," and "mammals" is irrelevant in detecting the fallacy. The problem may be traced to the second premise. If the letters C and B are interchanged, the form becomes valid, and the original argument, with the same change introduced, also becomes valid (but unsound). This particular fallacy, together with certain others, will be discussed in later chapters.

Informal fallacies are those that can be detected only through analysis of the content of an argument. Consider the following example:

> All factories are plants.
> All plants are things that contain chlorophyll.
> Therefore, all factories are things that contain chlorophyll.

From a mere inspection of the form, this argument might appear valid. But clearly it is invalid (and thus contains a fallacy) because it has true premises and a false conclusion. An inspection of the content, that is, the meaning of the words, reveals that the term "plants" is used in two different senses. In the first premise it means a building where something is manufactured; in the second it means a life form. Such a fallacy is called "equivocation" and is discussed in Section 3.3.

Informal fallacies are frequently backed by some motive on the part of the arguer to deceive the reader or listener. The arguer may not have sufficient evidence to support a certain conclusion and as a result may attempt to win its acceptance by resorting to a trick. Sometimes the trick fools even the arguer. The arguer may delude himself into thinking that he is presenting genuine evidence when in fact he is not. For these reasons arguments that contain informal fallacies, while *being* bad, may *appear* good. In fact, some fallacious arguments may appear to be even better than other arguments that commit no fallacies. By studying some of the typical ways in which arguers deceive both themselves and others, one is less likely to be fooled by the fallacious arguments posed by others and is less likely to stumble blindly into fallacies when constructing arguments for one's own use.

Since the time of Aristotle, logicians have attempted to classify the various informal fallacies. Aristotle himself identified thirteen and separated them into two groups. The work of subsequent logicians has produced dozens more, which has rendered the task of classifying them even more difficult. The presentation that follows separates seventeen informal fallacies into four groups: fallacies of relevance, fallacies of presumption, fallacies of ambiguity, and fallacies of grammatical analogy. The final section of this chapter presents five additional fallacies that occur frequently in ordinary language usage. These are also classified in terms of the fourfold subdivision. Of course, this list is not complete, but most of the informal defects occurring in arguments may be interpreted as instances of one or more of these twenty-two fallacies.

3.2 FALLACIES OF RELEVANCE

The **fallacies of relevance** share the common characteristic that the arguments in which they occur have premises that are *logically* irrelevant to the conclusion. Yet the premises are relevant *psychologically,* so the conclusion may *seem* to follow from the premises, even though it does not follow logically. In a good argument the premises provide genuine evidence in support of the conclusion. In an argument that commits a fallacy of relevance, on the other hand, the connection between premises and conclusion is emotional. To identify a fallacy of relevance, therefore, one must be able to distinguish genuine evidence from various forms of emotional appeal.

Appeal to Force (*Argumentum ad Baculum*: Appeal to the "Stick")

The fallacy of **appeal to force** occurs whenever an arguer poses a conclusion to another person and tells that person either implicitly or explicitly that some harm will come to him or her if he or she does not accept the conclusion. The fallacy always involves a threat by the arguer to the physical or psychological well-being of the listener or reader, who may be either a single person or a group of persons. Obviously, such a threat is logically irrelevant to the subject matter of the conclusion, so any argument based on such a procedure is fallacious. The *ad baculum* fallacy often occurs when children argue with one another:

> *Child to playmate:* "Mister Rogers" is the best show on TV; and if you don't believe it, I'm going to call my big brother over here and he's going to beat you up.

But it occurs among adults as well:

> *Secretary to boss:* I'm sure you'll want to raise my salary for the coming year. After all, you know how friendly I am with your wife, and I'm sure you wouldn't want her to find out what's been going on between you and that sexpot client of yours.

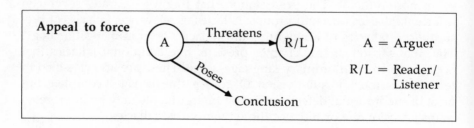

The first example involves a physical threat, the second a psychological threat. While neither threat provides any genuine evidence that the conclusion is true, both provide evidence that someone might be injured. If the two types of evidence are confused with each other, both arguer and listener may be deluded into thinking that the conclusion is supported by evidence, when in fact it is not.

Appeal to Pity (*Argumentum ad Misericordiam*)

The fallacy of **appeal to pity** occurs whenever an arguer poses a conclusion and then attempts to evoke pity from the reader or listener in an effort to get him or her to accept the conclusion. Example:

> *Taxpayer to judge:* Your Honor, I admit that I declared thirteen
> children as dependents on my tax return, even though I have
> only two, and I realize that this was wrong. But if you find
> me guilty of tax evasion, my reputation will be ruined. I'll
> probably lose my job, my poor wife will not be able to have
> the operation that she desperately needs, and my kids will
> starve. Surely you will find me not guilty.

The conclusion of this argument is, "Surely you will find me not guilty." Obviously, the conclusion is not *logically* relevant to the arguer's set of pathetic circumstances, although it *is psychologically* relevant. If the arguer succeeds in evoking pity from the listener or reader, the latter is liable to exercise his or her desire to help the arguer by accepting the argument. In this way the reader or listener may be fooled into accepting a conclusion that is not supported by any evidence. The appeal to pity is quite common and is frequently used by students on their instructors at exam time and by lawyers on behalf of their clients before judges and juries.

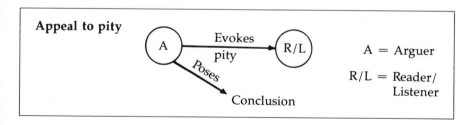

Appeal to the People (*Argumentum ad Populum*)

Nearly everyone wants to be loved, esteemed, admired, valued, recognized, and accepted by others. The **appeal to the people** uses these desires to get the reader or listener to accept a conclusion. Two approaches are involved, one of them direct, the other indirect.

The *direct approach* occurs when an arguer, addressing a large group of people, excites the emotions and enthusiasm of the crowd to win acceptance for his conclusion. The objective is to arouse a kind of mob mentality. This is the strategy used by nearly every propagandist and demagogue. Adolf Hitler was a master of the technique, but it is also used with some measure of success by speechmakers at Democratic and Republican national conventions. Waving flags and blaring music add to the overall effect. Because the individuals in the audience want to share in the camaraderie, the euphoria, and the excitement, they find themselves accepting any number of conclusions with ever-increasing fervor.

The direct approach is not limited to verbal argumentation, of course; a similar effect can be accomplished in writing. By employing such emotionally charged phraseology as "fighter of communism" "champion of the free enterprise system," and "defender of the working man," a polemicist can awaken the same kind of mob mentality as he would if he were speaking.

In the *indirect approach* the arguer directs his appeal not to the crowd as a whole but to one or more individuals separately, focusing upon some aspect of their relationship to the crowd. The indirect approach includes such specific forms as the bandwagon argument, the appeal to vanity, and the appeal to snobbery. All are standard techniques of the advertising industry. Here is an example of the **bandwagon argument**:

> Of course you want to buy Zest toothpaste. Why, 90 percent
> of America brushes with Zest.

The idea is that you will be left behind or left out of the group if you do not use the product.

The **appeal to vanity** often associates the product with a certain celebrity who is admired and pursued, the idea being that you, too, will be admired and pursued if you use it. Example:

> Only the ultimate in fashion could compliment the face of
> Bianca Jagger. Spectrum sunglasses—for the beautiful people
> in the jet set.

And here is an example of the **appeal to snobbery**:

> A Rolls Royce is not for everyone. If you qualify as one of the
> select few, this distinguished classic may be seen and driven
> at British Motor Cars, Ltd. (By appointment only, please.)

Needless to say, the indirect approach is used by others besides advertisers:

A CONCISE INTRODUCTION TO LOGIC

Mother to child: You want to grow up and be just like Wonder Woman, don't you? Then eat your liver and carrots.

Both the direct and indirect approaches of the *ad populum* fallacy have the same basic structure:

You want to be accepted/included in the group/loved/esteemed.... Therefore, you should accept XYZ as true.

In the direct approach the arousal of a mob mentality produces an immediate feeling of belonging for each person in the crowd. Each person feels united with the crowd, which evokes a sense of strength and security. When the crowd roars its approval of the conclusions that are then offered, anyone who does not accept them automatically cuts himself or herself off from the crowd and risks the loss of his or her security, strength, and acceptance. The same thing happens in the indirect approach, but the context and technique are somewhat subtler.

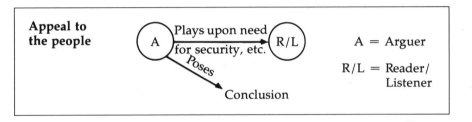

Argument Against the Person (*Argumentum ad Hominem*)

This fallacy always involves two arguers. One of them advances (either directly or implicitly) a certain argument, and the other then responds by directing his or her attention not to the first person's argument but to the first person *himself.* When this occurs, the second person is said to commit an **argument against the person.**

The argument against the person occurs in three forms: the *ad hominem* abusive, *ad hominem* circumstantial, and the *tu quoque.* In the **ad hominem abusive,** the second person responds to the first person's argument by verbally abusing the first person. Example:

Smith and Jones are both running for the State Senate. They present their respective positions at the county fair. Smith has finished speaking, and Jones replies: "Ladies and Gentlemen, you have just heard my opponent speak on the importance of fiscal responsibility; but I would urge you to take what he has said with a grain of salt. Most of you are well aware of the fact that Mr. Smith is an acknowledged homosexual, and you also know that he has been seen many times smoking marijuana at private parties."

Because Smith's being a marijuana-smoking homosexual has little bearing on the logic of his arguments in favor of fiscal responsibility, Jones's argument is fallacious.

The **ad hominem** circumstantial begins the same way as the *ad hominem* abusive, but instead of heaping verbal abuse on his or her opponent, the respondent attempts to discredit the opponent's argument by alluding to certain circumstances that affect the opponent. By doing so the respondent hopes to show that the opponent is predisposed to argue the way he or she does and should therefore not be taken seriously. Here is an example:

> The chief of police has presented an argument to the city council in favor of raising police officers' salaries. The chief's opponent, the mayor, now responds: "Ladies and gentlemen of the council, you have just heard the chief present his position. But surely you cannot take his argument seriously. The chief is an officer himself, and if you raise the officers' salaries, then you raise his salary, too. So it is only natural that he should argue the way he does."

The mayor does not attack the chief's argument directly, but he attempts to discredit it indirectly by calling attention to certain circumstances that affect the chief, namely, the fact that he is himself one of the officers whose salaries would be raised. The *ad hominem* circumstantial is easy to recognize because it always takes this form: "Of course Mr. X argues this way; just look at the circumstances that affect him." Merely because a person happens to be affected by certain circumstances is not sufficient reason to think that the person is incapable of arguing logically. Any attempt to discredit such an argument in this way therefore involves a fallacy.

The **tu quoque** ("you, too") fallacy begins the same way as the other two varieties of the *ad hominem* except that the first person's argument causes the respondent to appear guilty. The respondent then replies by attempting to shift the burden of guilt back to the first person. The response usually takes the form, "Your argument cannot be taken seriously because you are no better than I." Example:

> A parent admonishes his or her child for having stolen candy from the corner store. The child responds: "Your argument is no good. You told me yourself just a week ago that you, too, stole candy when you were a kid."

The *tu quoque* is otherwise called the "two wrongs make a right" fallacy. Obviously, two wrongs do not make a right. Whether the parent stole candy when he or she was a child is irrelevant to whether the child should steal candy.

The three forms of the *ad hominem* fallacy are often convincing because they catch the immediate attention of the reader or listener and they do introduce some kind of evidence into the picture. The fact that Smith is a marijuana-smoking homosexual is eyecatching, and it does constitute evidence in support of some conclusion about Smith's lifestyle. But it is totally irrelevant to the conclusion of the argument. If the reader or listener is not careful to distinguish relevant evidence from irrelevant evidence, he or she is likely to be persuaded by such an argument.

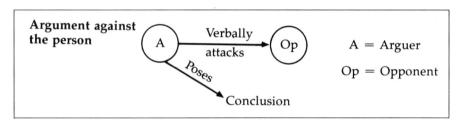

The various forms of the argument against the person should not be confused with the appeal to force. In the appeal to force only one person need present an argument, and that person *threatens* the listener or reader in an effort to make him or her accept the conclusion. In the argument against the person two people must present arguments (the first person at least by implication), and the second person attempts to discredit the first's argument by verbally abusing him, by citing circumstances that affect him, or by shifting the burden of guilt onto him.

Appeal to Authority (*Argumentum ad Verecundiam*)

The **appeal to authority** typically involves three persons: the arguer, the listener or reader, and the person whom the arguer cites as an authority. The structure of this fallacy is simple: the arguer presents a conclusion and cites the testimony of an unqualified authority in support of it. Example:

> Jupiter's third satellite, Europa, very probably has life on it. Why, none other than Joe Slugger, the great baseball player, has come out in support of this idea.

Because it is highly unlikely that a great baseball player should be an expert in astrobiology, we are justified in concluding that this argument is fallacious.

The appeal to authority occurs when the subject matter of the conclusion falls outside the authority's range of expertise. If the authority of Joe Slugger had been cited in support of some matter relating to baseball, it is unlikely that any fallacy would exist. Similarly, if the authority of an informed accountant were cited in support of a conclusion about the financial condition of a corporation, the argument would probably be a good one.

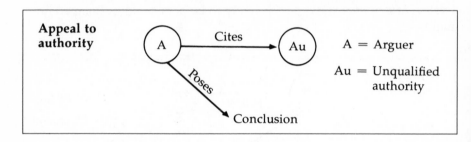

In deciding whether someone is a legitimate authority in a certain field, there are two important facts one should keep in mind: (a) one person might be an authority in more than one field, and (b) someone who is an authority in relation to one group of people might not be an authority in relation to another group. For example, a woman might be an authority in both law and medicine. But this same woman, while she might be an authority in relation to any number of nonlawyers, might not be an authority in relation to her colleagues within the legal profession. Thus, in deciding whether a person is being cited legitimately as an authority, one must know that person's full range of expertise and also something about the expertise of the people to whom the argument is posed.

Appeal to Ignorance (*Argumentum ad Ignorantiam*)

When the premises of an argument tell us that nothing can be known with certainty one way or the other about a certain subject, and the conclusion then states something definite about that subject, the argument commits an **appeal to ignorance**. Example:

> People have been trying for centuries to provide conclusive
> evidence for the claims of astrology, and no one has ever
> succeeded. Therefore, we must conclude that astrology is a lot
> of nonsense.

Conversely, the following argument commits the same fallacy.

> People have been trying for centuries to disprove the claims of astrology, and no one has ever succeeded. Therefore, we must conclude that the claims of astrology are true.

The premises of an argument are supposed to provide positive evidence for the conclusion. The premises of these arguments, however, tell us nothing about astrology; rather, they tell us about what certain unnamed and unidentified people have tried unsuccessfully to do. In each case the premises are irrelevant to the conclusion, and so the argument is fallacious.

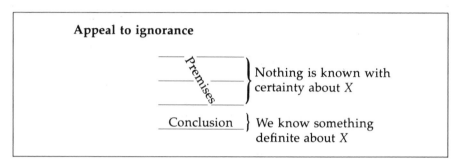

Appeal to ignorance

Premises } Nothing is known with certainty about X

Conclusion } We know something definite about X

These examples do, however, lead us to the first of two important exceptions to the appeal to ignorance. The first stems from the fact that if qualified researchers investigate a certain phenomenon within their range of expertise and fail to turn up any evidence that the phenomenon exists, this fruitless search by itself constitutes positive evidence about the question. Consider, for example, the following argument:

> Teams of scientists attempted over a number of decades to detect the existence of the luminiferous aether, and all failed to do so. Therefore, the luminiferous aether does not exist.

The premises of this argument are true. Given the circumstances, it is likely that the scientists in question would have detected the aether if in fact it did exist. Since they did not detect it, it probably does not exist. Thus, we can say that the above argument is inductively strong (but not deductively valid).

As for the two arguments about astrology, if the attempts to prove or disprove the astrological claims had been done in a systematic way by qualified experts, it is more likely that the arguments would be good. Exactly what is required to qualify someone to investigate astrological claims is, of course, difficult to say. But as these arguments stand, the premises state nothing about the qualifications of the investigators, and so the arguments remain fallacious.

It is not *always* necessary, however, that the investigators have *special* qualifications. The kinds of qualifications needed depend on the situation. Sometimes the mere ability to see and report what one sees is sufficient. Example:

> No one has ever seen Mr. Andrews drink a glass of wine,
> beer, or any other alcoholic beverage. Probably Mr. Andrews
> is a nondrinker.

Because it is highly probable that if Mr. Andrews were a drinker, somebody would have seen him drinking, this argument is inductively strong. No special qualifications are needed to be able to see someone take a drink.

The second exception to the appeal to ignorance relates to courtroom procedure. In the United States, among other countries, a person is presumed innocent until proven guilty. If the prosecutor in a criminal action fails to prove the guilt of the defendant, beyond reasonable doubt, counsel for the defense may justifiably argue that his or her client is innocent. Example:

> *Defense counsel to jury:* "Ladies and gentlemen of the jury, you
> have heard the prosecution present its case against my client.
> Nothing, however, has been proven beyond reasonable
> doubt. In the eyes of the law, therefore, my client is inno-
> cent."

This argument does not commit an appeal to ignorance because of the special provisons of American criminal law. According to these provisions, certain words and phrases take on a special meaning. The phrase "innocent under the law" in the United States means "guilt has not been proven." A defendant may indeed have committed the crime of which he is accused, but if the prosecutor fails to prove him guilty, he is innocent under the law.

Accident

The fallacy of **accident** is committed when a general rule is applied wrongly to a specific case. Typically, the general rule is cited (either directly or implicitly) in the premises and then wrongly applied to the specific case mentioned in the conclusion. Because of the "accidental" features of the specific case, the general rule does not fit. Two examples:

> Freedom of speech is a constitutionally guaranteed right.
> Therefore, John Q. Radical should not be arrested for his
> speech that incited that riot last week.

Property should be returned to its rightful owner. That drunken sailor who is starting a fight with his opponents at the pool table lent you his .45-caliber pistol, and now he wants it back. Therefore, you should return it to him now.

The right of freedom of speech has its limits, as does the rule that property be returned to its rightful owner. These rules are obviously misapplied in the above circumstances. The arguments therefore commit the fallacy of accident.

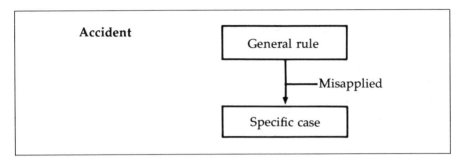

Hasty Generalization (Converse Accident)

Hasty generalization is a fallacy that affects inductive generalizations. In Chapter 1 we saw that an inductive generalization is an argument that draws a conclusion about all the members of a group from evidence that pertains to a selected sample. The fallacy occurs when there is a likelihood that the sample is not representative of the group. Such a likelihood may arise if the sample is either too small or not randomly selected. Here are two examples:

> After only one year the alternator went out in Mr. O'Grady's new Chevrolet. Mrs. Dodson's Oldsmobile developed a transmission problem after only six months. The conclusion is obvious that cars made by General Motors are just a pile of junk these days.

> Two weeks ago the Ajax Pharmacy was robbed and the suspect is a black man. Yesterday a black teenager snatched an old lady's purse while she was waiting at the corner bus stop. Clearly, blacks are nothing but a pack of criminals.

In these arguments a conclusion about a whole group is drawn from premises that mention only two instances. Because such small, atypical samples are not sufficient to support a general conclusion, each argument commits a hasty generalization. The second example indicates how hasty generalization plays a role in racial (and religious) prejudice.

The mere fact that a sample may be small, however, does not necessarily entail that it is atypical. Sometimes other factors intervene that cause the argument to be strong in spite of the fact that the sample may be small. Examples:

> Ten milligrams of substance Z was fed to four mice, and within two minutes all four went into shock and died. Probably substance Z, in this amount, is fatal to the average mouse.

> On three separate occasions I drank a bottle of Figowitz beer and found it flat and bitter. Probably I would find every bottle of Figowitz beer flat and bitter.

Neither of these arguments commits the fallacy of hasty generalization because in neither case is there any likelihood that the sample is atypical of the group. In the first argument the fact that the mice died in only two minutes suggests the existence of a causal connection between eating substance Z and death. If there is such a connection, it would hold for other mice as well. In the second example the fact that the taste of beer typically remains fairly constant from bottle to bottle causes the argument to be strong, even though only three bottles were sampled.

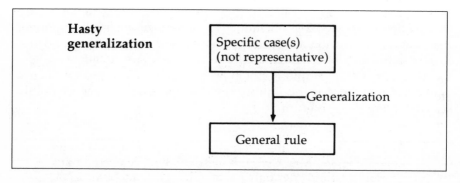

Hasty generalization is otherwise called "converse accident" because it proceeds in a direction opposite to that of accident. Whereas accident proceeds from the general to the particular, converse accident moves from the particular to the general. The premises cite some characteristic affecting one or more atypical instances of a certain class, and the conclusion then applies that characteristic to all members of the class.

False Cause

The fallacy of **false cause** occurs whenever the link between premises and conclusion depends on some imagined causal connection that does not in fact exist. Whenever an argument is suspected of committing the false cause fallacy, the reader or listener should be able to say that the conclusion depends on the supposition that X causes Y, whereas X does not really cause Y at all. Examples:

> During the past two months, every time that the cheerleaders have worn blue ribbons in their hair, the basketball team has been defeated. Therefore, to prevent defeats in the future, the cheerleaders should get rid of those blue ribbons.

> Successful business executives are paid salaries in excess of $50,000. Therefore, the best way to insure that Ferguson will become a successful executive is to raise his salary to at least $50,000.

> There are more laws on the books today than ever before, and more crimes are being committed than ever before. Therefore, to reduce crime we must eliminate the laws.

The first argument depends on the supposition that the blue ribbons caused the defeats, the second on the supposition that a high salary causes success, and the third on the supposition that laws cause crime. In none of them does any genuine causal connection exist.

The first argument illustrates a variety of the false cause fallacy called *post hoc ergo propter hoc* ("after this, therefore on account of this"). This variety of the fallacy presupposes that just because one event happens after another event the first event causes the second. Obviously, mere temporal succession is not sufficient to establish a causal connection. Nevertheless, this kind of reasoning is quite common and lies behind most forms of superstition. (Example: "A black cat crossed my path and later I tripped and sprained my ankle. It must be that black cats really are bad luck.")

The second and third arguments illustrate a variety of the false cause fallacy called *non causa pro causa* ("not the cause for the cause"). This variety is committed when what is taken to be the cause of something is not really the cause at all and the mistake is based on something other than mere temporal succession. In reference to the second argument, success as an executive causes increases in salary—not the other way around—so the argument mistakes the cause for the effect. In reference to the third argument, the increase in crime is, for the most part, only coincidental with the increase in the number of laws. Obviously, the mere fact that one event is coincidental with another is not sufficient reason to think that one caused the other.

The false cause fallacy is often convincing because it is sometimes difficult to determine whether two phenomena are causally related; and even when they are related, it is sometimes difficult to tell which is the cause and which the effect. One point that should be kept in mind when attempting to settle these issues is that statistical correlations by themselves often reveal little about what is actually going on. For example, if all that we knew about smoking and lung cancer is that the two frequently occur together, we might conclude any number of things. We might conclude that both have a common cause, such as a genetic predisposition, or we might conclude that lung cancer is a disease contracted early in life and that it manifests itself in its early stages by a strong desire for tobacco. Fortunately, in the case of smoking and lung cancer there is more evidence than a mere statistical correlation. This additional evidence inclines us to believe that the smoking is a cause of the cancer.

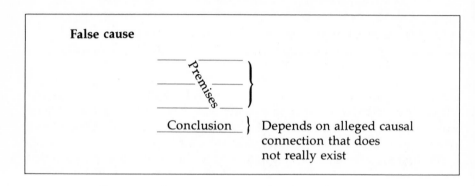

False cause

Conclusion } Depends on alleged causal connection that does not really exist

Missing the Point (*Ignoratio Elenchi*)

All the fallacies we have discussed thus far have been instances of cases where the conclusion of an argument is irrelevant to the premises. **Missing the point** illustrates a special form of irrelevance. This fallacy occurs when the premises of an argument appear to lead up to one particular conclusion, but then a completely different conclusion is drawn. Whenever one suspects that such a fallacy is being committed, he or she should be able to identify the *correct* conclusion, the conclusion that the premises *logically* imply. This conclusion must be completely different from the conclusion that is actually drawn. Examples:

> Crimes of theft and robbery have been increasing at an alarming rate lately. The conclusion is obvious: we must reinstate the death penalty immediately.

> Abuse of the welfare system is rampant nowadays. Our only alternative is to abolish the system altogether.

At least two correct conclusions are entailed by the premise of the first argument: either "We should provide increased police protection in vul-

A CONCISE INTRODUCTION TO LOGIC

nerable neighborhoods" or "We should initiate programs to eliminate the causes of the crimes." Reinstating the death penalty is not a logical conclusion at all. Among other things, theft and robbery are not capital crimes. In the second argument the premises logically suggest some systematic effort to eliminate the cheaters rather than eliminating the system altogether.

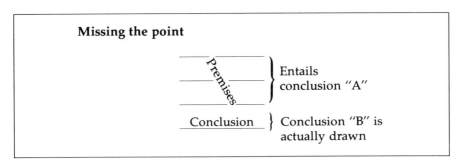

Missing the point

Premises } Entails conclusion "A"

Conclusion } Conclusion "B" is actually drawn

Ignoratio elenchi means "ignorance of the proof." The arguer is ignorant of the logical implications of his or her own premises and, as a result, draws a conclusion that misses the point entirely. The fallacy has a distinct structure all its own, but in some ways it serves as a catchall for arguments that are not clear instances of one or more of the other fallacies of relevance.

EXERCISE 3.2

I. Identify the fallacies of relevance committed by the following arguments. Some arguments may be interpreted as committing more than one fallacy. If no fallacy is committed, write "good argument."

★1. Professor Glazebrook's theory about the origin of the Martian craters is undoubtedly true. Rudolf Orkin, the great concert pianist, announced his support of the theory in this morning's newspaper.

2. Whoever thrusts a knife into another person should be arrested. But surgeons do precisely this when operating. Therefore, surgeons should be arrested.

3. There are more churches in New York City than in any other city in the nation, and more crimes are committed in New York City than anywhere else. So, if we are to eliminate crime, we must abolish the churches.

4. Susanna's dentist advised her to have extensive work done on her teeth. She should not take this advice seriously, however, because if she has this work done, the dentist will receive an excellent fee.

★5. It is financially advisable for you to join our protective organization. Think of the money you will lose in broken windows, overturned trucks, and damaged merchandise in the event of your not joining.

6. The position open in the accounting department should be given to Frank Thompson. Frank has six hungry children to feed, and his wife was recently blinded in one eye in an automobile accident.

7. Most of the graduates of Heathcliff College command excellent salaries upon graduation. Mary Edwards was in the top 10 percent of this year's graduating class at Heathcliff. In addition she is ambitious, talented, charming, and self-confident. Mary can probably look forward to a job that pays an excellent salary.

8. No one has ever been able to prove the existence of extrasensory perception. We must therefore conclude that extrasensory perception is a myth.

9. Something is seriously wrong with high school education these days. SAT scores have declined steadily over the past ten years, and current high school graduates are practically incapable of reading and writing. The obvious conclusion is that we should close the schools.

★10. You should read George Bishop's latest novel right away. It's sold over a million copies, and practically everyone in the Manhattan cocktail circuit is talking about it.

11. The *Daily News* carried an article this morning about three local teenagers who were arrested on charges of drug possession. Teenagers these days are nothing but a bunch of junkies.

12. A few minutes after Senator Harrison finished his speech on television, a devastating earthquake struck southern Alaska. For the safety of the people up there it is imperative that Senator Harrison keep his mouth shut.

13. Friedrich Nietzsche's philosophy is not worth the paper it's printed on. Nietzsche was an immoral reprobate who went completely insane from syphilis before he died.

14. The Nobel prize-winning biologist Herbert Ralls has stated that chlorinated hydrocarbons in our water supply constitute a major threat to public health. We conclude that the presence of these chemicals is indeed a threat and that the issue should be investigated thoroughly.

★15. What the farmer sows in the spring he reaps in the fall. In the spring he sows $8-per-bushel soybeans. Therefore, in the fall he will reap $8-per-bushel soybeans.

16. I know that some of you oppose the appointment of David Cole as the new sales manager. Upon further consideration, however, I am confident you will change your minds. If Cole is not appointed, it may become necessary to make severe personnel cutbacks in your department.

17. The editors of the *Daily Register* have accused our company of being one of the city's worst water polluters. But the *Daily Register* is responsible for much more pollution than we are. They own the Western Paper Company, you know, and Western Paper discharges tons of chemical residue into the city's river every day.

18. Surely you will not hold architect Norris responsible for the collapse of the building. Norris has had nothing but trouble lately. His daughter eloped with a junkie, his son committed suicide, and his alcoholic wife recently left for Las Vegas with his retirement savings.

19. No life exists on Venus. Teams of scientists have conducted exhaustive studies of the planet's surface and atmosphere, and no living organisms have been found.

★20. Jeffrey Noland's *History of the American Civil War* cannot be trusted. As a historian from Alabama, Noland could not possibly present an accurate account.

21. Governor Turner is prejudiced against Catholics. During his first week in office, he appointed three people to important commissions, and all three were Protestants.

22. Mr. Rhodes is currently suffering from amnesia and has no recollection whatever of the events of the past two weeks. We can only conclude that he did not commit the crime of murdering his wife, as he has been accused of doing.

23. Professor Pearson's arguments in favor of the theory of evolution should be discounted. Pearson is a cocaine-snorting sex pervert and, according to some reports, a member of the Communist Party.

24. Since a one-to-one correspondence can be set up between the odd integers and the integers, it follows that there are as many odd integers as there are integers.

★25. Of course you want to buy a pair of Slinky jeans. Slinky jeans really show off your figure, and all the Hollywood starlets down on the Strip can be seen wearing them these days.

II. Answer "true" or "false" to the following statements:

1. A formal fallacy may be detected through mere inspection of the form of an argument.

2. In the appeal to force (*ad baculum*), the arguer physically attacks the listener.

3. In the direct approach of the appeal to the people (*ad populum*), the arguer attempts to create a kind of mob mentality.

4. In the indirect approach of the *ad populum* fallacy, the arguer need not address more than a single individual.

5. The argument against the person (*argumentum ad hominem*) always involves two arguers.

6. In the *argumentum ad hominem* circumstantial, the circumstances cited by the second arguer are intended precisely to malign the character of the first arguer.

7. In the *tu quoque* fallacy, the arguer threatens the reader or listener.

8. In the appeal to authority (*argumentum ad verecundiam*) the arguer cites a legitimate authority in support of a conclusion.

9. In the appeal to ignorance (*argumentum ad ignorantiam*), the arguer accuses the reader or listener of being ignorant.

10. If an attorney for the defense in an American criminal trial argues that the attorney for the prosecution has proved nothing beyond reasonable doubt about the guilt of his client, he commits an appeal to ignorance.

11. In the fallacy of accident, a general rule is applied to a specific case where it does not fit.

12. Hasty generalization always proceeds from the particular to the general.

13. The *post hoc ergo propter hoc* variety of the false cause fallacy presupposes that X causes Y merely because X happens before Y.

14. If an argument presupposes that X causes Y when in fact Y causes X, the argument commits the *non causa pro causa* variety of the false cause fallacy.

15. Whenever one suspects that the fallacy of missing the point (*ignoratio elenchi*) is being committed, he or she should be able to state the conclusion that is logically implied by the premises.

3.3 FALLACIES OF PRESUMPTION, AMBIGUITY, AND GRAMMATICAL ANALOGY

The **fallacies of presumption** include begging the question and complex question. These fallacies arise not because the premises are irrelevant to the conclusion, as was the case with the ten fallacies of relevance, but because the premises presume what they purport to prove. Begging the question attempts to hide the fact that a certain premise may not be true, and complex question attempts to trick the respondent into making some statement that will establish the truth of the presumption hidden in the question.

The **fallacies of ambiguity** include equivocation, amphiboly, and accent. These fallacies arise from the occurrence of some form of ambiguity in either the premise or the conclusion (or both). In Chapter 2 we distinguished ambiguity from vagueness. We said that a term is vague if its meaning is blurred so that one cannot tell with any degree of precision whether or not it applies to a given situation. A term is ambiguous, on the other hand, if it is susceptible to different interpretations in a given context. Terms such as "light," "bank," and "race" lend themselves to ambiguous interpretations, while "love," "conservative," and "happiness" are often vague. As we will see in this section, ambiguity can affect not only terms but whole statements. When the conclusion of an argument depends on a certain interpretation being given to an ambiguous term or statement, the argument commits a fallacy of ambiguity.

The **fallacies of grammatical analogy** include composition and division. Arguments that commit these fallacies are grammatically analogous to other arguments that are good in every respect. Because of this similarity in linguistic structure, such fallacious arguments may appear good, yet be bad.

Begging the Question (*Petitio Principii*)

Begging the question occurs when an arguer uses some artifice (or trick) to deceive the reader or listener into thinking that a certain premise is true when in fact it may not be. Three requirements must be met for this fallacy to occur:

 a. The argument must be valid.
 b. One premise must be either false, or at least questionable.
 c. Some artifice must be used to hide the fact that this premise may not be true.

The kind of artifice used varies from argument to argument, but it often involves using the conclusion to support the questionable premise. One way of accomplishing this is to phrase the argument so that the premise and conclusion say the same thing in two slightly different ways. Example:

> Capital punishment is justified for the crimes of murder and kidnapping because it is quite legitimate and appropriate that someone be put to death for having committed such hateful and inhuman acts.

To say that capital punishment is "justified" means the same thing as to say that it is "legitimate and appropriate." Because premise and conclusion mean the same thing, it is obvious that if the premise is true, the conclusion is also true; so the argument is valid. The only question that remains is whether the premise is true. When read apart from the context of the argument, the premise is questionable, at best. But when it is preceded by the conclusion, as it is here, the alleged truth is strengthened. This strengthening is caused by the psychological illusion that results from saying the same thing in two slightly different ways. When a single proposition is repeated in two or more ways without the repetition becoming obvious, the suggested truth of the proposition is reinforced.

Another form of begging the question affects chains of arguments. Example:

> Ford Motor Company clearly produces the finest cars in the
> United States. We know they produce the finest cars because
> they have the best design engineers. The reason why they
> have the best design engineers is because they can afford to
> pay them more than other manufacturers. Obviously, they
> can afford to pay them more because they make the finest
> cars in the United States.

In this chain of arguments the final conclusion is stated first. The truth of this conclusion depends on each link in the chain, and ultimately on the first premise (stated last), which asserts the same thing as the final conclusion (stated first). This example illustrates why begging the question is frequently called circular reasoning. The artifice used in arguments such as these depends on the fact that several statements intervene between the final conclusion and the first premise. The reader or listener tends to get lost in the maze of arguments, and since every statement appears to be supported by some other statement, he or she is fooled into thinking that the final conclusion is necessarily true. What the reader or listener may fail to recognize is that the truth of the final conclusion is really supported only by itself, and therefore by nothing at all.

A third form of begging the question occurs when a questionable premise is hidden in the middle of a clearly valid argument. It usually follows another premise that is clearly true. Example:

> Murder is morally wrong, and since abortion is a form of
> murder, it follows that abortion is morally wrong.

If the reader or listener concentrates on the obvious truth of the first premise and on the obvious validity of the argument, he will be inclined to accept the conclusion without further question. The question that the argument begs is, "How do you know that abortion is a form of murder?"

An essential characteristic of begging the question is that some artifice is used to hide the fact that a key premise may not be true. If this premise is obviously true, no such artifice is relevant, and the fallacy cannot occur. Consider the following argument:

A CONCISE INTRODUCTION TO LOGIC

> Snow is white.
> Therefore, snow is white.

This argument is valid and the premise is true. The argument is therefore sound and contains no fallacies. Many logic texts consider arguments such as this to be instances of begging the question, but according to the position taken here, these views are mistaken. Obviously, the argument is trivial, but mere triviality is not a fallacy.

Here is another example:

> Snow is black.
> Therefore, snow is black.

This argument is valid but has a false premise. Accordingly, the argument is unsound, but it commits no fallacy. Although the premise is false, there is clearly no attempt made to hide this fact, and so begging the question is not committed.

Literally, *petitio principii* means "postulation of the beginning." In other words, what the argument sets out to do in the beginning is postulated instead of proven. "Begging the question" means the same thing. The argument begs the question at issue; it asks that the statement to be proved be granted beforehand.

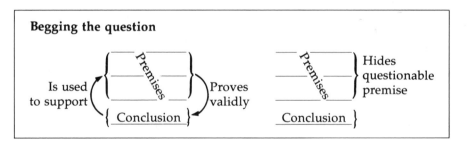

Begging the question

Is used to support {Premises} Proves validly {Conclusion}

{Premises} Hides questionable premise {Conclusion}

Complex Question

The fallacy of **complex question** is committed when a single question that is really two (or more) questions is asked and the single answer is then applied to both questions. Every complex question presumes the existence of a certain condition. When the respondent's answer is added to the complex question, an argument emerges that establishes the presumed condition. Thus, although not an argument as such, a complex question involves an implicit argument. This argument is usually intended to trap the respondent into acknowledging something that he or she might otherwise not want to acknowledge. Examples:

Have you stopped cheating on exams?
Where did you hide the cookies you stole?

Let us suppose the respondent answers "yes" to the first question and "under the bed" to the second. The following arguments emerge:

You were asked whether you have stopped cheating on exams. You answered "yes." Therefore, it follows that you have cheated in the past.

You were asked where you hid the cookies you stole. You replied "under the bed." It follows that you did in fact steal the cookies.

On the other hand, let us suppose that the respondent answers "no" to the first question and "nowhere" to the second. We then have the following arguments:

You were asked whether you have stopped cheating on exams. You answered "no." Therefore, you continue to cheat.

You were asked where you hid the cookies you stole. You answered "nowhere." It follows that you must have stolen them and eaten them.

Obviously, each of the above questions is really two questions:

Did you cheat on exams in the past? If you did cheat in the past, have you stopped now?

Did you steal the cookies? If you did steal them, where did you hide them?

If respondents are not sophisticated enough to identify a complex question when one is put to them, they may answer quite innocently and be trapped by a conclusion that is supported by no evidence at all; or, they may be tricked into providing the evidence themselves. The correct response lies in resolving the complex question into its component questions and answering each separately.

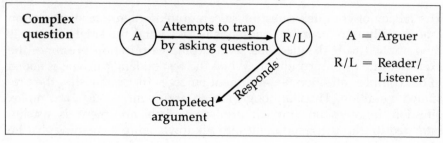

Complex question

A — Attempts to trap by asking question — R/L

Completed argument — Responds

A = Arguer

R/L = Reader/ Listener

The fallacy of complex question should be distinguished from another kind of question known in law as a leading question. A *leading question* is one in which the answer is in some way suggested in the question. Whether or not a question is a leading one is important in the direct examination of a witness by counsel. Example:

> Tell us, on April 9, did you
> see the defendent shoot the
> deceased?   (leading question)
>
> Tell us, what did you see on
> April 9?   (straight question)

Leading questions differ from complex questions in that they involve no logical fallacies; that is, they do not attempt to trick the respondent into admitting something he or she does not want to admit. To distinguish the two, however, it is sometimes necessary to know whether prior questions have been asked. Here are some additional examples of complex questions:

> Are you going to be a good little boy and eat your hamburger?
> Is George Hendrix still smoking marijuana?
> How long must I put up with your snotty behavior?
> When are you going to stop talking nonsense?

Equivocation

The fallacy of **equivocation** occurs when the conclusion of an argument depends on the fact that one or more words are used, either explicitly or implicitly, in two different senses in the argument. Examples:

> Some triangles are obtuse. Whatever is obtuse is ignorant. Therefore, some triangles are ignorant.

> Any law can be repealed by the legislative authority. But the law of gravity is a law. Therefore, the law of gravity can be repealed by the legislative authority.

> We have a duty to do what is right. We have the right to speak out as we choose. Therefore, we have a duty to speak out as we choose.

> A mouse is an animal. Therefore, a large mouse is a large animal.

In the first argument "obtuse" is used in two different senses. In the first premise it describes a certain kind of angle, while in the second it means dull or stupid. The second argument equivocates on the word "law." In the first premise it means statutory law, and in the second it means law of nature. The third argument uses "right" in two senses. In the first premise "right" means morally correct, but in the second it means a just claim or power. The fourth argument illustrates the ambiguous use of a relative term. The word "large" means different things depending on the context. Other relative terms that are susceptible to this same kind of ambiguity include "small," "good," "bad," "light," "heavy," "difficult," "easy," "tall," "short," and so on.

For an argument that commits an equivocation to be convincing, it is essential that the equivocal term be used in two ways that are subtly related. For this reason the triangle argument would probably not convince anyone. It takes but a moment for the reader or listener to realize that something is wrong with this argument and only a few additional seconds to see that the problem stems from the equivocal use of a word. For the same reason, few would be fooled by the second example either; but there are some who might be taken in by the third. In the third example, both senses of the word "right" pertain to ethics, and the conclusion, if not true, is at least plausible. If the reader or listener fails to distinguish the two meanings of "right," he or she is liable to think that the conclusion follows from the premises, when in fact it does not.

Most actual occurrences of the fallacy of equivocation do not, however, occur in succinct, straightforward arguments such as those above. Rather, they occur in protracted, drawn out arguments of the sort found in political speeches. If a certain word gradually shifts in meaning throughout the duration of a lengthy speech, and different conclusions are drawn from the different meanings, detection of the fallacy becomes more difficult. Terms that lend themselves to this kind of meaning shift include "disarmament," "equal opportunity," "gun control," "national security," "balanced budget," and "environmental protection."

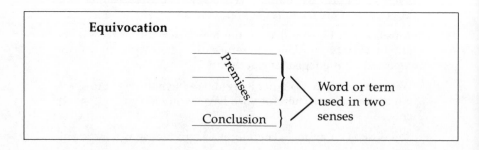

Another strategy used by speechmakers is to use a certain word in one sense when addressing one group of people and in quite another sense when addressing an opposing group. Depending on the specific usage, completely different conclusions may be drawn. For example, a speechmaker addressing a group of defense contractors might argue in favor of disarmament, but the context of the speech would make it clear that by "disarmament" he or she means the limitation of only a narrow range of weaponry. Such an interpretation would certainly please those in attendance. That same speechmaker, later addressing a group of anti-war militants, might again argue in favor of disarmament, but this time meaning the curtailment of all forms of weaponry. To detect the fallacy the listener would have to compare the two speeches.

Amphiboly

The fallacy of **amphiboly** occurs when the arguer misinterprets a statement that is ambiguous owing to some structural defect and proceeds to draw a conclusion based on this faulty interpretation. The original statement is usually asserted by someone other than the arguer, and the structural defect is usually a mistake in grammar or punctuation—a dangling modifier, an ambiguous antecedent of a pronoun, or some other careless arrangement of words. Because of this defect, the statement may be understood in two clearly distinguishable ways. The arguer typically selects the unintended interpretation and proceeds to draw a conclusion based upon it. Here are some examples:

> The tour guide said that standing in Greenwich Village, the Empire State Building could easily be seen. It follows that the Empire State Building is in Greenwich Village.
>
> John told Henry that he had made a mistake. It follows that John has at least the courage to admit his own mistakes.
>
> Professor Johnson said that he will give a lecture about heart failure in the biology lecture hall. It must be the case that a number of heart failures have occurred there recently.

The premise of the first argument contains a dangling modifier. Is it the observer or the Empire State Building that is supposed to be standing in Greenwich Village? The correct interpretation is the former. In the second argument the pronoun "he" has an ambiguous antecedent; it can refer either to John or to Henry. Perhaps John told Henry that *Henry* had made a mistake. In the third argument the ambiguity concerns what takes place in the biology lecture hall; is it the lecture or the heart failures? The correct interpretation is probably the former. The ambiguity can be eliminated by inserting commas ("Professor Johnson said that he will give a lecture, about heart failure, in the biology lecture hall") or by moving the ambiguous modifier ("Professor Johnson said that he will give a lecture in the biology lecture hall about heart failure").

Amphiboly differs from equivocation in two important ways. First, equivocation is always traced to an ambiguity in the meaning of one or more *words,* whereas amphiboly involves a structural defect in a *statement.* The second difference is that amphiboly usually involves a mistake made by the arguer in interpreting an ambiguous statement made by someone else, whereas the ambiguity in equivocation is typically the arguer's own creation. If these distinctions are kept in mind, it is usually easy to distinguish amphiboly from equivocation. Occasionally, however, the two fallacies occur together, as the following example illustrates:

> The *Great Western Cookbook* recommends that we serve the oysters when thoroughly stewed. Apparently the delicate flavor is enhanced by the intoxicated condition of the diners.

First, it is unclear whether "stewed" refers to the oysters or to the diners, and so the argument commits an amphiboly. But if "stewed" refers to the oysters it means "cooked," and if it refers to the diners it means "intoxicated." Thus, the argument also involves an equivocation.

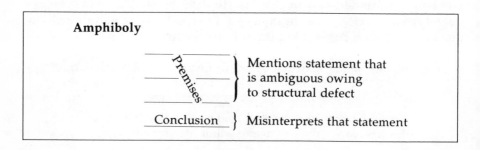

Accent

Like amphiboly, **accent** is a fallacy that arises from the mistaken interpretation of a statement. But whereas amphiboly results from an ambiguity in the *structure* of the statement, accent arises from an ambiguity in the way the statement should be *spoken.* With most occurrences of this fallacy the original statement is expressed in written form by someone other than the arguer, and because it is written, an ambiguity may exist as to which word or words, if any, should be given verbal stress when the statement is spoken. Stressing one word usually gives one meaning, while stressing another gives a quite different meaning. The fallacy of accent occurs when the arguer illegitimately stresses one or more words in the given statement and then proceeds to draw a conclusion based on the resultant interpretation.

For an illustration of this fallacy, imagine that a person named Catherine leaves a note for someone stating that she did not drive her car today. The person who finds the note proceeds to construct the following arguments, alternately stressing different words in the message:

> Catherine said *she* did not drive her car today. Therefore, someone else must have driven it.
>
> Catherine said she did not *drive* her car today. Therefore, she may have washed it.
>
> Catherine said she did not drive *her* car today. Therefore, she must have driven someone else's.
>
> Catherine said she did not drive her *car* today. Therefore, she must have driven her truck.
>
> Catherine said she did not drive her car *today*. Therefore, she must have driven it yesterday.

Since the words in the message did not come supplied with accent marks, there is no reason to think that Catherine intended any one of them to be given more stress than any other. Accordingly, when the arguer gives verbal stress to one of the words and then draws a conclusion based on the altered meaning, a fallacy results.

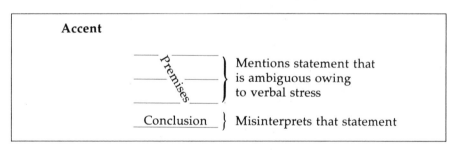

A variation on the fallacy of accent occurs when the person who makes the original statement entices the arguer into a certain misinterpretation and thereby tricks him into constructing a fallacious argument. Consider, for example, the following statements:

> Mrs. Owens was sober today.
> Mr. Darby didn't try to commit suicide today.

Upon reading (or, possibly, hearing) these statements, the arguer is liable to construct the following fallacious arguments:

> It was reported that Mrs. Owens was *sober today*. It must be the case that she is not usually that way.

It was reported that Mr. Darby *didn't* try to commit suicide *today*. Therefore, he has probably tried to commit suicide in the recent past.

This same strategy is frequently used by advertisers to trick prospective purchasers into constructing fallacious arguments about the products advertised. For example, when it is asserted that Anacin contains the ingredient doctors recommend most (with "Anacin" printed in bold letters), the reader is liable to emphasize "Anacin" and conclude that *only* Anacin has this ingredient (common aspirin), which is false.

Composition

The fallacy of **composition** is committed when the conclusion of an argument depends on the erroneous transference of a characteristic from the parts of something onto the whole. In other words, the fallacy occurs when it is argued that because the parts have a certain characteristic, it follows that the whole has that characteristic, too, and the situation is such that the characteristic in question cannot be legitimately transferred from parts to whole. Examples:

> A feather is light. Therefore, a plastic bag containing a billion feathers is light.

> Each player on this basketball team is an excellent athlete. Therefore, the team as a whole is excellent.

> Each atom in this piece of chalk is invisible. Therefore, the chalk is invisible.

> Sodium and chlorine, the atomic components of salt, are both deadly poisons. Therefore, salt is a deadly poison.

In these arguments the characteristics that are transferred from the parts onto the whole are designated by the terms "light," "excellent," "invisible," and "deadly poison," respectively. In each case the transference is illegitimate, and so the argument is fallacious.

Not every such transference is illegitimate, however. Consider the following arguments:

> Every atom in this piece of chalk has mass. Therefore, the piece of chalk has mass.

> Every picket in this picket fence is white. Therefore, the whole fence is white.

In each case a characteristic (having mass, being white) is transferred from the parts onto the whole, but these transferences are quite legitimate. Indeed, the fact that the atoms have mass is the very reason *why* the chalk has mass. The same reasoning extends to the fence. Thus, the validity of these arguments is attributable, at least in part, to the *legitimate* transference of a characteristic from parts onto whole.

These examples illustrate the fact that the fallacy of composition is indeed an informal fallacy. It cannot be discovered by a mere inspection of the form of an argument; that is, by the mere observation that a characteristic is being transferred from parts onto whole. In addition, detecting this fallacy requires a general knowledge of the situation and of the nature of the characteristic being transferred. The critic must be certain that, given the situation, the tranference of this particular characteristic is not allowed.

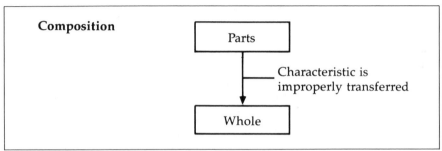

Further caution is required by the fact that composition is sometimes confused with hasty generalization. The only time this confusion is possible is when the "whole" is a class (such as the class of people in a city or the class of trees in a forest), and the "parts" are the members of the class. In such a case composition proceeds from the members of the class to the class itself. Hasty generalization, on the other hand, proceeds from the specific to the general. Because it is sometimes easy to mistake a statement about a class for a general statement, composition can be mistaken for hasty generalization. Such a mistake can be avoided if one is careful to keep in mind the distinction between a general statement and a class statement. This distinction falls back on the difference between the **collective** and the **distributive** predication of an attribute. Consider the following statements:

> Fleas are small.
> Fleas are numerous.

The first statement is a general statement. The attribute of being small is predicated distributively; that is, it is assigned (or distributed) to each and every flea in the class. Each and every flea in the class is said to be small. The second statement, on the other hand, is a class statement. The attribute of being numerous is predicated collectively; in other words, it is assigned not to the individual fleas but to the *class* of fleas. The meaning of the statement is not that each and every flea is numerous but that the class of fleas is large.

To distinguish composition from hasty generalization, therefore, the following procedure should be followed. Examine the conclusion of the argument. If the conclusion is a general statement, that is, a statement in which an attribute is predicated distributively to each and every member of a class, the fallacy committed is hasty generalization. But if the conclusion is a class statement, that is, a statement in which an attribute is predicated collectively to a class as a whole, the fallacy is composition. Example:

> Less gasoline is consumed by a car than by a truck. Therefore, less gasoline is consumed in the United States by cars than by trucks.

At first sight this argument might appear to proceed from the specific to the general and, consequently, to commit a hasty generalization. But in fact the conclusion is not a general statement at all but a class statement. The conclusion states that the whole class of cars uses less gas than does the whole class of trucks (which is false, because there are many more cars than trucks). Since the attribute of using less gasoline is predicated collectively, the fallacy committed is composition.

Division

The fallacy of **division** is the exact reverse of composition. As composition goes from parts to whole, division goes from whole to parts. The fallacy is committed when the conclusion of an argument depends on the erroneous transference of a characteristic from a whole (or a class) onto its parts (or members). Examples:

> Salt is a nonpoisonous compound. Therefore, its component elements, sodium and chlorine, are nonpoisonous.

> This jigsaw puzzle, when assembled, is circular in shape. Therefore, each piece is circular in shape.

> The Royal Society is over 300 years old. Professor Thompson is a member of the Royal Society. Therefore, Professor Thompson is over 300 years old.

In each case a characteristic, designated respectively by the terms "nonpoisonous," "circular in shape," and "over 300 years old," is illegitimately transferred from the whole or class onto the parts or members. As with the fallacy of composition, however, this kind of transference is not always illegitimate. The following arguments are valid:

This piece of chalk has mass. Therefore, the atoms that compose this piece of chalk have mass.

This field of poppies is uniformly orange in color. Therefore, the individual poppies are orange in color.

Obviously, one must be acquainted with the situation and the nature of the characteristic being transferred to decide whether the fallacy of division is actually committed.

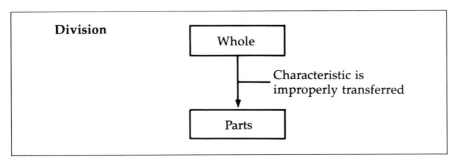

Just as composition is sometimes prone to being confused with hasty generalization (converse accident), division is sometimes prone to being confused with accident. As with composition, this fallacy can occur only when the "whole" is a class. In such a case, division proceeds from the class to the members, while accident proceeds from the general to the specific. Thus, if a class statement is mistaken for a general statement, division may be mistaken for accident. To avoid such a mistake, one should analyze the premises of the argument. If the premises contain a general statement, the fallacy committed is accident; but if they contain a class statement, the fallacy is division. Example:

> Stanley Steamers have almost disappeared.
> This car is a Stanley Steamer.
> Therefore, this car has almost disappeared.

The first premise is not a general statement but a class statement. The attribute of having almost disappeared is predicated collectively. Accordingly, the fallacy committed is division, not accident. Sometimes, however, it is more difficult to decide whether a certain statement is a general statement or a class statement. Consider the following argument:

> The average American family has 2.5 children.
> The Jones family is an average American family.
> Therefore, the Jones family has 2.5 children.

Is the statement "The average American family has 2.5 children" a general statement or a class statement? While at first glance it might appear to make an assertion about each and every family, the sense of the statement is clearly *not* that each and every family has 2.5 children. In other words, the attribute of having 2.5 children is not predicated distributively, so the statement is not a general statement. Upon further analysis we see that saying that the *average* family has 2.5 children is equivalent to saying that the *class* of families is reducible to 55% children and 45% adults. In other words, the first premise is really a class statement, and so, once again, the fallacy is division, not accident.

In the foregoing account of composition and division, we have presented examples of arguments that commit these fallacies in conjunction with other, structurally similar arguments that do not. Because of the structural similarity between arguments that do and do not commit these fallacies, composition and division are classified as fallacies of grammatical analogy.

EXERCISE 3.3

I. Identify the fallacies of presumption, ambiguity, and grammatical analogy committed by the following arguments. If no fallacy is committed, write "good argument."

★1. George said that he was interviewing for a job drilling oil wells in the supervisor's office. I conclude that the supervisor must have an awfully messy office.

2. All men are mortal. Therefore, some day man will disappear from the earth.

3. Are you still drinking excessively?

4. Picasso is the greatest artist of the twentieth century. We know this is so because certain art critics have described him in these terms. These art critics are correct in their assessment because they have a more keenly developed sense of appreciation than the average critic. This is true because it takes a more keenly developed sense of appreciation to realize that Picasso is the greatest artist of the twentieth century.

★5. Rhubarb pie is a dessert. Therefore, whoever eats rhubarb pie eats a dessert.

6. If Thomas gives Marie a ring, then Thomas and Marie will be engaged. Thomas did give Marie a ring. In fact, he phoned her just the other night. Therefore, Thomas and Marie are engaged.

7. Alexander said that he did not intend to study his calculus tonight. Therefore, he apparently intends to study something else.

8. Spain is 99 percent Catholic. Alfonso Rodriguez is a Spaniard. Therefore, Alfonso Rodriguez is 99 percent Catholic.

9. Each and every cell in this carrot is 90 percent water. Therefore, the entire carrot is 90 percent water.

★10. A salesman is a human being. Therefore, a good salesman is a good human being.

11. Every sentence in this paragraph is well written. Therefore, the paragraph is well written.

12. Good steaks are rare these days, so don't order yours well done.

13. Water will quench one's thirst. Water is composed of hydrogen and oxygen. Therefore, hydrogen and oxygen will quench one's thirst.

14. Hydrogen is combustible; therefore, it burns.

★15. Why did you lie on the witness stand?

16. It was reported that Mr. Foster arrived on time today. It must be that he is usually late.

17. The author warns against numerous computational errors in his accounting text. Therefore, he must have written it very carelessly.

18. Molecules are in constant random motion. The Statue of Liberty is composed of molecules. Therefore, the Statue of Liberty is in constant random motion.

19. Central City is north of Springtown, and Springtown is north of Greenville. Therefore, Central City is north of Greenville.

★20. Philosophers are highly intelligent individuals because if they weren't highly intelligent they wouldn't be philosophers.

21. A crust of bread is better than nothing. Nothing is better than true love. Therefore, a crust of bread is better than true love.

22. A line is composed of points. Points have no length. Therefore, a line has no length.

23. How long have you been dealing in drugs?

24. The travel brochure states that walking up O'Connell Street, the Statue of Parnell comes into view. Apparently that statue has no trouble getting around.

★25. California condors are practically extinct. This bird is a California condor. Therefore, this bird is practically extinct.

II. Answer "true" or "false" to the following statements:

1. Arguments that commit the fallacy of begging the question have conclusions that genuinely follow from the premises.

2. The effect of begging the question is to hide the fact that a premise may not be true.

3. The correct way of responding to a complex question is to divide the question into its component questions and answer each separately.

4. The fallacy of equivocation arises from a structural defect in a statement.

5. The fallacy of amphiboly usually involves the ambiguous use of a single word.

6. The fallacy of accent arises from the verbal stress that the arguer may place on a certain word or group of words in a statement.

7. Both amphiboly and accent usually arise from the arguer's misinterpreting a statement made by someone else.

8. The fallacy of composition always proceeds from whole to parts.

9. The fallacy of division always proceeds from parts to whole.

10. A general statement makes an assertion about each and every member of a class.

11. A class statement makes an assertion about a class as a whole.

12. In the statement, "Divorces are increasing," an attribute is predicated distributively.

13. In the statement, "Waistlines are increasing," an attribute is predicated distributively.

14. In the fallacy of begging the question, the conclusion is irrelevant to the premises.

15. Equivocation, amphiboly, and accent are classified as fallacies of ambiguity.

III. Identify the fallacies of relevance, presumption, ambiguity, and grammatical analogy committed by the following arguments. Some arguments may commit more than one. If no fallacy is committed, write "good argument."

★1. What goes up must come down. The price of gold has been going up for months. Therefore, it will surely come down soon.

2. Everything that runs has feet. The Columbia River runs very swiftly. Therefore, the Columbia River has feet.

3. On Monday I drank ten rum and cokes, and the next morning I woke up with a headache. On Wednesday I drank eight gin and cokes, and the next morning I woke up with a headache. On Friday I drank nine bourbon and cokes, and the next morning I woke up with a headache. Obviously, to prevent further headaches I must give up coke.

4. Senator Bradshaw's arguments in favor of legislation to create jobs for the poor should be ignored. Bradshaw is a hypocrite who supports this kind of legislation only to get his name in the newspapers.

★5. India recently suffered a serious drought, thousands of children are dying of starvation in their mothers' arms, and homeless beggars line the streets of the major cities. Surely these poor downtrodden people should be given the chance of bettering their condition in America, the land of wealth and opportunity.

6. Every member of the Delta Club is over 70 years old. Therefore, the Delta Club is over 70 years old.

7. The Book of Mormon is true because it was written by Joseph Smith. Joseph Smith wrote the truth because he was divinely inspired. We know that Joseph Smith was divinely inspired because the Book of Mormon says that he was and the Book of Mormon is true.

8. As a businessman you certainly want a subscription to *Forbes Magazine*. Virtually all the successful business executives in the country subscribe to it.

9. Each and every brick in the brick-faced building has a reddish-brown color. Therefore, the building has a reddish-brown color.

★10. Johnny, I know you'll lend me your bicycle for the afternoon. After all, I'm sure you wouldn't want your mother to find out that you played hooky today.

11. No one has ever proved that the human fetus is not completely human. Therefore, abortion is morally wrong.

12. Are you in favor of the ruinous economic policy of the Democratic Platform Committee?

13. White sheep eat more than black sheep (because there are more of them). Therefore, this white sheep eats more than that black sheep.

14. Ambulances race through the streets at breakneck speed and some of them even go through red lights. Therefore, there is nothing wrong with everyone breaking traffic regulations.

★15. One should not pay too much attention to Clark's arguments against the draft. As a conscientious objector he would be expected to argue that way.

16. This administration is not anti-German, as it has been alleged. Germany is a great country. Goethe, Schiller, and Bach were all Germans.

17. James said that he saw a picture of a beautiful girl stashed in Stephen's locker. We can only conclude that Stephen has broken the rules, because girls are not allowed in the locker room.

18. Extensive laboratory tests failed to reveal any deleterious side effects of the new pain killer, lexaprine. We conclude that lexaprine is safe for human consumption.

19. It is ridiculous to hear that man from Peru complaining about America's poverty. Peru has twice as much poverty as America has ever had.

★20. Sylvia said she is not inviting Jim's brother to her party. Therefore, she must be inviting his sister.

INFORMAL FALLACIES

21. Surely God must exist. My minister, stockbroker, and personal physician are all staunch believers.

22. Freedom of speech is guaranteed by the First Amendment. Therefore, your friend was acting within his rights when he shouted "Fire! Fire!" in that crowded theater, even though it was only a joke.

23. Of all people, you should eat Wheaties. Wheaties is the Breakfast of Champions, you know.

24. Mr. Mayor, I'm sure you will want to support the proposal to build ten new municipal swimming pools in black neighborhoods. If you don't, there will be riots that you won't believe next summer.

★25. Why is it so difficult for you to reach a decision?

26. Johnson is employed by the General Services Administration, and everyone knows that the GSA is the most inefficient branch of the government. Therefore, Johnson must be an inefficient worker.

27. Everybody loves a lover. Michael is a lover. Therefore, Michael loves himself.

28. Mr. Wilson said that on July 4 he went out on the veranda and watched the fireworks go up in his pajamas. We conclude that Mr. Wilson must have had an exciting evening.

29. During the time that General Grant was winning battles in the West, President Lincoln received numerous complaints about Grant's being a drunkard. When a delegation told him that Grant was hopelessly addicted to whiskey, Lincoln is reported to have replied, "I wish General Grant would send a barrel of his whiskey to each of my other generals."

★30. There must be something to psychical research. Three famous physicists, Oliver Lodge, James Jeans, and Arthur Stanley Eddington, took it seriously.

31. An atomic bomb causes more damage than a conventional bomb. Therefore, during World War II more damage was caused by atomic bombs than by conventional bombs.

32. Professor Andrews, surely you can find it in your heart to give me a "B" in Logic. I know I deserve an "F," but if you give me that, I will lose my scholarship. That will force me to drop out of school, and the last thing my aged parents want in life is to attend my graduation.

33. Judge Adams is going soft on dope peddlers. The other day he gave a suspended sentence to a 15-year-old girl after he heard that the girl's father had forced her to sell marijuana.

34. Marylou said that she wasn't baking a cake for dessert. So she must be baking a pie.

★35. No one has proved conclusively that nuclear power plants constitute a danger for people living in their proximate vicinity. Therefore, it is perfectly safe to continue to build nuclear power plants near large metropolitan centers.

36. Emeralds are seldom found in this country, so you should be careful not to misplace your emerald ring.

37. The students attending this university come from every one of the fifty states. George attends this university. Therefore, George comes from every one of the fifty states.

38. Mr. Fleming's arguments against the rent control initiative on the September ballot should be taken with a grain of salt. As a landlord he would naturally be expected to oppose the initiative.

39. Gentlemen prefer blondes. I know this is so because a gentleman once told me. Furthermore, I know that he was a gentleman because he preferred blondes.

★40. Certainly Miss Malone will be a capable and efficient manager. She has a great figure, a gorgeous face, and tremendous poise, and she dresses very fashionably.

41. Mr. Scott's arguments in favor of increasing teacher salaries are totally worthless. Scott, as you all know, has a criminal record as long as my arm, and only a week ago he was released from the state prison after having served a two-year term for car theft.

42. This twenty-story apartment building is constructed of concrete blocks. Each and every concrete block in the structure can withstand an earthquake of 9.5 on the Richter scale. Therefore, the building can withstand an earthquake of 9.5 on the Richter scale.

43. We know that induction will provide dependable results in the future because it has always worked in the past. Whatever has consistently worked in the past will continue to work in the future, and we know that this is true because it has been established by induction.

44. Pauline said that after she had removed her new mink coat from the shipping carton she threw it into the trash. We conclude that Pauline has no appreciation for fine furs.

★45. Motives and desires exert forces on people, causing them to choose one thing over another. But force is a physical quantity, governed by the laws of physics. Therefore, human choices are governed by the laws of physics.

3.4 FALLACIES IN ORDINARY LANGUAGE

Most of the informal fallacies that we have seen thus far have been clear-cut, easily recognizable instances of a specific mistake. When fallacies occur in ordinary usage, however, they are often neither clear-cut nor easily recognizable. The reason is that there are innumerable ways of making mistakes in arguing, and variations inevitably occur that may not be exact instances of any specifically named fallacy. In addition, one fallacious mode of arguing may be mixed together with one or more others, and the strands of reasoning may have to be disentangled before the fallacies can be named. Yet another problem arises from the fact that arguments in ordinary language are rarely presented in complete form. It often happens that a premise or conclusion is left unexpressed, which may obscure the nature of the evidence that is presented or the strength of the link between premises and conclusion.

In this section five additional fallacies are described. These fallacies occur more frequently in ordinary usage than some of those we have seen thus far, but they are typically more difficult to detect and evaluate than the others. They sometimes occur over an interval of several paragraphs, thus requiring close critical attention if they are to be detected. Furthermore, greater judgment is usually needed to determine whether one of them has been committed or whether the argument in question is actually a good one.

The categories presented earlier may be used to classify these five fallacies. False analogy, slippery slope, straw man, and red herring are fallacies of relevance, and suppressed evidence is a fallacy of presumption.

False Analogy

This fallacy affects inductive arguments from analogy. As we saw in Chapter 1, an argument from analogy is an argument in which the conclusion depends on the existence of an analogy, or similarity, between two things or situations. The fallacy of **false analogy** is committed when the analogy is not strong enough to support the conclusion that is drawn. Example:

> Harper's new car is bright blue, has leather upholstery, and gets excellent gas mileage. Crowley's new car is also bright blue and has leather upholstery. Therefore, it probably gets excellent gas mileage, too.

Because the color of a car and the choice of upholstery have nothing to do with gasoline consumption, this argument is fallacious.

The basic structure of an argument from analogy is as follows:

> Entity A has attributes a, b, c, and z.
> Entity B has attributes a, b, c.
> Therefore, entity B probably has attribute z also.

Evaluating an argument having this form requires a two-step procedure: (1) Identify the attributes a, b, c, . . . that the two entities A and B share in common, and (2) determine how the attribute z, mentioned in the conclusion, relates to the attributes $a, b, c, \ldots$ If some causal or systematic relation exists between z and $a, b,$ or $c,$ the argument is strong; otherwise it is weak. In the argument above, the two entities share the attributes of being cars, the attributes entailed by being a car, such as having four wheels, and the attributes of color and upholstery material. Because none of these attributes is systematically or causally related to good gas mileage, the argument is fallacious.

In addition to this criterion, arguments from analogy should always be analyzed for instances of equivocation. It often happens that such arguments use a term in more than one sense. The term may be used in its literal sense in one occurrence and in a metaphorical sense in another. Because of this double meaning, the conclusion may appear to follow from the premises when in fact it does not. Such arguments commit the fallacy of equivocation and not false analogy.

Let us now apply these criteria to some arguments from analogy. Consider the following:

> By means of the Louisiana Purchase the United States acquired from France the land that now comprises the greater part of thirteen states. Similarly, the United States acquired through purchase from Panama the land that provided the site for the Panama Canal. Today it would be improper to give the Louisiana Territory back to France. Similarly, it would be improper today to give the Canal Zone back to Panama.

This argument depends on the analogy that exists between the Canal Zone and the states that presently occupy the Louisiana Territory. The attributes shared by these entities include being purchased by the United States, consisting of over 1,000 acres, lying in the Western Hemisphere, and so on. Proceeding to the second step, we ask how the attribute of not being a proper gift relates to these other attributes. While there *is* a systematic relation between the attribute of not being a proper gift and the attribute of being a *state,* there is no such relation between this attribute and any of the attributes *shared* by the two entities. Accordingly, the argument commits the fallacy of false analogy. This means that the conclusion does not follow probably from the premises; but it may, of course, be true independently of the premises.

Here is another example:

> Some strains of cattle are more desirable than others, and the more desirable strains may be produced by eugenic practices such as selective breeding. Similarly, in man the more desirable strains may be produced by eugenic practices such as selective breeding.

This argument depends on the analogy between cattle and humans. The attributes shared by the members of these two groups include those of being mammals, having a heart, liver, and other internal organs, needing food and air to survive, and so on. Because there is no systematic relation between any of these attributes and that of being a desirable strain producible by eugenic practices, the argument commits the fallacy of false analogy. There is, of course, a systematic relation between being a desirable strain and being owned by someone. The more desirable strains of cattle bring a higher price in the marketplace. But since being owned by someone is not an attribute of humans, the argument is fallacious.

By an alternate analysis this argument may be seen to commit the fallacy of equivocation. The strength of the argument clearly depends on the supposition that "desirable strain" is used in the same sense in both occurrences. When it is used in connection with cattle, this term means being large, being well-proportioned, and having a certain protein distribution; but when it is used in connection with humans, it might mean being honest, courageous, of upright character, and so on. If the term is indeed used in this double sense, the argument commits the fallacy of equivocation, not false analogy.

Another example:

> When an individual is diagnosed as having cancer, every effort is made to kill the cancerous growth, whether by surgery, radiation treatment, or chemotherapy. But murderers and kidnappers are cancerous growths on society. Therefore, when these criminals are apprehended and convicted, they should be treated like any other cancer and eliminated by capital punishment.

Like the previous argument, this argument may be analyzed in two different ways. One way is to interpret it as depending on the analogy between the individual and society. These two entities share the attribute of having an interest in self-preservation, and there is a systematic relation between this attribute and the elimination of life-threatening factors. Thus, as so analyzed the argument does not appear to commit the fallacy of false analogy. But it does commit the fallacy of equivocation. "Cancerous growth" is used in a literal sense when referring to the disease and in a highly metaphorical sense when referring to murderers and kidnappers. The latter are not cancers in the former sense at all.

Analyzed from another angle, the argument may be seen to depend on the analogy between cancer and criminals. These two entities share the attribute of being life-threatening, but there is only a rather loose connection between this attribute and that of deserving to die. Automobiles can be life-threatening, but in no sense do automobiles deserve to die. Cancerous tumors are killed by surgery because there is neither the capacity nor the good reason to allow them to live. Criminals, on the other hand, are human beings, and there is good reason to allow human beings to live. Thus, from this standpoint, the argument commits the fallacy of false analogy.

A final example:

> After ingesting one milligram of substance alpha per day for 90 days, white mice developed genetic abnormalities. Since white mice are similar in many ways to humans, it follows that substance alpha probably produces genetic abnormalities in humans.

White mice share a number of attributes with humans and, given the truth of the premise, there is most likely a causal connection between ingesting substance alpha and certain attributes possessed by white mice that results in genetic damage. The question is whether these attributes are among those that white mice share with humans. If these attributes are not shared by humans, it might be the case that substance alpha is completely harmless to humans even though it causes genetic damage in white mice. Since it is not known whether this causal connection pertains to the *shared* attributes, we must evaluate this argument as having *undecided* strength. A great many arguments in ordinary language are of this kind. Because of the complexity of the subject matter, it may be impossible to determine with any precision the attributes between which the causal relationships lie.

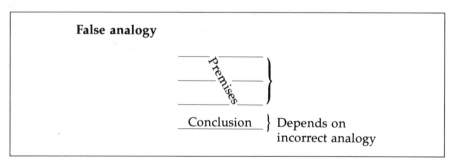

False analogy

Premises

Conclusion } Depends on incorrect analogy

Slippery Slope

The fallacy of **slippery slope** is a variety of the false cause fallacy. It occurs when the conclusion of an argument rests upon the claim that a certain event will set off a chain reaction, leading in the end to some undesirable consequence, yet there is not sufficient reason to think that the chain reaction will actually take place. Here is an example:

Immediate steps should be taken to outlaw pornography once and for all. The continued manufacture and sale of pornographic material will almost certainly lead to an increase in sex-related crimes such as rape and incest. This in turn will gradually erode the moral fabric of society and result in an increase in crimes of all sorts. Eventually a complete disintegration of law and order will occur, leading in the end to the total collapse of civilization.

Because there is no good reason to think that the mere failure to outlaw pornography will result in all these dire consequences, this argument is fallacious. An equally fallacious counterargument is as follows:

Attempts to outlaw pornography threaten basic civil rights and should be summarily abandoned. If pornography is outlawed, censorship of newspapers and news magazines is only a short step away. After that there will be censorship of textbooks, political speeches, and the content of lectures delivered by university professors. Complete mind control by the central government will be the inevitable result.

Both arguments attempt to persuade the reader or listener that the welfare of society rests on a "slippery slope" and that a single step in the wrong direction will result in an inevitable slide all the way to the bottom.

The slippery slope fallacy is frequently backed by an emotional conviction on the part of the arguer that a certain action or policy is bad, and the arguer attempts to trump up support for his position by citing all sorts of dire consequences that will result if his or her conclusion is not accepted. When these dire consequences stretch the imagination, the fallacy is easy to detect. But not all candidates for slippery slope are of this type. It may be that there is at least some reason to believe that the chain reaction will actually occur, in which case the argument may be a good one. The following argument is a case in point:

It has been argued that euthanasia (mercy killing) should be permissible in cases where the party concerned has signed a document stating his or her desire to be given a lethal injection if afflicted by terminal cancer, crippling stroke, or irreversible brain damage. Let us suppose that such a policy were made law. In cases where no document had been signed it would then be argued that the afflicted party *would* have signed one if the opportunity had arisen. This would open the door to such decisions by proxy. Should this be allowed, little imagination is required to envision grown children and other interested parties doing away with their aged parents or grandparents when the latter became a burden. A gradual deterioration in respect for human life would result, and in the end, all undesired persons might be put out of their misery, including mental defectives in state hospitals, convicted criminals, and unwanted children. The conclusion is obvious that euthanasia must never be permitted.

This argument is more difficult to evaluate. If some form of limited euthanasia were allowed by law, it is quite possible that some such chain of events would occur. Deciding the question more definitely would require a close study of society's commitment to the value of human life.

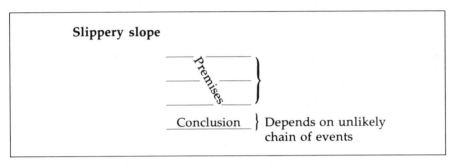

A slippery slope argument that was used with some measure of success during the early days of the Viet Nam War was expressed in the so-called "domino theory." It was argued that if South Viet Nam were allowed to go communist, Laos and Cambodia would follow, then Thailand, Burma, and the rest of Southeast Asia. Developments since the end of the war have not supported these claims.

Suppressed Evidence

The fallacy of **suppressed evidence** is committed when an arguer ignores evidence that would tend to undermine the premises of an otherwise good argument, causing it to be unsound or uncogent. Suppressed evidence is a fallacy of presumption and is closely related to begging the question. As such, its occurrence does not affect the relationship between premises and conclusion but rather the alleged truth of the premises. The fallacy consists in passing off what are at best half-truths as if they were the whole truth, thus making what is actually a defective argument appear to be good. The fallacy is especially common among arguers who have a vested interest in the situation to which the argument pertains. Consider, for example, the following argument dealing with the sale of a used car:

> *Used car salesman to buyer:* Mrs. Webb, I have just the car you need. This 1978 Chevrolet was recently traded in by a little

old lady who kept it in the garage most of the time. The odometer reads low mileage, and the engine was recently tuned up. If you buy this car, it will give you trouble-free service for years.

Mrs. Webb accepts the salesman's argument and buys the car, only to have it fall apart two months later. Unfortunately, the salesman had failed to tell her that whenever the car was not in the garage the little old lady was driving it cross-country, that the odometer had rolled around twice, and that even though the engine was recently tuned up, it had two cracked pistons and a burned valve. By suppressing this evidence, the salesman made it appear that Mrs. Webb was getting a good deal, whereas in fact she was getting a pile of junk for her money.

Another form of suppressed evidence is committed by arguers who quote passages out of context from sources such as the Bible, the Constitution, and the Bill of Rights to support a conclusion that the passage was not intended to support. Consider, for example, the following argument against gun control:

> The Second Amendment to the Constitution states that the right of the people to keep and bear arms shall not be infringed. But a law controlling handguns would infringe on the right to keep and bear arms. Therefore, a law controlling handguns would be unconstitutional.

In fact, the Second Amendment reads, "A well regulated militia, being necessary to the security of a free state, the right of the people to keep and bear arms, shall not be infringed." In other words, the amendment states that the right to bear arms shall not be infringed when the arms are necessary for the preservation of a militia. Because a law controlling handguns (pistols) would have little effect on the preservation of a militia, it is unlikely that such a law would be unconstitutional. By ignoring the militia qualification, the first premise of the above argument makes it appear that *any* law controlling guns would be unconstitutional, which is clearly not the case. In fact, the Supreme Court has upheld a federal law banning the interstate shipment of sawed-off shotguns because these arms are unrelated to the preservation of a militia.

For the fallacy of suppressed evidence to occur, the evidence that is ignored must be the kind that would undermine the premises. Many arguments ignore evidence that would support an opposing conclusion, but because the evidence is not the sort that would undermine the premises, the fallacy is not committed. Consider, for example, the following pair of arguments that reach opposite conclusions:

> Heroin addicts steal millions of dollars every year to support their habits, and thousands of addicts die every year from over-

dose. Methadone is a legal drug that relieves the craving for heroin, and its strength and quality can be precisely controlled. If methadone were supplied to heroin addicts, it would eliminate the constant need to steal and reduce the number of deaths from overdose. Therefore, methadone treatment centers should be set up for heroin addicts.

Methadone is just as addictive as heroin, and its distribution to heroin addicts would only result in one form of addiction being replaced by another. Such a solution would undercut any effort to treat the psychological causes of the addiction. Furthermore, methadone programs would almost certainly be abused. Persons pretending to be addicts would obtain methadone for the illicit purpose of selling it on the streets. Therefore, methadone treatment centers should not be set up for heroin addicts.

Neither of these arguments commits the fallacy of suppressed evidence because the evidence that each argument ignores is not the sort that would undermine the premises. The fact that methadone is addictive and that it might be misused does not cause the premises of the first argument to be any less true. Conversely, the fact that heroin addicts steal millions of dollars annually to support their habits and die by the thousands from overdose does not cause the premises of the second argument to be any less true.

Just the reverse is the case with the examples that commit the suppressed evidence fallacy. In the argument against handguns, the fact that the right to bear arms is related to the preservation of a militia restricts the truth of the first premise. Similarly, in the used car argument, the fact that the odometer had rolled around twice and that the engine had two cracked pistons and a burned valve affects the overall sense of the premises. If the buyer had been aware of this evidence, she would not have bought the car.

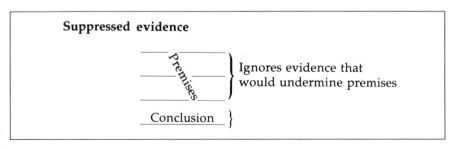

Suppressed evidence

Ignores evidence that would undermine premises

Conclusion

To detect the fallacy of suppressed evidence, the reader or listener must be cautious that the arguer is not ignoring evidence that has a bearing on the premises. This, in turn, requires a general knowledge of the topic to which the argument pertains and a familiarity with the devices used by unscrupulous individuals to pass off half-truths as the whole truth.

Straw Man

The **straw man** fallacy is committed when the arguer misinterprets an opponent's argument for the purpose of more easily attacking it, demolishes the misinterpreted argument, and then proceeds to conclude that the opponent's real argument has been demolished. By so doing the arguer is said to have set up a straw man and knocked it down, only to conclude that the real man (opposing argument) has been knocked down as well. Example:

> Supporters of the Equal Rights Amendment have advanced a number of arguments in favor of its passage. But the question is, are identical roles for men and women really what we want? If women are forced into combat roles in the armed forces, won't this weaken our nation's defenses? And if men and women are required to share the same restroom facilities in public buildings, won't this encourage crimes related to sex? Most thoughtful Americans would have to answer "yes" to these questions. Thus, upon analysis, it appears that the arguments supporting the ERA are not really so good after all.

In fact, the real argument in favor of the ERA has nothing to do with identical roles for men and women. Rather, it has to do with ensuring fairness for women in the labor market. What the above argument does is to switch a straw argument for the real one, show that the straw argument entails undesirable consequences, and then conclude that the real argument entails undesirable consequences as well.

Here is another example:

> Consumer groups that argue in favor of increased product safety are deluding themselves. Practically any car, no matter how carefully designed, will kill the driver and passengers when driven into a brick wall at 90 miles per hour. Similarly, almost any toy will cause injury if a child uses it to beat another child over the head. No matter how much these products are improved, it will be impossible to eliminate every conceivable cause of injury.

The real issue, of course, is whether cars should be designed so that they explode on impact, spewing burning gasoline over the driver and passengers, and whether toys should be made of materials that slowly poison the child who puts them into his or her mouth or that burst into

A CONCISE INTRODUCTION TO LOGIC

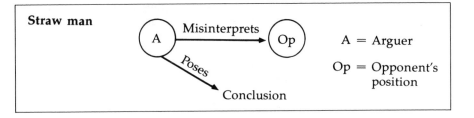

Straw man

A — Misinterprets → Op

Poses → Conclusion

A = Arguer

Op = Opponent's position

flames when touched with a burning match. The above argument substitutes straw issues for real ones.

Red Herring

This fallacy is closely associated with missing the point (*ignoratio elenchi*). The **red herring** fallacy is committed when the arguer diverts the attention of the reader or listener by addressing a number of extraneous issues and ends by presuming that some conclusion has been established. The fallacy gets its name from a procedure used to train hunting dogs to follow a scent. A red herring (or bag of them) is dragged across the trail with the aim of leading the animal astray. Red herrings have an especially potent scent, caused in part by the smoking process used to preserve them. Here is an example of the fallacy:

> Minority pressure groups have argued that the Beta General
> Corporation should employ a larger number of minority
> workers. But Beta General already has plenty of minority
> workers. The problem is that these pressure groups have too
> much power. Pretty soon they'll be taking over the country.
> For some strange reason these groups think that we have a
> negative attitude toward minorities. But this is simply not
> true. Minority employees are hard workers. And besides that,
> America is a nation of minorities. Members of the minority
> work force pay taxes, just like everyone else, and many of
> these people have distinguished records in the armed forces.
> A few have even won the Congressional Medal of Honor.

The conclusion of this argument is that the Beta General Corporation already has plenty of minority employees. Obviously, the issues raised by the company spokesperson are irrelevant to this conclusion. Their purpose is to throw the reader or listener off the track.

Another example:

> Environmental groups have argued that the construction of
> the new Chattsworth Dam will have an adverse impact on
> the scenic beauty of the surrounding parklands. But if we
> followed the advice of every environmentalist, the economy

would come to a halt. Some of these people go into a state of shock over the idea that some obscure species of bird or fish, whose very existence might have been unknown only a few days earlier, might become extinct. Such concerns are ridiculous. The passage into extinction and emergence of plant and animal species is an evolutionary commonplace. A short time ago the scientific community patted itself on the back over the eradication of smallpox. Did the environmentalists complain then about the threatened extinction of the smallpox virus?

The intended conclusion is that the construction of the Chattsworth Dam will not affect the scenic beauty of the parklands. The premises are totally irrelevant to this question and are intended only to sidetrack the reader or listener.

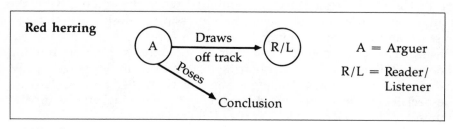

The red herring and the straw man are similar in that they both draw the reader/listener off the track. They differ, though, in the way in which they accomplish this purpose. In the straw man the arguer begins by misinterpreting an opponent's argument and concludes by knocking down the misinterpretation. In the red herring, on the other hand, the arguer ignores the opponent's argument and subtly changes the subject. Thus, in deciding which fallacy has been committed, the reader/listener must attempt to determine whether the arguer has misinterpreted something or simply changed the subject. Because it is often hard to decide which is the case, the two fallacies are sometimes difficult to distinguish.

The red herring frequently occurs in protracted, drawn out arguments, so to detect it the reader or listener must pay close attention to the logic of the passage. The intended conclusion must be kept constantly in mind, and the relevance of this conclusion to the evidence presented must be carefully evaluated.

EXERCISE 3.4

I. Evaluate the following arguments in light of the five fallacies presented in this section.

★1. A number of persuasive arguments have been advanced in favor of the unification of Ireland. But if all the Protestants in the north are forced to become Catholic, this will only increase the tensions and hatred. Surely, if anything is true, a person should have the right to practice the religion of his or her choice. Thus, in light of these facts it appears that the arguments in favor of unification are not so good after all.

2. General American Savings and Loan is a great place to put your money. For a $1,000 minimum balance you receive a checking account with no service charges, and for an additional $1,000 they give you a free safety deposit box. On top of that you receive 5¼ percent interest on your deposit, and every account is insured for up to $100,000.

3. Recently Congressional leaders have argued in favor of increasing the excise tax on cigarettes. But the excise tax is already too high. This is the so-called sin tax that is often supported by those holier-than-thou type Christians such as Jerry Falwell and the Moral Majority. If these people had their way, everyone would live exactly as they dictate. But one of the things that has made this country great is its tremendous variety of lifestyles and ways of thinking. If everyone in America starts thinking and living the same way, then this country is doomed.

4. In comparing my own behavior with that of others I notice many common features. Other people laugh, cry, solve problems, write letters, and make decisions just as I do. It therefore follows that other people have minds and experience self-awareness just as I do.

5. There is a lot discussion these days about the rights of animals. For example, it is argued that chickens and cows have a right not to be kept in tiny cages that prevent them from moving about and cause them to fatten more quickly on less food. But if chickens and cows are acknowledged as having rights, it won't be long before a case is made for fish and insects. And then we'll be giving rights to plants and bacteria. Rivers, lakes, and mountains will follow close behind. In the end the concept of rights will have become completely meaningless.

II. The following letters to the editor were taken from newspapers and magazines. All of them contain arguments, but in many cases the arguments are not explicit. Analyze these arguments in light of the material presented in this chapter. Some of the arguments may be good ones.

★1. No one forced Bobby Sands [who died in a Belfast jail] to fast to death. It was his own choice. Before long, murderers and rapists will be declaring themselves a special class of prisoners, and will be demanding concessions. They are all criminals, and as such should be punished. They should not expect privileges for their crimes.

2. In 1976 Jimmy Carter smiled a lot and talked in folksy platitudes. In 1980 he did little of either, concentrating instead on issues and the shortcomings of his opponent. Naturally, therefore, he lost to Ronald Reagan—a man who smiles a lot and talks folksy platitudes.

3. About 27 percent of eligible voters in the United States, little more than half of the 52 percent who voted, chose Ronald Reagan. This was said to be a "landslide" showing that the people "overwhelmingly" wanted him. In 1979 about 33 percent of eligible voters in Scotland, out of the 64 percent who voted, won a referendum for a Scottish legislature—which was denied them on the ground that the election showed the people did not want one. Which is correct?

4. According to Reagan's White House lawyer, the ACLU is part of a "criminals' lobby." Actually, ACLU represents some persons whose constitutional rights might have been violated; and there is a constitutional right to representation in criminal cases. It follows that all criminal defense lawyers are part of the "criminals' lobby." We should therefore eliminate ACLU and eliminate all criminal defense lawyers.

    Without criminal defense lawyers, there would be no need for prosecutors. With neither prosecutors nor defense lawyers around, we could abolish our criminal courts. Everyone arrested by the police would simply be jailed for whatever term the police felt appropriate. The police would also decide who should be executed.

    The no-criminals-lobby-no-criminal-courts policy would also apply to the federal government. We would only need the FBI. We would reduce crime. At the same time, government would become more efficient, less fat and relieve more weight from our backs.

★5. I strongly protest the Reagan Administration's condemnation of the Israeli raid. The Iraqis, a lunatic nation, professed themselves innocent of any intention to use their nuclear plant to produce weapons. India showed the world what "peaceful" nuclear plants can accomplish.

    The simple fact is that without the Israeli raid the nuclear plant would still exist. Only a moron would think that diplomatic efforts would convince the Iraqis to shelve their nearly completed $250 million operation. The state of Israel is not geographically large enough to survive a nuclear first strike, and its existence must not depend on the whim of madmen like Iraq's Saddam or Libya's Kadafi.

6. How can you say in your editorial that Israel may have made the Middle East a somewhat safer place? Are you saying that Hitler would have made Europe a safer place? How much longer until Israel will have concentration camps?

7. When will Prime Minister Menachem Begin take his mind-reading act to the circus where it will do no harm?

    Will Begin's planes next bomb the U.N. Building in New York City, because the U.N. may take action threatening the security of Israel?

Does the United States invade Mexico, because we believe that at some future time she might restrict her flow of oil to us?

Can we object if Russia marches into Poland?

Carried to its sick conclusion, all nations, then business and individuals may adopt this policy of preemptive strikes and chaos will be the order of the day.

When will this lunacy be stopped?

8. First the raid on Iraq's atomic reactor; then, a few days later, the worldwide meeting of Holocaust survivors in Jerusalem—very much a media-reported event.

One would simply call this a coincidence, were it not for Begin's repeated references to the Holocaust in justifying the bombing of the Iraq reactor—both right after the raid and later in an address to the Holocaust survivors.

Somehow, there is creeping suspicion that the raid on Iraq was so timed that the meeting of Holocaust survivors shortly afterwards would bring for Begin's government a maximum of understanding and even sympathy for its military "adventure" in Iraq.

It is appalling to think that Begin may well have manipulated the emotional outfall from such a universal tragedy as the martyrdom of 6 million Jews in order to serve his own political ends.

9. I think we should nominate the woman who killed one of her [unborn] twins because it had Down's Syndrome for the "Mother of the Year" award. She can be an inspiration to mothers everywhere and we can honor her for her bravery in the handling of a crisis situation.

Maybe we should take what she did one step further and allow mothers who do not approve of their grown children's lifestyles to kill them also—the children who abuse sex and drugs, thus causing more damage to their minds and bodies than a birth defect could. Surely these children cause their mothers more anguish for more years than a Mongoloid child ever could.

There are so many problems that could be eliminated by killing the problem-person that we may have the "solution of the '80s."

★10. For the benefit of Leon Smith [who wrote an earlier letter], there was no "German army, navy or air force" left in Germany after July 20, 1944. On the day Count Claus Stauffenberg made his daring attempt to assassinate Adolf Hitler and the German general staff failed to rise up and finish the job they all became equally guilty with Hitler and became a Nazi army, not a German army.

11. When will these upper-crust intellectuals realize that the masses of working people are not in cozy, cushy, interesting, challenging, well-paying jobs, professions and businesses? My husband is now 51; for most of the last 33 years he has worked in the same factory job, and only the thought of retiring at 62 has sustained him. When he reaches that age in 11 years, who will tell him that his aging and

physically wracked body must keep going another two years? My heart cries out for all the poor souls who man the assembly lines, ride the trucks or work in the fields or mines, or in the poorly ventilated, hot-in-summer, cold-in-winter factories and garages. Many cannot afford to retire at 62, 65, or even later. Never, never let them extend the retirement age. It's a matter of survival to so many.

12. My 16-year-old daughter is traveling to Ireland this fall and needed my signature to get a passport. According to the Supreme Court, she could have gotten an abortion the same day without my knowledge or permission. When are we going to get our priorities straight?

13. I want to discuss your editorial on abortion, but it's difficult to know how to go about it. The English language seems to have lost its meaning. You find it "indecent," "brutal" and "callous" to object to the killing of an unborn child—a human being with a heartbeat, a nervous system, its own individual fingerprints. True, he or she has not yet reached full development, but this is also true of a newborn baby, a 2-year-old, or a 10-year-old. From the very beginning nothing is added but time and nourishment.

    Rape is a terrible crime, but we don't rectify anything by adding a second—murder. You would not advocate capital punishment for the man, but you do for the innocent child.

    We should do all we can to prevent rape or punish it severely. But once a child is present, its life must be respected.

14. I was incensed to read in your article about the return of anti-Semitism that New York City Moral Majority Leader Rev. Dan C. Fore actually said that "Jews have a God-given ability to make money, almost a supernatural ability . . ." I find it incredibly ironic that he and other Moral Majority types conveniently overlook the fact that they, too, pack away a pretty tidy sum themselves through their fundraising efforts. It is sad that anti-Semitism exists, but to have this prejudice voiced by leaders of religious organizations is deplorable. These people are in for quite a surprise come Judgment Day.

★15. Mexico's President Lopez Portillo expresses legitimate concern when he questions supplying oil to Americans who are unwilling to apply "discipline" in oil consumption. In view of the fact that his country's population is expected to double in only 22 years, isn't it legitimate for us to ask when Mexicans will apply the discipline necessary to control population growth and quit dumping their excess millions over our borders?

16. There has been a recent and long overdue concern about the population growth of our country, which contributes to many of our social problems. There is one solution that would help to solve the population growth as well as relieve a portion of the tax burden.

    We should instigate a ruling that welfare will pay support for only two children of families on welfare. This does not prohibit them from having a larger family; however, it does put them in the same posi-

A CONCISE INTRODUCTION TO LOGIC

tion as the working family, whether or not they can afford more children.

It seems unfair and discriminatory to place the taxpayer in the position of having to limit his family while the government continues to reward the welfare family with increased monthly payments and additional benefits for each child.

17. How would you feel to see your children starving, and have all doors slammed in your face? Isn't it time that all of us who believe in freedom and human rights stop thinking in terms of color and national boundaries? We should open our arms and hearts to those less fortunate and remember that a time could come when we might be in a similar situation.

18. As a refugee from Nazism in the '30s, I thought the world was anti-Semitic. Today, reading about the plight of the boat people I know I was wrong. The world is not anti-Semitic, it is inhumane.

19. Contrary to Lord Snowdon's view, I think photography is art. Certainly the camera is a tool, but it is used for creating a photograph much as a brush is used to paint a picture. Creativity is the essence of art, and to say that photography does not belong in museums is to misunderstand the nature of artistic expression.

★20. When will they ever learn—that the Republican Party is not for the people who voted for it?

21. Before I came to the United States in July, 1922, I was in Berlin where I visited the famous zoo. In one of the large cages were a lion and a tiger. Both respected each other's strength. It occurred to me that it was a good illustration of "balance of power." Each beast followed the other and watched each other's moves. When one moved, the other did. When one stopped, the other stopped.

In today's world, big powers or groups of powers are trying to maintain the status quo, trying to be as strong as or stronger than the other. They realize a conflict may result in mutual destruction. As long as the countries believe there is a balance of power we may hope for peace. But when Iraq thought it had a preponderance of power over Iran, it started a war.

22. The media likes to equate President Reagan with President Franklin D. Roosevelt. I believe this is inaccurate. Reagan is more like Roosevelt's predecessor, President Hoover.

The Great Depression started during Hoover's time in office.

Hoover's effort to solve the financial woes of the country was to loan money to the banks with the idea in mind that money would trickle down to the poor. "Prime the pump from the top" was the way Hoover put it.

Reagan's current income tax plan involving a 10 percent tax cut across the board does the same thing. He states it is necessary to give people with the largest income the same tax write-off as the poor people so a surplus of money will be created at the top that can be used for investment, thus stimulating the economy.

Reagan is doing just like Hoover. He is "priming the pump from the top." The money did not trickle down for Hoover nor will it trickle for Reagan.

Once Reagan's four years are over, he will then need another FDR to straighten out the economy.

23. September 17 marked the 193rd anniversary of the signing of the U.S. Constitution. How well have we, the people, protected our rights? Consider what has happened to our private-property rights.

"Property has divine rights, and the moment the idea is admitted into society that property is not as sacred as the laws of God, anarchy and tyranny begin." John Quincy Adams, 1767–1848, Sixth President of the United States.

Taxes and regulations are the two-edged sword which gravely threatens the fabric of our capitalistic republic. The tyranny of which Adams speaks is with us today in the form of government regulators and regulations which have all but destroyed the right to own property. Can anarchy be far behind?

24. My gun has protected me, and my son's gun taught him safety and responsibility long before he got hold of a far more lethal weapon— the family car. Cigarettes kill many times more people yearly than guns and, unlike guns, have absolutely no redeeming qualities. If John Lennon had died a long, painful and expensive death from lung cancer, would you have devoted a page to a harangue against the product of some of your biggest advertisers—the cigarette companies?

★25. A drunk driver kills people; a drunk with no car just falls down. An angry man with a gun shoots his neighbor; an angry man with no gun is just angry. Most handgun killings are crimes of passion that take place because a gun is immediately available.

26. You take half of the American population every night and set them down in front of a box watching people getting stabbed, shot and blown away. And then you expect them to go out into the streets hugging each other?

27. If a car or truck kills a person, do politicians call for car control or truck control? And call in all cars/trucks?

If a child burns down a house do we have match control or child control and call in all of each?

Gun control and confiscation is equally as pathetic a thought process in an age of supposed intelligence.

28. If Castro had any regard for the Cubans, he would throw the Soviets and their bankrupt economics out and welcome Western capitalism. But no; the macho image prevails: the cigar, the beard, the fatigues, the whole clown act. Can one person's egotism lead to the creation of such monumental economic and historical illiteracy? Apparently so.

29. We cannot rally with enthusiasm around a man beseeching help. A president [Carter] who lists our faults and weaknesses does not inspire us. We need a clarion call: Come on, America! We've done it before and we can do it again. We can solve our energy problem. Nothing is impossible for 220 million Americans pulling together. We went to the moon; we shall not let OPEC bring us to our knees! Oh, for a buoyant, confident leader who can make us feel invincible.

★30. Kennedy is now and always has been the darling of a liberal press. Because of this bias, the Kennedy family has been able to blow the Bay of Pigs, instigate the Vietnam War, cheat at Harvard, conspire at Chappaquiddick with impunity. One would otherwise be hard pressed to discern why a President could be hounded from office for participation in the cover-up of a mere break-in (the extent of which remains questionable), while a Kennedy could, without media retribution, conspire to cover up or to mitigate his duplicity in the death of a fellow human being.

31. As the oldest of eleven children (all married), I'd like to point out our combined family numbers more than 100 who vote only for pro-life candidates. Pro-lifers have children, pro-choicers do not.

32. Castro does great violence to the intelligence of the world. His extreme criticism of the U.S. for not sending aid to the hungry and shoeless children cannot be countenanced. What is Cuba's record? Castro's dictatorship exports armies, hate and killing on command of the Kremlin. Where in the world does Communism feed and clothe little children without demanding their bodies and souls in payment?

33. Tom Hayden honored our fair city on May 20 (again) with a speech to a grand total of 100 people in Clairemont. You reported the event with a four-column headline and a photo.

    By any stretch of the imagination, Hayden is not an expert or an authority. He holds no degrees in economics or political science. He's never held (for any length of time) a traditional job. And he has never been elected to a political office.

    He tours the West speaking to a few misguided liberals and impressionable, young students only because his foolish wife pays his expenses from her movie career earnings.

    Anyway you slice it, Tom Hayden is not news—and should be ignored accordingly.

III. The following essay, titled "There Goes the Sun," which has been condensed slightly, appeared in *Newsweek* magazine ("My Turn," December 3, 1979, copyright 1979 by Newsweek, Inc. All rights reserved. Reprinted by permission). The author is associate editor of *London Oil Reports*. Analyze the argument in terms of the material presented in this section.

Solar energy is potentially the most polluting and ecologically threatening form of commercial power being proposed in the world today.

You saw that right. Solar energy can be dangerous to everybody's health and the time has come for its advocates to stop strumming their amplified guitars in its behalf and start listening to some quiet truths.

I am not discussing solar in terms of wind, hydropower or agriculture, for to paraphrase Keynes, in the long run we are all solar. For the purpose of this essay, solar energy is sunlight converted directly to electricity or to commercially usable heat.

Arriving free of charge, leaving no residue and making no smoke, this energy nonetheless may turn out to be more hazardous than nuclear, more polluting than coal, and more costly to the consuming public than petroleum.

Laws: Some elementary facts on the physical world in which we live, compiled recently by Resources for the Future under Ford Foundation sponsorship, are pertinent. Remember, now, we are dealing with the laws of nature and not of society, and we can neither repeal nor amend them.

Here is Fact One: Sunlight reaches the ground at a global average of 160 watts per square meter. The most optimistic engineers say that by the time we allow for variations in cloud and atmospheric cover, the natural resistance of materials, and the need to convert the electricity to alternating current, we are not likely to exceed a recovery efficiency of 5 to 10 percent.

That computes to an average power output of about 25 megawatts per square mile. Thus the entire estimated U.S. power requirement for the year 2000 could be met by covering an area equivalent to that of the state of Oregon with solar collectors. Or, less extreme, all existing and projected nuclear power plants for the year 2000 could be replaced by solar collectors covering a much smaller area—approximately that of West Virginia.

Here is Fact Two: The sun will not give up its energy for nothing. As we have shown, we are going to have an area equivalent to that of Oregon or West Virginia with solar conversion cells. Whether of the sunlight-to-electricity or sunlight-to-commercial-heat type, these cells will not be made out of guitar picks.

Direct-conversion photovoltaic units will contain larger—truly large—tonnages of cadmium, silicon, germanium, selenium, gallium, copper, arsenic, sulfur, and/or other conducting, semiconducting and nonconducting materials of varying availability on world markets. Thermal-conversion units will be made of thousands of tons of glass, plastics and rubber, and will house uncommonly great volumes of ethylene glycol, liquid metals, Freon and/or other heat movers.

Exotic materials: If we settle on cadmium-sulfide cells for direct photovoltaic conversion, for instance, it would require the entire 1978 world production of cadmium to produce only 180,000 megawatts of installed capacity, or about 10 percent of the capacity the world had in place last year.

On the other hand, if we opt for solar-heat transfer, from where will the medium come? I'm not referring to the few ounces of Freon in your refrigerator, or the four gallons of coolant in your car radiator. I'm referring to millions of tons of a toxic material coursing through miles of complicated plumbing out there in the hinterlands.

Now we are ready for the first set of serious questions: How much energy will it require to manufacture enough solar cells—either photovoltaic or heat-transfer—to cover an area the size of Oregon or West Virginia? How much oil or coal must we burn in the process? How much pollution will be belched into the atmosphere as a result? How much silicate matter? How much sulfur? How much arsenic?

Hazards: And now for the second set of serious questions: What will be the ecological price of covering an area the size of Oregon or West Virginia with solar cells? What will be the effect on land where sunlight has shone unimpeded but for clouds and eclipses for uncounted trillions of days? What of its wildlife? Its flora? What will be the effect on neighboring lands? What are the hazards of a massive ethylene glycol spill?

There is a third set of serious questions: Of what real value is a source of energy that operates only in the daytime and whose output is subject to unpredictable deterioration by the vagaries of weather and season? What kind of buffer and storage systems must we develop to accommodate such variations in output? Can we really devise a battery-powered assembly line to provide work for the night shift?

Which leads us to the polemical coda of this essay. Please answer for me the following questions:

Why do so many of the people who fear the effect of drugstore de-odorant-spray cans on the ozone layer rush to risk a massive Freon spill on earth?

Why are so many of those who tremble in terror over the Three Mile Island accident, which killed nobody, ecstatic about the prospect of putting tons of silicate particles into the air we breathe?

Why are those so quick to protect the wilderness from a single pipeline so anxious to smother it with solar cells?

I don't have the answers. But it is clear that in energy as in life itself there is no free lunch. Our access to commercial solar power is only slightly more promising than the Ancient Mariner's to potable water. And the shrill, facile sun worship to which we are increasingly subjected had better give way to more serious reflection on the energy mess in which we find ourselves.

Donald C. Winston

IV. The following guest editorial appeared in the *San Diego Tribune* (May 21, 1981). The author is associate editor of *American Firearms Industry News*. Analyze the argument in terms of the material presented in this section.

It's about time that people in the news media stop their self-righteous preaching and grandstanding, speaking as though they reflect the views of the entire population.

The anti-firearms cause sounds good, looks good in print and seems the honorable course to take, but it is mostly the view of media personnel, not the view of the majority of U.S. citizens. It's fairly easy to blame the National Rifle Association for all of our country's crime and firearm incidents, and easier yet to focus on firearms themselves. But behind all their breast-beating and cries for "gun control," the media thrive on the misuse of firearms.

The week after John Lennon's death, every major newspaper and magazine, along with the major broadcasting networks, produced Lennon tributes. Everybody got their buck's worth. Very few major news publications devoted entire sections to Lennon after the Beatles' breakup, but they all had their special sections on the presses the day after his death. Yet, for all their articles and columns on gun control, the news publications are not dealing with the real Lennon story: the assailant, Mark David Chapman. If he's convicted, it's likely to be only second-degree murder—another way of saying he'll be walking the streets in a few years.

In a recent column in the Chicago *Sun-Times*, journalist Michael J. McManus mentioned an incident from his childhood: He found his father's revolver, pulled out the clip and pulled the trigger, firing a shot. To correct him: A revolver does not have a clip but a cylinder, which contains the cartridges. It's evident McManus knows nothing about firearms, yet he insists on instructing his readers on the use and misuse of them. I must agree, though, that anyone who leaves firearms loaded and unlocked should not have them around. Even as a youngster, in a house full of firearms, I was never stupid enough to place one in my mouth, as McManus claims to have done.

Probably the most important consideration for any firearms problem does not lie in new laws or regulations, but in mandatory enforcement of existing laws. We in the American firearms industry do not sanction the free-for-all sale of firearms, nor do we argue against fair and reasonable firearms laws aimed at seriously restricting the criminal and his use of firearms to pursue his trade. But very few people charged with crimes in connection with firearms are prosecuted for violating existing firearms laws; the federal Bureau of Alcohol, Tobacco and Firearms will confirm this. Regardless of what FBI statistics show or what law enforcement officials claim, you can get away with murder.

Firearms homicides are tolerated by the courts. Examples of such limpid justice are the cases of Sirhan Sirhan and David Berkowitz, the Son of Sam. Both murderers live a fairly comfortable life in prison, without regrets. Sirhan is eligible for parole in another year and Berkowitz collects Social Security benefits. Were their horrible crimes adequately punished? I think not. The Puerto Rican terrorists who killed a security guard in an attempted assassination of President Truman were pardoned by President Carter. They expressed no regrets for their action and hinted they would be willing to do it again. Not much of a deterrent, is it?

I suggest we concentrate on crime control instead of so-called gun control. The courts should be forced to impose mandatory jail terms for firearms offenses, without exception. Capital punishment should be mandatory for any firearm homicide in connection with a crime and for multiple crimes connected with firearms, without exception.

There are not too many people in the firearms business who would complain about a workable computer system that would record serial numbers of firearms. Any Chicago area dealer will tell you he gets very little support from police in using the National Crime Information Center to trace serial numbers on suspected stolen firearms.

We at the National Association of Federally Licensed Firearms Dealers have written to the federal Bureau of Alcohol, Tobacco and Firearms many times concerning this problem and the lack of support for dealers who try to run an honest business.

As for Sen. Edward M. Kennedy's anti-firearm propaganda and "ban all guns" philosophy, forget it. He was born very wealthy, never had to work to support his family, travels with heavily armed bodyguards and lives in the closed society of the super-rich that most Americans only dream about.

A man who has never struggled to earn a living, never lived in the real world of violence and crime and never experienced the blue-collar way of life has no right to impose his anti-firearm vendetta on all America. He talks a good line, but has never encountered life in Harlem or inner-city Chicago.

Kennedy cannot speak for the common man because he has never walked in his shoes.

R. A. Lesmeister

V. Turn to the editorial pages of a newspaper and find an instance of a fallacious argument in the editorials or letters to the editor. Identify the premises and conclusion of the argument and write an analysis at least one paragraph in length stating why the argument is fallacious and identifying the fallacy or fallacies committed.

4
CATEGORICAL PROPOSITIONS

4.1 THE COMPONENTS OF CATEGORICAL PROPOSITIONS

In Chapter 1 we saw that a proposition (or statement—here we are ignoring the distinction) is a sentence that is either true or false. A proposition that relates two classes, or categories, is called a **categorical proposition.** The classes in question are denoted respectively by the **subject term** and the **predicate term,** and the proposition asserts that either all or part of the class denoted by the subject term is included in or excluded from the class denoted by the predicate term. Here are some examples of categorical propositions:

> Ostriches are birds.
> Oak trees can't read.
> Lions live in the zoo.
> Rainy days are always cloudy.
> Not all students like algebra.
> Herbert Hoover was a Republican.

The first statement asserts that the entire class of ostriches is included in the class of birds, the second that the entire class of oak trees is excluded from the class of things that can read, and the third that part of the class of lions is included in the class of things that live in the zoo. The fourth statement asserts that the whole class of rainy days is included in the class of cloudy days, and the fifth asserts that part of the class of students is excluded from the class of persons who like algebra. The last example asserts that the single individual denoted by the term "Herbert Hoover" is a member of the class denoted by the term "Republican."

Since any categorical proposition asserts that either all or part of the class denoted by the subject term is included in or excluded from the class denoted by the predicate term, it follows that there are exactly four types of categorical propositions: (1) those that assert that the whole subject class is included in the predicate class, (2) those that assert that part of the subject class is included in the predicate class, (3) those that assert that the whole subject class is excluded from the predicate class, and (4) those that assert that part of the subject class is excluded from the predicate class. A categorical proposition that expresses these relations with complete clarity is one that is in **standard form.** A categorical proposition is in standard form if and only if it is a substitution instance of one of the following four forms:

All *S* are *P.*
No *S* are *P.*
Some *S* are *P.*
Some *S* are not *P.*

Many categorical propositions, of course, are not in standard form because, among other things, they do not begin with the words "all," "no," or "some." In the final section of this chapter we will develop techniques for translating categorical propositions into standard form, but for now we may restrict our attention to those that are already in standard form.

The words "all," "no," and "some" are called **quantifiers** because they specify how much of the subject class is included in or excluded from the predicate class. The first form above asserts that the whole subject class is included in the predicate class, the second that the whole subject class is excluded from the predicate class, and so on. (Incidentally, in formal deductive logic the word "some" always means at least one.) The letters "*S*" and "*P*" stand respectively for the subject and predicate terms, and the words "are" and "are not" are called the **copula** because they link the subject term with the predicate term.

Consider the following example:

All members of the American Medical Association are persons holding degrees from recognized academic institutions.

This standard-form categorical proposition is analyzed as follows:

quantifier: all
subject term: members of the American Medical Association
copula: are

predicate term: persons holding degrees from recognized academic institutions

In resolving standard-form categorical propositions into their four components, one must keep these components separate. They do not overlap each other. In this regard it should be noted that "subject term" and "predicate term" do not mean the same thing in logic that "subject" and "predicate" mean in grammar. The *subject* of the above statement includes the quantifier "all," but the *subject term* does not. Similarly, the *predicate* includes the copula "are," but the *predicate term* does not.

Two additional points should be noted about standard-form categorical propositions. The first is that the form "All *S* are not *P*" is *not* a standard form. This form is usually correctly rendered as "No *S* are *P*." The second point is that there are exactly three forms of quantifiers and two forms of copulas. Other texts allow the various forms of the verb "to be" (such as "is," "is not," "will," and "will not") to serve as the copula. For the sake of uniformity, this book restricts the copula to "are" and "are not." The last section of this chapter describes techniques for translating these alternate forms into the two accepted ones.

EXERCISE 4.1

In the following categorical propositions identify the quantifier, subject term, copula, and predicate term.

★1. Some pigs are wild animals.

2. No canaries are melancholy creatures.

3. All lobsters that are found in the North Atlantic are strange and unreasonable crustaceans.

4. Some teetotalers who have recently gone on the wagon are not persons who have a craving for sugar.

5. All elderly members of the Phoenix Club are inveterate prattlers.

6. Some shops in the tourist district of Fayette are hopelessly crowded places.

7. No busy and industrious employees are persons who are always talking about their grievances.

8. Some holidays spent in the mountains are not stimulating and refreshing vacations.

4.2 QUALITY, QUANTITY, AND DISTRIBUTION

Quality and quantity are attributes of categorical propositions. In order to see how these attributes pertain, it is useful to rephrase the meaning of categorical propositions in class terminology:

Proposition	Meaning in Class Notation
All S are P.	Every member of the S class is a member of the P class; that is, the S class is included in the P class.
No S are P.	No member of the S class is a member of the P class; that is, the S class is excluded from the P class.
Some S are P.	At least one member of the S class is a member of the P class.
Some S are not P.	At least one member of the S class is not a member of the P class.

The **quality** of a categorical proposition is either affirmative or negative depending on whether it affirms or denies class membership. Accordingly, "All S are P" and "Some S are P" have **affirmative** quality, and "No S are P" and "Some S are not P" have **negative** quality.

The **quantity** of a categorical proposition is either universal or particular depending on whether the statement makes a claim about *every* member or just *some* member of the class denoted by the subject term. "All S are P" and "No S are P" each assert something about every member of the S class and thus are **universal.** "Some S are P" and "Some S are not P" assert something about one or more members of the S class and hence are **particular.**

Note that the quantity of a categorical proposition may be determined through mere inspection of the quantifier. "All" and "no" immediately imply universal quantity, while "some" implies particular. But categorical propositions have no "qualifier." In universal propositions the quality is determined by the quantifier, and in particular propositions it is determined by the copula.

It should also be noted that particular propositions mean no more and no less than the meaning assigned to them in class notation. The statement "Some S are P" does *not* imply that some S are not P, and the statement "Some S are not P" does *not* imply that some S are P. It often *happens*, of course, that substitution instances of these statement forms are both true. For example, "Some apples are red" is true, as is "Some apples are not red." But the fact that one is true does not *necessitate* that the other be true. "Some zebras are animals" is true (because at least one zebra is an animal), but "Some zebras are not animals" is false. Similarly, "Some turkeys are not fish" is true, but "Some turkeys are fish" is false. Thus, the fact that one of these statement forms is true does not *logically imply* that the other is true, as these substitution instances clearly prove.

Since the early Middle Ages the four kinds of categorical propositions have commonly been designated by letter names corresponding to the first four vowels of the Roman alphabet: **A, E, I, O.** The universal affirmative is called an **A** proposition, the universal negative an **E** proposition, the particular affirmative an **I** proposition, and the particular negative an **O** proposition. Tradition has it that these letters were derived from the first two vowels in the Latin words *affirmo* ("I affirm") and *nego* ("I deny"), thus:

Universal			Particular				
	|**A**|	f	f	|**I**|	r	m o	(affirmative)
n	|**E**|		g	|**O**|			(negative)

The material presented thus far in this section may be summarized as follows:

Proposition	Letter name	Quantity	Quality
All *S* are *P*.	**A**	universal	affirmative
No *S* are *P*.	**E**	universal	negative
Some *S* are *P*.	**I**	particular	affirmative
Some *S* are not *P*.	**O**	particular	negative

Unlike quality and quantity, which are attributes of *propositions*, **distribution** is an attribute of the *terms* (subject and predicate) of propositions. A term is said to be distributed if and only if the proposition makes an assertion about every member of the class denoted by the term; otherwise, it is undistributed. Stated another way, a term is distributed if and only if the statement assigns (or distributes) an attribute to every member of the class denoted by the term. Thus, if a statement asserts something about every member of the *S* class, then *S* is distributed; if it asserts something about every member of the *P* class, then *P* is distributed; otherwise *S* and *P* are undistributed.

Let us imagine that the members of the classes denoted by the subject and predicate terms of a categorical proposition are contained respectively in circles marked with the letters "*S*" and "*P*." The meaning of the statement "All *S* are *P*" may then be represented by the following diagram:

The *S* circle is contained in the *P* circle, which represents the fact that every member of S is a member of P. (Of course, should S and P represent terms denoting identical classes, the two circles would overlap exactly.) Through reference to the diagram, it is clear that "All S are P" makes a claim about every member of the S class, since the statement says that every member of S is in the P class. But the statement does not make a claim about every member of the P class, since there may be some members of P that are outside of S. Thus, by the definition of "distributed term" given above, S is distributed and P is not. In other words, for any universal affirmative (A) proposition, the subject term, whatever it may be, is distributed, and the predicate term is undistributed.

Let us now consider the universal negative (E) proposition. "No S are P" states that the S and P classes are separate, which may be represented as follows:

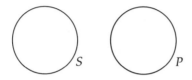

This statement makes a claim about every member of S and every member of P. It asserts that every member of S is separate from every member of P, and also that every member of P is separate from every member of S. Accordingly, by the definition above, both the subject and predicate terms of universal negative (E) propositions are distributed.

The particular affirmative (I) proposition states that at least one member of S is a member of P. If we represent this one member of S that we are certain about by an asterisk, the resulting diagram looks like this:

Since the asterisk is inside the P class, it represents something that is simultaneously an S and a P; in other words, it represents a member of the S class that is also a member of the P class. Thus, the statement "Some S are P" makes a claim about one member (at least) of S and also one member (at least) of P, but not about all members of either class. Hence, by the definition of distribution, neither S nor P is distributed.

The particular negative (O) proposition asserts that at least one member of S is not a member of P. If we once again represent this one member of S by an asterisk, the resulting diagram is as follows:

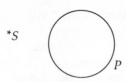

*S

P

Since the other members of S may or may not be outside of P, it is clear that the statement "Some S are not P" does not make a claim about every member of S, so S is not distributed. But, as may be seen from the diagram, the statement does assert that the entire P class is separated from this one member of S that is outside; that is, it does make a claim about every member of P. Thus, in the particular negative (**O**) proposition, P is distributed and S is undistributed.

At this point the notion of distribution may be somewhat vague and elusive. Unfortunately, there is no simple and easy way to make the idea graphically clear. The best that can be done is to repeat some of the things that have already been said. First of all, distribution is an attribute or quality that the subject and predicate terms of a categorical proposition may or may not possess, depending on the kind of proposition. If the proposition in question is an **A** type, then the subject term, whatever it may be, is distributed. If it is an **E** type, then both terms are distributed; if an **I** type, then neither; and if an **O** type, then the predicate. If a certain term is *distributed* in a proposition, this simply means that the proposition says something about every member of the class that the term denotes. If a term is *undistributed*, the proposition does not say something about every member of the class. The attribute of distribution, while not particularly important in relation to subsequent developments in this chapter, is essential to the evaluation of syllogisms in the next chapter.

The material of this section may now be summarized as follows:

Proposition	Letter name	Quantity	Quality	Terms distributed
All S are P.	A	universal	affirmative	S
No S are P.	E	universal	negative	S and P
Some S are P.	I	particular	affirmative	none
Some S are not P.	O	particular	negative	P

EXERCISE 4.2

I. For each of the following categorical propositions identify the letter name, quantity, and quality. Then state whether the subject and predicate terms are distributed or undistributed.

★1. No rich men are persons who beg in the street.

2. All ducks are birds that waddle.

3. Some medicines are nasty substances.

4. Some bald people are not persons who wear wigs.

5. All eggshells are delicate objects.

6. No nightmares are pleasant experiences.

7. Some battles are noisy affairs.

8. Some critical remarks are not suitable responses.

II. Change the quality but not the quantity of the following statements:

★1. All pigs are greedy creatures.

2. No coins are square objects.

3. Some professors are terrible bores.

4. Some donkeys are not bipeds.

III. Change the quantity but not the quality of the following statements:

★1. All sandwiches are satisfying meals.

2. No elderly ladies are talkative people.

3. Some spiders are web spinners.

4. Some clear explanations are not satisfactory answers.

IV. Change both the quality and the quantity of the following statements:

★1. All rabbits are furry animals.

2. No soldiers are quadrupeds.

3. Some miners are happy people.

4. Some concerts are not enjoyable affairs.

4.3 THE TRADITIONAL SQUARE OF OPPOSITION

The **traditional square of opposition,** in essence originated by Aristotle more than 2,000 years ago, is a calculating device that in many cases allows one to determine the truth or falsity of three categorical propositions when the truth or falsity of a fourth proposition is known. Of course, the four categorical propositions must be such that each has the same subject term and predicate term as the others. For example, given the true statement "All leopards are animals," the truth value of the corresponding **E** statement, "No leopards are animals," may readily be computed, as can the truth value of the corresponding **I** and **O** statements. But the truth value of the statement "No leopards are mammals" cannot be computed from the truth value of the given statement because it has a different predicate term. The traditional square of opposition is represented as follows:

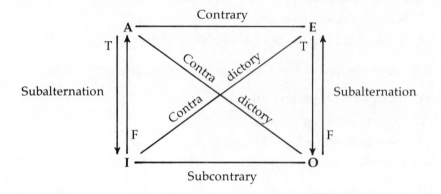

The four different categorical propositions are related to one another in terms of four different inferential relations. Here are the definitions of three of these relations (the fourth will be defined shortly):

contradictory = opposite truth value
contrary = not both true (at least one is false)
subcontrary = not both false (at least one is true)

Now suppose that we are presented with the categorical proposition "All Sadlerians are politicians," and let us further suppose that we are told that this statement is true. Without knowing anything at all about Sadlerians, we can use the square of opposition to compute the truth value of the three related propositions. The given proposition is an **A** proposition. By the *contradictory* relation we know immediately that the **O** proposition, "Some Sadlerians are not politicians," has the opposite truth value of the **A** proposition and is therefore false. By the *contrary* relation we know that the **A** and the **E** are not both true. Since we know that the **A** is true, it follows that the **E** proposition, "No Sadlerians are politicians," is false. Finally, since the **E** is false, it follows via the contradictory relation that the **I** proposition, "Some Sadlerians are politicians," is true. The truth value of the **I** proposition could also have been determined via the *subcontrary* relation: because the **O** was found to be false, and because the **O** and the **I** are not both false, it follows that the **I** is true. Thus, from the knowledge that "All Sadlerians are politicians" is true, we have determined the truth value of the other three propositions.

A CONCISE INTRODUCTION TO LOGIC

A word of caution is needed here concerning contrary and subcontrary. These relations work by the method of elimination. The **A** and **E** propositions are not both true, so if one is true, the other is false. But what happens if one is given as false? In such a case the method of elimination cannot be used, and the square of opposition tells us nothing about the truth value of the other proposition. In this case the other proposition is said to have **undetermined** truth value. Thus, for example, if the **E** proposition is given as false, the **A** has undetermined truth value. Analogous reasoning extends to the subcontrary relation. If the **O** proposition is given as false, by method of elimination the **I** is true. But if the **O** is given as true, the method of elimination cannot be used, and the **I** has undetermined truth value. Thus, in order to use the contrary relation, we must first be told that either the **A** or **E** proposition is *true;* to use the subcontrary relation we must first be told that either the **I** or **O** proposition is *false*.

As we have seen, it is possible to use the square of opposition quite successfully without at any time depending on the relation of **subalternation.** This relation is needed only if one wishes to make immediate inferences between the **A** and **I** propositions or between the **E** and **O** propositions. Of course, it also serves as a useful supplement to the other three relations. Note that the subalternation relation is represented by two arrows, the downward arrow marked with the letter "T" (true) and the upward one with "F" (false). These arrows may be thought of as pipelines through which truth values "flow." The downward arrow transmits only truth, the upward arrow only falsity. Thus, if the **A** proposition is given as true, we may conclude that the **I** proposition is also true; conversely, if the **I** is given as false, we may conclude that the **A** proposition is also false. But if the **A** proposition is given as false, the downward arrow, which transmits only truth, is useless and, of course, the upward arrow goes in the wrong direction. So in this case we conclude that the **I** proposition has undetermined truth value. Similarly, if the **I** proposition is given as true, the **A** proposition has undetermined truth value. Analogous reasoning prevails for the subalternation relation between the **E** and **O** propositions.

Rather than attempt a rigorous proof of the four inferential relations involved in the square of opposition, let us settle for a less rigorous illustration of their correctness. For reasons that will become apparent in Section 4.5, it is important that the categorical propositions to which the traditional square of opposition is applied have subject terms that denote actually existing things. But this hardly constitutes a severe restriction on its use. Let us first consider the statement "All tigers are mammals." This statement is in fact true, and the results given by the square of opposition are quite expected: "Some tigers are mammals" (subalternation) is true, "Some tigers are not mammals" (contradictory) is false, and "No tigers are mammals" (contrary) is false. Next, consider the statement "Some apples are red." This statement is actually true. Accordingly, it is hardly unexpected that "No apples are red" (contradiction) should be false. By the other three relations, contrary, subcontrary, and subalternation, the corresponding A and E propositions are undetermined. This means that the square of opposition alone will not tell us the truth value of these statements. But, of course, we know from having actually experienced green apples that "All apples are red" is false, and "Some apples are not red" is true. Thus, we have a case where the A and E propositions are both false and the I and O propositions both true: a result quite consistent with the square of opposition.

In applying the square of opposition, one should always refer to the relation of contradiction first. If, for example, a certain A proposition is given as true and we wish to determine the truth value of the corresponding O proposition, one possible procedure is to infer that the E statement is false, and from there proceed to the O statement. But subalternation from a false E statement yields undetermined results, and we might therefore be persuaded that the truth value of the O statement is undetermined. The relation of contradiction, however, tells us immediately that the O statement is false. This example illustrates the fact that the relation of contradiction is stronger than the others and gives concrete results when the combination of two other relations does not.

Another point that should be kept in mind is that when undetermined truth values do turn up, they always do so in pairs across the diagonal of the square. This is only natural, of course. For if we were to say that a certain E statement, for example, has undetermined truth value, and that the corresponding I statement is, let us say, true, we could then conclude via contradiction that the E statement is really false. Such an inference would necessarily involve some prior mistake in the use of the square.

The following table may be used to check results when using the square of opposition:

If A is given as true, then: E is false, I is true, O is false.
If E is given as true, then: A is false, I is false, O is true.
If I is given as true, then: E is false, A is undetermined, O is undetermined.
If O is given as true, then: A is false, E is undetermined, I is undetermined.

If A is given as false, then: E is undetermined, I is undetermined, O is true.
If E is given as false, then: A is undetermined, I is true, O is undetermined.
If I is given as false, then: A is false, E is true, O is true.
If O is given as false, then: A is true, E is false, I is true.

A CONCISE INTRODUCTION TO LOGIC

EXERCISE 4.3

I. Use the traditional square of opposition to find the answers to these problems.

★1. If "All girls are discontented individuals" is true, what is the truth value of the following statements:
   a. No girls are discontented individuals.
   b. Some girls are discontented individuals.
   c. Some girls are not discontented individuals.

2. If "All girls are discontented individuals" is false, what is the truth value of the following statements:
   a. No girls are discontented individuals.
   b. Some girls are discontented individuals.
   c. Some girls are not discontented individuals.

3. If "No geraniums are blue flowers" is true, what is the truth value of the following statements:
   a. All geraniums are blue flowers.
   b. Some geraniums are blue flowers.
   c. Some geraniums are not blue flowers.

4. If "No geraniums are blue flowers" is false, what is the truth value of the following statements:
   a. All geraniums are blue flowers.
   b. Some geraniums are blue flowers.
   c. Some geraniums are not blue flowers.

★5. If "Some oysters are silent creatures" is true, what is the truth value of the following statements:
   a. All oysters are silent creatures.
   b. No oysters are silent creatures.
   c. Some oysters are not silent creatures.

6. If "Some oysters are silent creatures" is false, what is the truth value of the following statements:
   a. All oysters are silent creatures.
   b. No oysters are silent creatures.
   c. Some oysters are not silent creatures.

7. If "Some judges are not fair officials" is true, what is the truth value of the following statements:
   a. All judges are fair officials.
   b. No judges are fair officials.
   c. Some judges are fair officials.

8. If "Some judges are not fair officials" is false, what is the truth value of the following statements:
   a. All judges are fair officials.
   b. No judges are fair officials.
   c. Some judges are fair officials.

II. Use the traditional square of opposition to determine whether the following arguments are valid or invalid. By definition, a valid argument is one in which the conclusion is necessarily true when the premises are assumed true. Thus, you should begin by assuming the premise is true, enter this information on the square of opposition, and then determine if the conclusion is necessarily true. If it is, the argument is valid; otherwise, it is invalid.

★1. All lions are fierce creatures.
    Therefore, some lions are fierce creatures.

2. It is false that no songs are melodic pieces.
   Therefore, some songs are not melodic pieces.

3. Some pirates are daring men.
   Therefore, some pirates are not daring men.

4. All dictionaries are useful books.
   Therefore, it is false that no dictionaries are useful books.

★5. Some wasps are unfriendly insects.
    Therefore, it is false that no wasps are unfriendly insects.

6. It is false that all professors are ignorant fools.
   Therefore, no professors are ignorant fools.

7. It is false that some monkeys are soldiers.
   Therefore, it is false that all monkeys are soldiers.

8. It is false that some bankers are not misers.
   Therefore, it is false that some bankers are misers.

9. Some idlers are not employees.
   Therefore, all idlers are employees.

★10. It is false that some muffins are not wholesome foods.
     Therefore, some muffins are wholesome foods.

III. Use the traditional square of opposition to determine whether the following arguments are valid or invalid. Then determine whether they are sound or unsound.

★1. Some coins are things made of silver.
    Therefore, some coins are not things made of silver.

2. All sharks are mammals.
   Therefore, it is false that no sharks are mammals.

3. It is false that no office buildings are skyscrapers.
   Therefore, some office buildings are skyscrapers.

4. Some daisies are flowers.
   Therefore, all daisies are flowers.

★5. It is false that some chemists are not scientists.
    Therefore, all chemists are scientists.

6. No cameras are things made in Japan.
   Therefore, it is false that some cameras are not things made in Japan.

7. It is false that some diamonds are not hard substances.
   Therefore, some diamonds are hard substances.

8. No women are grandmothers.
   Therefore, it is false that all women are grandmothers.

4.4 CONVERSION, OBVERSION, AND CONTRAPOSITION

Many statements expressed in ordinary English contain negated terms that sometimes obscure the meaning of the statements involved. Consider the following example:

> Some employees who are not currently on the payroll are not ineligible for workers' benefits.

As it stands, this statement is rather complicated, and its meaning may not be immediately clear; but it may be shown to be equivalent to the much simpler statement:

> Some of those eligible for workers' benefits are not currently on the payroll.

To justify this equivalence, and others like it, we need the operations of conversion, obversion, and contraposition.

Conversion, the simplest of the three, consists in switching the subject term with the predicate term. For example, if the **E** statement "No foxes are hedgehogs" is converted, the resulting statement is "No hedgehogs are foxes." This new statement is called the converse of the given statement and has the same truth value as the given statement. Similarly, converting the **I** statement "Some women are lawyers" gives us "Some lawyers are women," which has the same truth value as the given statement. Generalizing these results we obtain the following rule: *Converting an **E** or **I** statement gives a new statement that is logically equivalent to the given statement.* Two statements are said to be **logically equivalent** when they *necessarily* have the same truth value. Thus, converting an **E** or **I** statement gives a new statement that always has the same truth value as the original statement.

When we convert an **A** or **O** statement, on the other hand, the resulting statement does not necessarily have the same truth value as the given statement. For example, converting the true **A** statement "All carnations are flowers" gives the false statement "All flowers are carnations," and converting the true **O** statement "Some birds are not robins"

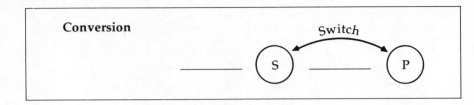

Conversion

Switch

———— (S) ———— (P)

gives the false statement "Some robins are not birds." But converting the true **A** statement "All bachelors are unmarried men" gives the *true* statement "All unmarried men are bachelors," and converting the true **O** statement "Some apples are not oranges" gives the *true* statement "Some oranges are not apples." Thus, as these examples illustrate, the truth value of the converse of an **A** or **O** statement depends on the terms in the statement. In some cases the converse may happen to have the same truth as the original statement and in other cases not. Since logic alone cannot decide which is the case, from the standpoint of logic the converse of an **A** or **O** statement has *undetermined* truth value.*

Conversion may be used to provide the link between the premise and conclusion of an argument. The following argument forms are valid:†

> No *A* are *B*.
> Therefore, no *B* are *A*.
>
> Some *A* are *B*.
> Therefore, some *B* are *A*.

Since the premise of each argument form necessarily has the same truth value as the conclusion, if the premise is assumed true, the conclusion is necessarily true. On the other hand, the next two argument forms are invalid. Each commits the fallacy of **illicit conversion:**

> All *A* are *B*.
> Therefore, all *B* are *A*.
>
> Some *A* are not *B*.
> Therefore, some *B* are not *A*.

Obversion is more complicated than conversion and involves a two-step process: (1) changing the quality (without changing the quantity),

---

*Some textbooks include treatment of an operation called "conversion by limitation," by which a true **A** statement entails a true **I** statement. Because this operation is merely a synthesis of ordinary conversion and subalternation, no special treatment is given it in this text. For analogous reasons, no special treatment is given to a similar operation called "contraposition by limitation."

†Some texts interpret arguments such as these as instances of begging the question. This text does not. See Section 3.3.

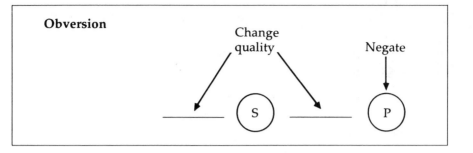

Obversion

Change quality   Negate

S   P

and (2) negating the predicate. The first part of this operation was dealt with in the exercise at the end of Section 4.2. For example, the following pairs of propositions have different quality but the same quantity:

| All birds are animals. | No birds are animals. |
| Some foxes are animals. | Some foxes are not animals. |

The second step involves negating the predicate. This is typically done by affixing the prefix "non-" to the predicate. When the two operations are performed together, the given proposition is said to be obverted, and the resulting proposition is called the "obverse" of the given proposition. Examples:

Given statement	**Obverse**
All horses are animals.	No horses are non-animals
No cats are dogs.	All cats are non-dogs.
Some trees are maples.	Some trees are not non-maples.
Some birds are not robins.	Some birds are non-robins.

Note that in each case (**A, E, I, O**) the obverse has the same truth value as the given statement. These results may be generalized to obtain this rule: *The obverse of an **A, E, I,** or **O** statement is logically equivalent to, and therefore necessarily has the same truth value as, the given statement.*

If a proposition is obverted and then obverted again, the predicate will have been negated twice. Example:

All horses are animals.	
No horses are non-animals.	(obverse)
All horses are non-non-animals.	(obverse of the obverse)

The prefix "non-non" is called double negation and may be deleted. The obverse of the obverse thus yields a statement identical in all respects to the given statement (as does the converse of the converse and the contrapositive of the contrapositive). However, while "non-non" may be deleted, the phrase "are not non-" should be left as it is. The word "not" is part of the copula, and "non-" is part of the predicate. These two components of categorical propositions must be kept separate.

As is the case with conversion, obversion may be used to supply the link between premise and conclusion in deductive arguments. The following argument forms are valid:

> All *A* are *B*.
> Therefore, no *A* are non-*B*.
>
> No *A* are *B*.
> Therefore, all *A* are non-*B*.
>
> Some *A* are *B*.
> Therefore, some *A* are not non-*B*.
>
> Some *A* are not *B*.
> Therefore, some *A* are non-*B*.

The premise of each argument form has the same truth value as the conclusion; accordingly, if the premise is assumed true, the conclusion must necessarily be true.

Contraposition also involves a two-step process: (1) switching subject and predicate terms, and (2) negating subject and predicate terms. When a given statement is contraposed, the resulting statement is called the "contrapositive" of the given statement. Examples:

Given statement	**Contrapositive**
All goats are animals.	All non-animals are non-goats.
Some birds are not parrots.	Some non-parrots are not non-birds.

A little reflection will reveal that each of these statements has the same truth value as its contrapositive. These results may be generalized to obtain this rule: *The contrapositive of an* **A** *or* **O** *statement is logically equivalent to, and therefore necessarily has the same truth value as, the given statement.*

When we contrapose an **E** or **I** statement, on the other hand, the contrapositive does not necessarily have the same truth value as the given statement. For example, the truth value of the contrapositives of the following statements is different from that of the given statements:

Given statement	**Contrapositive**
No dogs are cats.	No non-cats are non-dogs.
Some birds are non-parrots.	Some parrots are non-birds.

In each case the given statement is true and the contrapositive is false. For example, an instance of both a non-cat and a non-dog is a pig. Thus the statement "No non-cats are non-dogs" implies that "no pigs are pigs"—which is clearly false. As for the second pair of statements, "Some parrots are non-birds" is also clearly false because it implies that some parrot is not a bird.

On the other hand, contraposing the true **E** statement "No fish are non-fish" gives the *true* (and identical) statement "No fish are non-fish," and contraposing the true **I** statement "Some apples are red things" gives the *true* statement "Some non-red things are non-apples." Thus, the truth value of the contrapositive of an **E** or **I** statement, as with the converse of an **A** or **O** statement, depends on the terms in the statement. In other words, the contrapositive of an **E** or **I** statement is not logically equivalent to the given statement, and so from the standpoint of logic, it has *undetermined* truth value.

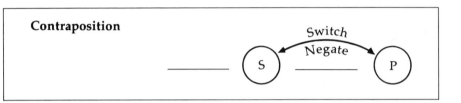

Contraposition

As with conversion and obversion, contraposition may provide the link between the premise and the conclusion of an argument. The following argument forms are valid:

All *A* are *B*.
Therefore, all non-*B* are non-*A*.

Some *A* are not *B*.
Therefore, some non-*B* are not non-*A*.

On the other hand, the following argument forms are invalid. Each commits the fallacy of **illicit contraposition:**

Some *A* are *B*.
Therefore, some non-*B* are non-*A*.

No *A* are *B*.
Therefore, no non-*B* are non-*A*.

Both illicit contraposition and illicit conversion are formal fallacies; that is, they can be detected through mere examination of the form of an argument.

Conversion, obversion, and contraposition may be used in conjunction with the traditional square of opposition to establish the validity of certain arguments. Consider the following:

All non-*A* are *B*.
Therefore, some *B* are not *A*.

Proving this argument valid requires three steps. Each step is derived from the one preceding it, and the justification for each is written to the immediate right:

All non-*A* are *B*.
Some non-*A* are *B*.   subalt.
Some *B* are non-*A*.   conv.
Some *B* are not *A*.   obv.

Various strategies may be used to obtain the conclusion of arguments such as this, but one procedure is to concentrate first on obtaining the individual terms as they appear in the conclusion. The order of the terms may be attended to next, and finally the square of opposition may be used to adjust the quality and quantity. As the above proof illustrates, however, variations on this procedure are sometimes necessary. The conclusion of the above argument requires that the "non-*A*" in the premise be negated, thus suggesting obversion. But to use obversion to accomplish this, the "non-*A*" must be moved into the predicate position via conversion. The latter operation, however, is valid only on **E** and **I** statements. The fact that the conclusion is a particular statement suggests subalternation as an intermediate step, thus yielding an **I** statement that can be converted.

The results of this section are summarized in the following table:

Conversion: Switch subject and predicate terms.

Given statement	Converse	Truth value
E: No *S* are *P*.	No *P* are *S*.	Same truth
I: Some *S* are *P*.	Some *P* are *S*.	value as given statement
A: All *S* are *P*.	All *P* are *S*.	Undetermined
O: Some *S* are not *P*.	Some *P* are not *S*.	truth value

Obversion: Change quality, negate predicate term.

Given statement	Obverse	Truth value
A: All *S* are *P*.	No *S* are non-*P*.	Same truth
E: No *S* are *P*.	All *S* are non-*P*.	value as given
I: Some *S* are *P*.	Some *S* are not non-*P*.	statement
O: Some *S* are not *P*.	Some *S* are non-*P*.	

Contraposition: Switch and negate subject and predicate terms.

Given statement	Contrapositive	Truth value
A: All S are P.	All non-P are non-S.	Same truth
O: Some S are not P.	Some non-P are not non-S.	value as given statement
E: No S are P.	No non-P are non-S.	Undetermined
I: Some S are P.	Some non-P are non-S.	truth value

EXERCISE 4.4

I. Perform the operations of conversion, obversion, and contraposition as indicated.

1. Convert the following propositions and state whether the converse is logically equivalent or not logically equivalent to the given proposition.
   ★a. All bores are dreaded creatures.
   b. No bankrupts are rich men.
   c. Some eagles are large birds.
   d. Some bonbons are not chocolate creams.

2. Obvert the following propositions and state whether the obverse is logically equivalent or not logically equivalent to the given proposition.
   ★a. All thieves are dishonest individuals.
   b. No policemen are persons less than four feet tall.
   c. Some analgesics are inefficient pain relievers.
   d. Some porcupines are not nonswimmers.

3. Contrapose the following propositions and state whether the contrapositive is logically equivalent or not logically equivalent to the given proposition.
   ★a. All uneducated people are persons who are incapable of being managers.
   b. No children who don't obey are good children.
   c. Some unauthorized reports are false reports.
   d. Some sailboats longer than 40 feet are not things that weigh at least four tons.

II. Use conversion, obversion, and contraposition to determine whether the following arguments are valid or invalid. If the conclusion is logically equivalent to the premise, the argument is valid; otherwise, invalid.

★1. All kangaroos are marsupials.
   Therefore, all marsupials are kangaroos.

2. No pillows are hard objects.
   Therefore, all pillows are soft objects.

3. Some birds are not peacocks.
   Therefore, some non-peacocks are not non-birds.

4. Some careless people are undependable individuals.
   Therefore, some dependable individuals are careful people.

★5. Some apples are not ripe fruits.
   Therefore, some apples are unripe fruits.

6. No emperors are dentists.
   Therefore, no dentists are emperors.

7. All uninteresting poems are unpopular poems.
   Therefore, all popular poems are interesting poems.

8. Some bluejays are not reptiles.
   Therefore, some reptiles are not bluejays.

9. All mares are female horses.
   Therefore, no mares are male horses.

★10. No illogical people are successful people.
   Therefore, no unsuccessful people are logical people.

III. In 1 through 10 you are given a statement, its truth value in parentheses, and an operation to be performed on that statement. You must supply the new statement and the truth value of the new statement. In 11 through 20 you are given a statement, its truth value in parentheses, and a new statement. You must determine how the new statement was derived from the given statement and supply the truth value of the new statement. Some of these exercises involve the traditional square of opposition.

Given statement	Operation	New statement	Truth value
★1. All non-A are B. (T)	contrap.	_____	____
2. Some A are non-B. (F)	subalt.	_____	____
3. No A are non-B. (T)	obv.	_____	____
4. Some non-A are not B. (T)	subcon.	_____	____
★5. No A are non-B. (F)	contradic.	_____	____
6. No A are B. (T)	contrap.	_____	____
7. All non-A are B. (T)	contrary	_____	____
8. Some A are not non-B. (F)	obv.	_____	____
9. No A are non-B. (F)	conv.	_____	____
★10. Some non-A are non-B. (F)	subcon.	_____	____
11. Some non-A are not B. (T)	_____	All non-A are B.	____
12. Some A are non-B. (T)	_____	Some non-B are A.	____
13. All non-A are B. (F)	_____	No non-A are non-B.	____
14. Some non-A are not B. (T)	_____	No non-A are B.	____

Given statement	Operation	New statement	Truth value
★15. All A are non-B. (F)	————	All non-B are A.	———
16. Some non-A are non-B. (F)	————	No non-A are non-B.	———
17. Some A are not non-B. (T)	————	Some B are not non-A.	———
18. No non-A are B. (T)	————	Some non-A are not B.	———
19. No A are non-B. (F)	————	All A are non-B.	———
★20. Some non-A are B. (F)	————	Some non-A are not B.	———

IV. Use conversion, obversion, contraposition, and the traditional square of opposition to prove that the following arguments are valid. Show each intermediate step in the deduction.

★1. All artichokes are vegetables.
   Therefore, some vegetables are artichokes.

2. No non-metals are conductors.
   Therefore, some non-conductors are not metals.

3. It is false that some admirals are non-sailors.
   Therefore, all admirals are sailors.

4. All non-workers are executives.
   Therefore, it is false that all executives are workers.

★5. No non-writers are editors.
   Therefore, it is false that some editors are not writers.

6. It is false that some non-surgeons are non-physicians.
   Therefore, some physicians are non-surgeons.

7. Some secretaries are not non-typists.
   Therefore, it is false that no typists are secretaries.

8. It is false that no non-trees are plants.
   Therefore, some plants are not trees.

9. It is false that some non-violinists are not musicians.
   Therefore, some musicians are not violinists.

★10. It is false that some oysters are not fish.
   Therefore, it is false that all fish are non-oysters.

4.5 THE MODERN SQUARE OF OPPOSITION AND THE EXISTENTIAL FALLACY

As was suggested in Section 4.3, a problem arises if the traditional square of opposition is used in connection with statements that make assertions about things that do not actually exist. Consider, for example, the statement "All unicorns are one-horned animals." If this statement is considered to be false (because there are no unicorns), the traditional square of opposition, via the relation of contradiction, tells us that "Some unicorns are not one-horned" is true. But this latter statement asserts that at least one unicorn is not one-horned—which is false, because no unicorns exist. And if "All unicorns are one-horned animals" is considered to be true (because if there were any unicorns, by definition they would be one-horned), the relation of subalternation tells us that "Some unicorns are one-horned animals" is true. But once again, because no unicorns exist, this statement is false. Thus, as this example illustrates, the traditional square of opposition simply cannot be used in conjunction with statements that make assertions about things that do not exist. In these cases we must use what is called the **modern square of opposition.**

The modern square of opposition is based on an interpretation of categorical statements introduced by the nineteenth-century logician George Boole. According to this interpretation, universal statements are equivalent to conditional statements:

> All *S* are *P*. = If there are any *S*, then they are *P*.
> No *S* are *P*. = If there are any *S*, then they are not *P*.

Thus, from the Boolean standpoint, universal statements make no assumption about whether or not their subject terms denote actually existing things.

Particular statements, on the other hand, mean the same thing from the Boolean standpoint as they do from the standpoint of the traditional square of opposition:

> Some *S* are *P*. = At least one *S* exists, and that *S* is a *P*.
> Some *S* are not *P*. = At least one *S* exists, and that *S* is not a *P*.

The square of opposition that results from the Boolean interpretation of categorical statements—that is, the modern square of opposition—is presented in this way:

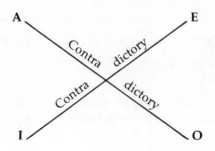

The only relation that exists in the modern square of opposition is the contradictory relation—the relations of contrary, subcontrary, and subalternation do not apply. Thus, the modern square of opposition provides for fewer inferences than the traditional square—which is only natural, since it makes fewer assumptions.

Let us now apply the modern square of opposition to the statement "All unicorns are one-horned animals." According to the Boolean interpretation of universal propositions, this statement means "If there are any unicorns, then they are one-horned animals"—which is true.* By the contradictory relation, therefore, "Some unicorns are not one-horned animals" is false—which is exactly what we would expect it to be. No additional inferences are possible.

Now that we have two squares of opposition, the traditional and the modern, the question naturally arises of when to use one and when to use the other. The answer is that although the modern square may be used on all categorical propositions, it is preferable to use the traditional square on categorical propositions that make assertions about actually existing things, because it provides for more inferences. On categorical propositions that make assertions about things that do not actually exist (such as unicorns or leprechauns), the traditional square cannot be used; only the modern square may be used.

The **existential fallacy** is a formal fallacy that occurs when the traditional square of opposition is used in conjunction with propositions that make assertions about things that do not actually exist. In other words, it occurs when the relations of contrary, subcontrary, and subalternation are used (in a manner that would normally yield a determinate truth value) to draw inferences from propositions whose subject terms denote empty classes. Under these conditions, as I have pointed out, only the modern square of opposition may be used, and the modern square does not include these relations. The existential fallacy is a formal fallacy in that, once the Boolean standpoint has been adopted, it may be detected through mere inspection of the form of an argument. The following arguments commit the existential fallacy:

> All unicorns are one-horned animals.
> Therefore, some unicorns are one-horned animals.
>
> No leprechauns are German citizens.
> Therefore, it is not the case that all leprechauns are German citizens.

The first argument depends on the subalternation relation, the second on the contrary relation.

---

*Actually, the truth of this statement rests upon the fact that no unicorns exist; in other words, the statement is *vacuously* true. The logic behind this concept is developed in Chapters 6 and 8.

EXERCISE 4.5

Use the traditional and modern squares of opposition to determine whether the following arguments are valid or invalid. Identify the arguments that commit the existential fallacy.

★1. All eagles are birds.
Therefore, some eagles are birds.

2. No mermaids are brunettes.
Therefore, some mermaids are not brunettes.

3. It is false that some rabbits are turtles.
Therefore, some rabbits are not turtles.

4. All leprechauns are clever individuals.
Therefore, it is false that some leprechauns are not clever individuals.

★5. Some books are not romances.
Therefore, no books are romances.

6. It is false that some gnomes are hard workers.
Therefore, some gnomes are not hard workers.

7. No wood nymphs are dependable creatures.
Therefore, it is false that some wood nymphs are dependable creatures.

8. It is false that all gluttons are reprobates.
Therefore, no gluttons are reprobates.

9. No centaurs are friendly animals.
Therefore, it is false that all centaurs are friendly animals.

★10. It is false that some ducks are not birds.
Therefore, it is false that no ducks are birds.

4.6 VENN DIAGRAMS

The nineteenth-century logician John Venn, following the interpretation of universal statements introduced earlier by George Boole, developed a system of diagrams to represent the information contained in categorical propositions. These diagrams have come to be known as **Venn diagrams.**

A Venn diagram is an arrangement of overlapping circles. Each circle represents the class denoted by a term in a categorical proposition. Since each categorical proposition has exactly two terms, the Venn diagram consists of two circles. Once the circles are drawn, they are labeled with letters corresponding to the terms in the statement. The left-hand circle is usually selected to represent the subject term, and the right-hand circle, the predicate term, but the exact order is not important. The first

A CONCISE INTRODUCTION TO LOGIC

letter in each term is usually selected for labeling the circles, but if two terms begin with the same letter, this convention is modified.

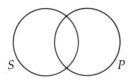

The members of the class denoted by the subject term (if any such members exist) are conceived as being located in the S circle, and the members of the class denoted by the predicate term (if any such members exist) are conceived as being located in the P circle. The members of the S class may all be located in the part of the S circle that is outside the P circle, or in the part that the P circle overlaps, or in both; and the members of the P class may all be located in the part of the P circle that is outside the S circle, or in the part that the S circle overlaps, or in both.

Conversely, if an entity is inside the S circle, it is a member of the S class, and if it is inside the P circle, it is a member of the P class. Obviously, if something is in the central area where the S and P circles overlap, it is a member of both the S and P classes. For example, in the diagram below, if the letter "A" represents the term "Americans" and "F" the term "farmers," then anything in the area marked "1" is an American but not a farmer, anything in the area marked "2" is both an American and a farmer, and anything in the area marked "3" is a farmer but not an American. The area marked "4" is the area outside both circles—anything in this area is neither a farmer nor an American.

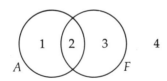

Unless an exception is made to the contrary, categorical propositions represented in Venn diagrams are given the Boolean interpretation:

All S are P. = If there are any S, then they are P.
No S are P. = If there are any S, then they are not P.
Some S are P. = At least one S exists, and that S is a P.
Some S are not P. = At least one S exists, and that S is not a P.

Each proposition is represented by making a single mark in a pair of overlapping circles. Two kinds of marks are allowed: shading an area and placing an "X" in an area. Shading an area means that the shaded area is empty, and placing an "X" in an area means that at least one thing exists in that area.* The "X" may be thought of as representing that one thing. If no mark appears in a certain area, nothing is known about that area; it may contain members or it may be empty. Shading is always used in connection with universal propositions, and placing an "X" is used in connection with particular propositions. The content of the four kinds of categorical propositions is represented as follows:

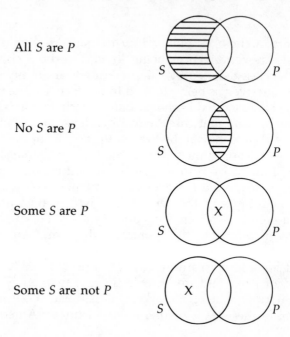

All S are P

No S are P

Some S are P

Some S are not P

These four diagrams exactly represent the Boolean interpretations of the four propositions. The first diagram states that the portion of the S circle that is outside the P circle is empty; so if there are any S, they are in the part of the S circle that is inside the P circle. The second diagram states that the area where the S and P circles overlap is empty (in other words, nothing is both an S and a P); so if there are any S, they are outside the P circle. The third diagram states that there is at least one thing that is both an S and a P, and the fourth diagram states that at least one thing exists in the S circle that is not a P.

It should be noted that the diagrams that represent the universal propositions state nothing about existence. For example, the one that represents the **A** proposition states that the portion of S that is outside P

---

*In many mathematics texts shading an area of a Venn diagram indicates that the area is *not* empty. The significance of shading in logic is exactly the opposite.

is empty; but it does not say that the part of S that is inside P is not empty. Because no marks are made in these areas, we know nothing of their contents. They may be empty or they may have members. All of this is in conformity with the nonexistential character of the Boolean interpretation. Similarly, it should be noted that the diagrams that represent the particular propositions tell us that something exists in one single area. For example, the diagram that represents the I proposition tells us that something exists in the central area; but since no marks appear in either of the other two areas, we know nothing about their possible content.

EXERCISE 4.6

Draw Venn diagrams for the following propositions:

★1. No debaters are prejudiced people.

2. All pigs are fat animals.

3. Some newspapers are worthless endeavors.

4. Some misers are not cheerful individuals.

5. All sailors are adventuresome spirits.

6. No bridges are things made of sugar.

7. Some philosophers are conceited fools.

8. Some college graduates are not educated people.

4.7 VENN DIAGRAMS: FURTHER APPLICATIONS

Venn diagrams provide a convenient illustration of, and proof for, the inferences involved in both the traditional and the modern squares of opposition, as well as the operations of conversion, obversion, and contraposition. Let us first consider the modern square of opposition, shown on page 158.

The meaning of the contradictory relation is clearly illustrated by the diagrams. The diagram for the **A** statement says that the left-hand part of the S circle is empty, and the diagram for the **O** statement says that it is not empty. This is the strictest form of opposition. Similarly, the diagram for the **E** statement says that the central area is empty, while the diagram for the **I** statement says that it is not empty.

The relations of contrary, subcontrary, and subalternation do not hold in this diagram. This may be illustrated through the (quite legitimate) supposition that the S class is empty. If this is so, then we may imagine the entire S circle as shaded, in which case the diagrams for both the **A** and the **E** statements make a true assertion. This violates the definition

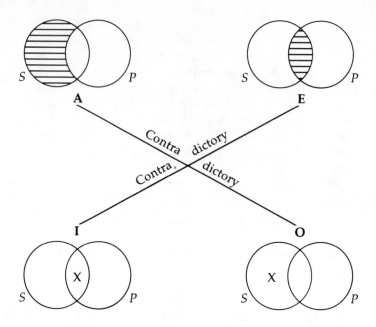

of contrary. Continuing, if the entire *S* circle is empty, then the diagrams for both the **I** and **O** statements (which claim that some portion of the *S* circle is not empty) are false. This violates the definition of subcontrary. Finally, if the **A** and **E** statements are both true, and the **I** and **O** statements both false, the definition of subalternation is violated.

Now let us turn to the traditional square of opposition. What distinguishes the traditional square from the modern one is the supposition that the universal statements to which it is applied make an assertion about things that actually exist. In other words, it is assumed that the classes denoted by the subject terms of these statements are not empty. In the diagram representing the **A** statement, this means that since the left-hand portion of the *S* circle is empty, the right-hand portion is not empty. This fact is represented by placing an "X" in the right-hand portion of the *S* circle. In addition, a small circle may be placed around this "X" to indicate that it comes not from the statement as such but from the special assumption peculiar to the traditional square of opposition. By similar reasoning, in the diagram that represents the **E** statement, a circled "X" is placed in the left-hand portion of the *S* circle.

Now, by inspecting the diagrams, we see that the **A** and **E** statements cannot both be true, because one says that an area is empty while the other says that that same area is not empty. Thus, the contrary relation prevails. Turning to subalternation, if the **A** statement is true, then the right-hand portion of the *S* circle has at least one member, making the **I** statement true. By similar reasoning, if the **E** statement is true, then the **O** statement is also true. Conversely, if the **I** statement is false, then the

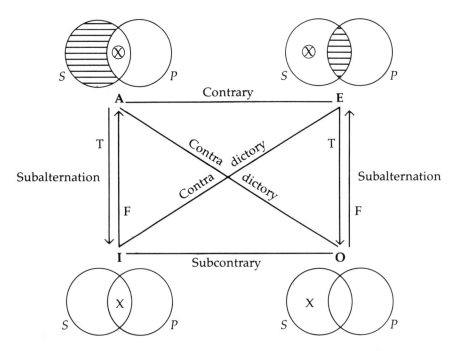

A ——————— Contrary ——————— E

T · · · Contradictory · · · T

Subalternation · · · Contradictory · · · Subalternation

F · · · · F

I ——————— Subcontrary ——————— O

right-hand portion of the S circle is empty, making the **A** statement false; and if the **O** statement is false, then the left-hand portion of the S circle is empty, making the **E** statement false. Finally, turning to subcontrary, if the **I** statement is false, the right-hand portion of the S circle is empty, and (since the entire S circle has at least one thing in it) this means that the left-hand portion of the S circle is not empty, making the **O** statement true. By similar reasoning, if the **O** statement is false, the right-hand portion of the S circle is not empty, making the **I** statement true. Thus, the relation of subcontrary prevails.

The diagrams for the traditional square show how contrary, subcontrary, and subalternation come back into the picture when the assumption is made that at least one S exists. Unfortunately, these diagrams obscure the meaning of contradiction; but since contradiction is established by the diagrams for the modern square, which make no existential assumptions, contradiction remains valid when existential assumptions are made. This same line of thinking underlies the use of Venn diagrams to prove the operations of conversion, obversion, and contraposition. Since these operations hold from the modern standpoint, proving them from this standpoint is sufficient to prove that they hold from the traditional standpoint as well.

Let us begin with conversion. The diagram for "No S are P" is clearly identical to that for "No P are S," and the diagram for "Some S are P" is clearly identical to that for "Some P are S." The operation of conversion thus yields equivalent results for **E** and **I** statements. But the diagram for

CATEGORICAL PROPOSITIONS

"All S are P" is clearly different from that for "All P are S," and the diagram for "Some S are not P" is clearly different from that for "Some P are not S." Thus, in general, conversion does not yield equivalent results for **A** and **O** statements.

Conversion

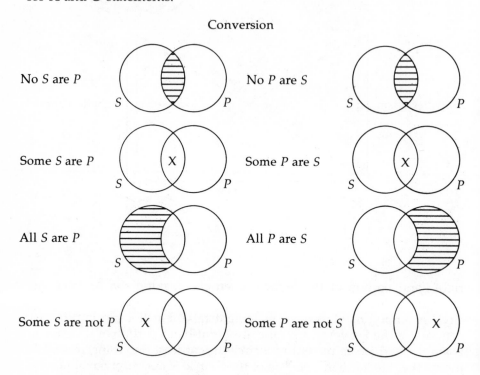

No S are P · No P are S

Some S are P · Some P are S

All S are P · All P are S

Some S are not P · Some P are not S

In the case of obversion, the diagrams are identical for all four kinds of categorical propositions. When drawing these diagrams, keep in mind that the area corresponding to "non-P" is everything outside the P circle. In the diagram corresponding to the statement "No S are non-P" the area is shaded where S overlaps the area outside P. In the diagram corresponding to "All S are non-P" the area of S that is inside P is shaded. This has the effect of moving the members of S outside the P circle. In the diagram corresponding to "Some S are not non-P" there is a member of S that is not outside P; that is, there is a member of S that is inside P. And in the diagram corresponding to "Some S are non-P" there is a member of S that is outside P.

In reference to contraposition, the diagram corresponding to "All non-P are non-S" states that the members in the area outside the P circle are also outside the S circle. In other words, the area where the outside of the P circle overlaps the S circle is empty.

Obversion

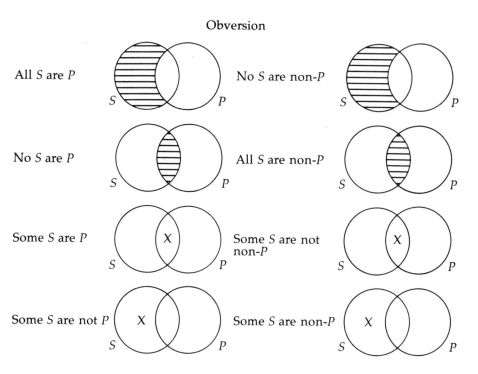

All S are P	No S are non-P
No S are P	All S are non-P
Some S are P	Some S are not non-P
Some S are not P	Some S are non-P

The following diagram illustrates contraposition for the **A** proposition. Diagrams for the other kinds of categorical propositions are left to an exercise.

Contraposition

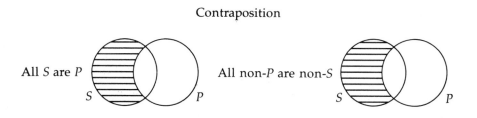

All S are P   All non-P are non-S

EXERCISE 4.7

I. Use Venn diagrams to show that contraposition yields logically equivalent results for **O** propositions and that it does not yield logically equivalent results for **I** and **E** propositions. For the diagrams corresponding to statements that include negated terms, supply a written explanation.

II. Draw Venn diagrams for the following statement forms, labeling the circles "S" and "P." Then check your results by using conversion, obversion, or contraposition to eliminate the negated terms and by then comparing the diagram with the new statement form. Of course, these operations must be used only when they yield a statement that is logically equivalent to the given statement.

★1. All P are non-S.

2. Some non-P are S.

3. All non-P are non-S.

4. Some S are not non-P.

★5. Some non-P are not non-S.

6. No non-P are S.

7. All S are non-P.

8. Some P are not non-S.

4.8 TRANSLATING ORDINARY LANGUAGE STATEMENTS INTO CATEGORICAL FORM

Few statements that occur in ordinary written and oral expression are categorical propositions, strictly speaking. If the operations and inferences pertinent to categorical propositions are to be applied to these statements, they must first be translated into categorical form. As with any kind of translation, no set of specific rules can be given that will cover every possible form of phraseology; yet one general rule always applies: Understand the *meaning* of the given statement, and then re-express it in a new statement that has a quantifier, subject term, copula, and predicate term. Some of the forms of phraseology that are typically encountered are terms without nouns, nonstandard verbs, singular propositions, adverbs and pronouns, unexpressed and nonstandard quantifiers, conditional statements, exclusive propositions, "the only," and exceptive propositions.

Terms Without Nouns

The subject and predicate terms of a categorical proposition must contain either a noun or noun substitute that serves to denote the class indicated by the term. Nouns and noun substitutes denote classes, while adjectives (and participles) connote attributes. If a term consists of only an adjective, a noun or noun substitute should be introduced to make the term genuinely denotative. Examples:

Some roses are red.	Some roses are red *flowers*.
All tigers are carnivorous.	All tigers are carnivorous *animals*.

Nonstandard Verbs

According to the position adopted earlier in this chapter, the only copulas that are allowed in categorical propositions are "are" and "are not." Statements in ordinary usage often incorporate other forms of the verb "to be." Such statements may be corrected as the following examples illustrate:

Some persons who go to college will become educated.	Some persons who go to college *are persons who* will become educated.
Some dogs would rather bark than bite.	Some dogs *are animals that* would rather bark than bite.

In other statements no form of the verb "to be" occurs at all. These may be translated as the following examples indicate:

Some birds fly south during the winter.	Some birds *are animals that* fly south during the winter.
All ducks swim.	All ducks *are swimmers*.
	or
	All ducks *are animals that* swim.

Singular Propositions

A singular proposition is a proposition that makes an assertion about a specific person, place, thing, or time. Singular propositions are typically translated into universals by means of a parameter. A **parameter** is a phrase that, when introduced into a statement, affects the form but not the meaning. Some parameters that may be used to translate singular propositions are:

persons identical to
places identical to
things identical to
cases identical to
times identical to

For example, the statement "Socrates is mortal" may be translated as "All persons identical to Socrates are persons who are mortal." Because only one person is identical to Socrates, namely Socrates himself, the term "persons identical to Socrates" denotes the class that has Socrates as its only member. In other words, it simply denotes Socrates. Other examples:

George went home.	All *persons identical to* George are *persons who* went home.
There is a radio in the back bedroom.	All *places identical to* the back bedroom are *places where* there is a radio.
The moon is full tonight.	All *things identical to* the moon are *things that* are full tonight. <div align="center">or</div> All *times identical to* tonight are *times* the moon is full.
I hate gin.	All *persons identical to* me are *persons who* hate gin. <div align="center">or</div> All *things identical to* gin are *things that* I hate.

Adverbs and Pronouns

When a statement contains a spatial adverb such as "where," "wherever," "everywhere," or "nowhere," or a temporal adverb such as "when," "whenever," "always," or "never," it may be translated in terms of "places" or "times," respectively. Statements containing pronouns such as "who," "whoever," "what," or "whatever" may be translated in terms of "persons" or "things," respectively. Examples:

He always wears a suit to work.	All *times* he goes to work are *times* he wears a suit.
He is always clean shaven.	All *times* are *times* he is clean shaven.
She never brings her lunch to school.	No *times* she goes to school are *times* she brings her lunch. <div align="center">or</div> No *times* are *times* she brings her lunch to school.

Nowhere are there any unicorns.	No *places* are *places* there are unicorns.
Whoever works hard will succeed.	All *persons* who work hard are *persons* who will succeed.
He glitters when he walks.	All *times* he walks are *times* he glitters.
She goes where she chooses.	All *places* she chooses to go are *places* she goes.
She does what she wants.	All *things* she wants to do are *things* she does.

Notice the order of the terms in the last three examples. When one of the aforenamed adverbs or pronouns occurs in the middle of a statement, the order of the terms must be reversed in the categorical form.

Unexpressed Quantifiers

Many statements in ordinary usage have quantifiers that are implied but not expressed. In introducing the quantifiers one must be guided by the most probable meaning of the statement. Examples:

Emeralds are green gems.	*All* emeralds are green gems.
There are lions in the zoo.	*Some* lions are animals in the zoo.
A tiger is a mammal.	*All* tigers are mammals.
A fish is not a mammal.	*No* fish are mammals.
A tiger roared.	*Some* tigers are animals that roared.
Children are human beings.	*All* children are human beings.
Children live next door.	*Some* children are persons who live next door.

Nonstandard Quantifiers

Sometimes the quantity of a statement is indicated by a word or words other than the three quantifiers that are allowed. Furthermore, statements having the form "All S are not P" are *not* in standard categorical form. Depending on the meaning, statements having this form must be rendered as either "No S are P" or "Some S are not P." Examples:

A few soldiers are heroes.	*Some* soldiers are heroes.

Anyone who votes is a citizen.	*All* voters are citizens.
Not everyone who votes is a Democrat.	*Some* voters are not Democrats.
Not a single dog is a cat.	*No* dogs are cats.
All race horses can't be winners.	*Some* race horses are not winners.
All goats are not sheep.	*No* goats are sheep.
Few sailors entered the regatta.	*Some* sailors are persons who entered the regatta *and some* sailors are not persons who entered the regatta.

Notice that statements beginning with "few" (and some statements beginning with "a few") cannot be translated as single categorical propositions. They must be translated as a compound arrangement of an **I** proposition and an **O** proposition. Statements beginning with "almost all" and "not quite all" must be handled in the same way. When these statements occur in arguments, the arguments must be treated in the same way as those containing exceptive propositions, which will be discussed shortly.

Conditional Statements

When the antecedent and consequent of a conditional statement have subject terms that denote the same thing, the statement can usually be translated into categorical form. The Boolean interpretation of categorical propositions provides the key: such statements are always rendered as universals. Examples:

If it's a mouse, then it's a mammal.	All mice are mammals.
If an animal has four legs, then it is not a bird.	No four-legged animals are birds.
If Los Angeles is in California, then Los Angeles is a large city.	All California cities identical to Los Angeles are large cities.

Conditional statements such as "If Los Angeles is in California, then Houston is a large city" cannot be translated into categorical form.

When the word "if" occurs in the middle of a conditional statement, the statement must be restructured so that it occurs at the beginning. For example, "An animal is a fish if it has gills" means "If an animal has gills, then it is a fish." This is then translated, "All animals having gills are fish." Other examples:

A person will succeed if he perseveres.	All persons who persevere are persons who will succeed.
Jewelry is expensive if it is made of gold.	All pieces of jewelry made of gold are expensive things.

In translating conditional statements it is sometimes useful to employ a rule called **transposition**. According to this rule, the antecedent and consequent of a conditional statement may switch places if both are negated. For example, the statement "If something is not valuable, then it is not scarce" is logically equivalent to "If something is scarce, then it is valuable." This is then translated as "All scarce things are valuable things." Examples:

If it's not a mammal, then it's not a mouse.	All mice are mammals.
If a company is not well managed, then it is not a good investment.	All companies that are good investments are well-managed companies.

The word "unless" means "if ... not." For example, the statement "An applicant is not eligible unless he has a college degree" means "An applicant is not eligible if he does not have a college degree," which means "If an applicant does not have a college degree, then he is not eligible." By transposition, this means "If an applicant is eligible, then he has a college degree," which is translated as "All eligible applicants are applicants with college degrees." Other examples:

Tomatoes are edible unless they are spoiled.	All inedible tomatoes are spoiled tomatoes. or All unspoiled tomatoes are edible tomatoes.
Unless a boy misbehaves he will be treated decently.	All boys who do not misbehave are boys who will be treated decently.

Exclusive Propositions

Propositions that involve the words "only" and "none but" are exclusive propositions. Efforts to translate them into categorical propositions frequently lead to confusion of the subject term with the predicate term. Such confusion can be avoided if the statement is phrased as a conditional statement first, then as a categorical statement. For example, the statement "Only executives can use the silver elevator" is equivalent to "If a person can use the silver elevator, he is an executive." The correct categorical proposition is "All persons who can use the silver elevator are executives." If the statement were translated "All executives are persons who can use the silver elevator," it would clearly be wrong. Thus, the occurrence of "only" and "none but" at the beginning of a statement indicates a reversal in the order of the terms when the statement is translated into categorical form. Examples:

Only elected officials will attend the convention.	All persons who will attend the convention are elected officials.
None but the brave deserve the fair.	All persons who deserve the fair are brave persons.

When "only" and "none but" occur in the middle of a statement, the statement must first be restructured so that the term preceded by "only" or "none but" occurs first. Then the statement can be translated as those above. For example, the statement "Executives can use only the silver elevator" is equivalent to "Only the silver elevator can be used by executives." This, in turn, is equivalent to "If an elevator can be used by executives, then it is the silver elevator," which is translated: "All elevators that can be used by executives are elevators identical to the silver elevator." Other examples:

He owns only the shirt on his back.	All shirts owned by him are shirts identical to the one on his back.
She invited only wealthy socialites.	All persons invited by her are wealthy socialites.

"The Only"

Statements beginning with the words "the only" are translated differently from those beginning with "only." For example, the statement "The only cars that are available are Chevrolets" means "If a car is available, then it is a Chevrolet." This, in turn, is translated as "All cars that are available are Chevrolets." In other words, "The only," when it occurs at the beginning of a statement, can simply be replaced with "all," and the order of the terms is *not* reversed in the translation.

When "the only" occurs in the middle of a statement, the statement must be restructured so that it occurs at the beginning. For example, "Romances are the only books he sells" is equivalent to "The only books he sells are romances." This is then translated as "All books that he sells are romances." Other examples:

The only animals that live in this canyon are skunks.	All animals that live in this canyon are skunks.
Accountants are the only ones who will be hired for the job.	All those who will be hired for the job are accountants.

Exceptive Propositions

Propositions of the form "All except S are P" and "All but S are P" are exceptive propositions. They must be translated not as single categorical propositions but as pairs of conjoined categorical propositions. Statements that include the phrase "none except," on the other hand, are exclusive (not exceptive) propositions. "None except" is synonymous with "none but." Some examples of exceptive propositions are:

All except students are invited.	No students are invited persons, and all nonstudents are invited persons.
All but managers must report to the President.	No managers are persons who must report to the president, and all nonmanagers are persons who must report to the president.

Because exceptive propositions cannot be translated into single categorical propositions, many of the simple inferences and operations pertinent to categorical propositions cannot be applied to them. Arguments that contain exceptive propositions as premises or conclusion can be evaluated only through the application of extended techniques. This topic is taken up in Section 5.5 of the next chapter.

EXERCISE 4.8

Translate the following statements into categorical propositions:

★1. A prudent man shuns tigers.

2. Ostriches do not feed on mince pies.

3. No idlers win fame.

4. Sugar is sweet.

★5. Not all bores are uneducated.

6. Everyone who is sane can do logic.

7. If it's a duck, then it can't waltz.

8. A kitten that loves fish is playful.

9. Kangaroos are not suitable for pets.

★10. None but carnivores kill mice.

11. Warmth always relieves pain.

12. John is in the house.

13. Only literate people write poetry.

14. A few rabbits live in these woods.

★15. The only people who do mischief are thoughtless people.

16. Mount Everest has been climbed by Americans.

17. If a person is clever, he will invest in profitable stocks.

18. No birds except peacocks are proud of their tails.

19. Only wasps and ants came to the picnic.

★20. Lions are wild.

21. Occasionally, there are concerts in the park.

22. St. Louis is south of Chicago.

23. Cheaters never win.

24. The only way to get rid of a temptation is to yield to it.

★25. Where there's life, there's hope.

26. Short stories are not interesting unless they are romantic.

27. She gets fat when she eats too much.

28. If it isn't graceful, it isn't an antelope.

29. All but the rats left the sinking ship.

★30. A cat is contented if it is well fed.

31. She likes only rich foods.

32. He who fails is slothful.

33. Philosophers are all mad.

34. Only gentlemen prefer blondes.

★35. Unless he has an honest face, a gambler is not to be trusted.

36. All except employees are eligible to enter the contest.

37. Few novels are worth reading.

38. Monkeys live in this jungle.

39. Monkeys are mammals.

★40. I like strawberries.

5
CATEGORICAL SYLLOGISMS

5.1 STANDARD FORM, MOOD, AND FIGURE

In the general sense of the term, a **syllogism** is a deductive argument consisting of two premises and one conclusion. A **categorical syllogism** is a special type of syllogism in which all three statements are categorical propositions. In addition, these three propositions must contain a total of three different terms, each of which appears twice in distinct propositions. The following argument is a categorical syllogism:

> All civic leaders are wealthy individuals.
> No wealthy individuals are paupers.
> Therefore, no civic leaders are paupers.

The requirement that the premises and conclusion contain exactly three terms, each of which appears twice, needs two qualifications. The first is that an argument containing more than three terms qualifies as a categorical syllogism if it can be translated into an equivalent argument having exactly three terms. For example, if, in the argument above, the term "wealthy individuals" were changed in the second premise to "well-to-do individuals," the argument would have four terms. But since "well-to-do" is synonymous with "wealthy," the argument could easily be translated into the form above. Thus, the argument would still qualify as a categorical syllogism, even though, technically speaking, it had more than three terms. As we will see in Section 5.4, negated terms sometimes present similar problems, and techniques are developed in that section to reduce the number of terms when some of them are negated.

The second qualification is that each of the three terms must be used in the same sense throughout the argument. If a term is used in one sense in one statement and in a different sense in another statement, the argument really contains more than three terms. An argument containing the term "men," for example, might use the term in the sense of human beings in one statement and of male humans in another. Such an argument would commit the informal fallacy of equivocation and would therefore not qualify as a categorical syllogism.

It is not necessary that all three statements in an argument be standard-form categorical propositions for the argument to qualify as a categorical syllogism. If they are, however, the analysis is greatly simplified. Accordingly, all of the syllogisms presented in the next three sections of this chapter will consist of statements that are standard-form categorical propositions. In later sections, techniques will be developed for translating arguments involving nonstandard propositions into equivalent arguments composed of standard-form propositions.

The three terms in a categorical syllogism are given names depending on their role in the argument. The **major term,** by definition, is the predicate of the conclusion, and the **minor term** is the subject of the conclusion. The **middle term,** which provides the middle ground between the two premises, is the one that does not occur in the conclusion. For example, in the categorical syllogism

> All soldiers are patriots.
> No traitors are patriots.
> Therefore, no traitors are soldiers.

the major term is "soldiers," the minor term is "traitors," and the middle term is "patriots."

The premises of a categorical syllogism are also given names. The **major premise,** by definition, is the one that contains the major term, and the **minor premise** is the one that contains the minor term. This terminology enters into the definition of standard form. A categorical syllogism is said to be in **standard form** when the following three conditions are met:

1. All three statements are standard-form categorical propositions.
2. The two occurrences of each term are identical.
3. The major premise is listed first, the minor premise second, and the conclusion last.

CATEGORICAL SYLLOGISMS

The syllogism about soldiers is in standard form, but the one at the beginning of the chapter is not because the premises are not listed in the right order. In conformity with the third condition, the premise containing the predicate of the conclusion ("paupers") must be listed first, and the premise containing the subject of the conclusion ("civic leaders") must be listed second.

Standard form of a syllogism

1. Quantifier _____ copula _____ $\left\{\begin{array}{l}\text{Major premise} \\ \text{(contains major term)}\end{array}\right.$

2. Quantifier _____ copula _____ $\left\{\begin{array}{l}\text{Minor premise} \\ \text{(contains minor term)}\end{array}\right.$

3. Quantifier _____ copula _____ $\left\{\text{Conclusion}\right.$

     Minor   Major
      term   term

After a categorical syllogism has been checked for instances of equivocation, its validity or invalidity may be determined through mere inspection of the form. The individual form of a syllogism consists of two factors: mood and figure. The **mood** of a categorical syllogism is determined by the kind of propositions (**A, E, I, O**) that make it up. For example, if the major premise is an **A** proposition, the minor premise an **O** proposition, and the conclusion an **E** proposition, the mood is **AOE**. To determine the mood of a categorical syllogism, one must first put the syllogism into standard form; the letter name of the statements may then be noted to the side of each. The mood of the syllogism is then designated by the order of these letters.

The **figure** of a categorical syllogism is determined by the placement of the middle term. Four different arrangements are possible. If we let S represent the subject of the conclusion (minor term), P the predicate of the conclusion (major term), and M the middle term, the four possible arrangements may be illustrated as follows:

Figure 1		Figure 2		Figure 3		Figure 4	
— M	— P	— P	— M	— M	— P	— P	— M
— S	— M	— S	— M	— M	— S	— M	— S
— S	— P	— S	— P	— S	— P	— S	— P

The blanks indicate the places for the quantifiers and copulas. In the first figure the middle term is top left, bottom right; in the second, top right, bottom right, and so on. Example:

No painters are sculptors.
Some sculptors are artists.
Therefore, some artists are not painters.

This syllogism is in standard form. The mood is **EIO** and the figure is four. The form of the syllogism is therefore designated as **EIO-4**.

If you have difficulty remembering the correspondence between the arrangements of the middle term and the figure numbers, you may find the "shirt collar model" useful. To use this analogical device, you may imagine the arrangement of the middle term in the four figures as depicting the outline of a shirt collar:

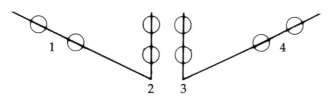

The only problem with this device is that it may lead you to confuse the second figure with the third. To avoid this confusion, keep in mind that for these two figures the S and P terms go on the same "collar flap" as the middle term. Thus, for the second figure, S and P are to the left of the middle term, and for the third figure they are to the right.

Since there are four kinds of categorical propositions and there are three categorical propositions in a categorical syllogism, there are 64 possible moods (4 × 4 × 4 = 64). And since there are four different figures, there are 256 different forms of categorical syllogisms (4 × 64 = 256).

Because the validity of a syllogism is purely a function of the form, if the form is known, the validity of the syllogism can be determined. Two lists of valid syllogistic forms are presented below. The first list contains the fifteen forms that are valid from the Boolean standpoint—that is, valid without making any existential assumptions, or unconditionally valid. The second list contains an additional nine forms that are invalid from the Boolean standpoint but that become valid when a certain existential assumption is made. The exact nature of the assumption is indicated in the fifth column. Of course, the forms in the first list remain valid under these assumptions.

Unconditionally valid

Figure 1	Figure 2	Figure 3	Figure 4
AAA	EAE	IAI	AEE
EAE	AEE	AII	IAI
AII	EIO	OAO	EIO
EIO	AOO	EIO	

Conditionally valid

Figure 1	Figure 2	Figure 3	Figure 4	Presupposition required
AAI EAO	AEO EAO		AEO	*S* exist
		AAI EAO	EAO	*M* exist
			AAI	*P* exist

For example, **AEO**-2 is invalid from the Boolean standpoint but becomes valid in the second list, if we assume that *S* (the subject of the conclusion, the minor term) denotes at least one existing thing. **AAI**-3 becomes valid if we assume that *M* (the middle term) denotes at least one existing thing, and so on. If these letters stand for a word such as "dogs" or "cats," the argument would be valid. But if they stand for a word such as "unicorns" or "leprechauns," the argument would be invalid.

It is interesting, from a historical perspective, to recall that logic students during the Middle Ages used to memorize a little poem that served as a rule of thumb for distinguishing valid from invalid syllogisms. The vowels in the words identified the mood, and the words "prioris," "secundae," and so on the figure.

> Barbara, Celarent, Darii, Ferioque prioris;
> Cesare, Camestres, Festino, Baroco secundae;
> Tertia, Darapti, Disamis, Datisi, Felapton,
> Bocardo, Ferison habet: quarta insuper addit
> Bramantip, Camenes, Dimaris, Fesapo, Fresison.

For example, the "Barbara" syllogism (this designation is still encountered today) is **AAA**-1, "Celarent" is **EAE**-1, and so on. This poem conforms substantially to the two lists above, except that five forms have been left out. The reason these forms were left out is that the logicians of that time considered them weak: They draw a particular conclusion from premises that would support a (stronger) universal conclusion. For example, the weaker **AAI**-1 is left out in favor of the stronger **AAA**-1. Needless to say, few students today depend on this poem to distinguish valid from invalid syllogisms.

We have seen how, given the syllogism, we can obtain the mood and figure. But sometimes we need to go in the reverse direction: from the mood and figure to the syllogistic form. Let us suppose we are given the form **EIO**-4. To reconstruct the syllogistic form is easy. First use the mood to determine the skeleton of the form:

A CONCISE INTRODUCTION TO LOGIC

E	No _____ are _____.
I	Some _____ are _____.
O	Some _____ are not _____.

Then use the figure to determine the arrangement of the middle terms:

E	No _____ are M.
I	Some M are _____.
O	Some _____ are not _____.

Finally, supply the major and minor terms, using the letters "S" and "P" to designate the subject and predicate of the conclusion. The predicate of the conclusion is always repeated in the first premise, and the subject of the conclusion in the second premise:

E	No P are M.
I	Some M are S.
O	Some S are not P.

EXERCISE 5.1

I. Put the following syllogisms into standard form using letters to represent the terms, name the mood and figure, and determine whether valid or invalid by checking the mood and figure against the two lists of valid syllogistic forms.

★1. No sailors are romantic individuals, so no sailors are poets, since all poets are romantic individuals.

2. Some lions are not coffee drinkers, for some fierce creatures are lions and no coffee drinkers are fierce creatures.

3. No uncles of mine are epicures and all epicures are generous people. Therefore, some uncles of mine are generous people.

4. Some healthy animals are not animals that jump, since no young lambs are animals that jump and all young lambs are healthy animals.

★5. No thieves are honest individuals and some people who are caught are thieves. Thus, some honest individuals are people who are caught.

6. Some wheelbarrows are not comfortable vehicles, for some wheelbarrows are not popular vehicles and all comfortable vehicles are popular vehicles.

7. All ducks are birds, so some griffins are birds, since all griffins are ducks.

8. Some pigs are not winged creatures, for some turtles are not winged creatures and no turtles are pigs.

9. No wise men are fast talkers and all people who walk on their hands are fast talkers. Hence, no people who walk on their hands are wise men.

★10. Some bankers are prudent women because all bankers are good managers and some good managers are not prudent women.

II. Reconstruct the syllogistic forms from the following combinations of mood and figure.

★1. OAE-3

2. EIA-4

3. AII-3

4. IAE-1

★5. AOO-2

6. EAO-4

7. AAA-1

8. EAO-2

9. OEI-3

★10. OEA-4

III. Answer "true" or "false" to the following statements:

1. Every syllogism is a categorical syllogism.

2. A categorical syllogism may contain a term that is used in two different senses.

3. The statements in a categorical syllogism need not be expressed in standard form.

4. The statements in a standard-form categorical syllogism need not be expressed in standard form.

5. In a standard-form categorical syllogism the two occurrences of each term must be identical.

6. The major premise of a standard-form categorical syllogism contains the subject of the conclusion.

7. To determine the mood and figure of a categorical syllogism, the syllogism must first be put into standard form.

8. In a standard-form syllogism having Figure 2, the middle terms are on the right.

9. The unconditionally valid syllogistic forms remain valid when existential assumptions are made.

10. The conditionally valid syllogistic forms are invalid if no existential
    assumptions are made.

5.2 VENN DIAGRAMS

Venn diagrams provide the most intuitively evident and, in the long
run, easiest to remember technique for testing the validity of categorical
syllogisms. The technique is basically an extension of the one developed
in Chapter 4 to represent the information content of categorical propositions. Because syllogisms contain three terms, whereas propositions contain only two, the application of Venn diagrams to syllogisms requires
three overlapping circles. These circles should be drawn so that seven
areas are clearly distinguishable within the diagram. The second step is
to label the circles, one for each term. The precise order of the labeling is
not important.

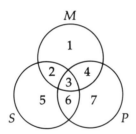

Anything in the area marked "1" is an M but neither an S nor a P,
anything in the area marked "2" is both an S and an M but not a P,
anything in the area marked "3" is a member of all three classes, and so
on.

The test procedure consists in transferring the information content of
the premises to the diagram and then inspecting the diagram to see
whether it necessarily implies the truth of the conclusion. If the information in the diagram does do this, the argument is valid; otherwise it is
invalid.

The use of Venn diagrams to evaluate syllogisms usually requires a
little practice before it can be done with facility. Perhaps the best way of
presenting the technique is through illustrative examples, but a few preliminary pointers are needed:

1. Marks (shading or placing an "X") are entered only for the
   premises. No marks are made for the conclusion.
2. If the argument contains one universal premise, this prem-

ise should be entered first in the diagram. If there are two universal premises, either one can be done first.

3. When entering the information contained in a premise, one should concentrate on the circles corresponding to the two terms in the statement. While the third circle cannot be ignored altogether, it should be given only minimal attention.

4. When inspecting a completed diagram to see whether it supports a particular conclusion, one should remember that particular statements assert two things. "Some S are P" means "At least one S exists *and* that S is a P"; "Some S are not P" means "At least one S exists *and* that S is not a P."

5. When shading an area, one must be careful to shade *all* of the area in question. Examples:

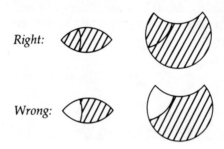

6. The area where an "X" goes is always initially divided into two parts. If one of these parts has already been shaded, the "X" goes in the unshaded part. Examples:

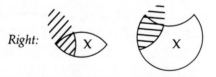

If one of the two parts is not shaded, the "X" goes on the line separating the two parts. Examples:

This means that the "X" may be in either (but not both) of the two areas—but it is not known which one.

7. An "X" should never be placed in such a way that it dangles outside of the diagram altogether, and it should never be placed on the intersection of two lines.

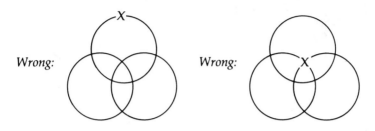

Wrong: *Wrong:*

Let us now consider some examples.

> 1. No *P* are *M*.   **EAE-2**
>   All *S* are *M*.
>   No *S* are *P*.

Since both premises are universal, it makes no difference which premise we enter first in the diagram. Beginning with the major premise, we have:

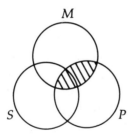

We may now complete the diagram by entering the information of the minor premise:

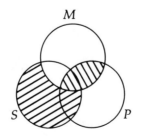

CATEGORICAL SYLLOGISMS   **181**

The conclusion states that the area where *S* and *P* overlap is empty. Inspection of the diagram reveals that this area is indeed empty, so the argument is valid.

2. No *M* are *P*. **EAE-3**
   All *M* are *S*.
   No *S* are *P*.

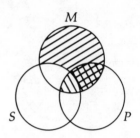

Again, the conclusion states that the area where *S* and *P* overlap is empty. Inspection of the diagram reveals that only part of this area is empty, so the syllogism is invalid.

3. No *M* are *P*. **EIO-1**
   Some *S* are *M*.
   Some *S* are not *P*.

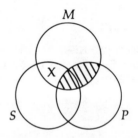

The universal premise is entered first. The shaded part of the area where the *S* and *M* circles overlap leaves only a single area for the "X." The conclusion states that there is an "X" that is inside the *S* circle but outside the *P* circle. Inspection of the diagram reveals that this is indeed the case, so the syllogism is valid.

4. All *M* are *P*. **AII-1**
   Some *S* are *M*.
   Some *S* are *P*.

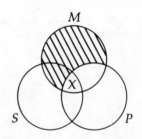

Again, only a single area is left for the "X." The conclusion states that there is an "X" in the *S* circle that is also in the *P* circle. There is such an "X," so the argument is valid.

5. Some *M* are *P*.   **IAI-1**
   All *S* are *M*.
   ――――――――――――
   Some *S* are *P*.

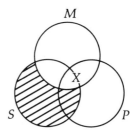

Even though the universal premise is entered first, there are still two possible areas for the "X." That is, the areas where the *M* and *P* circles overlap is divided into two parts, neither of which has been shaded. The "X" therefore goes on the line (the arc of the *S* circle) that separates the two parts. The conclusion states that there is an "X" that is in the *S* circle and also in the *P* circle. The one "X" in the diagram, however, is on the boundary of the *S* circle. We do not know whether it is in or out. Hence, the syllogism is invalid.

6. All *M* are *P*.   **AOO-1**
   Some *S* are not *M*.
   ――――――――――――――
   Some *S* are not *P*.

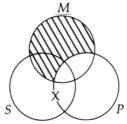

Again, there are two possible areas for the "X." That is, there are two unshaded parts of the *S* circle that are outside the *M* circle. The "X" goes on the line (arc of the *P* circle) separating the two areas. The conclusion states that there is an "X" in the *S* circle that is outside the *P* circle. There *is* an "X" in the *S* circle, but we do not know whether it is inside or outside the *P* circle. Hence, the argument is invalid.

7. All *M* are *P*.   **AAA-1**
   All *S* are *M*.
   ――――――――――――
   All *S* are *P*.

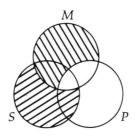

This is the "Barbara" syllogism. The conclusion states that if there is anything in the S circle it is also in the P circle. Inspection of the diagram reveals that the only area of the S circle that may contain members is indeed part of the P circle. Thus, the syllogism is valid.

8. Some M are not P.   **OIO**-1
Some S are M.
Some S are not P.

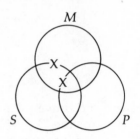

Since there are always initially two areas for placing an "X," and since none of these areas has been shaded, the "X"s from both premises go on the lines separating the two areas. The "X" from the first premise is on the arc of the S circle, and the "X" from the second premise is on the arc of the P circle. The conclusion states that there is an "X" in the S circle that is outside the P circle. We have no certainty that the "X" from the first premise is inside the S circle, and while the "X" from the second premise is inside the S circle, we have no certainty that it is outside the P circle. Hence, the argument is invalid.

We have yet to explain the rationale for placing the "X" on the boundary separating two areas when neither of the areas is shaded. Consider this argument:

No P are M.
Some S are not M.
Some S are P.

Wrong
M

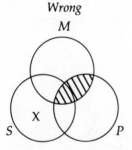

Wrong
M

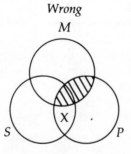

Right
M

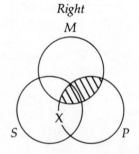

In each of the three diagrams the content of the first premise is represented correctly. The problem concerns placing the "X" from the second premise. In the first diagram the "X" is placed inside the S circle but outside both the M circle and the P circle. This diagram asserts: "At least one S is not an M and it is also not a P." Clearly the diagram says more than the premise does, and so it is incorrect. In the second diagram the "X" is placed inside the S circle, outside the M circle, and inside the P circle. This diagram asserts: "At least one S is not an M, but it is a P." Again, the diagram says more than the premise says, and so it is incorrect. In the third diagram, which is done correctly, the "X" is placed on the boundary between the two areas. This diagram asserts: "At least one S is not an M, and it may or may not be a P." In other words, nothing at all is said about P, and so the diagram represents exactly the content of the second premise.

All of the examples of syllogisms that we have considered thus far have been unaffected by the existential standpoint; that is, it makes no difference to their validity whether or not we assume that the component propositions assert something about things that really exist. Of the 256 different syllogisms, there are nine that are so affected; namely, those that are included in the second list presented in Section 5.1. These syllogisms are invalid from the Boolean standpoint but become valid when the existential standpoint is adopted. Venn diagrams may be used in a special way to evaluate these nine syllogisms. Example:

No M are P. **EAO-3**
All M are S.
Some S are not P.

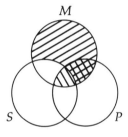

The conclusion asserts that there is an "X" that is inside the S circle and outside the P circle. Inspection of the diagram reveals no "X"s at all, so the syllogism is invalid from the Boolean standpoint. But let us now suppose that the universal statements in the syllogism (the two premises) make an assertion about really existing things; that is, let us assume that M denotes at least one existing thing. We may represent this one existing thing by placing an "X" in the one area of the M circle that is not shaded:

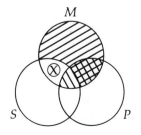

We place a small circle around this "X" to indicate that it comes from a special assumption about universal propositions. We now have an "X" that is inside the S circle and outside the P circle, and so the syllogism is valid from the existential standpoint. Another example:

All M are P.   **AAI-1**
All S are M.
Some S are P.

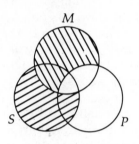

The conclusion asserts that there is an "X" in the S circle that is also in the P circle. The diagram contains no "X"s at all so the syllogism is invalid from the Boolean standpoint. But let us now assume that the subjects (S and M) of the universal premises denote one existing thing. If we consider the M circle first, we see that the "X" could go in either of two areas and should therefore be placed on the boundary between them. Since this "X" is not sufficient to make the syllogism valid, we turn to the S circle. Here only one unshaded area remains, and we place the "X" in that area:

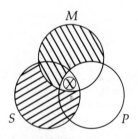

We now have an "X" that is inside the S circle and also inside the P circle, and so the syllogism is valid from the existential standpoint.

These two examples illustrate an important point about the use of Venn diagrams: If the premises of an argument are universal and the conclusion particular, and if after shading the diagram it turns out that one circle is completely shaded except for one area, then it should be determined whether placing an "X" in that one remaining area will make the argument valid. If, after this addition, the argument becomes valid, the argument is one of those that is invalid from the Boolean standpoint but valid from the existential standpoint.

EXERCISE 5.2

I. Use Venn diagrams to determine whether the following standard-form categorical syllogisms are valid or invalid. Identify any that may be invalid from the Boolean standpoint but valid from the existential standpoint, and determine which standpoint is preferable. Determine the mood and figure, and cross-check your answers with the lists of valid forms found in Section 5.1.

★1. All conceited children are greedy brats.
   Some greedy brats are Girl Scouts.
   Therefore, some Girl Scouts are conceited children.

2. No students anxious to learn are failures.
   Some students anxious to learn are romantics.
   Therefore, some romantics are not failures.

3. No operettas are grand operas.
   All operas written by Wagner are grand operas.
   Therefore, some operas written by Wagner are not operettas.

4. All things made of gold are heavy objects.
   Some heavy objects are not statues.
   Therefore, some statues are not things made of gold.

★5. No concertos are symphonies.
   No symphonies are string quartets.
   Therefore, no string quartets are concertos.

6. All greyhounds are fast runners.
   All dogs owned by Marylou are greyhounds.
   Therefore, all dogs owned by Marylou are fast runners.

7. All badly managed businesses are unprofitable ventures.
   No airlines are unprofitable ventures.
   Therefore, no airlines are badly managed businesses.

8. Some idlers are not persons who win fame.
   Some persons who win fame are artists.
   Therefore, some artists are not idlers.

9. Some Impressionist paintings are works by Renoir.
   All works by Renoir are masterpieces.
   Therefore, some masterpieces are Impressionist paintings.

★10. No bald eagles are lizards.
   Some parakeets are not lizards.
   Therefore, some parakeets are not bald eagles.

11. All banshees are wailers.
   All banshees are females.
   Therefore, some females are wailers.

12. All legislators are citizens.
   All congressmen are citizens.
   Therefore, all congressmen are legislators.

CATEGORICAL SYLLOGISMS   **187**

II. Use Venn diagrams to obtain the conclusion that is validly implied by each of the following sets of premises. If no conclusion can be validly drawn, write "no conclusion."

★1. No P are M.
   All S are M.

2. Some M are S.
   Some P are not M.

3. All M are P.
   No S are M.

4. Some M are not P.
   All M are S.

★5. Some P are M.
   All M are S.

6. No M are P.
   Some S are not M.

7. All M are P.
   All S are M.

8. All P are M.
   All S are M.

9. No P are M.
   No M are S.

★10. No P are M.
    Some M are S.

III. Answer "true" or "false" to the following statements:

1. In the use of Venn diagrams to test the validity of syllogisms, marks are sometimes entered in the diagram for the conclusion.

2. When inspecting a completed diagram, if an "X" lies on the arc of a circle, the argument cannot be valid.

3. When an "X" is placed on the arc of a circle, it means that the "X" could be in either (but not both) of the two areas that the arc separates.

4. When representing a universal statement in a Venn diagram, one always shades two of the seven areas in the diagram (unless one of these areas is already shaded).

5. If a completed diagram contains two "X"s, the argument cannot be valid.

6. If the conclusion asserts that a certain area is shaded, and inspection of the diagram reveals that only half that area is shaded, the argument is valid.

7. If the conclusion asserts that a certain area contains an "X" and inspection of the diagram reveals that only half an "X" appears in that area, the argument is valid.

8. If the conclusion is in the form "All S are P," and inspection of the diagram reveals that the part of the S circle that is outside the P circle is shaded, then the argument is valid.

9. If, in a completed diagram, three areas of a single circle are shaded, and placing an "X" in the one remaining area would make the conclusion true, then the argument is valid from the existential standpoint but not from the Boolean standpoint.

10. If, in a completed diagram, three areas of a single circle are shaded, but the argument is not valid from the Boolean standpoint, then it must be valid from the existential standpoint.

5.3 RULES AND FALLACIES

The idea that valid syllogisms conform to certain rules was first expressed by Aristotle. Many such rules are discussed in Aristotle's own account, but logicians of today generally settle on five or six.* If any one of these rules is violated, a specific formal fallacy is committed and, accordingly, the syllogism is invalid. These rules may be used as a convenient cross-check against the method of Venn diagrams. Of the five rules presented in this section, the first two depend on the concept of distribution, explained in Chapter 4, and the last three on the concepts of quality and quantity. In applying the first two rules, remember that **A** statements distribute the subject, **E** statements distribute both subject and predicate, **I** statements distribute neither, and **O** statements distribute the predicate.

> Rule 1: *The middle term must be distributed at least once.*
>
> Fallacy: Undistributed middle.

---

*Some texts include a rule stating that the three terms of a categorical syllogism must be used in the same sense throughout the argument. In this text this requirement is included as part of the definition of "categorical syllogism." See Section 5.1.

Example: All sharks are fish.
All salmon are fish.
All salmon are sharks.

In this standard-form categorical syllogism the middle term is "fish." In both premises "fish" occurs as the predicate of an **A** proposition and, therefore, by the rule developed in Chapter 4, is not distributed in either premise. (Only the subject term in an **A** proposition is distributed.) Thus, the syllogism commits the fallacy of undistributed middle and is invalid. If the major premise were rewritten to read "All fish are sharks," then "fish" would be distributed in that premise and the syllogism would be valid. But, of course, it would still be unsound because the rewritten premise would be false.

In applying this rule, note that from the Boolean standpoint the middle term must be distributed once and *only* once; but those arguments in which the middle term is distributed in both premises break some other rule.

The logic behind Rule 1 may be explained by recounting how the middle term accomplishes its intended purpose, which is to provide a common ground for establishing some necessary relation between the subject and predicate terms of the conclusion. Let us designate the minor, major, and middle terms by the letters "S," "P," and "M," respectively, and let us suppose that M is distributed in the major premise. By definition, P is related to the *whole* of the M class. Then, when the M class is related either in whole or in part to S, S and P necessarily become related. But if M is undistributed in both premises, S and P may be related to *different parts* of the M class, in which case there is no common ground for relating S and P. This is exactly what happens in our fish example. The terms "salmon" and "sharks" are related to different parts of the fish class, so no common ground exists for relating them together.

Rule 2:   *If a term is distributed in the conclusion, then it must be distributed in the premise.*

Fallacy: Illicit major; illicit minor.

Examples: All horses are animals.
Some dogs are not horses.
Some dogs are not animals.

All tigers are mammals.
All mammals are animals.
All animals are tigers.

In the first example the major term, "animals," is distributed in the conclusion but not in the major premise, so the syllogism commits the fallacy of illicit major, or, more precisely, "illicit process of the major term."

In the second example the minor term, "animals," is distributed in the conclusion but not in the minor premise. The second example therefore commits the fallacy of illicit minor, or "illicit process of the minor term."

In applying this rule, one must always examine the conclusion first. If no terms are distributed in the conclusion, Rule 2 cannot be violated. If one or both terms in the conclusion are distributed, then the appropriate premise must be examined. If the term distributed in the conclusion is also distributed in the premise, then the rule is not violated. But, if the term is not distributed in the premise, the rule is violated and the syllogism is invalid. In applying Rule 2 (and also Rule 1), you may find it helpful to begin by marking all the distributed terms in the syllogism— either by circling them or by labeling them with a small letter "d."

The logic behind Rule 2 is easy to understand. Let us once again designate the minor, major, and middle terms by the letters "S," "P," and "M," respectively, and let us suppose that a certain syllogism commits the fallacy of illicit major. The conclusion of that syllogism then makes an assertion about every member of the P class, but the major premise makes an assertion about only some members of the P class. Because the minor premise, by itself, says nothing at all about the P class, the conclusion clearly contains information not contained in the premises, and the syllogism is therefore invalid. Analogous reasoning applies to the fallacy of illicit minor.

Rule 3:   *Two negative premises are not allowed.*

Fallacy: Exclusive premises.

Example: No fish are mammals.
            Some dogs are not fish.
            Some dogs are not mammals.

This syllogism may be seen to be invalid because it has true premises and a false conclusion. The defect is attributable to the fact that it has two negative premises.

Upon reflection, Rule 3 should be fairly obvious. Let "S," "P," and "M" once again designate the minor, major, and middle terms. Now, if the P class and the M class are separate either wholly or partially, and the S class and the M class are separate either wholly or partially, nothing is said about the relation between the S class and the P class. These two classes may be either distinct or identical in whole or in part. Venn diagrams may be used effectively to illustrate the fact that no conclusion can be validly drawn from two negative premises.

Rule 4:   *One negative premise is allowed if and only if the conclu-
           sion is negative.*

CATEGORICAL SYLLOGISMS   **191**

Fallacy:	Drawing an affirmative conclusion from a negative premise.
	or
	Drawing a negative conclusion from affirmative premises.
Examples:	All crows are birds.
	Some wolves are not crows.
	Some wolves are birds.
	All triangles are three-angled polygons.
	All three-angled polygons are three-sided polygons.
	Some three-sided polygons are not triangles.

These arguments may be seen to be invalid because each has true premises and a false conclusion. The first draws an affirmative conclusion from a negative premise, and the second draws a negative conclusion from affirmative premises.

If "S," "P," and "M" once again designate the minor, major, and middle terms, an affirmative conclusion always states that the S class is contained either wholly or partially in the P class. The only way that such a conclusion can follow is if the S class is contained either wholly or partially in the M class, and the M class wholly in the P class. In other words, it follows only when both premises are affirmative. But if, for example, the S class is contained either wholly or partially in the M class, and the M class is separate either wholly or partially from the P class, such a conclusion will never follow. Thus, an affirmative conclusion cannot be drawn from negative premises.

Conversely, a negative conclusion asserts that the S class is separate either wholly or partially from the P class. But if both premises are affirmative, they assert class inclusion rather than separation. Thus, a negative conclusion cannot be drawn from affirmative premises.

Rule 5:	*If both premises are universal, the conclusion cannot be particular.*
Fallacy:	Existential fallacy.
Examples:	All mammals are animals.
	All unicorns are mammals.
	Some unicorns are animals.
	All mammals are animals.
	All tigers are mammals.
	Some tigers are animals.

If a categorical syllogism breaks only Rule 5, it is valid from the existential standpoint but not from the Boolean standpoint. The syllogistic forms that fall into this category are those that are included in the "conditionally valid" list in Section 5.1. In the first example above, if we

A CONCISE INTRODUCTION TO LOGIC

make the assumption that one unicorn exists, the syllogism is valid. But since unicorns probably do not exist, it is preferable to adopt the Boolean standpoint and judge the syllogism invalid. It commits the existential fallacy. In the second example we must assume that one tiger exists for the syllogism to be valid. Since this assumption is justified, it is preferable in this case to adopt the existential standpoint and call the syllogism valid. From the existential standpoint there is no such thing as an existential fallacy, and the syllogism breaks no other rules.

The rationale behind Rule 5 is quite easy to understand. From the Boolean standpoint, universal statements make no assertions about existence, while particular statements do. Thus, if a syllogism is made up of universal premises and a particular conclusion, the conclusion asserts that something exists, while the premises do not. Thus the conclusion contains more information than the premises, and the syllogism is invalid. From the existential standpoint, on the other hand, the assumption is made that the subject term of a universal statement denotes at least one existing thing. Thus, under this assumption the mere fact that a syllogism has universal premises and a particular conclusion is not sufficient grounds for claiming that the conclusion contains more information than the premises. Provided that such a syllogism breaks no other rules, therefore, it is valid.

You may recall that the term "existential fallacy" first occurred in Section 4.5, where it was used in connection with the Boolean interpretation of the square of opposition. The existential fallacy that appears in connection with Rule 5 stems from the same idea, applied in this case to syllogisms.

EXERCISE 5.3

I. Reconstruct the following syllogistic forms and use the five rules for syllogisms to determine which are valid and which are invalid. For those that are invalid, name the fallacy or fallacies committed. Check your answers by constructing Venn diagrams. Finally, if any forms are invalid from the Boolean standpoint but valid from the existential standpoint, use the Venn diagrams to determine the existential assumption that must be made.

★1.	AAA-3	11.	AII-2
2.	IAI-2	12.	EEE-1
3.	EIO-1	13.	AEE-4
4.	AAI-2	14.	OAA-4
★5.	IEO-1	★15.	EAO-3
6.	EOO-4	16.	AEO-3
7.	EAA-1	17.	EAE-1
8.	AII-3	18.	OAI-3
9.	AAI-4	19.	AOO-2
★10.	IAO-3	★20.	EAO-1

II. Answer "true" or "false" to the following statements:

1. If an argument violates one of the first four rules, it may still be valid.
2. In arguments that are valid from the Boolean standpoint, the middle term is distributed in only one premise.
3. If a term is distributed in a premise but not in the conclusion, the second rule is violated.
4. If both premises are negative, then no conclusion follows validly.
5. If no terms are distributed in the conclusion, then Rule 2 cannot be violated.
6. If, in a valid argument, one premise is negative, then the conclusion must be negative.
7. If, in a valid argument, the conclusion is negative, then one and only one premise must be negative.
8. If an argument breaks only Rule 5 and the three terms denote actually existing things, then the argument is valid.
9. If an argument breaks only Rule 5 and the three terms have empty extension (i.e., they denote nonexistent things), the argument is valid.
10. Some syllogisms that are valid from the Boolean standpoint are not valid from the existential standpoint.

5.4 REDUCING THE NUMBER OF TERMS

Categorical syllogisms, as they occur in ordinary spoken and written expression, are seldom phrased according to the precise norms of the standard-form syllogism. Sometimes quantifiers, premises, or conclusions are left unexpressed, chains of syllogisms are strung together into single arguments, and terms are mixed together with their negations in a single argument. The final three sections of this chapter are concerned with developing techniques for reworking such arguments in order to render them testable by Venn diagrams or by the rules for syllogisms.

In this section we consider arguments that contain more than three terms but that can be modified to reduce the number of terms to three. Consider the following:

> All photographers are non-writers.
> Some editors are writers.
> Therefore, some non-photographers are not non-editors.

This syllogism is clearly not in standard form because it has six terms: "photographers," "editors," "writers," "non-photographers," "non-editors," and "non-writers." But because three of the terms are negations of the other three, the number of terms can be reduced to a total of three, each used twice in distinct propositions. To accomplish the reduction, we can use the three operations of conversion, obversion, and contraposition discussed in Chapter 4. But, of course, since the reworked syllogism must be equivalent in meaning to the original one, we must use these operations only on the kinds of statements for which they yield equivalent results. That is, we must use conversion only on **E** and **I** statements and contraposition only on **A** and **O** statements. Obversion yields equivalent results for all four kinds of categorical statements.

Let us rewrite our six-term argument using letters to represent the terms, and then obvert the first premise and contrapose the conclusion in order to eliminate the negated letters:

Symbolized argument	Reduced argument
All *P* are non-*W*.	No *P* are *W*.
Some *E* are *W*.	Some *E* are *W*.
Some non-*P* are not non-*E*.	Some *E* are not *P*.

Because the first premise of the original argument is an **A** statement and the conclusion an **O** statement, the reduced argument is equivalent in meaning to the original argument. The reduced argument is in standard syllogistic form and may be evaluated either with a Venn diagram or by the five rules for syllogisms. The application of these methods indicates that the reduced argument is valid. We conclude, therefore, that the original argument is also valid.

It is not necessary to eliminate the negated terms in order to reduce the number of terms. It is equally effective to convert certain non-negated terms into negated ones. Thus, instead of obverting the first premise of the above argument and contraposing the conclusion, we could have contraposed the first premise and converted and then obverted the second premise. The operation is performed as follows:

Symbolized argument	Reduced argument
All *P* are non-*W*.	All *W* are non-*P*.
Some *E* are *W*.	Some *W* are not non-*E*.
Some non-*P* are not non-*E*.	Some non-*P* are not non-*E*.

The reduced argument is once again equivalent to the original one, but now we must reverse the order of the premises to put the syllogism into standard form:

Some *W* are not non-*E*.
All *W* are non-*P*.
Some non-*P* are not non-*E*.

When tested with a Venn diagram or by means of the five rules, this argument will, of course, also be found valid, and so the original argument is valid. When using a Venn diagram no unusual method is needed; the diagram is simply lettered with the three terms "W," "non-E," and "non-P."

The most important point to remember in reducing the number of terms is that conversion and contraposition must never be used on statements for which they yield undetermined results. That is, conversion must never be used on **A** and **O** statements, and contraposition must never be used on **E** and **I** statements.

EXERCISE 5.4

Rewrite the following arguments using letters to represent the terms, reduce the number of terms, and put the arguments into standard form. Then test the new forms with Venn diagrams or by means of the five rules for syllogisms to determine the validity or invalidity of the original arguments.

★1. Some intelligible statements are true statements, because all unintelligible statements are meaningless statements and some false statements are meaningful statements.

2. No laws are inappropriate regulations, so some appropriate regulations are not necessary measures because some unnecessary measures are laws.

3. No thoughtful individuals are prejudiced people, for no unprejudiced people are residents of this neighborhood and all residents of this neighborhood are thoughtless individuals.

4. Some vehicles are not uncomfortable cars and all foreign cars are comfortable cars. It follows that some vehicles are not domestic cars.

★5. No careless hunters are prudent individuals because all hunters who shun hyenas are careful hunters and all hunters who fail to shun hyenas are imprudent individuals.

6. No frogs weighing at least eight ounces are frogs capable of jumping ten feet. Therefore, some frogs weighing less than eight ounces are not losers, since some frogs incapable of jumping ten feet are not winners.

7. All unicorns are stately creatures and no unicorns are dancers. Therefore, some nondancers are not unstately creatures.

8. Some uneducated individuals are not effective speakers, for all ineffective speakers are unpopular leaders and some popular leaders are not educated individuals.

9. Some even numbers are squares and all primes are odd numbers. Thus, some non-primes are not non-squares.

★10. Some athletes are not eligible for Olympic competition because some swimmers are ineligible for Olympic competition and all non-athletes are non-swimmers.

5.5 ORDINARY LANGUAGE ARGUMENTS

Many categorical syllogisms that are not in standard form as written can be translated into standard-form syllogisms. Such translation often involves making some of the corrective measures discussed in the last section of Chapter 4—namely, inserting quantifiers, modifying subject and predicate terms, and correcting copulas. The goal, of course, is to produce an argument consisting of three standard-form categorical propositions that contain a total of three different terms, each of which is used twice in distinct propositions. Since this task involves not only the translation of the component statements into standard form but the adjustment of these statements one to another so that their terms occur in matched pairs, a certain amount of practice is usually required before it can be done with any facility. In reducing the terms to three matched pairs it is often helpful to identify some factor common to two or all three propositions and express this common factor through the strategic use of parameters. Consider the following argument:

> Henry must have overslept this morning because he was late
> for work, and he is never late for work unless he oversleeps.

All three statements are about Henry, but if the parameter "persons identical to Henry" were selected it would have to be used more than twice. The temporal adverbs in the argument, "this morning" and "never," suggest that "times" might be used. Following this suggestion, we have:

> All times identical to this morning are times Henry overslept,
> because all times identical to this morning are times Henry is
> late for work, and all times Henry is late for work are times
> Henry overslept.

We now have a standard-form categorical syllogism. If we adopt the following convention,

> A = times identical to this morning
> B = times Henry overslept
> C = times Henry is late for work

the syllogism may be symbolized as follows:

> All C are B.
> All A are C.
> All A are B.

This is the so called "Barbara" syllogism and is, of course, valid. Here is another example:

> Iron is heavier than water because it doesn't float, and whatever doesn't float in water is heavier than water.

For this argument the parameter "things" suggests itself:

> All things identical to iron are things that are heavier than water, because all things identical to iron are things that don't float, and all things that don't float are things that are heavier than water.

The first statement is, of course, the conclusion. When the syllogism is written in standard form, it will be seen that it has, like the previous syllogism, the form **AAA-1**.

Another example:

> If a book is interesting, then it is worth reading. Books by George Stone are not interesting; therefore, they are not worth reading.

The word "books" will serve as the common parameter:

> All interesting books are books worth reading.
> No books by George Stone are interesting books.
> Therefore, no books by George Stone are books worth reading.

This syllogism commits the fallacy of illicit major and is therefore invalid.

As was mentioned in Section 4.8, arguments containing an exceptive proposition must be handled in a special way. Let us consider one that contains an exceptive proposition as a premise:

> All except employees are eligible to enter the contest. Catherine is not eligible, so it follows that she is an employee.

The first premise is translated as two conjoined categorical propositions: "No employees are persons eligible to enter the contest, and all non-employees are persons eligible to enter the contest." These in turn give rise to two syllogisms:

> No employees are persons eligible to enter the contest.
> No persons identical to Catherine are persons eligible to enter the contest.
> Therefore, all persons identical to Catherine are employees.

A CONCISE INTRODUCTION TO LOGIC

All nonemployees are persons eligible to enter the contest.
No persons identical to Catherine are persons eligible to enter
the contest.
Therefore, all persons identical to Catherine are employees.

The first syllogism, which is in standard form, is invalid because it has two negative premises. The second one, on the other hand, is not in standard form because it has four terms. If the conclusion is obverted, so that it reads "No persons identical to Catherine are nonemployees," the syllogism is reduced to standard form. Testing by the usual methods shows that the syllogism is valid.

Each of these two syllogisms may be viewed as a pathway in which the conclusion of the original argument might follow necessarily from the premises. Since it does follow via the second syllogism, the original argument is valid. If both of the resulting syllogisms turned out to be invalid, the original argument would be invalid.

If the conclusion of an argument is an exceptive proposition, and both premises are categorical propositions, it is easy to see that the argument is invalid because both of the categorical syllogisms would have to be valid—and this is impossible. A more extended analysis can be used to show that an argument having an exceptive proposition for its conclusion and for either or both of its premises is also invalid. Thus, any argument having an exceptive proposition for its conclusion is invalid.

EXERCISE 5.5

Translate the following arguments into standard-form categorical syllogisms, then use Venn diagrams or the rules for syllogisms to determine whether each is valid or invalid. See Section 4.8 for help with the translation.

★1. Only good students can pass this exam. Since Theresa passed it, it follows that she's a good student.

2. It must have rained lately because the streets are wet, and the streets are always wet after it rains.

3. Hummingbirds are all very small, so this can't be a hummingbird, because it's quite large.

4. Charles suffers cardiac irregularities whenever he gets angry, and he's suffering cardiac irregularities now. It follows that Charles is angry now.

★5. Where there's smoke there's fire; so there's no fire in the warehouse, because there's no smoke there.

6. The only people who can use the rear door are maintenance men. Since Harry is a maintenance man, it follows that he can use the rear door.

7. Susana likes only Impressionist paintings, and yesterday she said she likes Renoir's "Little Irene." It follows that "Little Irene" is an Impressionist painting.

8. Since canaries are birds and there is a canary in the kitchen, it follows that there is a bird in the kitchen.

9. Not all biographies are worthwhile reading. Since *Moby Dick* is worthwhile reading, it must not be a biography.

★10. The Blue Fox Tavern features live music on Saturdays. Wherever there's live music on Saturdays there's dancing. Therefore, there's dancing in the Blue Fox on Saturdays.

11. If an automobile is well engineered, it won't break down prematurely. Sammy's Chevrolet broke down only two days after he bought it new, so it can't be well engineered.

12. Experienced mountain climbers are the only ones allowed to go on this hike. Since Barbara Harris is not allowed to go, she must be an inexperienced mountain climber.

13. Jascha does what he wants. Since Jascha practices the violin, it follows that he must want to practice the violin.

14. All except the garbanzo beans go into the chef's salad. Since the black-eyed peas are clearly not garbanzo beans, they go into the chef's salad.

★15. A business is unprofitable unless it is well managed. Since the Alpha General Corporation is well managed, it follows that it is profitable.

5.6 ENTHYMEMES AND SORITES

An **enthymeme** is an argument that is expressible as a categorical syllogism but that is missing a premise or a conclusion. Examples:

> Smith must be an American citizen; after all, he's a California State Senator.

> This statue is made of solid gold, and anything made of gold is extremely expensive.

The first argument is missing the premise "All California State Senators are American citizens," and the second argument is missing the conclusion "This statue is extremely expensive."

Enthymemes occur frequently in ordinary spoken and written English for a number of reasons. Sometimes it is simply boring to express every statement in an argument. The listener or reader's intelligence is called into play when he or she is required to supply a missing statement, and his or her interest is thereby sustained. On other occasions the arguer may want to slip an invalid argument past an unwary lis-

A CONCISE INTRODUCTION TO LOGIC

tener or reader, and this aim may be facilitated by leaving a premise or conclusion out of the picture.

Enthymemes are usually quite easy to evaluate. The reader or listener must first determine what is missing, whether premise or conclusion, and then introduce the missing statement with the aim of converting the enthymeme into a good argument. Attention to indicator words will usually provide the clue as to the nature of the missing statement, but a little practice usually renders this task virtually automatic. The missing statement need not be expressed in categorical form; expressing it in the general context of the other statements is sufficient and is often the easier alternative. Once this is done, the entire argument may be translated into categorical form and then tested with a Venn daigram or by the rules for syllogisms. Example:

> Ms. Jackson must be a businesswoman because she subscribes to the *Wall Street Journal*.
>
> *Missing premise:* Any woman who subscribes to the *Wall Street Journal* is a businesswoman.

Translating this argument into categorical form, we have:

> All women who subscribe to the *Wall Street Journal* are businesswomen.
> All women identical to Ms. Jackson are women who subscribe to the *Wall Street Journal*.
> All women identical to Ms. Jackson are businesswomen.

This syllogism is valid.

A **sorites** is a chain of categorical syllogisms in which the intermediate conclusions have been left out. The name is derived from the Greek word *soros*, meaning "heap," and is pronounced "sō rī tēz." The plural form is also "sorites." Here is an example:

> All bloodhounds are dogs.
> All dogs are mammals.
> No fish are mammals.
> Therefore, no fish are bloodhounds.

The first two premises validly imply the intermediate conclusion "All bloodhounds are mammals." If this intermediate conclusion is then treated as a premise and put together with the third premise, the final conclusion follows validly. The sorites is thus composed of two valid categorical syllogisms and is therefore valid. The rule in evaluating a sorites is based on the idea that a chain is only as strong as its weakest link. If any of the component syllogisms in a sorites is invalid, the entire sorites is invalid.

A sorites is in **standard form** when each of the component propositions is in standard form, when each term occurs twice, when the predicate of the conclusion is in the first premise, and when each successive premise has a term in common with the preceding one.* The sorites presented above, for example, is in standard form. Each of the propositions is in standard form, each term occurs twice, the predicate of the conclusion, "bloodhounds," is in the first premise, the other term in the first premise, "dogs," is in the second premise, and so on.

The procedure to be followed in evaluating a sorites is: (1) put the sorites into standard form, (2) introduce the intermediate conclusions, and (3) test each component syllogism for validity. If each component is valid, the sorites is valid. Consider the following sorites form:

> No B are C.
> Some E are A.
> All A are B.
> All D are C.
> _____
> Some E are not D.

To put the sorites form into standard form, the premises must be rearranged:

> All D are C.
> No B are C.
> All A are B.
> Some E are A.
> _____
> Some E are not D.

Next, the intermediate conclusions are drawn. Venn diagrams are useful in performing this step, and they serve simultaneously to check the validity of each component syllogism:

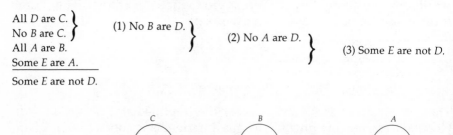

All D are C. ⎱
No B are C. ⎰   (1) No B are D. ⎱
All A are B.   ⎰   (2) No A are D. ⎱
Some E are A.   ⎰   (3) Some E are not D.
_____
Some E are not D.

---

*Actually, there are two definitions of standard form: the Goclenian and the Aristotelian. The one given here is the Goclenian. In the Aristotelian version, the premises are arranged so that the *subject* of the conclusion occurs in the first premise.

The first intermediate conclusion, "No *B* are *D*," is drawn from the first two premises. The second, "No *A* are *D*" is drawn from the first intermediate conclusion and the third premise. And the third conclusion, which is identical to the final conclusion, is drawn from the second intermediate conclusion and the fourth premise. Since all conclusions are drawn validly, the sorites is valid.

If, at any designated step in the procedure, no conclusion can be validly drawn, as, for example, if the first two premises are negative or contain undistributed middle terms, then the sorites is invalid. Sometimes immediate inspection will disclose that a certain sorites is invalid. For example, any sorites having two (or more) negative premises or two (or more) particular premises is invalid. Before any such inspection is attempted, however, one must be certain that the terms occur in pairs. Sometimes the operations of conversion, obversion, and contraposition must be used to reduce the number of terms in a sorites, and obversion, of course, affects the quality of the statements on which it is used.

EXERCISE 5.6

I. In the following enthymemes determine whether the missing statement is a premise or conclusion. Then supply the missing statement, attempting whenever possible to convert the enthymeme into a valid argument.

★1. All of my students are intelligent, so George can't be one of my students.

2. Only geraniums grow in the east garden, and those flowers on the table were picked from there this morning.

3. The woman who committed the robbery had long blonde hair; but Mary is a curly-headed brunette.

4. Dictatorial people aren't popular, so Judy can't be dictatorial.

★5. Karen dresses very stylishly, and we know what that implies because all successful businesswomen dress stylishly.

6. Someone must be burning leaves because the scent of burning leaves is in the air.

7. Dr. Jones can't be a psychiatrist because his name isn't listed in the *Medical Directory*.

8. You know the saying—"None but the brave deserve the fair"—and Jerry's bravery is beyond question.

9. Whenever word of inflation spreads, the price of gold shoots up. And the price of gold is shooting up right now.

★10. This is not a good time to invest in stocks because the market has been off every day for the past month.

11. The only vegetables I raised this year were tomatoes, and those have all been killed by the frost.

12. Whenever it snows, Annie gets excited about skiing, and it's snowing now.

13. This can't be a rosebush because it doesn't have thorns.

14. This is the best musical of the year. It's won practically all of the Tony awards.

★15. No topless dancers are Campfire Girls, so we can be sure that Marylou is not a Campfire Girl.

II. Translate the enthymemes in Part I of this exercise into standard-form categorical syllogisms and test them for validity.

III. Rewrite the following sorites in standard form, reducing the number of terms when necessary. Then supply the intermediate conclusions and test with Venn diagrams.

★1. No *B* are *C*.
   Some *D* are *C*.
   All *A* are *B*.
   Some *D* are not *A*.

2. No *C* are *D*.
   All *A* are *B*.
   Some *C* are not *B*.
   Some *D* are not *A*.

3. No *A* are non-*B*.
   No *C* are *B*.
   All non-*A* are non-*D*.
   No *D* are *C*.

4. All *M* are non-*P*.
   Some *M* are *S*.
   All *K* are *P*.
   Some non-*K* are not non-*S*.

★5. All non-*U* are non-*V*.
   No *U* are non-*W*.
   All *V* are *Y*.
   No *X* are *W*.
   All *Y* are non-*X*.

6. All *D* are non-*C*.
   All non-*B* are non-*A*.
   Some *E* are *D*.
   All *B* are *C*.
   Some non-*A* are not non-*E*.

7. All non-*L* are non-*K*.
   Some *K* are *M*.
   All *P* are non-*L*.
   No non-*N* are *M*.
   No *Q* are non-*P*.
   Some *N* are not *Q*.

8. All *R* are *S*.
   No non-*V* are *T*.
   No *Q* are non-*R*.
   No non-*Q* are *P*.
   All *T* are non-*S*.
   All *V* are non-*P*.

IV. The following sorites are taken from Lewis Carroll's *Symbolic Logic*. All are valid. Rewrite each sorites in standard form, using letters to represent the terms and reducing the number of terms whenever necessary. Then use Venn diagrams to prove each one valid.

★1. No ducks waltz.
   No officers ever decline to waltz.
   All my poultry are ducks.
   My poultry are not officers.

2. No experienced person is incompetent.
   Jenkins is always blundering.
   No competent person is always blundering.
   Jenkins is inexperienced.

3. No terriers wander among the signs of the zodiac.
   Nothing that does not wander among the signs
      of the zodiac is a comet.
   Nothing but a terrier has a curly tail.
   No comet has a curly tail.

4. All hummingbirds are richly colored.
   No large birds live on honey.
   Birds that do not live on honey are dull in color.
   All hummingbirds are small.

★5. All unripe fruit is unwholesome.
   All these apples are wholesome.
   No fruit grown in the shade is ripe.
   These apples were grown in the sun.

6. All my sons are slim.
   No child of mine is healthy who takes no exercise.
   All gluttons who are children of mine are fat.
   No daughter of mine takes any exercise.
   All gluttons who are children of mine are unhealthy.

7. The only books in this library that I do not recommend for
      reading are unhealthy in tone.
   The bound books are all well-written.
   All the romances are healthy in tone.
   I do not recommend you to read any of the unbound books.
   All the romances in this library are well-written.

8. No interesting poems are unpopular among people of real taste.
   No modern poetry is free from affectation.
   All your poems are on the subject of soap bubbles.
   No affected poetry is popular among people of real taste.
   No ancient poem is on the subject of soap bubbles.
   All your poems are uninteresting.

9. All writers who understand human nature are clever.
   No one is a true poet unless he can
      stir the hearts of men.
   Shakespeare wrote *Hamlet*.
   No writer who does not understand human nature can
      stir the hearts of men.
   None but a true poet could have written *Hamlet*.
   Shakespeare was clever.

6

PROPOSITIONAL LOGIC

6.1 SYMBOLS AND TRANSLATION

In earlier chapters we saw that the validity of a deductive argument is purely a function of its form. By knowing the specific form we can often tell immediately whether an argument is valid or invalid. Unfortunately, however, ordinary language usage frequently obscures the form of an argument. To correct for this, logic introduces various simplifying procedures that facilitate form recognition. In Chapter 5 letters were used to represent the terms in a syllogism, and techniques were developed to reduce syllogisms to what is called standard form. In this chapter form recognition is facilitated through the introduction of special symbols called **connectives.** When arguments are expressed in terms of these connectives, the determination of validity or invalidity often becomes a matter of mere visual inspection.

Propositional logic marks a break with the logic of the previous two chapters in that the fundamental elements are not terms, but whole statements (or propositions). Statements are represented by letters, and these letters are then combined with one another by means of the connectives to form more complex arrangements. To explain how this is done, it is necessary to distinguish between what are called simple, or "atomic," statements and compound, or "molecular," statements. A **simple** (atomic) **statement** is one that does not contain any other statement as a component. Here are some examples:

Butane is a hydrogen compound.
James Joyce wrote *Ulysses*.
Parakeets are colorful birds.
The monk seal is threatened with extinction.

Any convenient upper-case letter may be selected to represent each statement. Thus, *B* might be selected to represent the first, *J* the second, *P* the third, and *M* the fourth. As will be explained shortly, the lower-case letters are reserved for use as propositional variables.

A **compound** (molecular) **statement** is one that contains at least one atomic statement as a component. Here are some examples:

It is not the case that Shakespeare wrote *Vanity Fair*.

If acorns are planted in the spring, then oak trees will grow in the fall.

Either Peterson committed the murder or Conrad lied on the witness stand.

Detroit is in Michigan and Atlanta is in Georgia.

If the first letters in the atomic statements are selected to represent these statements, the molecular statements may be represented as follows:

It is not the case that *S*.
If *A* then *O*.
Either *P* or *C*.
D and *A*.

The words "it is not the case that," "if ... then," and so on, may be translated through the introduction of connective symbols. In all, five symbols are needed, and they are listed, together with their meanings, in the following table:

Connective	Name	Meaning	Sample translations
~	negation	not	$\sim P$ = it is not the case that P
•	conjunction	and	$P \cdot Q$ = P and Q
v	disjunction	or	$P \lor Q$ = P or Q
⊃	conditional *or* implication	if ... then ... *or* implies	$P \supset Q = \begin{cases} \text{if } P \text{ then } Q \\ or \\ P \text{ implies } Q \end{cases}$
≡	biconditional *or* equivalence	if and only if *or* is equivalent to	$P \equiv Q = \begin{cases} P \text{ if and only if } Q \\ or \\ P \text{ is equivalent to } Q \end{cases}$

In the expression $P \cdot Q$ the propositions P and Q are called **conjuncts;** in $P \vee Q$ they are called **disjuncts;** and in $P \supset Q$ they are called the **antecedent** and **consequent,** respectively.

Let us now use these symbols to translate some typical statements found in ordinary English expression. In the examples that follow, the first letters in the names "Alfred," "Blake," "Clark," "David," and "Edward" are used to represent the respective atomic propositions.

Typically, the **negation sign** is used to translate any negated atomic proposition:

Alfred will not be elected president:	$\sim A$
It is not the case that Alfred will be elected president:	$\sim A$
It is false that Alfred will be elected president:	$\sim A$

The **conjunction sign** is used equivalently to translate such conjunctions as "and," "however," "yet," "but," "also," "moreover," "although," "nevertheless," and "still":

Alfred will be elected president and Blake will retire:	$A \cdot B$
Alfred will be elected president but Blake will retire:	$A \cdot B$
Alfred will be elected president; however, Blake will retire:	$A \cdot B$
Blake and Clark will retire:	$B \cdot C$

Note that the last example is equivalent to the statement "Blake will retire and Clark will retire." To translate such a statement as a conjunction of two atomic statements, the original statement must be equivalent to a compound statement in English. For example, the statement "Blake and Clark are friends" is *not* equivalent to "Blake is a friend and Clark is a friend," so this statement *cannot* be translated as $B \cdot C$.

The word "or" in English has two meanings. "Or" is used *inclusively* when it means "one or the other and possibly both." It is used *exclusively* when it means "one or the other but not both." For example, "or" is used inclusively in the statement "Anyone who owns a car or a truck needs insurance" and exclusively in the statement "The Orient Express is on track one or track two." In the first statement it is intended that anyone who owns a car *and* a truck also needs insurance, but in the second it is *not* intended that the Orient Express should be on *both* tracks. In propositional logic the **disjunction sign** is given the *inclusive* meaning of "or." This is the weaker of the two meanings, and if ever the exclusive meaning is intended, it may be constructed from the inclusive meaning by simply adding the phrase "but not both."

Two other words that deserve some comment are "either" and "unless." In propositional logic the word "either" has primarily a punctuational meaning. As we will see shortly, the use of this word often tells us where parentheses or brackets should be introduced in the symbolic expression. If parentheses are not needed, "either" does not usually affect the translation. The word "unless," on the other hand, is equivalent to "or." In an earlier chapter we saw that "unless" could be translated as "if not." This rule holds true in propositional logic as well; but as we will see, "if not" can be proven to be equivalent to "or."

Alfred will be elected president or Blake will retire: $A \lor B$

Either Alfred will be elected president or Blake will retire: $A \lor B$

Alfred will be elected president unless Edward is promoted: $A \lor E$

Unless Edward is promoted, Alfred will be elected president: $A \lor E$

From the sense of these statements in English it should be clear that $A \cdot B$ is logically equivalent to $B \cdot A$. Similarly, $A \lor B$ is logically equivalent to $B \lor A$. Later in this chapter techniques will be developed for proving these equivalences.

The **conditional sign** is used to translate "if . . . then," "implies that," "entails that," and similar phrases indicating a conditional statement. When the word "if" occurs in the middle of a conditional statement, the statement should be mentally rearranged so that the proposition following the "if" (that is, the antecedent) occurs first. The phrases "in case," "provided that," "given that," and "on the condition that" are synonymous with "if." The phrases "only if" and "entails that" are synonymous with "implies that." As was mentioned earlier, "unless" may also be translated as "if not." Finally, it should be noted that the order of antecedent and consequent is essential in translating conditional statements. In other words, $A \supset B$ is not logically equivalent to $B \supset A$.

If David is appointed to the board, then Clark will retire:	$D \supset C$
David's being appointed to the board implies that Clark will retire:	$D \supset C$
Blake will retire if Clark will retire:	$C \supset B$
Blake will retire only if Clark will retire:	$B \supset C$
Blake will retire provided that Edward is promoted:	$E \supset B$
Blake will retire on the condition that Edward is promoted:	$E \supset B$
David will retire unless Edward is promoted:	$\sim E \supset D$

The conditional sign is also used to translate statements phrased in terms of sufficient conditions and necessary conditions. An event A is said to be a **sufficient condition** for an event B whenever the occurrence of A is all that is required for the occurrence of B. On the other hand, an event A is said to be a **necessary condition** for an event B whenever B cannot occur without the occurrence of A. For example, having the flu is a sufficient condition for feeling miserable, whereas having air to breath is a necessary condition for survival. Other things besides having the flu might cause a person to feel miserable, but that by itself is sufficient; and other things besides having air to breathe are required for survival, but without air survival is impossible. In other words, air is necessary. To translate statements involving sufficient and necessary conditions into symbolic form, the statement that names the sufficient condition is placed in the antecedent of the conditional, and the statement that names the necessary condition is placed in the consequent*:

Blake's retiring is a sufficient condition for Clark to retire:	$B \supset C$
Blake's retiring is a necessary condition for Clark to retire:	$C \supset B$

---

*The mnemonic device "SUN" may be conveniently used to keep this rule in mind: When the "U" is turned sideways we have $S \supset N$, where S and N designate sufficient and necessary conditions, respectively. Whatever is given as a sufficient condition goes in the place of the S, and whatever is given as a necessary condition goes in the place of the N.

PROPOSITIONAL LOGIC

The **biconditional sign** is used to translate the phrases "is equivalent to," "if and only if," and "is a sufficient and necessary condition for":

Blake will retire if and only
if Clark will retire: $B \equiv C$

Blake's retiring is a sufficient
and necessary condition for
Clark's retiring: $B \equiv C$

"Blake will retire" is equiv-
alent to "Clark will retire": $B \equiv C$

In propositional logic, when one statement is said to be equivalent to another, as in the third example above, the meaning is that of **truth functional equivalence** (otherwise called "material equivalence"). As will be explained in the next section, such a statement asserts merely that the two component propositions have the same truth value—not that they have the same meaning.

Analysis of the first two examples reveals that $B \equiv C$ is logically equivalent to $(B \supset C) \cdot (C \supset B)$. Thus, for example, "Blake will retire only if Clark will retire" is translated $B \supset C$, and "Blake will retire if Clark will retire" is translated $C \supset B$. Putting the two English statements together we have $(B \supset C) \cdot (C \supset B)$, which is otherwise translated as $B \equiv C$. Because the order of the two conjuncts may be reversed, $B \equiv C$ is logically equivalent to $C \equiv B$.

Whenever more than two letters appear in a translated statement, parentheses, brackets, or braces must be used to indicate the proper range of the connectives. The statement $A \cdot B \lor C$, for example, is ambiguous. When parentheses are introduced, this statement becomes either $(A \cdot B) \lor C$ or $A \cdot (B \lor C)$. These new statements have a distinct meaning, and they are not logically equivalent. Thus, with statements such as these, some clue must be found in the English statement that indicates the correct placement of the parentheses in the symbolic statement. Such clues are usually given by commas and semicolons, by such words as "either" and "both," and by the use of a single predicate in conjunction with two or more subjects. The following examples illustrate the correct placement of parentheses and brackets:

Alfred is elected president and Blake
will retire, or Clark will retire: $(A \cdot B) \lor C$

Alfred is elected president, and Blake
will retire or Clark will retire: $A \cdot (B \lor C)$

Either Alfred is elected president and
Blake will retire or Clark will retire: $(A \cdot B) \lor C$

Alfred is elected president and either Blake will retire or Clark will retire:	$A \cdot (B \lor C)$
Alfred is elected president or both Blake will retire and Clark will retire:	$A \lor (B \cdot C)$
Alfred is elected president or Blake and Clark will retire:	$A \lor (B \cdot C)$
If Alfred is elected president, then if Edward is promoted, then Blake will retire:	$A \supset (E \supset B)$
If Alfred's being elected president implies that Edward is promoted, then Blake will retire:	$(A \supset E) \supset B$
If either Blake and Clark retire or Alfred is elected president, then Edward will be promoted:	$[(B \cdot C) \lor A] \supset E$

When a negation sign appears in a symbolic expression, by convention it is considered to affect only the unit that immediately follows it. Thus, for example, in the expression $\sim P \lor Q$ the negation sign affects only the P, while in the expression $\sim(P \lor Q)$ it affects the entire expression inside the parentheses. Analogously, the English expression "It is not the case that P or Q" is translated $\sim P \lor Q$—not as $\sim(P \lor Q)$. On the contrary, "It is not the case that: P or Q" is translated $\sim(P \lor Q)$. The occurrence of the colon makes the difference.

Expressions of the form "Not both P and Q" are translated alternately as $\sim(P \cdot Q)$ or $\sim P \lor \sim Q$, and those of the form "Not either P or Q" (i.e., "Neither P nor Q") are translated alternately as $\sim(P \lor Q)$ or $\sim P \cdot \sim Q$. A little reflection reveals that these alternate forms are equivalent to one another; in other words, $\sim(P \cdot Q)$ is equivalent to $\sim P \lor \sim Q$, and $\sim(P \lor Q)$ is equivalent to $\sim P \cdot \sim Q$. As will be seen in the next chapter, these equivalences express an important rule, called DeMorgan's Rule. In this connection it is important to note that $\sim(P \cdot Q)$ is *not* equivalent to $\sim P \cdot \sim Q$ and $\sim(P \lor Q)$ is *not* equivalent to $\sim P \lor \sim Q$. As is indicated in the following examples, expressions of the form "Not both" are *not* the same as those of the form "Both ... not," and expressions of the form "Not either" are *not* the same as those of the form "Either ... not."

It is not the case that Blake will retire and Clark will retire:	$\sim B \cdot C$
It is not the case that: Blake will retire and Clark will retire:	$\sim(B \cdot C)$
Not both Blake and Clark will retire:	$\sim(B \cdot C)$
Both Blake and Clark will not retire:	$\sim B \cdot \sim C$

Not either Blake or Clark will retire
(Neither Blake nor Clark will retire): $\sim(B \vee C)$

Either Blake or Clark will not retire: $\sim B \vee \sim C$

EXERCISE 6.1
Translate the following English expressions into symbolic form:

★1. It is not the case that Austria embargoes steel imports.

2. Austria embargoes steel imports and Belgium does not develop nuclear weapons.

3. Either Canada curtails grain exports or Denmark decreases military spending.

4. Both Austria and Belgium embargo steel imports.

★5. If England increases oil production, then France drops out of NATO.

6. England increases oil production if France drops out of NATO.

7. England increases oil production only if France drops out of NATO.

8. France's dropping out of NATO implies that England increases oil production.

9. Austria does not embargo steel imports unless Belgium develops nuclear weapons.

★10. Austria embargoes steel imports and either Belgium develops nuclear weapons or Canada curtails grain exports.

11. Either Austria embargoes steel imports and Belgium develops nuclear weapons or Canada curtails grain exports.

12. Not both Canada and Denmark decrease military spending.

13. Canada and Denmark both do not decrease military spending.

14. Either England or France does not drop out of NATO.

★15. Not either England nor France drops out of NATO.

16. Neither England nor France drops out of NATO.

17. If Austria embargoes steel imports, then if Belgium develops nuclear weapons, then Canada curtails grain exports.

18. If Austria's embargoing steel imports implies that Belgium develops nuclear weapons, then Canada curtails grain exports.

19. Austria embargoes steel imports only if neither Belgium develops nuclear weapons nor Canada curtails grain exports.

★20. If Austria embargoes steel imports, then either Belgium develops nuclear weapons or Canada curtails grain exports.

21. If Austria embargoes steel imports and Belgium develops nuclear weapons, then Canada curtails grain exports.

22. Canada and Denmark decrease military spending unless England does not increase oil production.

23. Canada curtails grain exports unless Austria and Belgium embargo steel imports.

24. Either Canada curtails grain exports or, if Denmark decreases military spending, then France drops out of NATO.

★25. Either Canada and Denmark decrease military spending or it is not the case that either England or France drops out of NATO.

26. If either Canada or Denmark decreases military spending, then neither England nor France drops out of NATO.

27. If both Canada and Denmark decrease military spending, then England and France both do not drop out of NATO.

28. Austria embargoes steel imports, and Belgium develops nuclear weapons or Canada curtails grain exports.

29. Austria embargoes steel imports and Belgium develops nuclear weapons, or Canada curtails grain exports.

★30. Austria embargoes steel imports or Belgium develops nuclear weapons, and either Canada curtails grain exports or Denmark decreases military spending.

31. If Denmark decreases military spending, then England increases oil production or France drops out of NATO.

32. If Denmark decreases military spending, then England increases oil production; and France drops out of NATO.

33. If Canada curtails grain exports, then Denmark decreases military spending unless England increases oil production.

34. Canada curtails grain exports or Denmark decreases military spending, or both England increases oil production and France drops out of NATO.

★35. Austria embargoes steel imports; however, if Belgium develops nuclear weapons, then either Canada curtails grain exports or Denmark decreases military spending.

36. If Austria embargoes steel imports, then if Belgium develops nuclear weapons, then both Canada curtails grain exports and Denmark decreases military spending.

37. England's increasing oil production is a sufficient condition for France to drop out of NATO.

38. England's increasing oil production is a necessary condition for France to drop out of NATO.

39. If Austria's embargoing steel imports is a sufficient condition for Belgium to develop nuclear weapons, then Canada's curtailing grain exports is a necessary condition for Denmark to decrease military spending.

★40. Austria's embargoing steel imports is a sufficient and necessary condition for Belgium to develop nuclear weapons.

41. If Austria's embargoing steel imports is a sufficient and necessary condition for Belgium to develop nuclear weapons, then not both Canada curtails grain exports and Denmark decreases military spending.

42. It is not the case that England increases oil production provided that France drops out of NATO.

43. It is not the case that: England's increasing oil production entails that France drops out of NATO.

44. Austria embargoes steel imports or Belgium develops nuclear weapons but they do not both do so.

★45. Austria embargoes steel imports on condition that Belgium develops nuclear weapons; moreover, Canada and Denmark decrease military spending only if it is not the case that: England's increasing oil production is a sufficient condition for France not to drop out of NATO.

46. If both Austria's embargoing steel imports and Belgium's not developing nuclear weapons is a sufficient and necessary condition for Canada to curtail grain exports, then neither Denmark decreases military spending nor England increases oil production.

6.2 TRUTH FUNCTIONS

The truth value of a molecular proposition symbolized in terms of one or more connectives is said to be a **function** of the truth value of its atomic components. This means that the truth value of the molecular proposition is determined by the truth value of its components. To see how this happens, we will consider examples of statements involving each of the five connectives.

The statement "It is not the case that Milton wrote *Paradise Lost*" may be symbolized ∼*M*, where *M* designates the atomic statement "Milton wrote *Paradise Lost*." Since Milton did write *Paradise Lost*, *M* is true, and consequently the molecular statement ∼*M* is false. Conversely, the statement "It is not the case that Shakespeare wrote *Huckleberry Finn*" is true, because the atomic component "Shakespeare wrote *Huckleberry Finn*" is false. No matter what the content of a statement may be, its negation will always have a truth value opposite to that of the statement itself. We may express this principle in a rule that says that for any statement *p*, ∼*p* will have the opposite truth value of *p*. In this rule the

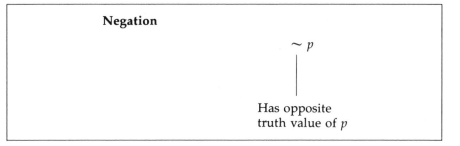

Negation

$$\sim p$$

Has opposite
truth value of p

lower-case letter p is called a **statement variable;** it can represent any statement we choose, either simple or compound. The expression $\sim p$, on the other hand, is called a **statement form,** and any statement having this form is called a **substitution instance** of this form.

Let us next consider a conjunction. The statement "London is the capital of England and Madrid is the capital of Spain" may be symbolized $L \cdot M$. This statement is true because both conjuncts L and M are true. On the other hand, "London is the capital of England and Paris is the capital of Spain" is false, because one of the conjuncts is false. Similarly, "Dublin is the capital of England and Paris is the capital of Spain" is also false because both conjuncts are false. The principle illustrated by these statements may be expressed in the following rule: The statement form $p \cdot q$ is true if and only if both p and q are true. In other words, if one or both conjuncts is false, the whole conjunction is false. This rule, like the previous one and the ones that follow, expresses the fact that truth functions, like validity and invalidity, are determined by the *form* of a statement. Regardless of what the content might be, once the truth values of the atomic components are known, the truth value of a molecular statement can be determined merely from a knowledge of its form.

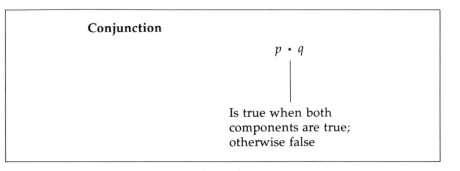

Conjunction

$$p \cdot q$$

Is true when both
components are true;
otherwise false

Turning now to disjunctions, the statement "Thomas Jefferson was a Spaniard or Alexander Hamilton was a Frenchman," symbolized $T \vee A$, is false because both disjuncts, T and A, are false. On the other hand, "Thomas Jefferson was an American or Alexander Hamilton was a

---

Disjunction

$$p \lor q$$

|

Is true when at least
one component is true;
otherwise false

Frenchman" is true because one of the disjuncts is true. In the previous section it was noted that the symbol "v" designates the inclusive sense of "or." This means that the possibility is left open for both disjuncts to be true. Accordingly, the statement "Thomas Jefferson was an American or Alexander Hamilton was an American" is likewise true. Generalizing these results, we have the following rule: The statement form $p \lor q$ is true if and only if either p or q (or both) is true. In other words, $p \lor q$ is false only when both p and q are false.

The analysis of conditional statements is somewhat more complex than that of conjunction or disjunction because conditional statements may be used to express different kinds of relationships. Here are some examples:

1. If no S are P, then no P are S.   (logical)

2. If all A are B and all B are C, then all A are C.   (logical)

3. If figure A is a triangle, then figure A has three sides.   (definitional)

4. If the temperature rises above 32°F, then the ice on the lake will begin to melt.   (causal)

5. If George brings flowers, then Marsha will be thrilled.   (factual)

The first two examples express logical relationships. In the first statement, whatever terms one chooses may be substituted in place of S and P, and the antecedent will be logically equivalent to the consequent. As a result, this conditional statement is necessarily true. In the second statement, although antecedent and consequent are not logically equivalent, the antecedent logically implies the consequent. Thus, like the first statement, this one is also necessarily true. The third example expresses the fact that a triangle, by definition, has three sides. Accordingly, the statement is true by definition. The fourth example expresses

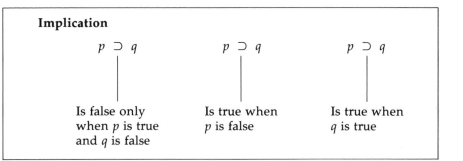

Implication

$p \supset q$ — Is false only when p is true and q is false

$p \supset q$ — Is true when p is false

$p \supset q$ — Is true when q is true

the causal relationship that exists between rising temperature and melting. Thus, its truth rests upon a physical law. The fifth example asserts the existence of a factual relation between George's bringing flowers and Marsha's being thrilled.

Turning to the last of these examples, let us suppose that George does in fact bring flowers. If Marsha is then thrilled, the statement correctly reports the facts and is therefore true. In other words, if both antecedent and consequent are true, the conditional statement is true. Such a result is consistent with the other four conditional statements as well. Conversely, if George does in fact bring flowers but Marsha is not thrilled, the statement does not correctly report the facts and is therefore false. Thus, if the antecedent is true and the consequent false, the conditional statement is false. Such an arrangement of truth values cannot occur, of course, in the other four statements, because the consequent follows either logically, definitionally, or causally from the antecedent. But such an interpretation in no way misrepresents these other statements.

The question that arises next is, what happens when the antecedent is false? If we ask this question of the fifth example, no ready answer is available. If George does not in fact bring flowers, it would seem that there is as much reason for saying that the statement is true as there is for saying that it is false. But the other statements do provide an answer. Since the first statement is necessarily true, it remains true even when the antecedent is false. If, for example, S were to stand for "dogs" and P for "animals," both antecedent and consequent would be false, and yet the statement itself would be true. But what happens when the antecedent is false and the consequent true? Such an arrangement cannot occur in the first statement, because antecedent and consequent are logically equivalent. For an answer we must turn to the second statement. If, in that statement, A, B, and C should stand respectively for "dogs," "birds," and "mammals," the antecedent would be false and the consequent true. Yet, the statement itself would remain true.

From these examples we can derive the following rule: The statement form $p \supset q$ is false if and only if p is true and q is false. As an immediate consequence, if p is false, $p \supset q$ is automatically true, regardless of the

> **Equivalence**
>
> $$p \equiv q$$
>
> Is true when both components
> have the same truth value;
> otherwise false

truth value of q. This rule may be understood as expressing the least common denominator of meaning among the five statements above. As we have seen, the various arrangements of truth values for antecedent and consequent are not equally relevant to these statements, but the rule in no sense violates the meaning of any of them. In this respect the procedure we have followed with implication parallels the one for disjunction. In Section 6.1 we saw that the word "or" could have either an inclusive or an exclusive sense but that the weaker, inclusive sense was part of the meaning of statements expressing the exclusive sense. In a similar way, the truth functional rule for implication expresses a common part of the meaning of the various kinds of conditional statements.

In Section 6.1 we saw that the statement form $p \equiv q$ is an alternate way of translating statements having the form $(p \supset q) \cdot (q \supset p)$. Now that we have a rule for implication we may use it together with the rule for conjunction to provide a rule for equivalence. If p and q are either both true or both false, then $p \supset q$ and $q \supset p$ are both true, making their conjunction true. But if p is true and q is false, then $p \supset q$ is false, making the conjunction false. Similarly, if p is false and q is true, then $q \supset p$ is false, making the conjunction false. Thus, we have the following rule for equivalence: $p \equiv q$ is true if and only if p and q have the same truth value. This rule makes it clear that truth functional equivalence is quite different from equivalence of meaning. If two statements are truth functionally equivalent, they need only have the same truth value. Apart from this the statements may be totally unrelated to one another.

The rules of the five truth functional connectives are summarized as follows:

$\sim p$ has the opposite truth value of p

$p \cdot q$ is true if and only if both p and q are true

$p \vee q$ is true if and only if either p or q (or both) is true

$p \supset q$ is false if and only if p is true and q is false

$p \equiv q$ is true if and only if p and q have the same truth value

We may use these rules to compute the truth values of molecular propositions having varying degrees of complexity. The procedure to be followed is this: Enter the truth values of the atomic components directly beneath the letters. Then use these truth values to compute the truth values of the molecular components. The truth value of a molecular statement is written beneath the connective representing it. Let us suppose, for example, that we are told in advance that the atomic propositions A, B, and C are true, and D, E, and F are false. We may then compute the truth value of the following molecular proposition:

$$(A \lor D) \supset E$$

First we write the truth values of the atomic propositions immediately below the respective letters:

$$(A \lor D) \supset E$$
$$\ \ T \ \ \ \ F \ \ \ \ \ \ F$$

Next we compute the truth value of the proposition in parentheses:

$$(A \lor D) \supset E$$
$$\ \ T \ \ \ \ F \ \ \ \ \ \ F$$
$$\ \ \ \ \ \diagdown \diagup$$
$$\ \ \ \ \ \ \ T$$

Finally, we use the truth value of the disjunction together with the truth value of the consequent to compute the truth value of the conditional:

The final answer is circled. This is the truth value of the molecular proposition given that A is true and D and E are false.

The general strategy is to build the truth values of the larger components from the truth values of the smaller ones. In general, the order to be followed in entering truth values is this:

1. Individual letters representing atomic propositions.
2. Negation signs immediately preceding individual letters.
3. Connectives joining letters or negated letters.
4. Negation signs immediately preceding parentheses.

5. Connectives joining parentheses or negated parentheses with letters, negated letters, parentheses, or negated parentheses.
6. Negation signs immediately preceding brackets.
7. And so on.

Here are some additional examples. As above, let A, B, and C be true, D, E, and F false. Note that the computed truth values are written below the connectives to which they pertain. The final answers are circled.

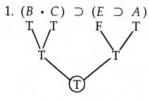

1. (B · C) ⊃ (E ⊃ A)

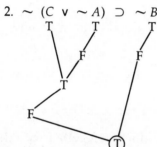

2. ~ (C v ~ A) ⊃ ~ B

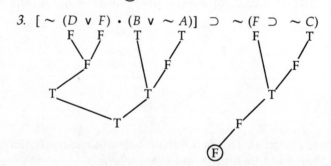

3. [~ (D v F) · (B v ~ A)] ⊃ ~ (F ⊃ ~ C)

If preferred, the truth values of the molecular components may be entered directly beneath the connectives, without using the "tree" approach illustrated in these examples. The following examples illustrate this second approach, which prepares for truth tables in the next section:

4. [(D ≡ ~ A) · ~ (C · ~ B)] ≡ ~ [(A ⊃ ~ D) v (C ≡ E)]
   F T FT T T TF F T Ⓕ F   T T T F T T F F

5. $\sim \{[(C \cdot \sim E) \supset \sim (A \cdot \sim B)] \supset [\sim (B \lor D) \equiv (\sim C \lor E)]\}$
   (F) T T T F T T T F F T T F T T F T F T F F

EXERCISE 6.2

I. Write the following molecular statements in symbolic form, then use your knowledge of the historical events referred to by the atomic statements to determine the truth value of the molecular statements.

★1. Napoleon was not defeated at Waterloo.

2. Napoleon was defeated at Waterloo and Caesar conquered Gaul.

3. Caesar conquered Gaul or Washington was assassinated.

4. Napoleon was defeated at Waterloo and Caesar did not conquer Gaul.

★5. Edison invented the telephone or Napoleon was not defeated at Waterloo.

6. Edison invented the telephone if Caesar conquered Gaul.

7. Washington was assassinated only if Edison invented the telephone.

8. Napoleon was defeated at Waterloo if and only if Washington was assassinated.

9. It is not the case that either Washington was assassinated or Edison invented the telephone.

★10. If Napoleon was defeated at Waterloo, then either Caesar conquered Gaul or Edison invented the telephone.

11. Either Napoleon was defeated at Waterloo and Washington was assassinated or both Caesar conquered Gaul and Edison did not invent the telephone.

12. Napoleon's being defeated at Waterloo is a sufficient condition for Edison to have invented the telephone if and only if Washington's being assassinated is a necessary condition for Caesar to have conquered Gaul.

13. Both Napoleon was defeated at Waterloo and Caesar conquered Gaul only if neither Washington was assassinated nor Edison invented the telephone.

14. It is not the case that: Caesar conquered Gaul and either Edison invented the telephone or Washington was not assassinated.

★15. Napoleon was defeated at Waterloo, and Caesar's having conquered Gaul implies that either Washington was assassinated or Edison invented the telephone.

II. Determine the truth values of the following symbolized statements. Let A, B, and C be true; X, Y, and Z, false. Circle your answer.

★1. $A \cdot X$

2. $B \cdot \sim Y$

3. $X \vee \sim Y$

4. $\sim C \vee Z$

★5. $B \supset \sim Z$

6. $Y \supset \sim A$

7. $\sim X \supset Z$

8. $B \equiv Y$

9. $\sim C \equiv Z$

★10. $\sim (A \cdot \sim Z)$

11. $\sim B \vee (Y \supset A)$

12. $A \supset \sim (Z \vee \sim Y)$

13. $(A \cdot Y) \vee (\sim Z \cdot C)$

14. $\sim (X \vee \sim B) \cdot (\sim Y \vee A)$

★15. $(Y \supset C) \cdot \sim (B \supset \sim X)$

16. $(C \equiv \sim A) \vee (Y \equiv Z)$

17. $\sim (A \cdot \sim C) \supset (\sim X \supset B)$

18. $\sim [(B \vee \sim C) \cdot \sim (X \vee \sim Z)]$

19. $\sim [\sim (X \supset C) \equiv \sim (B \supset Z)]$

★20. $(X \supset Z) \supset [(B \equiv \sim X) \cdot \sim (C \vee \sim A)]$

21. $[(\sim X \vee Z) \supset (\sim C \vee B)] \cdot [(\sim X \cdot A) \supset (\sim Y \cdot Z)]$

22. $\sim [(A \equiv X) \vee (Z \equiv Y)] \vee [(\sim Y \supset B) \cdot (Z \supset C)]$

23. $[(B \cdot \sim C) \vee (X \cdot \sim Y)] \supset \sim [(Y \cdot \sim X) \vee (A \cdot \sim Z)]$

24. $\sim \{\sim [(C \vee \sim B) \cdot (Z \vee \sim A)] \cdot \sim [\sim (B \vee Y) \cdot (\sim X \vee Z)]\}$

★25. $(Z \supset C) \supset \{[(\sim X \supset B) \supset (C \supset Y)] \equiv [(Z \supset X) \supset (\sim Y \supset Z)]\}$

III. When possible, determine the truth values of the following symbolized statements. Let A and B be true, Y and Z false. P and Q have unknown truth value. If the truth value of the statement cannot be determined, write "undetermined."

★1. $A \vee P$

2. $Q \vee Z$

3. $Q \cdot Y$

4. $Q \cdot A$

★5. $P \supset B$

6. $Z \supset Q$

7. $A \supset P$

8. $P \equiv {\sim}P$

9. $(P \supset A) \supset Z$

★10. $(P \supset A) \equiv (Q \supset B)$

11. $(Q \supset B) \supset (A \supset Y)$

12. ${\sim}(P \supset Y) \vee (Z \supset Q)$

13. ${\sim}(Q \cdot Y) \equiv {\sim}(Q \vee A)$

14. $[(Z \supset P) \supset P] \supset P$

★15. $[Q \supset (A \vee P)] \equiv [(Q \supset B) \supset Y]$

6.3 TRUTH TABLES FOR PROPOSITIONS

A **truth table** is an arrangement of truth values that shows how the truth value of a molecular proposition varies depending on the truth value of its atomic components. In the previous section we showed how the truth value of a molecular proposition could be determined, given a *designated* truth value for each atomic component. A truth table gives the truth value of a molecular proposition for *every possible* truth value of its atomic components. Each line in the truth table represents one such possible arrangement of truth values.

In constructing a truth table the first factor that must be determined is the number of lines. Because each line represents one possible arrangement of truth values, the total number of lines is equal to the number of possible combinations of truth values for the atomic propositions. Where L designates the number of lines and n the number of *different* atomic propositions, the number of lines may be computed by the following formula:

$$L = 2^n$$

By means of this formula we obtain the following table:

Number of different atomic propositions	Number of lines in truth table
1	2
2	4
3	8
4	16
5	32
6	64

Let us now construct a truth table for a molecular proposition. We may begin with a fairly simple one:

$$(P \lor \sim Q) \supset Q$$

The number of different atomic propositions is two. Thus, the number of lines in the truth table is four. We draw these lines beneath the proposition as follows:

$$(P \lor \sim Q) \supset Q$$

The next step is to divide the number of lines in half and assign "T" to the first half of the lines beneath P and "F" to the remaining half. Since the number of lines is four, we have two T's and two F's:

$(P \lor \sim Q) \supset Q$
T
T
F
F

Next we divide that number (two) in half and, since the result is one, write one T, one F, one T, and one F beneath Q.

$(P \lor \sim Q) \supset Q$	
T	T
T	F
F	T
F	F

Inspection of the truth table at this stage reveals that every possible combination of truth and falsity has now been assigned to P and Q. In other words, the truth table exhausts the entire range of possibilities.

The next step is to duplicate the Q column under the second Q.

$(P \lor \sim Q) \supset Q$		
T	T	T
T	F	F
F	T	T
F	F	F

This much has been automatic. Now, using the principles developed in the previous section, we compute the remaining columns: first the column for the negation sign (which will be exactly opposite to the column beneath Q), then the column beneath the disjunction sign, and finally the column beneath the conditional sign:

$$(P \lor \sim Q) \supset Q$$

P	$\lor$	$\sim$	$Q)$	$\supset$	Q
T	T	F	T	T	T
T	T	T	F	F	F
F	F	F	T	T	T
F	T	T	F	F	F

We outline the last column completed to indicate that it represents the entire molecular proposition. Inspecting the completed truth table, we see that the truth value of the molecular proposition is true when Q is true and false when Q is false, irrespective of the truth value of P.

Let us consider another example: $(P \cdot \sim Q) \supset R$. The number of different letters is three, so the number of lines is eight. Under P we make half this number true, half false (that is, four true, four false). Then, under Q, we make half *this* number true, half false, and so on (two true, two false, two true, two false). Finally, under R the truth value alternates on every line. The truth table thus exhausts every possible arrangement of truth values:

$(P$	$\cdot$	$\sim$	$Q)$	$\supset$	R
T			T		T
T			T		F
T			F		T
T			F		F
F			T		T
F			T		F
F			F		T
F			F		F

Now we compute the truth values for the remaining columns—first for the negation sign, then for the conjunction sign, and finally for the conditional sign:

$(P$	$\cdot$	$\sim$	$Q)$	$\supset$	R
T	F	F	T	T	T
T	F	F	T	T	F
T	T	T	F	T	T
T	T	T	F	F	F
F	F	F	T	T	T
F	F	F	T	T	F
F	F	T	F	T	T
F	F	T	F	T	F

Inspecting the completed truth table, we see that the molecular proposition is false only when P is true and Q and R are false.

PROPOSITIONAL LOGIC   227

Truth tables may be used to determine whether the truth value of a molecular statement depends solely upon its form or whether it also depends on the specific truth values of its components. A molecular statement is said to be **logically true** or **tautologous** if it is true regardless of the truth values of its components. It is said to be **logically false** or **self-contradictory** if it is false regardless of the truth value of its components. And it is said to be **contingent** if its truth value varies depending on the truth value of the components. By inspecting the final column of the truth table (that is, the column that is *completed* last), we can determine how the molecular proposition should be classified.

Statement classification	Final column of truth table
tautology (or logical truth)	all true
self-contradiction (or logical falsehood)	all false
contingent	at least one true, at least one false

As the truth table we developed indicates, $(P \cdot \sim Q) \supset R$ is a contingent proposition. The final column of the truth table contains at least one T and at least one F. In other words, the truth value of the molecular proposition is "contingent" upon the truth values of its components. Sometimes it is true, sometimes false, depending on the truth value of the components.

On the other hand, consider the following truth tables:

```
[(P ⊃ Q) • P] ⊃ Q            ·(P ∨ Q) ≡ (~ P • ~ Q)
 T  T  T  T T  T  T           T T T  F  F T  F F T
 T  F  F  F T  T  F           T T F  F  F T  F T F
 F  T  T  F F  T  T           F T T  F  T F  F F T
 F  T  F  F F  T  F           F F F  F  T F  T T F
```

The proposition on the left is a tautology (or logical truth) because the final column is all true, and the one on the right is a self-contradiction (or logical falsehood) because the final column is all false. In neither case is the truth value of the molecular proposition contingent upon the truth value of the components. The one on the left is true irrespective of the truth value of its components—in other words, *necessarily* true; and the one on the right is *necessarily* false.

If a proposition is either logically true or logically false, its truth value depends merely upon its form and has nothing to do with its content. As a result, such statements do not make any genuine assertions about things in the world. For example, the tautologous statement "It is either raining or it is not raining" says nothing about the weather. Similarly, the self-contradictory statement "It is raining and it is not raining" says nothing about the weather. On the other hand, the contingent statement "It is raining in the mountains" does say something about the weather.

Truth tables may also be used to determine how two propositions are related to one another. Two propositions are said to be **logically equivalent** if they have the same truth value regardless of the truth values of their atomic components. They are **contradictory** if they have opposite truth values regardless of the truth values of their atomic components. And they are *neither* logically equivalent nor contradictory if they sometimes have the same truth value and sometimes opposite truth values, depending on the truth values of the components. By comparing the final columns on the respective truth tables one can determine which is the case:

Relation	Final columns of truth tables
logically equivalent	same truth value on each line
contradictory	opposite truth value on each line
neither logically equivalent nor contradictory	same truth value on at least one line; opposite truth value on at least one line

For example, the following pair of propositions are logically equivalent. The final columns of their respective truth tables are identical. Note that for proper comparison the columns under P must be identical and the columns under Q must be identical:

```
P ⊃ Q            ~ Q ⊃ ~ P
T T T            F T  T  F T
T F F            T F  F  F T
F T T            F T  T  T F
F T F            T F  T  T F
```

The next two propositions are mutually contradictory:

```
P ⊃ Q            P · ~ Q
T T T            T F F T
T F F            T T T F
F T T            F F F T
F T F            F F T F
```

Finally, the next two propositions are neither logically equivalent nor contradictory. On two lines the truth values in the final columns are the same but on the two other lines they are opposite:

P	v	Q
T	T	T
T	T	F
F	T	T
F	F	F

P	·	Q
T	T	T
T	F	F
F	F	T
F	F	F

As these examples illustrate, there is a distinction between two statements merely having the same truth value and their being logically equivalent. For example, the statements "Water boils at 100°C" and "The current population of the United States is over 200 million" have the same truth value; they are both true. But they are not *logically* equivalent because their truth values are not *necessarily* the same. The truth value of the second one might change while the first remains constant. The same holds true, incidentally, for the distinction between two statements having opposite truth values and their being contradictory.

EXERCISE 6.3

I. Use truth tables to determine whether the following symbolized statements are tautologous, self-contradictory, or contingent:

★1. $A \supset (A \supset A)$

2. $(D \supset D) \supset D$

3. $(R \supset S) \cdot (R \cdot \sim S)$

4. $[(E \supset F) \supset F] \supset E$

★5. $(H \supset J) \equiv (H \cdot \sim J)$

6. $(N \supset P) \vee (P \supset N)$

7. $[(X \supset Z) \cdot (X \vee Z)] \supset Z$

8. $[(C \supset D) \cdot \sim C] \supset \sim D$

9. $[G \supset (N \supset \sim G)] \cdot [(G \equiv N) \cdot (G \vee N)]$

★10. $[F \supset (T \supset X)] \equiv [(F \supset T) \supset X]$

11. $[(P \supset Q) \cdot (\sim P \supset R)] \cdot \sim (Q \vee R)$

12. $[(H \supset N) \cdot (T \supset N)] \supset [(H \vee T) \supset N]$

13. $[S \cdot (T \vee U)] \equiv [(\sim S \vee \sim T) \cdot (\sim S \vee \sim U)]$

14. $\{[(G \cdot H) \supset N] \cdot [(G \supset N) \supset P]\} \supset (H \supset P)$

★15. $[(E \vee F) \cdot (G \vee H)] \equiv [(E \cdot G) \vee (F \cdot H)]$

II. Use truth tables to determine whether the following pairs of symbolized statements are logically equivalent, contradictory, or neither:

★1. $\sim D \vee T$ $\sim (D \cdot \sim T)$

2. $\sim K \supset L$ $K \supset \sim L$

3. $R \vee \sim S$ $S \cdot \sim R$
4. $\sim A \equiv X$ $(X \cdot \sim A) \vee (\sim X \cdot A)$
★5. $N \supset \sim P$ $N \cdot P$
6. $G \equiv \sim H$ $(H \cdot G) \vee (\sim G \cdot \sim H)$
7. $(E \supset F) \supset G$ $E \supset (F \supset G)$
8. $J \supset (K \supset L)$ $(K \cdot J) \supset L$
9. $P \cdot (R \vee S)$ $(S \vee P) \cdot (R \vee P)$
★10. $H \cdot (J \vee K)$ $(J \cdot H) \vee (H \cdot K)$

6.4 ARGUMENT FORMS AND FALLACIES

Many of the arguments that occur in propositional logic have forms that bear specific names and can be immediately recognized as either valid or invalid. The first part of this section presents some of the more common ones and explains how they are recognized. The second part discusses ways of refuting two of these forms, constructive and destructive dilemmas.

Common Argument Forms

A **disjunctive syllogism** is an argument that consists of a disjunctive premise, a premise that denies one of the disjuncts, and a conclusion that affirms the other disjunct. Example:

> Thomas will apologize or Michelle will be angry. $T \vee M$
> Thomas will not apologize. $\underline{\sim T}$
> Therefore, Michelle will be angry. M

It is easy to see that this argument is valid. The first premise presents two alternatives, and the second premise eliminates one of them, leaving the other for the conclusion. This is the so-called "method of elimination" and is essential to the validity of a disjunctive syllogism. If the second premise were to affirm one of the disjuncts instead of denying it, the argument would be invalid. Example:

> Chicago is in Illinois or Boston is in Massachusetts. $C \vee B$
> Chicago is in Illinois. $\underline{C}$
> Therefore, ...

It makes no difference whether the conclusion is "Boston is in Massachusetts" or "Boston is not in Massachusetts"; the argument is invalid in either case. Unless explicitly stated to the contrary, the word "or" is always understood in the inclusive sense that includes the possibility of both disjuncts being true. Thus, if one disjunct is not denied by the second premise, as in the above example, no conclusion follows.

In the broad sense of the term, each of the above arguments is a disjunctive syllogism in that the first premise of each is a disjunctive statement. This text, however, opts to use the term "disjunctive syllogism" only in the narrower sense of denoting the valid form of the argument. In accordance with this convention we may define "disjunctive syllogism" in terms of the following **argument form.** Any argument having this form—that is, any substitution instance—will be a valid argument:

disjunctive syllogism (DS):
$$\begin{array}{l} p \lor q \\ \underline{\sim p} \\ q \end{array}$$

Incidentally, the mere fact that this argument form is called a "syllogism" should not be cause for assuming it to be a categorical syllogism. As was noted in Chapter 5, the term "syllogism," in the broad sense, means simply an argument having two premises and one conclusion. If the premises and conclusion are categorical statements, then the argument is a categorical syllogism; if not, then it is some other kind of syllogism. Apart from the mere fact that both have two premises and one conclusion, there is little similarity between categorical syllogisms and disjunctive syllogisms. They are essentially different kinds of arguments, and different methods and principles are used to evaluate each.

Another kind of syllogism that occurs frequently in propositional logic and that consists of one or more conditional statements is called a **hypothetical syllogism.** If all three statements in the argument are conditional statements, the argument is a **pure hypothetical syllogism;** if only one is a conditional statement, the argument is a **mixed hypothetical syllogism.** Here is an example of a pure hypothetical syllogism:

If tuition increases, enrollment will drop.	$T \supset E$
If enrollment drops, instructors will be laid off.	$E \supset I$
Therefore, if tuition increases, instructors will be laid off.	$\overline{T \supset I}$

This argument is valid because the premises link together like a chain; the consequent of the first is identical to the antecedent of the second. Under such conditions the antecedent of the first implies the consequent of the second. If this order is mixed up, however, the resulting argument is invalid. Example:

If New Orleans is in Louisiana, then Cleveland is in Ohio.	$N \supset C$
If Detroit is in Kansas, then Cleveland is in Ohio.	$D \supset C$
Therefore, if New Orleans is in Louisiana, then Detroit is in Kansas.	$\overline{N \supset D}$

By the rule for conditional statements the premises are true and the conclusion false. The argument is therefore clearly invalid. The problem stems from the fact that the antecedent and consequent of the second premise are in the wrong order. If they were to be reversed, the argument would become valid.

In the broad sense of the term, both of these arguments are pure hypothetical syllogisms. As with "disjunctive syllogism," however, this text prefers to use "pure hypothetical syllogism" to designate only the valid form of the argument. In accord with this convention we define "pure hypothetical syllogism" in terms of the following argument form. Any substitution instance of this form is a valid argument:

pure hypothetical syllogism (HS):
$$p \supset q$$
$$\frac{q \supset r}{p \supset r}$$

Mixed hypothetical syllogism comprises four forms, two of which are valid, two invalid. The two valid forms are called *modus ponens* ("asserting mode") and *modus tollens* ("denying mode"), and the two invalid forms are called affirming the consequent and denying the antecedent. These four forms are called "mixed" hypothetical syllogisms because only one of the premises is a conditional statement. Usually, however, the term "mixed hypothetical syllogism" is not used to name these forms; they are identified instead by their specific names. Here is an example of **modus ponens:**

If this flashlight works, then the batteries are good.	$F \supset B$
This flashlight does work.	F
Therefore, the batteries are good.	B

In *modus ponens* it is essential that the antecedent of the first premise be asserted in the second. The conclusion then asserts the consequent of the first premise. If, on the other hand, the consequent of the first premise is asserted in the second, the resulting argument is invalid, regardless of what the conclusion might be. It would commit the fallacy of **affirming the consequent.** The following example is clearly invalid:

If Napoleon was killed in a plane crash, then Napoleon is dead.	$K \supset D$
Napoleon is dead.	D
Therefore, Napoleon was killed in a plane crash.	K

In **modus tollens,** the consequent of the first premise is *denied* in the second premise, and the conclusion then denies the antecedent of the first premise. Example:

If this flashlight works, then the batteries are good.	$F \supset B$
The batteries are not good.	$\sim B$
Therefore, this flashlight does not work.	$\sim F$

Upon reflection this argument will be seen to be valid. If, on the other hand, the *antecedent* of the first premise is denied in the second, the resulting argument is invalid regardless of what the conclusion might be. Such an argument commits the fallacy of **denying the antecedent.** Example:

> If Napoleon was killed in a plane crash, then
>   Napoleon is dead. $K \supset D$
> Napoleon was not killed in a plane crash. $\sim K$
> Therefore, Napoleon is not dead. $\overline{\sim D}$

Modus ponens and *modus tollens* are defined in terms of the following argument forms. Any substitution instance of either of these forms is a valid argument:

> *modus ponens* (MP): $p \supset q$
> $\underline{p}$
> q
>
> *modus tollens* (MT): $p \supset q$
> $\underline{\sim q}$
> $\sim p$

The invalid forms are defined as follows. Any argument composed of distinct atomic propositions that correspond one-to-one with the letters in either of these forms is invalid*:

> affirming the consequent (AC): $p \supset q$
> $\underline{q}$
> $\cdots\cdots$
>
> denying the antecedent (DA): $p \supset q$
> $\underline{\sim p}$
> $\cdots\cdots$

The substitution instances given above for affirming the consequent and denying the antecedent provide a convenient illustration of the difference between a sufficient and a necessary condition. In the statement "If Napoleon was killed in a plane crash, then Napoleon is dead," Napoleon's being killed in a plane crash is a *sufficient* condition for his being dead. The fallacy of affirming the consequent mistakenly converts this sufficient condition into a necessary condition, with the effect that Napoleon's not being killed in a plane crash supposedly entails his not being dead. Conversely, Napoleon's being dead is actually a *necessary* condition for his being killed in a plane crash. The fallacy of denying the antecedent mistakenly converts this necessary condition into a suffi-

---

*See the comment regarding the real form of an argument at the end of Section 1.5.

cient condition and concludes that because Napoleon is dead he was therefore killed in a plane crash. Obviously, converting sufficient conditions into necessary conditions, and vice versa, is not legitimate.

In a **constructive dilemma,** the first premise consists of two conjoined conditional statements, and the second premise asserts the truth of one of the antecedents. The conclusion, which follows logically via two *modus ponens* steps, asserts the truth of at least one of the consequents. Example:

If this punch contains gin, then Elisa will like it, and if it contains vodka, then Carmen will like it.	$(G \supset E) \cdot (V \supset C)$
This punch contains either gin or vodka.	$G \lor V$
Therefore, either Elisa will like it or Carmen will like it.	$\overline{E \lor C}$

The **destructive dilemma** is similar in form to the constructive dilemma, but the second premise, instead of asserting the truth of at least one of the antecedents, asserts the falsity of at least one of the consequents. The conclusion, which follows validly via two *modus tollens* steps, asserts the falsity of at least one of the antecedents. Example:

If this punch contains gin, then Elisa will like it, and if it contains vodka, then Carmen will like it.	$(G \supset E) \cdot (V \supset C)$
Either Elisa will not like it or Carmen will not like it.	$\sim E \lor \sim C$
Therefore, either this punch does not contain gin or it does not contain vodka.	$\overline{\sim G \lor \sim V}$

The constructive and destructive dilemmas are defined in terms of the following argument forms. Any substitution instance of either of these forms is a valid argument:

constructive dilemma (CD): $(p \supset q) \cdot (r \supset s)$
$$\frac{p \lor r}{q \lor s}$$

destructive dilemma (DD): $(p \supset q) \cdot (r \supset s)$
$$\frac{\sim q \lor \sim s}{\sim p \lor \sim r}$$

In identifying substitution instances of the various argument forms one should use the following procedure. First, symbolize the argument using upper-case letters for the atomic propositions. Then see whether

PROPOSITIONAL LOGIC   **235** the symbolized argument fits the pattern of one of these forms. In doing so, one should keep three points in mind. The first is that the statement form $p \vee q$ is logically equivalent to $q \vee p$. (In the next chapter this equivalence will be expressed as a rule, but for now it may be assumed.) As a result, if an argument appears having the form

$$A \vee B$$
$$\underline{\sim B}$$
$$A$$

it may be reexpressed in the form

$$B \vee A$$
$$\underline{\sim B}$$
$$A$$

This second version is a substitution instance of disjunctive syllogism, and so the original argument may also be considered to be a substitution instance of disjunctive syllogism.

The second point is that negated letters, as well as non-negated letters, may be interpreted as substitution instances of the p, q, r, and s in the argument forms. Consider, for example, the following argument:

$$\sim A \supset B$$
$$\underline{\sim A}$$
$$B$$

When $\sim A$ is substituted in the place of p and B in the place of q, the above argument will be seen to be a substitution instance of *modus ponens*.

The third point to remember is that the simple statement form p is logically equivalent to $\sim \sim p$. Like the previous equivalence, this one will be expressed as a rule in the next chapter, but for now it may be assumed. In view of this equivalence, an argument having the form

$$A \supset \sim B$$
$$\underline{B}$$
$$\sim A$$

may be reexpressed as

$$A \supset \sim B$$
$$\underline{\sim \sim B}$$
$$\sim A$$

Now when A is substituted in place of p and $\sim B$ in place of q, this argument will be seen to be a substitution instance of *modus tollens*.

Here are some additional examples. In some cases the symbolized argument may have to be reexpressed, using one or more of these three logical equivalences, before it fits the pattern of the argument form indicated in parentheses:

$\sim A \supset \sim B$
$\underline{\sim B \supset C}$ (HS)
$\sim A \supset C$

$A \supset \sim B$
$\underline{B \supset \sim C}$ invalid
$A \supset \sim C$

$\sim A \vee \sim B$
$\underline{B}$ (MT)
A

$\sim A \supset B$
$\underline{A}$ (DA)
$\sim B$

$\sim A \supset \sim B$
$\underline{A}$ (DS)
$\sim B$

$\sim A \vee B$
$\underline{\sim A}$ invalid
$\sim B$

$(A \supset \sim B) \cdot (\sim C \supset D)$
$\underline{A \vee \sim C}$ (CD)
$\sim B \vee D$

$(\sim A \supset B) \cdot (C \supset \sim D)$
$\underline{B \vee \sim D}$ invalid
$A \vee \sim C$

$A \vee \sim B$
$\underline{B}$ (DS)
A

$A \supset \sim B$
$\underline{\sim B}$ (AC)
$\sim A$

Refuting Constructive and Destructive Dilemmas

Now that we are familiar with a number of argument forms in propositional logic, we may return for a closer look at two of them, constructive and destructive dilemmas. Arguments having these forms occur frequently in public debate, where they may be used by an arguer to trap an opponent. Since both forms are intrinsically valid, the only direct mode of defense available to the opponent is to prove the dilemma unsound. This can be done by proving at least one of the premises false. If the first premise (the conjunctive premise—otherwise called the "horns of the dilemma") is proven false, the opponent is said to have "grasped the dilemma by the horns." This, of course, may be done by proving either one of the conditional statements false. If, on the other hand, the second (disjunctive) premise is proven false, the opponent is said to have "escaped between the horns of the dilemma." The latter strategy often involves finding a third alternative to the two that are given in the disjunctive premise. If a third alternative can be found, then neither of these disjuncts need be true. Consider the following constructive dilemma:

> If taxes increase, the economy will suffer, and if taxes decrease, needed governmental services will be curtailed. Since taxes must either increase or decrease, it follows that the

economy will suffer or that needed governmental services
will be curtailed.

It is easy to escape between the horns of this dilemma by arguing that
taxes could be kept as they are, in which case they would neither increase nor decrease.

Some dilemmas, however, do not allow for the possibility of escaping
between the horns. Consider the following constructive dilemma:

> If we encourage competition, we will have no peace, and if
> we do not encourage competition, we will make no progress.
> Since we must either encourage competition or not encourage
> it, we will either have no peace or make no progress.

Since the second premise of this dilemma is a tautology, it cannot be
proven false. This leaves the strategy of grasping the dilemma by the
horns, which may be done by proving either of the conditional statements in the first premise false. A debater with conservative inclinations
might want to attack the first conditional and argue that competition
and peace can coexist, while one with liberal inclinations might want to
attack the second and argue that progress can be achieved through some
means other than encouraging competition.

The strategy to be followed in refuting a dilemma is therefore this:
Examine the disjunctive premise. If this premise is a tautology, attempt
to grasp the dilemma by the horns by attacking one or the other of the
conditional statements in the conjunctive premise. If the disjunctive
premise is not a tautology, then either escape between the horns by,
perhaps, finding a third alternative, or grasp the dilemma by the
horns—whichever is easier.

A third, indirect strategy for refuting a dilemma involves constructing
a counterdilemma. This is typically done by changing either the antecedents or the consequents of the conjunctive premise while leaving the
disjunctive premise as it is, so as to obtain a different conclusion. If the
dilemma in question is a constructive dilemma, the consequents of the
conjunctive premise are changed. Here are possible counterdilemmas
for the two dilemmas presented above:

> If taxes increase, needed governmental services will be ex-
> tended, and if taxes decrease, the economy will improve. Since
> taxes must either increase or decrease, it follows that needed
> governmental services will be extended or the economy will
> improve.

> If we encourage competition, we will make progress, and if we
> do not encourage competition, we will have peace. Since we
> must either encourage competition or not encourage it, we will
> either make progress or have peace.

A CONCISE INTRODUCTION TO LOGIC

Constructing a counterdilemma does not accomplish a complete refutation of a given dilemma because it merely shows that a different approach can be taken to a certain problem. Nevertheless, this strategy is often quite effective because it testifies to the cleverness of the debater who can accomplish it successfully. In the heat of debate the attending audience is often persuaded that the original argument has been thoroughly demolished.

The argument forms presented in this section may now be summarized. Any argument that has one of the following forms is valid:

$p \lor q$	disjunctive	$p \supset q$	pure hypotheti-
$\sim p$	syllogism	$q \supset r$	cal syllogism
q	(DS)	$p \supset r$	(HS)
$p \supset q$	*modus ponens*	$p \supset q$	*modus tollens*
p	(MP)	$\sim q$	(MT)
q		$\sim p$	
$(p \supset q) \cdot (r \supset s)$	constructive	$(p \supset q) \cdot (r \supset s)$	destructive di-
$p \lor r$	dilemma	$\sim q \lor \sim s$	lemma (DD)
$q \lor s$	(CD)	$\sim p \lor \sim r$	

Any argument composed of distinct atomic propositions that correspond one-to-one with the letters in the following forms is invalid:

$p \supset q$	affirming the consequent	$p \supset q$	denying the antecedent
q	(AC)	$\sim p$	(DA)
$\therefore$		$\therefore$	

EXERCISE 6.4

I. Identify the forms of the following arguments. If the form has no specific name, write "invalid form."

★1. If that bar of iron is magnetized, it will attract iron filings. Since it does not attract iron filings, it isn't magnetized.

2. If the fuel pump is defective, then this car won't run. This car won't run. Therefore, the fuel pump is defective.

3. If we build our home in the valley, it will be struck by floods, and if we build it on the hilltop, it will be struck by lightning. We must either build it in the valley or on the hilltop. Therefore, our home will either be struck by floods or by lightning.

4. Either Andrews excels in tonight's game or the Falcons won't make it to the playoffs. Andrews won't excel in tonight's game. Therefore, the Falcons won't make it to the playoffs.

★5. Either this painting is not an authentic Rembrandt or it should not be hung in the north gallery. This painting is not an authentic Rembrandt. Therefore, it should not be hung in the north gallery.

6. If the machinists do not accept their new contract, they will go on strike. If the machinists go on strike, the Ajax helicopter will not be completed on schedule. Therefore, if the machinists do not accept their new contract, the Ajax helicopter will not be completed on schedule.

7. If Chief O'Fallon is not supplied with adequate resources, he will not be able to protect vulnerable neighborhoods. Chief O'Fallon is not being supplied with adequate resources. Therefore, he will not be able to protect vulnerable neighborhoods.

8. If United Semiconductor vigorously advertises its new calculator, it will recover development costs within two months. United Semiconductor refuses to advertise. Therefore, it will not recover development costs within two months.

9. If the Andersons are invited to dinner, we cannot serve fish, and if the Petersons are invited, we cannot serve fowl. We will either serve fish or fowl. Therefore, either the Andersons or the Petersons will not be invited.

★10. If Kapellmeister Weiskopf selects the Mahler sixth, he will alienate the classicists, and if he selects the Haydn eighty-sixth he will disappoint the romanticists. Weiskopf will select neither the Mahler sixth nor the Haydn eighty-sixth. Therefore, he will neither alienate the classicists nor disappoint the romanticists.

11. If this toy is not made by Mattel, then it is unsafe for children. This toy is made by Mattel. Therefore, it is safe for children.

12. If Henderson doesn't read *Newsweek*, then he can't be well informed about current events. Henderson is well informed about current events. Therefore, he reads *Newsweek*.

13. If you enter the teaching profession, you will have no money for vacations, and if you do not enter the teaching profession, you will have no time for vacations. Since you must either enter or not enter the teaching profession, it follows that you will either have no money or no time for vacations.

14. Adrienne subscribes to either *Time* or *U.S. News & World Report*. But she does subscribe to *Time*. Therefore, she does not subscribe to *U.S. News & World Report*.

★15. If these flowers are impatiens, they should not be planted in full sunlight. These flowers should not be planted in full sunlight. Therefore, they are impatiens.

16. If Hans Schneider does not overexert himself in today's practice session, he should win the downhill slalom tomorrow. He will not overexert himself today. Therefore, he should win the downhill slalom tomorrow.

17. Either Thompson doesn't understand the problem or he's incapable of

solving it. Thompson does understand the problem. Therefore, he's incapable of solving it.

18. If Russia invades Poland, an international crisis will develop. If an international crisis develops, the price of gold will skyrocket. Therefore, if Russia invades Poland, the price of gold will skyrocket.

19. If Beverly has bronchitis, she will not be able to sing the part of Violetta. If she is able to sing the part of Violetta, she will win the Chicago Lyric Opera competition. Therefore, if Beverly does not have bronchitis she will win the Chicago Lyric Opera competition.

★20. If Rita Palermo does not receive a high score on the aptitude test, she will not be admitted to medical school; but if she earns a 4.0 average this semester she will be admitted. Since she will either be admitted or not admitted, it follows that she will either receive a high score on the aptitude test or not earn a 4.0 average this semester.

II. Identify the following dilemmas as either constructive or destructive. Then suggest a refutation for each one by either escaping between the horns, grasping by the horns, or constructing a counterdilemma.

★1. If Melinda spends the night studying, she will miss the party, and if she doesn't spend the night studying, she will fail the test tomorrow. She must either spend the night studying or not studying. Therefore, she will either miss the party or fail the test.

2. If the Western nations continue stockpiling, then OPEC will increase oil prices, and if consumption declines, then OPEC will not increase oil prices. OPEC will either increase or not increase oil prices. Therefore, either the Western nations will discontinue stockpiling or consumption will not decline.

3. If the Mitchells get a divorce, they will live separately in poverty, and if they stay married, they will live together in misery. Since they must either get a divorce or stay married, they will either live separately in poverty or together in misery.

4. If interest rates rise, the economy will stagnate, and if they fall, inflation will run rampant. Interest rates will either rise or fall. Therefore, either the economy will stagnate or inflation will run rampant.

★5. If you want flowers to enjoy through the summer, you must plant a flower garden, and if you want vegetables to eat during the winter, you must plant a vegetable garden. You cannot plant both a flower garden and a vegetable garden. Therefore, either you will have no flowers through the summer or no vegetables during the winter.

6. If the workers want to retain their wages, they must not go on strike, and if they want increased benefits, they must go on strike. Since they must do one or the other, they will either lose their wages or forgo increased benefits.

7. If you subscribe to the small local paper, you will miss the national news, and if you subscribe to the large urban paper, you will miss the local news. You must either subscribe to the small local paper or the large urban paper. Therefore, you will miss either the national news or the local news.

8. If Senator Rodriguez supports the deregulation bill, he will lose the Teamster vote, and if he supports the retirement bill, he will win the Teamster vote. Senator Rodriguez will either win or lose the Teamster vote. Therefore, he will either not support the deregulation bill or not support the retirement bill.

6.5 TRUTH TABLES FOR ARGUMENTS

Truth tables provide the standard technique for testing the validity of arguments in propositional logic. To construct a truth table for an argument, follow these steps:

1. Symbolize the argument, using letters to represent the atomic propositions.
2. Write out the symbolized argument, placing a single slash between the premises and a double slash between the last premise and the conclusion.
3. Draw a truth table for the symbolized argument as if it were a proposition broken into parts, outlining the columns representing the premises and conclusion.
4. Look for a line in which the premises are all true and the conclusion false. If such a line exists, the argument is invalid; if not, it is valid.

For example, let us test the following argument for validity:

If Detroit is in Kansas, then Krugerrands are made of copper.
Detroit is not in Kansas.
Therefore, Krugerrands are not made of copper.

The first step is to symbolize the argument:

$$D \supset K$$
$$\underline{\sim D}$$
$$\sim K$$

Now a truth table may be constructed. Since the symbolized argument contains two different letters, the truth table has four lines. Make sure that identical letters have identical columns beneath them. Here are the columns for the individual letters:

$$D \supset K \quad / \quad \sim D \quad // \quad \sim K$$

D	⊃	K		~	D		~	K
T		T			T			T
T		F			T			F
F		T			F			T
F		F			F			F

The truth table is now completed, and the columns representing the premises and conclusion are outlined:

$$D \supset K \quad / \quad \sim D \quad // \quad \sim K$$

D	⊃	K		~	D		~	K
T	**T**	T		**F**	T		**F**	T
T	**F**	F		**F**	T		**T**	F
F	**T**	T		**T**	F		**F**	T ✓
F	**T**	F		**T**	F		**T**	F

Inspection of the third line reveals that the premises are both true and the conclusion false. The argument is therefore invalid. A check mark is placed next to the line on which the argument fails.

Another example:

> If Lincoln was assassinated, then Caesar did not cross the Rubicon. If Caesar did not cross the Rubicon, then World War II was fought in Arkansas. Therefore, if Lincoln was assassinated, then World War II was fought in Arkansas.

The completed truth table is:

$$L \supset \sim C \quad / \quad \sim C \supset W \quad // \quad L \supset W$$

L	⊃	~	C		~	C	⊃	W		L	⊃	W
T	**F**	F	T		F	T	**T**	T		T	**T**	T
T	**F**	F	T		F	T	**T**	F		T	**F**	F
T	**T**	T	F		T	F	**T**	T		T	**T**	T
T	**T**	T	F		T	F	**F**	F		T	**F**	F
F	**T**	F	T		F	T	**T**	T		F	**T**	T
F	**T**	F	T		F	T	**T**	F		F	**T**	F
F	**T**	T	F		T	F	**T**	T		F	**T**	T
F	**T**	T	F		T	F	**F**	F		F	**T**	F

Inspection of the truth table reveals that there is no line on which the premises are both true and the conclusion false. The argument is therefore valid. It is, however, unsound, because it has a false premise.

The logic behind the method of truth tables is easy to understand. By definition, a valid argument is one in which the conclusion follows necessarily from the premises. In other words, in a valid argument it is not possible for the premises to be true and the conclusion false. A truth table presents every possible combination of truth values that the components of an argument may have. Therefore, if no line exists on which the premises are true and the conclusion false, then it is not possible for the premises to be true and the conclusion false, in which case the argument is valid. Conversely, if there *is* a line on which the premises are true and the conclusion false, then it *is* possible for the premises to be true and the conclusion false, and the argument is invalid.

Truth tables provide a convenient illustration of the fact that any argument having contradictory premises is valid regardless of what its conclusion may be, and any argument having a tautologous conclusion is valid regardless of what its premises may be. Example:

> The sky is blue.
> The sky is not blue.
> Therefore, Paris is the capital of France.

S	/	~	S	//	P
T		F	T		T
T		F	T		F
F		T	F		T
F		T	F		F

Since the premises of this argument are self-contradictory, there is no line on which the premises are both true. Accordingly, there is no line on which the premises are both true and the conclusion false, so the argument is valid. Of course, the argument is unsound, because it has a false premise. Another example:

> Bern is the capital of Switzerland. Therefore, it is either raining or it is not raining.

B	//	R	v	~	R
T		T	T	F	T
T		F	T	T	F
F		T	T	F	T
F		F	T	T	F

The conclusion of this argument is a tautology. Accordingly, there is no line on which the premise is true and the conclusion false, and so the argument is valid. Incidentally, it is also sound, because the premise is true.

EXERCISE 6.5

I. Translate the following arguments into symbolic form. Then determine whether each is valid or invalid by constructing a truth table for each.

★1. If Annie gets the pretzels, then Bob buys the beer. Therefore, if Annie does not get the pretzels, then Bob does not buy the beer.

2. Charles gets the chips. Therefore, either Charles gets the chips or Denise brings the dip.

3. If Annie gets the pretzels, then Bob brings the beer. If Bob brings the beer, then Charles gets the chips. Therefore, if Annie gets the pretzels, then Charles gets the chips.

4. If Esther brings the nuts, then Frank buys the pizza. Frank buys the pizza. Therefore, Esther brings the nuts.

★5. If Bob buys the beer, then Charles gets the chips. If Denise brings the dip, then Charles gets the chips. Therefore, if Bob buys the beer, then Denise brings the dip.

6. Sylvia sings a song. Therefore, if Charles gets the chips, then if Denise brings the dip, then Charles gets the chips.

7. Either Esther brings the nuts or Frank buys the pizza. Esther brings the nuts. Therefore, Frank does not buy the pizza.

8. If Charles gets the chips, then Denise brings the dip. Denise does not bring the dip and Charles gets the chips. Therefore, Sylvia sings a song.

9. Either Annie does not get the pretzels or Bob does not buy the beer. Therefore, it is not the case that either Annie gets the pretzels or Bob buys the beer.

★10. If Charles gets the chips, then Denise brings the dip, and if Esther brings the nuts, then Frank buys the pizza. Either Charles gets the chips or Esther brings the nuts. Therefore, either Denise brings the dip or Frank buys the pizza.

II. Determine whether the following symbolized arguments are valid or invalid by constructing a truth table for each:

★1. $K \supset {\sim}K$
$\frac{}{{\sim}K}$

2. $R \supset R$
$\frac{}{R}$

3. $E \supset F$
$\frac{}{E \supset (E \cdot F)}$

4. $G \cdot (I \lor J)$
$\frac{}{(G \cdot I) \lor (G \cdot J)}$

★5. ${\sim}(K \cdot L)$
$\frac{}{{\sim}K \cdot {\sim}L}$

6. S
$\frac{}{(T \supset U) \equiv ({\sim}T \lor U)}$

7. ${\sim}W \lor X$
${\sim}W$
$\frac{}{X}$

8. $C \equiv D$
$E \lor {\sim}D$
$\frac{}{E \supset C}$

9. $A \equiv (B \lor C)$
${\sim}C \lor B$
$\frac{}{A \supset B}$

★10. $J \supset (K \supset L)$
$K \supset (J \supset L)$
$\frac{}{(J \lor K) \supset L}$

11. $P \equiv Q$
$\frac{}{(P \cdot {\sim}Q) \lor (Q \cdot {\sim}P)}$

12. $E \supset (F \cdot G)$
$F \supset (G \supset H)$
$\frac{}{E \supset H}$

13. $(A \lor B) \supset (A \cdot B)$
   $\dfrac{\sim(A \lor B)}{\sim(A \cdot B)}$

14. $(X \lor Y) \supset Z$
   $\dfrac{Z \supset (X \cdot Y)}{(X \cdot Y) \supset (X \lor Y)}$

★15. $L \supset M$
   $M \supset N$
   $\dfrac{N \supset L}{L \lor N}$

16. $S \supset T$
   $S \supset \sim T$
   $\dfrac{\sim T \supset S}{S \lor \sim T}$

17. $P \supset Q$
   $R \supset S$
   $\dfrac{\sim Q \lor \sim S}{\sim P \lor \sim R}$

18. $A \supset B$
   $(A \cdot B) \supset C$
   $\dfrac{A \supset (C \supset D)}{A \supset D}$

19. $K \equiv (L \lor M)$
   $L \supset M$
   $M \supset K$
   $\dfrac{K \lor L}{K \supset L}$

★20. $W \supset X$
   $X \supset W$
   $X \supset Y$
   $\dfrac{Y \supset X}{W \equiv Y}$

6.6 INDIRECT TRUTH TABLES FOR ARGUMENTS

Indirect truth tables provide a shorter and faster method for testing the validity of arguments than that provided by ordinary truth tables. This method is especially applicable to arguments that contain a large number of different atomic propositions. For example, an argument containing five different atomic propositions would require an ordinary truth table having thirty-two lines. The indirect truth table for such an argument, on the other hand, would usually require only a single line and could be constructed in a fraction of the time required for the ordinary truth table.

To construct an indirect truth table for an argument, we begin by assuming that the argument is invalid. That is, we assume that it is possible for the premises to be true and the conclusion false. Truth values corresponding to true premises and false conclusion are entered beneath the symbols corresponding to the premises and conclusion. Then, working backward, the truth values of the separate components are derived. If no contradiction is obtained in the process, this means that it is indeed possible for the premises to be true and the conclusion false, as originally assumed, so the argument is therefore invalid. If, however, the attempt to make the premises true and the conclusion false leads to a contradiction, it is not possible for the premises to be true and the conclusion false, in which case the argument is valid. Consider the following symbolized argument:

$$\sim A \supset (B \lor C)$$
$$\underline{\sim B}$$
$$C \supset A$$

We begin as before by writing the symbolized argument on a single line, placing a single slash between the premises and a double slash between the last premise and the conclusion. Then we assign T to the premises and F to the conclusion, thus:

$$\sim A \supset (B \lor C) \ / \ \sim B \ // \ C \supset A$$
$$\quad \text{T} \qquad\qquad \text{T} \qquad\quad \text{F}$$

We can now obtain the truth values of B, C, and A, as follows:

$$\sim A \supset (B \lor C) \ / \ \sim B \ // \ C \supset A$$
$$\quad \text{T} \qquad\qquad \text{T F} \qquad \text{T F F}$$

These truth values are now transferred to the first premise:

$$\sim A \supset (B \lor C) \ / \ \sim B \ // \ C \supset A$$
$$\text{T F T} \quad \text{F T T} \qquad \text{T F} \qquad \text{T F F}$$

We thus have a perfectly consistent assignment of truth values, which makes the premises true and the conclusion false. The argument is therefore invalid. If an ordinary truth table were constructed for this argument, it would be seen that the argument fails on the line on which A is false, B is false, and C is true. This is the exact arrangement presented in the indirect truth table above.

Here is another example. As always, we begin by assigning T to the premises and F to the conclusion:

$$A \supset (B \lor C) \ / \ B \supset D \ / \ A \ // \ \sim C \supset D$$
$$\quad \text{T} \qquad\qquad\quad \text{T} \qquad\quad \text{T} \qquad\quad \text{F}$$

From the conclusion we can now obtain the truth values of C and D, which are then transferred to the first two premises:

$$A \supset (B \lor C) \ / \ B \supset D \ / \ A \ // \ \sim C \supset D$$
$$\quad \text{T} \qquad \text{F} \qquad\quad \text{T F} \qquad \text{T} \qquad \text{T F F F}$$

The truth value of B is now obtained from the second premise and transferred, together with the truth value of A, to the first premise:

$$A \supset (B \lor C) \ / \ B \supset D \ / \ A \ // \ \sim C \supset D$$
$$\text{T T} \quad \text{F F F} \qquad \text{F T F} \qquad \text{T} \qquad \text{T F F F}$$

A contradiction now appears in the truth values assigned to the first

PROPOSITIONAL LOGIC

247

premise. A slash mark is put through the inconsistent truth value. These results show that it is impossible for the premises to be true and the conclusion false. The argument is therefore valid.

Sometimes a single row of truth values is not sufficient to prove an argument valid. Example:

$$\sim A \supset B \ / \ B \supset A \ / \ A \supset \sim B \ // \ A \cdot \sim B$$
$$ T T T F$$

Since a conditional statement can be true in any one of three ways, and a conjunctive statement can be false in any one of three ways, merely assigning truth to the premises and falsity to the conclusion of this argument is not sufficient to obtain the truth values of any of the component statements. When faced with a situation such as this, we must list all of the possible ways that one of the premises can be true or the conclusion false, and proceed from there. If we list all of the possible ways the conclusion may be false, we obtain the following:

$\sim A \supset B$	/	$B \supset A$	/	$A \supset \sim B$	//	$A \cdot \sim B$
T		T		T		T F F T
T		T		T		F F T F
T		T		T		F F F T

Extending the truth values of A and B to the premises, we obtain the following result:

$\sim A \supset B$	/	$B \supset A$	/	$A \supset \sim B$	//	$A \cdot \sim B$
T		T		T T̸ F T		T F F T
T F T̸ F		T		T		F F T F
T		T T̸ F		T		F F F T

Since a contradiction is obtained on each line, the argument is valid. If a contradiction had not been obtained on every line, the argument would, of course, be invalid, because it would be possible for the premises to be true and the conclusion false. Note that in this argument it is not necessary to fill out all the truth values on any one line to be forced into a contradiction. On each line the contradiction is obtained within the context of a single premise.

Two final reminders are in order about indirect truth tables. First, if a contradiction is obtained in the assignment of truth values, it is essential that every step leading to it be logically implied by some prior step. In other words, the contradiction must be unavoidable. If a contradiction is obtained after truth values are assigned haphazardly or by guessing, then nothing has been proved. The objective is not merely to reach a contradiction but to be *forced* into one.

A CONCISE INTRODUCTION TO LOGIC

For example, in the following indirect truth table a contradiction is apparent in the first premise:

$$A \supset B \quad / \quad C \supset B \quad // \quad A \supset C$$
$$T\ \cancel{T}\ F \qquad F\ T\ F \qquad T\ F\ F$$

Yet the argument is invalid. The contradiction that appears is not *required* by the assignment of truth to the premises and falsity to the conclusion. The following indirect truth table, which is done correctly, proves the argument invalid:

$$A \supset B \quad / \quad C \supset B \quad // \quad A \supset C$$
$$T\ T\ T \qquad F\ T\ T \qquad T\ F\ F$$

The second point to remember is that it is essential that identical letters be assigned identical truth values. For example, if the letter A appears three times in a certain symbolized argument and the truth value T is assigned to it in one occurrence, then the same truth value must be assigned to it in the other occurrences as well. After the truth table has been completed, each letter should be rechecked to ensure that one and the same truth value has been assigned to its various occurrences.

EXERCISE 6.6

Use indirect truth tables to determine whether the following arguments are valid or invalid:

★1. $B \equiv C$
$\underline{\sim C \supset \sim B}$

2. $\sim E \lor F$
$\underline{\sim E}$
$\sim F$

3. $\sim(I \equiv J)$
$\underline{\sim(I \supset J)}$

4. $P \supset (Q \supset R)$
$\underline{(P \cdot Q) \supset R}$

★5. $W \supset (X \supset Y)$
$\underline{X \supset (Y \supset Z)}$
$W \supset (X \supset Z)$

6. $A \supset (B \lor C)$
$C \supset (D \cdot E)$
$\underline{\sim B}$
$A \supset \sim E$

7. $G \supset H$
$H \supset I$
$\sim J \supset G$
$\underline{\sim I}$
J

8. $J \supset (\sim L \supset \sim K)$
$K \supset (\sim L \supset M)$
$\underline{(L \lor M) \supset N}$
$J \supset N$

9. $P \cdot (Q \lor R)$
$(P \cdot R) \supset \sim(S \lor T)$
$\underline{(\sim S \lor \sim T) \supset \sim(P \cdot Q)}$
$S \equiv T$

★10. $F \supset G$
$\sim H \lor I$
$(G \lor I) \supset J$
$\underline{\sim J}$
$\sim(F \lor H)$

11. $(A \lor B) \supset (C \cdot D)$
$\dfrac{(\sim A \lor \sim B) \supset E}{(\sim C \lor \sim D) \supset E}$

12. $(M \lor N) \supset O$
$O \supset (N \lor P)$
$M \supset (\sim Q \supset N)$
$\dfrac{(Q \supset M) \supset \sim P}{N \equiv O}$

13. $(A \lor B) \supset (C \cdot D)$
$(X \lor \sim Y) \supset (\sim C \cdot \sim W)$
$\dfrac{(X \lor Z) \supset (A \cdot E)}{\sim X}$

14. $\sim G \supset (\sim H \cdot \sim I)$
$J \supset H$
$K \supset (L \cdot M)$
$\dfrac{K \lor J}{L \cdot G}$

★15. $N \lor \sim O$
$P \lor O$
$P \supset Q$
$(N \lor Q) \supset (R \cdot S)$
$S \supset (R \supset T)$
$\dfrac{O \supset (T \supset U)}{U}$

7

NATURAL DEDUCTION IN PROPOSITIONAL LOGIC

7.1 RULES OF IMPLICATION I

Natural deduction is a method for establishing the validity of propositional type arguments that is both simpler and more enlightening than the method of truth tables. By means of this method, the conclusion of an argument is actually derived from the premises through a series of discrete steps. In this respect natural deduction resembles the method used in geometry to derive theorems relating to lines and figures; but whereas each step in a geometrical proof depends on some mathematical principle, each step in a logical proof depends on a **rule of inference.** Eighteen rules of inference will be set forth in this chapter. The first four should be familiar from the previous chapter:

1. *Modus ponens* (MP):

$$p \supset q$$
$$\underline{p}$$
$$q$$

2. *Modus tollens* (MT):

$$p \supset q$$
$$\underline{\sim q}$$
$$\sim p$$

3. Hypothetical syllogism (HS):

$$p \supset q$$
$$\underline{q \supset r}$$
$$p \supset r$$

4. Disjunctive syllogism (DS):

$$p \vee q$$
$$\underline{\sim p}$$
$$q$$

For an illustration of the use of three of these rules, consider the following argument:

> If the Astros win the playoff, then the Braves will lose the pennant. If the Astros do not win the playoff, then either Connolly or Davis will be fired. The Braves will not lose the pennant. Furthermore, Connolly will not be fired. Therefore, Davis will be fired.

The first step is to symbolize the argument, numbering the premises and writing the conclusion to the right of the last premise, separated by a slash mark:

1. $A \supset B$
2. $\sim A \supset (C \lor D)$
3. $\sim B$
4. $\sim C$ / D

The conclusion is now derived from the premises via steps 5 through 7. The justification for each line is written to the immediate right:

5. $\sim A$ 1, 3, MT
6. $C \lor D$ 2, 5, MP
7. D 4, 6, DS

Line 5 is obtained from lines 1 and 3 via *modus tollens*. In other words, when A and B in these lines are substituted respectively for the p and q of the *modus tollens* rule, line 5 follows as the conclusion. Then, when $\sim A$ and $C \lor D$ in lines 2 and 5 are substituted respectively for the p and q of the *modus ponens* rule, line 6 follows as the conclusion. Finally, when C and D in lines 4 and 6 are substituted respectively for the p and q of the disjunctive syllogism rule, line 7 follows as the final conclusion. These lines constitute a valid derivation of the conclusion from the premises because each line is a substitution instance of a valid argument form.

Here is an example of another completed proof. The conclusion to be obtained is written to the right of the last premise (line 4). Lines 5 through 7 are used to derive the conclusion:

1. $F \supset G$
2. $F \lor H$
3. $\sim G$
4. $H \supset (G \supset I)$ / $F \supset I$
5. $\sim F$ 1, 3, MT
6. H 2, 5, DS
7. $G \supset I$ 4, 6, MP
8. $F \supset I$ 1, 7, HS

When the letters in lines 1 and 3 are substituted into the *modus tollens* rule, line 5 is obtained. Then, when the letters in lines 2 and 5 are substituted into the disjunctive syllogism rule, line 6 is obtained. Line 7 is obtained by substituting H and $G \supset I$ from lines 4 and 6 into the *modus ponens* rule. Finally, line 8 is obtained by substituting the letters in lines 1 and 7 into the hypothetical syllogism rule. Notice that the conclusion, stated to the right of line 4, is not (and never is) part of the proof. It merely indicates what the proof is supposed to yield in the end.

The successful use of natural deduction to derive a conclusion from one or more premises depends on the ability of the reasoner to visualize more or less complex arrangements of atomic propositions as instances of the basic rules of inference. Here is a slightly more complex example:

1. $\sim (A \cdot B) \vee [\sim (E \cdot F) \supset (C \supset D)]$
2. $\sim\sim (A \cdot B)$
3. $\sim (E \cdot F)$
4. $D \supset G$ / $C \supset G$
5. $\sim (E \cdot F) \supset (C \supset D)$ 1, 2, DS
6. $C \supset D$ 3, 5, MP
7. $C \supset G$ 4, 6, HS

Line 4 is the last premise. To obtain line 5, $\sim (A \cdot B)$ and $[\sim (E \cdot F) \supset (C \supset D)]$ are substituted respectively for the p and q of the disjunctive syllogism rule, yielding $[\sim (E \cdot F) \supset (C \supset D)]$ as the conclusion. Next, $\sim (E \cdot F)$ and $C \supset D$ are substituted respectively for the p and q of *modus ponens*, yielding $C \supset D$ on line 6. Finally, lines 6 and 4 are combined to yield line 7 via the hypothetical syllogism rule.

The proofs that we have investigated thus far have been presented in ready-made form. We turn now to the question of how the various lines are obtained, leading in the end to the conclusion. What strategy is used in deriving these lines? While the answer is somewhat complex, there are a few basic rules of thumb that should be followed. Always begin by looking at the conclusion and by then attempting to locate the conclusion in the premises. Let us suppose that the conclusion is a single letter L. We begin by looking for L in the premises. Let us suppose we find it in a premise that reads:

$$K \supset L$$

Immediately we see that we can obtain L via *modus ponens* if we first obtain K. We now begin searching for K. Let us suppose that we find K in another premise that reads

$$J \vee K$$

From this we see that we could obtain K via disjunctive syllogism if we first obtain $\sim J$. The process continues until we isolate the required statement on a line by itself. Let us suppose that we find $\sim J$ on a line by itself. The thought process is then complete, and the various steps may be written out in the reverse order in which they were obtained mentally. The proof would look like this:

1. $\sim J$
2. $J \vee K$
3. $K \supset L$ / L
4. K 1, 2, DS
5. L 3, 4, MP

Turning now to a different example, let us suppose that the conclusion is the conditional statement $R \supset U$. We begin by attempting to locate $R \supset U$ in the premises. If we cannot find it, we look for its separate components, R and U. Let us suppose we find R in the antecedent of the conditional statement

$$R \supset S$$

Furthermore, let us suppose we find U in the consequent of the conditional statement

$$T \supset U$$

We then see that we can obtain $R \supset U$ via a series of hypothetical syllogism steps if we first obtain $S \supset T$. Let us suppose that we find $S \supset T$ on a line by itself. The proof has now been completely thought through and may be written out as follows:

1. $S \supset T$
2. $T \supset U$
3. $R \supset S$ / $R \supset U$
4. $R \supset T$ 1, 3, HS
5. $R \supset U$ 2, 4, HS

At this point a word of caution is in order about the meaning of a proposition being "obtained." Let us suppose that we are searching for E and we find it in a premise that reads $E \supset F$. The mere fact that we have located the letter E in this line does not mean that we have obtained E. $E \supset F$ means that *if* we have E, then we have F; it does *not* mean that we *have* either E or F. From such a line we could obtain F (via *modus ponens*) if we first obtain E, or, we could obtain $\sim E$ (via *modus tollens*) if we first obtain $\sim F$. $E \supset F$ by itself gives us nothing, and even if we combine it with other lines, there is no way that we could ever obtain E from such a line.

Here is a sample argument:

1. $A \vee B$
2. $\sim C \supset \sim A$
3. $C \supset D$
4. $\sim D$ / B

We begin by searching for B in the premises. Finding it in line 1, we see that it can be obtained via disjunctive syllogism if we first obtain $\sim A$. This in turn can be gotten from line 2 via *modus ponens* if we first obtain $\sim C$, and this can be gotten from line 3 via *modus tollens* once $\sim D$ is obtained. Happily, the latter is stated by itself on line 4. The proof has now been completely thought through and can be written out as follows:

1. $A \vee B$
2. $\sim C \supset \sim A$
3. $C \supset D$
4. $\sim D$ / B
5. $\sim C$ 3, 4, MT
6. $\sim A$ 2, 5, MP
7. B 1, 6, DS

Another example:

1. $E \supset (K \supset L)$
2. $F \supset (L \supset M)$
3. $G \vee E$
4. $\sim G$
5. F / $K \supset M$

We begin by searching for $K \supset M$ in the premises. Not finding it, we search for the separate components, K and M, and locate them in lines 1 and 2. The fact that K appears in the antecedent of a conditional statement, and M in the consequent of another, immediately suggests hypothetical syllogism. But first we must obtain these conditional statements on lines by themselves. We can obtain $K \supset L$ via *modus ponens* if we first obtain E. This, in turn, we can obtain from line 3 via disjunctive syllogism if we first obtain $\sim G$. Since $\sim G$ appears by itself on line 4, the first part of the thought process is now complete. The second part requires that we obtain $L \supset M$. This we can get from line 2 via *modus ponens* if we can get F, and we do have F by itself on line 5. All of the steps leading to the conclusion have now been thought through, and the proof can be written out:

1. $E \supset (K \supset L)$
2. $F \supset (L \supset M)$
3. $G \vee E$

4. ~G
5. F   / K ⊃ M
6. E   3, 4, DS
7. K ⊃ L   1, 6, MP
8. L ⊃ M   2, 5, MP
9. K ⊃ M   7, 8, HS

The thought process behind these proofs illustrates an important point about the construction of proofs by natural deduction. As a rule, we should never write down a line in a proof unless we know why we are doing it and where it leads. Typically, good proofs are not produced haphazardly or by luck; rather, they are produced by organized logical thinking. Occasionally, of course, we may be baffled by an especially difficult proof, and random deductive steps noted on the side may be useful. But we should not commence the actual writing out of the proof until we have used logical thinking to discover the path leading to the conclusion.

EXERCISE 7.1

I. Supply the required justification for the derived steps in the following proofs. No justification, of course, is required for the premises. The last premise is always the line adjacent to the required conclusion.

★(1) 1. $J \supset (K \supset L)$
    2. $L \vee J$
    3. $\sim L$ / $\sim K$
    4. J _____
    5. $K \supset L$ _____
    6. $\sim K$ _____

(2) 1. $\sim(S \equiv T) \supset (\sim P \supset Q)$
    2. $(S \equiv T) \supset P$
    3. $\sim P$ / Q
    4. $\sim(S \equiv T)$ _____
    5. $\sim P \supset Q$ _____
    6. Q _____

(3) 1. $\sim A \supset (B \supset \sim C)$
    2. $\sim D \supset (\sim C \supset A)$
    3. $D \vee \sim A$
    4. $\sim D$ / $\sim B$
    5. $\sim A$ _____
    6. $B \supset \sim C$ _____
    7. $\sim C \supset A$ _____
    8. $B \supset A$ _____
    9. $\sim B$ _____

(4) 1. ~G ⊃ [G v (S ⊃ G)]
    2. (S v L) ⊃ ~G
    3. S v L   / L
    4. ~G   ——————
    5. G v (S ⊃ G)   ——————
    6. S ⊃ G   ——————
    7. ~S   ——————
    8. L   ——————

(5) 1. H ⊃ [~E ⊃ (C ⊃ ~D)]
    2. ~D ⊃ E
    3. E v H
    4. ~E   / ~C
    5. H
    6. ~E ⊃ (C ⊃ ~D) ——————
    7. C ⊃ ~D   ——————
    8. C ⊃ E   ——————
    9. ~C   ——————

II. Use the first four rules of inference to derive the conclusions of the following symbolized arguments:

★(1) 1. F v (D ⊃ T)
    2. ~F
    3. D   / T

(2) 1. (K • B) v (L ⊃ E)
    2. ~(K • B)
    3. ~E   / ~L

(3) 1. P ⊃ (G ⊃ T)
    2. Q ⊃ (T ⊃ E)
    3. P
    4. Q   / G ⊃ E

(4) 1. ~W ⊃ [~W ⊃ (X ⊃ W)]
    2. ~W   / ~X

★(5) 1. ~S ⊃ D
    2. ~S v (~D ⊃ K)
    3. ~D   / K

(6) 1. A ⊃ (E ⊃ ~F)
    2. H v (~F ⊃ M)
    3. A
    4. ~H   / E ⊃ M

(7) 1. N ⊃ (J ⊃ P)
    2. (J ⊃ P) ⊃ (N ⊃ J)
    3. N   / P

(8) 1. G ⊃ [~O ⊃ (G ⊃ D)]
    2. O v G
    3. ~O   / D

NATURAL DEDUCTION IN PROPOSITIONAL LOGIC   **257**

(9) 1. $\sim M \lor (B \lor \sim T)$
2. $B \supset W$
3. $\sim \sim M$
4. $\sim W$ / $\sim T$

★(10) 1. $(L \equiv N) \supset C$
2. $(L \equiv N) \lor (P \supset \sim E)$
3. $\sim E \supset C$
4. $\sim C$ / $\sim P$

(11) 1. $\sim J \supset [\sim A \supset (D \supset A)]$
2. $J \lor \sim A$
3. $\sim J$ / $\sim D$

(12) 1. $(B \supset \sim M) \supset (T \supset \sim S)$
2. $B \supset K$
3. $K \supset \sim M$
4. $\sim S \supset N$ / $T \supset N$

(13) 1. $(R \supset F) \supset [(R \supset \sim G) \supset (S \supset Q)]$
2. $(Q \supset F) \supset (R \supset Q)$
3. $\sim G \supset F$
4. $Q \supset \sim G$ / $S \supset F$

(14) 1. $\sim A \supset [A \lor (T \supset R)]$
2. $\sim R \supset [R \lor (A \supset R)]$
3. $(T \lor D) \supset \sim R$
4. $T \lor D$ / D

★(15) 1. $\sim N \supset [(B \supset D) \supset (N \lor \sim E)]$
2. $(B \supset E) \supset \sim N$
3. $B \supset D$
4. $D \supset E$ / $\sim D$

III. Translate the following arguments into symbolic form and use the first four rules of inference to derive the conclusion of each. The letters to be used for the atomic statements are given in parentheses after each exercise.

★1. If the Pirates lose their last game, then either the Cardinals or the Reds will take the pennant. The Pirates will lose their last game. Furthermore, the Cardinals will not take the pennant. Therefore, the Reds will take the pennant. (*P, C, R*)

2. If the Red Sox lose their fifth game, then the Orioles will move into first place. Either the Mariners will be rained out or the Orioles will not move into first place. The Mariners will not be rained out. Therefore, the Red Sox will not lose their fifth game. (*R, O, M*)

3. If the fact that the Tigers take the Triple Crown implies that the Royals do not win the most games, then the White Sox will finish with the most base hits only if the Brewers do not finish with the most stolen bases. The Tigers will have the highest team batting average only if the White Sox finish with the most base hits. If the White

Sox finish with the most base hits, then the Royals will not win the most games. Therefore, the Tigers will have the highest team batting average only if the Brewers do not finish with the most stolen bases. (T, R, W, B)

4. If the Padres finish last only if the Giants make the playoffs, then if the Giants make the playoffs, the Expos will finish with the most errors. The Expos will finish with the most errors unless the Padres' finishing last implies that the Giants make the playoffs. The Expos will not finish with the most errors. Therefore, the Padres will not finish last. (P, G, E)

★5. Either the Cubs will finish with the most homeruns or if the Dodgers lead in defense the Phillies will have the most base hits. The Braves will not finish with the most double plays unless the Phillies' having the most base hits implies that the Astros do not get the most shutouts. The Cubs will not finish with the most homeruns. In addition, it is not the case that the Braves will not finish with the most double plays. Therefore, the Astros will not get the most shutouts if the Dodgers lead in defense. (C, D, P, B, A)

6. Either the Rangers will not earn the highest batting average, or the Angels will have the most complete games unless the Twins do not lead in homeruns. The Angels will have the most complete games if the Rangers do not earn the highest batting average. But the Angels will not have the most complete games. Therefore, the Twins will not lead in homeruns. (R, A, T)

7. If both the Yankees and the Bluejays win their next game, then the A's will finish with the most strikeouts if and only if the Indians finish with the most RBI's. The Orioles will finish with the highest batting average unless both the Yankees and the Bluejays win their next game. The Orioles will not finish with the highest batting average. Therefore, the A's will finish with the most strikeouts if and only if the Indians finish with the most RBI's. (Y, B, A, I, O)

8. Either the Cardinals and the Astros will lose their next game or the Pirates and the Dodgers will make the playoffs. If the Mets' not getting the most base hits implies that the Expos finish with the most homeruns, then it is not the case that both the Cardinals and the Astros will lose their next game. The Braves will have the lowest team ERA if the Mets do not get the most base hits. Furthermore, the Expos will finish with the most homeruns if the Braves have the lowest team ERA. Therefore, both the Pirates and the Dodgers will make the playoffs. (C, A, P, D, M, E, B)

9. If the Royals lead the league in fielding percentage only if the Angels do not get a homerun in tomorrow's game, then either the Mariners or the Twins will have the most errors. The Yankees will have the most stolen bases if the Royals lead the league in fielding percentage. Furthermore, the Yankees will have the most stolen bases only if the Angels do not get a homerun in tomorrow's game. The Mariners will

not have the most errors. Therefore, the Twins will have the most errors. (*R, A, M, T, Y*)

★10. If the Tigers do not win the pennant then either the Tigers will win it or if the Rangers finish second the Brewers will lose their last game. If the Tigers win the pennant, then both the Indians will finish last and the A's will not have the best batting average. It is not the case that both the Indians will finish last and the A's will not have the best batting average. Moreover, the Brewers will not lose their last game. Therefore, the Rangers will not finish second. (*T, R, B, I, A*)

7.2 RULES OF IMPLICATION II

Four additional rules of inference are listed below. Constructive dilemma should be familiar from Chapter 6. The other three are new.*

5. Constructive dilemma (CD):

$$(p \supset q) \cdot (r \supset s)$$
$$\underline{p \vee r}$$
$$q \vee s$$

6. Simplification (Simp):

$$\underline{p \cdot q}$$
$$p$$

7. Conjunction (Conj):

$$p$$
$$\underline{q}$$
$$p \cdot q$$

8. Addition (Add):

$$\underline{p}$$
$$p \vee q$$

Like the previous four rules, these four are fairly easy to understand, but if there is any doubt about them their validity may be proven by means of a truth table.

Constructive dilemma involves two *modus ponens* steps. The first premise states that if we have *p* then we have *q*, and if we have *r* then we have *s*. But since, by the second premise, we do have either *p* or *r*, it follows by *modus ponens* that we have either *q* or *s*. Constructive dilemma is the only form of dilemma that will be included as a rule of inference. By the rule of transposition, which will be presented in Section 7.4, any argument that is a substitution instance of the destructive dilemma form can be easily converted into a substitution instance of constructive dilemma. Destructive dilemma, therefore, is not needed as a rule of inference.

Simplification states that if two propositions are given as true on a single line, then each of them is true separately. According to the strict interpretation of the simplification rule, only the left-hand conjunct may be stated in the conclusion. Once the commutativity rule for conjunction has been presented, however (see Section 7.3), we will be justified in

---

*Some texts include a rule called "absorption" by which the statement form $p \supset (q \cdot p)$ is deduced from $p \supset q$. This rule is necessary only if conditional proof is not presented. This text opts in favor of conditional proof.

replacing a statement such as $H \cdot K$ with $K \cdot H$. Having done this, the K now appears on the left, and the appropriate conclusion is K.

Conjunction states that two propositions—for example, H and K—asserted separately on different lines may be conjoined on a single line. The two propositions may be conjoined in whatever order we choose (either $H \cdot K$ or $K \cdot H$) without appeal to the commutativity rule for conjunction.

Addition states that whenever a proposition is asserted on a line by itself it may be joined disjunctively with any proposition we choose. In other words, if G is asserted to be true by itself, it follows that $G \vee H$ is true. This may appear somewhat puzzling at first, but once one realizes that $G \vee H$ is a much weaker statement than G by itself, the puzzlement should disappear. The new proposition must, of course, always be joined disjunctively (not conjunctively) to the given proposition. If G is stated on a line by itself, we are *not* justified in writing $G \cdot H$ as a consequence of addition.

The use of these four rules may now be illustrated. Consider the following argument form:

1. $A \supset B$
2. $(B \vee C) \supset (D \cdot E)$
3. A $/ D$

As usual, we begin by looking for the conclusion in the premises. D appears in the consequent of the second premise, which we can obtain via simplification if we first obtain $B \vee C$. This expression as such does not appear in the premises, but from lines 1 and 3 we see that we can obtain B by itself via *modus ponens*. Having obtained B, we can get $B \vee C$ via addition. The proof has now been thought through, and can be written out as follows:

1. $A \supset B$
2. $(B \vee C) \supset (D \cdot E)$
3. A $/ D$
4. B 1, 3, MP
5. $B \vee C$ 4, Add
6. $D \cdot E$ 2, 5, MP
7. D 6, Simp

Another example:

1. $K \supset L$
2. $(M \supset N) \cdot S$
3. $N \supset T$
4. $K \vee M$ $/ L \vee T$

Seeing that $L \vee T$ does not appear as such in the premises, we look for

NATURAL DEDUCTION IN PROPOSITIONAL LOGIC   **261**

the separate components. Finding L and T as the consequents of two distinct conditional statements causes us to think that the conclusion can be obtained via the constructive dilemma. If a constructive dilemma can be set up, it will need a disjunctive statement as its second premise, and such a statement appears on line 4. Furthermore, the components of this statement, K and M, each appear as the antecedent of a conditional statement, exactly as they should for a dilemma. The only statement that is missing now is $M \supset T$. Inspecting line 2 we see that we can obtain $M \supset N$ via simplification, and putting this together with line 3 gives us $M \supset T$ via hypothetical syllogism. The completed proof may now be written out.

1. $K \supset L$
2. $(M \supset N) \cdot S$
3. $N \supset T$
4. $K \vee M$ $/ L \vee T$
5. $M \supset N$ 2, Simp
6. $M \supset T$ 3, 5, HS
7. $(K \supset L) \cdot (M \supset T)$ 1, 6, Conj
8. $L \vee T$ 4, 7, CD

Another example:

1. $\sim M \cdot N$
2. $P \supset M$
3. $Q \cdot R$
4. $(\sim P \cdot Q) \supset S$ $/ S \vee T$

When we look for $S \vee T$ in the premises we find S in the consequent of line 4, but no T at all. This signals an important principle: Whenever the conclusion of an argument contains a letter not found in the premises, addition must be used to introduce the missing letter. Addition is the *only* rule of inference that can introduce new letters. To introduce T by addition, however, we must first obtain S on a line by itself. S can be obtained from line 4 via *modus ponens* if we first obtain $\sim P \cdot Q$. This, in turn, can be gotten via conjunction, but first $\sim P$ and Q must be obtained individually on separate lines. Q can be obtained from line 3 via simplication and $\sim P$ from line 2 via *modus tollens,* but the latter step requires that we first obtain $\sim M$ on a line by itself. Since this can be gotten from line 1 via simplification, the proof is now complete. It may be written out as follows:

1. $\sim M \cdot N$
2. $P \supset M$
3. $Q \cdot R$
4. $(\sim P \cdot Q) \supset S$ $/ S \vee T$
5. $\sim M$ 1, Simp

6. ~P	2, 5, MT
7. Q	3, Simp
8. ~P • Q	6, 7, Conj
9. S	4, 8, MP
10. S v T	9, Add

Addition is used together with disjunctive syllogism to derive the conclusion of arguments having contradictory premises. As we saw in Chapter 6, such arguments are always valid. The procedure is illustrated as follows:

1. S	
2. ~S	/ T
3. S v T	1, Add
4. T	2, 3, DS

With arguments of this sort the conclusion is always introduced via addition and then separated via disjunctive syllogism. Since addition can be used to introduce any letter or arrangement of letters we choose, it should be clear from this example that inconsistent premises validly entail any conclusion whatever.

To complete this presentation of the eight rules of implication, let us consider some of the typical ways in which they are *misapplied*. Examples are as follows:

1. $A \supset (B \supset C)$
2. B

_____

3. C 1, 2, MP (invalid—$B \supset C$ must first be obtained on a line by itself)

1. $P \lor (S \cdot T)$

_____

2. S 1, Simp (invalid—$S \cdot T$ must first be obtained on a line by itself)

1. K

_____

2. $K \cdot L$ 1, Add (invalid—the correct form of addition is "$K \lor L$")

1. $M \lor N$

_____

2. M 1, Simp (invalid—simplification is possible only with conjunctive premise; line 1 is a disjunction)

1. $G \supset H$

_____

2. $G \supset (H \lor J)$ 1, Add (improper—J must be added to the whole line, not just to the consequent: $(G \supset H) \lor J$)

1. $(W \supset X) \supset Y$
2. $\sim X$

_____

3. $\sim W$ 1, 2, MT (invalid—$W \supset X$ must first be obtained on a line by itself)

1. $L \supset M$
2. $L \supset N$
———————
3. $M \cdot N$ 1, 2, Conj (invalid—M and N must first
                           be obtained on lines by themselves)

1. $\sim(P \cdot Q)$
———————
2. $\sim P$ 1, Simp (invalid—parentheses must be
                           removed first)

1. $\sim(P \vee Q)$
2. $\sim P$
———————
3. $\sim Q$ 1, 2, DS (invalid—parentheses must be
                           removed first)

Regarding the last two examples, a rule will be presented in the next section (DeMorgan's Rule) that will allow us to remove parentheses preceded by negation signs. But even after the parentheses have been removed from these examples, the inferences remain invalid.

EXERCISE 7.2

I. Supply the required justification for the derived steps in the following proofs:

★(1)   1. $(\sim M \cdot \sim N) \supset [(\sim M \vee H) \supset (K \cdot L)]$
       2. $\sim M \cdot (C \supset D)$
       3. $\sim N \cdot (F \equiv G)$ / $K \cdot \sim N$
       4. $\sim M$ ————
       5. $\sim N$ ————
       6. $\sim M \cdot \sim N$ ————
       7. $(\sim M \vee H) \supset (K \cdot L)$ ————
       8. $\sim M \vee H$ ————
       9. $K \cdot L$ ————
     10. K ————
     11. $K \cdot \sim N$ ————

(2)   1. $(P \vee S) \supset (E \supset F)$
       2. $(P \vee T) \supset (G \supset H)$
       3. $(P \vee U) \supset (E \vee G)$
       4. P / $F \vee H$
       5. $P \vee S$ ————
       6. $E \supset F$ ————
       7. $P \vee T$ ————
       8. $G \supset H$ ————
       9. $P \vee U$ ————
     10. $E \vee G$ ————
     11. $(E \supset F) \cdot (G \supset H)$ ————
     12. $F \vee H$ ————

(3) 1. $(S \supset Q) \cdot (Q \supset {\sim}S)$
  2. $S \vee Q$
  3. ${\sim}Q$ / $P \cdot R$
  4. $Q \vee {\sim}S$ _____
  5. ${\sim}S$ _____
  6. Q _____
  7. $Q \vee (P \cdot R)$ _____
  8. $P \cdot R$ _____

(4) 1. $(D \supset B) \cdot (C \supset D)$
  2. $(B \supset D) \cdot (E \supset C)$
  3. $B \vee E$ / $D \vee B$
  4. $D \vee C$ _____
  5. $B \vee D$ _____
  6. $B \supset D$ _____
  7. $D \supset B$ _____
  8. $(B \supset D) \cdot (D \supset B)$ _____
  9. $D \vee B$ _____

(5) 1. $(R \supset H) \cdot (S \supset I)$
  2. $({\sim}H \cdot {\sim}L) \supset (R \vee S)$
  3. ${\sim}H \cdot (K \supset T)$
  4. $H \vee {\sim}L$ / $I \vee M$
  5. ${\sim}H$ _____
  6. ${\sim}L$ _____
  7. ${\sim}H \cdot {\sim}L$ _____
  8. $R \vee S$ _____
  9. $H \vee I$ _____
  10. I _____
  11. $I \vee M$ _____

II. Use the first eight rules of inference to derive the conclusions of the following symbolized arguments:

★(1) 1. ${\sim}M \supset Q$
  2. $R \supset {\sim}T$
  3. ${\sim}M \vee R$ / $Q \vee {\sim}T$

(2) 1. $E \supset (A \cdot C)$
  2. $A \supset (F \cdot E)$
  3. E / F

(3) 1. $G \supset (S \cdot T)$
  2. $(S \vee T) \supset J$
  3. G / J

(4) 1. $(L \vee T) \supset (B \cdot G)$
  2. $L \cdot (K \equiv R)$ / $L \cdot B$

★(5) 1. $({\sim}F \vee X) \supset (P \vee T)$
  2. $F \supset P$
  3. ${\sim}P$ / T

(6) 1. $(N \supset B) \cdot (O \supset C)$
  2. $Q \supset (N \vee O)$
  3. Q / $B \vee C$

(7) 1. $(U \vee W) \supset (T \supset R)$
  2. $U \cdot H$
  3. ${\sim}R \cdot {\sim}J$ / $U \cdot {\sim}T$

(8) 1. $(D \vee E) \supset (G \cdot H)$
  2. $G \supset {\sim}D$
  3. $D \cdot F$ / M

NATURAL DEDUCTION IN PROPOSITIONAL LOGIC   **265**

(9) 1. $(B \lor F) \supset (A \supset G)$
2. $(B \lor E) \supset (G \supset K)$
3. $B \cdot \sim H$ $\quad / A \supset K$

★(10) 1. $(P \supset R) \supset (M \supset P)$
2. $(P \lor M) \supset (P \supset R)$
3. $P \lor M$ $\quad / R \lor P$

(11) 1. $(C \supset N) \cdot E$
2. $D \lor (N \supset D)$
3. $\sim D$ $\quad / \sim C \lor P$

(12) 1. $[A \lor (K \cdot J)] \supset (\sim E \cdot \sim F)$
2. $M \supset [A \cdot (P \lor R)]$
3. $M \cdot U$ $\quad / \sim E \cdot A$

(13) 1. $\sim H \supset (\sim T \supset R)$
2. $H \lor (E \supset F)$
3. $\sim T \lor E$
4. $\sim H \cdot D$ $\quad / R \lor F$

(14) 1. $(U \cdot \sim\sim\sim P) \supset Q$
2. $\sim O \supset U$
3. $\sim P \supset O$
4. $\sim O \cdot T$ $\quad / Q$

★(15) 1. $(M \lor N) \supset (F \supset G)$
2. $D \supset \sim C$
3. $\sim C \supset B$
4. $M \cdot H$
5. $D \lor F$ $\quad / B \lor G$

(16) 1. $(F \cdot M) \supset (S \lor T)$
2. $(\sim S \lor A) \supset F$
3. $(\sim S \lor B) \supset M$
4. $\sim S \cdot G$ $\quad / T$

(17) 1. $(\sim K \cdot \sim N) \supset$
$\quad [(\sim P \supset K) \cdot (\sim R \supset G)]$
2. $K \supset N$
3. $\sim N \cdot B$
4. $\sim P \lor \sim R$ $\quad / G$

(18) 1. $(\sim A \lor D) \supset (B \supset F)$
2. $(B \lor C) \supset (A \supset E)$
3. $A \lor B$
4. $\sim A$ $\quad / E \lor F$

(19) 1. $(J \supset K) \cdot (\sim O \supset \sim P)$
2. $(L \supset J) \cdot (\sim M \supset \sim O)$
3. $\sim K \supset (L \lor \sim M)$
4. $\sim K \cdot G$ $\quad / \sim P$

★(20) 1. $(W \cdot X) \supset (Q \lor R)$
2. $(S \lor F) \supset (Q \lor W)$
3. $(S \lor G) \supset (\sim Q \supset X)$
4. $Q \lor S$
5. $\sim Q \cdot H$ $\quad / R$

III. Translate the following arguments into symbolic form and use the first eight rules of inference to derive the conclusion of each:

★1. Fiat will increase American sales only if both Datsun and Chrysler increase European sales. Both Fiat and Volvo will increase American sales. Therefore, either Datsun will increase European sales or General Motors will suffer a strike. (F, D, C, V, G)

2. Either Volkswagen or Porsche will merge with a competitor if either Leyland or Saab introduces a new model. Leyland will introduce a new model and BMW will curtail exports. If Volkswagen merges with a competitor, then Renault will reduce production, and if Porsche merges with a competitor, then Chrysler will reorganize. Therefore, Renault will reduce production unless Chrysler reorganizes. (V, P, L, S, B, R, C)

3. If American Motors withstands a takeover and Ford does not curtail exports, then Ford will curtail exports unless General Motors shows a profit. American Motors will withstand a takeover. Ford will not curtail exports. Therefore, General Motors will show a profit. (A, F, G)

4. Either BMW or Mercedes will reduce employment. Both Leyland and Fiat will increase European sales if either Mercedes reduces employment or Fiat increases European sales. BMW will not reduce employment. Therefore, Leyland will increase European sales. (B, M, L, F)

★5. If Citroen gets bought out, then if either Saab or Fiat issues additional stock, then Datsun will curtail exports. Datsun will not curtail exports if either Citroen or Renault gets bought out. Citroen will get bought out. Therefore, it is not the case that either Saab or Fiat will issue additional stock. (C, S, F, D, R)

6. If either Mercedes or Porsche shows a profit, then Ford will take over a competitor only if Chrysler reorganizes and American Motors will introduce a new model only if BMW curtails exports. If either Mercedes shows a profit or Ford takes over a competitor, then Ford will take over a competitor unless American Motors introduces a new model. Both Mercedes and Porsche will show a profit. Therefore, Chrysler will reorganize unless BMW curtails exports. (M, P, F, C, A, B)

7. If either Toyota does not drop an old model or Subaru changes management, then if Toyota does not drop an old model Datsun will modernize production. Toyota will drop an old model unless Datsun does not modernize production. Toyota will not drop an old model. Therefore, American Motors will merge with a competitor. (T, S, D, A)

8. If either Saab or Renault modernizes production, then both BMW and Mercedes will introduce a new model. Ford will increase exports only if Saab modernizes production, and General Motors will increase exports only if Renault modernizes production. Either Ford or General Motors will increase exports, and Volvo will change management. Therefore, BMW will introduce a new model. (S, R, B, M, F, G, V)

9. If either Ferarri merges with a competitor or Masserati does not increase American sales, then Lotus will not change management and Jaguar will increase European sales. Lotus will change management only if Ferrari merges with a competitor, and Porsche will not introduce a new model only if Masserati does not increase American sales. Lotus will change management unless Porsche does not introduce a new model. Therefore, Porsche will not introduce a new model. (F, M, L, J. P)

★10. Honda will sell its overseas facilities and either Toyota or Datsun will merge with a competitor. If both Honda and Volkswagen sell their overseas facilities, then if Honda sells its overseas facilities Fiat will reorganize. Volkswagen will sell its overseas facilities and Datsun will not merge with a competitor. Therefore, Fiat will reorganize. (H, T, D, V, F)

7.3 RULES OF REPLACEMENT I

The ten rules of replacement are stated in the form of logical equivalences. Underlying their use is an **axiom of replacement,** which asserts that within the context of a proof, logically equivalent expressions may replace one another. The first five rules of replacement are as follows:

9. DeMorgan's Rule (DM):

$$\sim(p \cdot q) \equiv (\sim p \vee \sim q)$$
$$\sim(p \vee q) \equiv (\sim p \cdot \sim q)$$

10. Commutativity (Com):

$$(p \vee q) \equiv (q \vee p)$$
$$(p \cdot q) \equiv (q \cdot p)$$

11. Associativity (Assoc):

$$[p \vee (q \vee r)] \equiv [(p \vee q) \vee r]$$
$$[p \cdot (q \cdot r)] \equiv [(p \cdot q) \cdot r]$$

12. Distribution (Dist):

$$[p \cdot (q \vee r)] \equiv [(p \cdot q) \vee (p \cdot r)]$$
$$[p \vee (q \cdot r)] \equiv [(p \vee q) \cdot (p \vee r)]$$

13. Double negation (DN):

$$p \equiv \sim\sim p$$

DeMorgan's Rule (named after the nineteenth-century logician Augustus DeMorgan) was discussed in Section 6.1 in connection with translation. There it was pointed out that "Not both p and q" is equivalent to "Not p or not q," and that "Not either p or q" is equivalent to "Not p and not q." When applying DeMorgan's Rule, one should keep in mind that it holds only for conjunction and disjunction (not for implication or equivalence). The rule may be summarized as follows: When moving a negation sign inside or outside a set of parentheses, "and" switches to "or," and conversely.

The **commutativity** rule asserts that the meaning of a conjunction or disjunction is unaffected by the order in which the components are listed. In other words, the component statements may be commuted, or switched for one another, without affecting the meaning. The validity of this rule should be immediately apparent.

The **associativity** rule states that the meaning of a conjunction or disjunction is unaffected by the placement of parentheses when the same connective is used throughout. In other words, the way in which the component propositions are grouped, or associated with one another, can be changed without affecting the meaning. The validity of this rule is quite easy to see, but if there is any doubt about it, it may be readily checked by means of a truth table.

The **distribution** rule, like DeMorgan's Rule, pertains only to conjunction and disjunction. In the first form of the rule, a statement is distributed through a disjunction, and in the second form, through a conjunction. While the rule may not be immediately obvious, it is easy to remember: The connective that is at first outside the parentheses goes inside, and the connective that is at first inside the parentheses goes outside.

The **double negation** rule is fairly obvious and needs little explanation. The rule states simply that pairs of negation signs immediately adjacent to one another may be either deleted or introduced without affecting the meaning of the statement.

There is an important difference between the rules of implication, treated in the first two sections of this chapter, and the rules of replacement. The **rules of implication** derive their name from the fact that each is an atomic argument form in which the premises imply the conclusion. To be applicable in natural deduction, certain lines in a proof must be interpreted as substitution instances of the argument form in question. Stated another way, the rules of implication are applicable only to *whole lines* in a proof. For example, step 3 in the following proof is not a legitimate application of *modus ponens,* because the first premise in the *modus ponens* rule is applied to only a *part* of line one.

1. $A \supset (B \supset C)$
2. B
3. C 1, 2 MP (incorrect)

The **rules of replacement,** on the other hand, are not rules of implication but rules of equivalence. Since, by the axiom of replacement, logically equivalent statement forms can always replace one another in a proof sequence, the rules of replacement can be applied either to a whole line or to any part of a line. Step 2 in the following proof is a quite legitimate application of DeMorgan's Rule, even though the rule is applied to only part of line 1:

1. $S \supset \sim(T \cdot U)$
2. $S \supset (\sim T \vee \sim U)$ 1, DM (valid)

Application of the first five rules of replacement may now be illustrated. Consider the following argument:

1. $A \supset \sim(B \cdot C)$
2. $A \cdot C$ / $\sim B$

Examining the premises, we find B in the consequent of line 1. This leads us to suspect that the conclusion can be obtained via *modus ponens.*

NATURAL DEDUCTION IN PROPOSITIONAL LOGIC   **269**

If this is correct, the negation sign would then have to be taken inside the parentheses via DeMorgan's Rule and the resulting $\sim C$ eliminated by disjunctive syllogism. The following completed proof indicates that this strategy yields the anticipated result:

$$
\begin{array}{lll}
1. & A \supset \sim(B \cdot C) & \\
2. & A \cdot C & /\ \sim B \\
3. & A & 2,\ \text{Simp} \\
4. & \sim(B \cdot C) & 1,\ 3,\ \text{MP} \\
5. & \sim B \vee \sim C & 4,\ \text{DM} \\
6. & C \cdot A & 2,\ \text{Com} \\
7. & C & 6,\ \text{Simp} \\
8. & \sim\sim C & 7,\ \text{DN} \\
9. & \sim C \vee \sim B & 5,\ \text{Com} \\
10. & \sim B & 8,\ 9,\ \text{DS}
\end{array}
$$

The rationale for line 6 is to get C on the left side so that it can be separated via simplification. Similarly, the rationale for line 9 is to get $\sim C$ on the left side so that it can be eliminated via disjunctive syllogism. Line 8 is required because, strictly speaking, the negation of $\sim C$ is $\sim\sim C$—not simply C. Thus, C must be replaced with $\sim\sim C$ to set up the disjunctive syllogism. For brevity, however, these steps may be combined together with other steps, as the following shortened proof illustrates:

$$
\begin{array}{lll}
1. & A \supset \sim(B \cdot C) & \\
2. & A \cdot C & /\ \sim B \\
3. & A & 2,\ \text{Simp} \\
4. & \sim(B \cdot C) & 1,\ 3,\ \text{MP} \\
5. & \sim B \vee \sim C & 4,\ \text{DM} \\
6. & C & 2,\ \text{Com, Simp} \\
7. & \sim B & 5,\ 6,\ \text{Com, DN, DS}
\end{array}
$$

Another example:

$$
\begin{array}{lll}
1. & D \cdot (E \vee F) & \\
2. & \sim D \vee \sim F & /\ D \cdot E
\end{array}
$$

The conclusion requires that we get D and E together. Inspection of the first premise suggests distribution as the first step in achieving this. The completed proof is as follows:

$$
\begin{array}{lll}
1. & D \cdot (E \vee F) & \\
2. & \sim D \vee \sim F & /\ D \cdot E \\
3. & (D \cdot E) \vee (D \cdot F) & 1,\ \text{Dist} \\
4. & \sim(D \cdot F) & 2,\ \text{DM} \\
5. & D \cdot E & 3,\ 4,\ \text{Com, DS}
\end{array}
$$

Sometimes it is useful to use distribution in the reverse manner. Consider this argument:

> 1. $(G \cdot H) \lor (G \cdot J)$
> 2. $(G \lor K) \supset L$ / L

The conclusion can be obtained from line 2 via *modus ponens* if we first obtain $G \lor K$ on a line by itself. Since K does not occur in the first premise at all, it must be introduced by addition. To do this requires in turn that we obtain G on a line by itself. Distribution applied to line 1 provides the solution:

> 1. $(G \cdot H) \lor (G \cdot J)$
> 2. $(G \lor K) \supset L$ / L
> 3. $G \cdot (H \lor J)$ 1, Dist
> 4. G 3, Simp
> 5. $G \lor K$ 4, Add
> 6. L 2, 5, MP

Application of the associativity rule is illustrated in the next proof:

> 1. $M \lor (N \lor O)$
> 2. $\sim O$ / $M \lor N$
> 3. $(M \lor N) \lor O$ 1, Assoc
> 4. $O \lor (M \lor N)$ 3, Com
> 5. $M \lor N$ 2, 4, DS

Before O can be eliminated via disjunctive syllogism from line 1, it must be moved over to the left side. Associativity and communtativity together accomplish this objective.

EXERCISE 7.3

I. Supply the required justifications for the derived steps in the following proofs:

★(1)   1. $(J \lor F) \lor M$
        2. $(J \lor M) \supset \sim P$
        3. $\sim F$ / $\sim(F \lor P)$
        4. $(F \lor J) \lor M$ _____
        5. $F \lor (J \lor M)$ _____
        6. $J \lor M$ _____
        7. $\sim P$ _____
        8. $\sim F \cdot \sim P$ _____
        9. $\sim(F \lor P)$ _____

(2) 1. $(K \cdot P) \lor (K \cdot Q)$
     2. $P \supset \sim K$ / $Q \lor T$
     3. $K \cdot (P \lor Q)$ _____
     4. K _____
     5. $\sim\sim K$ _____
     6. $\sim P$ _____
     7. $(P \lor Q) \cdot K$ _____
     8. $P \lor Q$ _____
     9. Q _____
   10. $Q \lor T$ _____

(3) 1. $E \lor \sim(D \lor C)$
     2. $(E \lor \sim D) \supset C$ / E
     3. $E \lor (\sim D \cdot \sim C)$ _____
     4. $(E \lor \sim D) \cdot (E \lor \sim C)$ _____
     5. $E \lor \sim D$ _____
     6. C _____
     7. $(E \lor \sim C) \cdot (E \lor \sim D)$ _____
     8. $E \lor \sim C$ _____
     9. $\sim C \lor E$ _____
   10. $\sim\sim C$ _____
   11. E _____

(4) 1. $(T \lor R) \lor P$
     2. $(T \lor P) \supset \sim S$
     3. $\sim R$ / $\sim(R \lor S)$
     4. $(R \lor T) \lor P$ _____
     5. $R \lor (T \lor P)$ _____
     6. $T \lor P$ _____
     7. $\sim S$ _____
     8. $\sim R \cdot \sim S$ _____
     9. $\sim(R \lor S)$ _____

(5) 1. $A \cdot (F \cdot L)$
     2. $A \supset (U \lor W)$
     3. $F \supset (U \lor X)$ / $U \lor (W \cdot X)$
     4. $(A \cdot F) \cdot L$ _____
     5. $A \cdot F$ _____
     6. A _____
     7. $U \lor W$ _____
     8. $F \cdot A$ _____
     9. F _____
   10. $U \lor X$ _____
   11. $(U \lor W) \cdot (U \lor X)$ _____
   12. $U \lor (W \cdot X)$ _____

II. Use the first thirteen rules of inference to derive the conclusions of the following symbolized arguments:

★(1) 1. $(\sim M \supset P) \cdot (\sim N \supset Q)$
    2. $\sim(M \cdot N)$ / $P \vee Q$

(2) 1. $J \vee (K \cdot L)$
    2. $\sim K$ / J

(3) 1. $R \supset \sim B$
    2. $D \vee R$
    3. B / D

(4) 1. $(O \vee M) \supset S$
    2. $\sim S$ / $\sim M$

★(5) 1. $Q \vee (L \vee C)$
    2. $\sim C$ / $L \vee Q$

(6) 1. $\sim(\sim E \cdot \sim N) \supset T$
    2. $G \supset (N \vee E)$ / $G \supset T$

(7) 1. $H \cdot (C \cdot T)$
    2. $\sim(\sim F \cdot T)$ / F

(8) 1. $(E \cdot I) \vee (M \cdot U)$
    2. $\sim E$ / M

(9) 1. $\sim(J \vee K)$
    2. $B \supset K$
    3. $S \supset B$ / $\sim S \cdot \sim J$

★(10) 1. $(G \cdot H) \vee (M \cdot G)$
    2. $G \supset (T \cdot A)$ / A

(11) 1. $(D \cdot S) \vee (C \cdot T)$
    2. $\sim T$ / S

(12) 1. $\sim(U \vee R)$
    2. $(\sim R \vee N) \supset (P \cdot H)$
    3. $Q \supset \sim H$ / $\sim Q$

(13) 1. $\sim(F \cdot A)$
    2. $\sim(L \vee \sim A)$
    3. $D \supset (F \vee L)$ / $\sim D$

(14) 1. $[(I \vee M) \vee G] \supset \sim G$
    2. $M \vee G$ / M

★(15) 1. $E \supset \sim B$
    2. $U \supset \sim C$
    3. $\sim(\sim E \cdot \sim U)$ / $\sim(B \cdot C)$

(16) 1. $\sim(K \vee F)$
    2. $\sim F \supset (K \vee C)$
    3. $(G \vee C) \supset \sim H$ / $\sim(K \vee H)$

(17) 1. $S \vee (I \cdot \sim J)$
    2. $S \supset \sim R$
    3. $\sim J \supset \sim Q$ / $\sim(R \cdot Q)$

(18) 1. $P \vee (I \cdot L)$
2. $(P \vee I) \supset \sim(L \vee C)$
3. $(P \cdot \sim C) \supset (E \cdot F)$ $/ F \vee D$

(19) 1. $B \vee (S \cdot N)$
2. $B \supset \sim S$
3. $S \supset \sim N$ $/ B \vee W$

★(20) 1. $(\sim M \vee E) \supset (S \supset U)$
2. $(\sim Q \vee E) \supset (U \supset H)$
3. $\sim(M \vee Q)$ $/ S \supset H$

(21) 1. $(\sim R \vee D) \supset \sim(F \cdot G)$
2. $(F \cdot R) \supset S$
3. $F \cdot \sim S$ $/ \sim(S \vee G)$

(22) 1. $\sim Q \supset (C \cdot B)$
2. $\sim T \supset (B \cdot H)$
3. $\sim(Q \cdot T)$ $/ B$

(23) 1. $\sim(A \cdot G)$
2. $\sim(A \cdot E)$
3. $G \vee E$ $/ \sim(A \cdot F)$

(24) 1. $(M \cdot N) \vee (O \cdot P)$
2. $(N \vee O) \supset \sim P$ $/ N$

★(25) 1. $(T \cdot K) \vee (C \cdot E)$
2. $K \supset \sim E$
3. $E \supset \sim C$ $/ T \cdot K$

III. Translate the following arguments into symbolic form and use the first thirteen rules of inference to derive the conclusion of each:

★1. Either Mexico will continue to develop its oil reserves and Panama will expand shrimp production, or Mexico will continue to develop its oil reserves and Honduras will suffer a banana failure. If Mexico continues to develop its oil reserves, then both Jamaica and the Dominican Republic will boost sugar production. Therefore, Mexico will continue to develop its oil reserves and the Dominican Republic will boost sugar production. (M, P, H, J, D)

2. Either Colombia will raise the price of coffee and Ecuador will not reduce oil production, or Brazil will mechanize gold recovery on the Amazon and Ecuador will not reduce oil production. If Paraguay increases soybean exports, then Ecuador will reduce oil production. Therefore, Paraguay will not increase soybean exports. (C, E, B, P)

3. It is not the case that either Cuba will continue to promote revolution abroad or El Salvador will experience a coup. If it is not the case that

both Cuba will continue to promote revolution abroad and Haiti will contend with illiteracy, then either El Salvador will experience a coup or Jamaica will inflate rum prices. Therefore, Jamaica will inflate rum prices. (C, E, H, J)

4. Guyana will subsidize diamond mining unless both Peru and Bolivia reduce silver exports. If either Guyana subsidizes diamond mining or Bolivia reduces silver exports, then Peru will not reduce silver exports. Therefore, Guyana will subsidize diamond mining unless Cuba undergoes a revolution. (G, P, B, C)

★5. Both Mexico and the Bahamas will fail to check unemployment; also, Uruguay will continue a policy of political repression. If Uruguay continues a policy of political repression and Mexico fails to check unemployment, then it is not the case that both the Bahamas will fail to check unemployment and Colombia will curb population growth. Therefore, Mexico will fail to check unemployment and Colombia will not curb population growth. (M, B, U, C)

6. If Bolivia expands tin production, then both Peru and Chile will reduce copper exports. Furthermore, if Argentina reduces beef prices, then both Guatemala and El Salvador will increase coffee production. Either Bolivia will expand tin production or Argentina will reduce beef prices. Therefore, either Peru will reduce copper exports or Guatemala will increase coffee production. (B, P, C, A, G, E)

7. If Uruguay increases wool exports, then either Nicaragua will reduce cotton production or Costa Rica will reduce sugar production. It is not the case that either Guatemala or Nicaragua will reduce cotton production. Also, it is not the case that either Haiti or Costa Rica will reduce sugar production. Therefore, it is not the case that Uruguay will increase wool exports. (U, N, C, G, H)

8. If either Cuba or the Dominican Republic expands nickel production, then Nicaragua will extend its gold mining operations. If either Guyana or Surinam curtails bauxite production, then Honduras will reduce silver mining. It is not the case that either Nicaragua will extend its gold mining operations or Honduras will reduce silver mining. Therefore, it is not the case that either the Dominican Republic will expand nickel production or Surinam will curtail bauxite production. (C, D, N, G, S, H)

9. It is not the case that either Argentina or Chile will succeed in controlling inflation. If Argentina and Brazil both do not succeed in controlling inflation, then Chile will. Therefore, Brazil will succeed in controlling inflation. (A, C, B)

★10. Brazil will continue to develop nuclear power unless both Ecuador and Venezuela reduce crude oil prices. Furthermore, Brazil will continue to develop nuclear power unless both Surinam and Paraguay reduce the price of hydroelectric power. Either Venezuela will not reduce crude oil prices or Paraguay will not reduce the price of hydroelectric power. Therefore, Brazil will continue to develop nuclear power. (B, E, V, S, P)

7.4 RULES OF REPLACEMENT II

The remaining five rules of replacement are as follows:

14. Transposition (Trans):

$(p \supset q) \equiv (\sim q \supset \sim p)$

15. Material implication (Impl):

$(p \supset q) \equiv (\sim p \vee q)$

16. Material equivalence (Equiv):

$(p \equiv q) \equiv [(p \supset q) \cdot (q \supset p)]$
$(p \equiv q) \equiv [(p \cdot q) \vee (\sim p \cdot \sim q)]$

17. Exportation (Exp):

$[(p \cdot q) \supset r] \equiv [p \supset (q \supset r)]$

18. Tautology (Taut):

$p \equiv (p \vee p)$
$p \equiv (p \cdot p)$

Transposition was first mentioned in Section 6.1, where it was introduced to assist in translation. The rule is fairly easy to understand and is provable via *modus tollens.* In applying the rule one need only remember that antecedent and consequent may switch places if and only if both are negated.

The rule of **material implication** is less obvious than transposition, but it can be illustrated by substituting actual statements in place of the letters. A little reflection should disclose that the statement "If the river rises, then there will be a flood" $(R \supset F)$ is logically equivalent to "Either the river doesn't rise or there will be a flood" $(\sim R \vee F)$. The rule states, in effect, that the implication sign may be switched for a conditional sign, and vice versa, if and only if the left-hand component is negated.

The **material equivalence** rule has two formulations. The first is the same as the definition of material equivalence given in Section 6.1. The second formulation is easy to remember through recalling the two ways in which $p \equiv q$ may be true. Either p and q are both true or p and q are both false. This, of course, is the meaning of $[(p \cdot q) \vee (\sim p \cdot \sim q)]$.

The **exportation** rule is also fairly easy to understand. It asserts that the statement "If we have p, then if we have q we have r" is logically equivalent to "If we have both p and q, we have r." Upon consideration, this rule should appear reasonable.

The last rule, **tautology,** is obvious. Its effect is to eliminate redundancy in disjunctions and conjunctions.

The following proofs illustrate the use of these five rules.

    1. $\sim A$ $/ A \supset B$

In this argument the conclusion contains a letter not found in the premise. Obviously, addition must be used to introduce the B. The material implication rule completes the proof:

    1. $\sim A$ $/ A \supset B$
    2. $\sim A \vee B$ 1, Add
    3. $A \supset B$ 2, Impl

Here is another example:

    1. $F \supset G$
    2. $F \vee G$ $/ G$

To derive the conclusion of this argument, some method must be found to link the two premises together and eliminate the F. Hypothetical syllogism provides the solution, but first the second premise must be converted into a conditional. Here is the proof:

    1. $F \supset G$
    2. $F \vee G$ $/ G$
    3. $\sim F \supset G$ 2, Impl
    4. $\sim G \supset F$ 3, Trans, DN
    5. $\sim G \supset G$ 1, 4, HS
    6. $G \vee G$ 5, Impl, DN
    7. G 6, Taut

Another example:

    1. $J \supset (K \supset L)$ $/ K \supset (J \supset L)$

The conclusion can be obtained by simply rearranging the components of the single premise. Exportation provides the simplest method:

    1. $J \supset (K \supset L)$ $/ K \supset (J \supset L)$
    2. $(J \cdot K) \supset L$ 1, Exp
    3. $(K \cdot J) \supset L$ 2, Com
    4. $K \supset (J \supset L)$ 3, Exp

Another example:

    1. $M \supset N$
    2. $M \supset O$ $/ M \supset (N \cdot O)$

As with the second example above, some method must be found to link the two premises together. In this case, however, hypothetical syllogism will not work. The solution lies in setting up a distribution step:

1. $M \supset N$
2. $M \supset O$ / $M \supset (N \cdot O)$
3. $\sim M \vee N$ 1, Impl
4. $\sim M \vee O$ 2, Impl
5. $(\sim M \vee N) \cdot (\sim M \vee O)$ 3, 4, Conj
6. $\sim M \vee (N \cdot O)$ 5, Dist
7. $M \supset (N \cdot O)$ 6, Impl

Another example:

1. $P \supset Q$
2. $R \supset (S \cdot T)$
3. $\sim R \supset \sim Q$
4. $S \supset (T \supset P)$ / $P \equiv R$

The conclusion is a biconditional, and there are only two ways that a biconditional can be obtained; namely, via the two formulations of the material equivalence rule. The fact that the premises are all conditional statements suggests the first formulation of this rule. Accordingly, we must try to obtain $P \supset R$ and $R \supset P$. Again, the fact that the premises are themselves conditionals suggests hypothetical syllogism to accomplish this. Premises 1 and 3 can be used to set up one hypothetical syllogism; premises 2 and 4 provide the other. Here is the proof:

1. $P \supset Q$
2. $R \supset (S \cdot T)$
3. $\sim R \supset \sim Q$
4. $S \supset (T \supset P)$ / $P \equiv R$
5. $Q \supset R$ 3, Trans
6. $P \supset R$ 1, 5, HS
7. $(S \cdot T) \supset P$ 4, Exp
8. $R \supset P$ 2, 7, HS
9. $(P \supset R) \cdot (R \supset P)$ 6, 8, Conj
10. $P \equiv R$ 9, Equiv

Occasionally, mere inspection of the premises of an argument provides little insight into how the conclusion should be derived. In such cases it often helps to apply the rules of replacement to the conclusion with the aim of bridging the gap between it and the premises. Once this is done, the strategy to be used for deriving the conclusion should become evident. Because the rules of replacement are biconditionals, the same rules applied to the conclusion may then be used in reverse order on the premises. For example, consider the following argument:

1. $K \supset M$
2. $L \supset M$ $/ (K \vee L) \supset M$

If it is not clear upon first inspection exactly how the conclusion of this argument should be derived, we may be able to obtain some insight by applying the rules of replacement to the conclusion and then attempting to work backward toward the premises. Beginning with the implication rule, we proceed as follows:

1. $(K \vee L) \supset M$
2. $\sim(K \vee L) \vee M$ 1, Impl
3. $(\sim K \cdot \sim L) \vee M$ 2, DM
4. $(\sim K \vee M) \cdot (\sim L \vee M)$ 3, Com, Dist, Com
5. $(K \supset M) \cdot (L \supset M)$ 4, Impl

Comparing line 5 with the original premises, it should now be completely clear how to proceed. The proof is as follows:

1. $K \supset M$
2. $L \supset M$ $/ (K \vee L) \supset M$
3. $(K \supset M) \cdot (L \supset M)$ 1, Conj
4. $(\sim K \vee M) \cdot (\sim L \vee M)$ 3, Impl
5. $(\sim K \cdot \sim L) \vee M$ 4, Com, Dist, Com
6. $\sim(K \vee L) \vee M$ 5, DM
7. $(K \vee L) \supset M$ 6, Impl

EXERCISE 7.4

I. Supply the required justifications for the derived steps in the following arguments.

★(1) 1. $K \equiv R$
       2. $K \supset (R \supset P)$
       3. $\sim P$ $/ \sim R$
       4. $(K \cdot R) \vee (\sim K \cdot \sim R)$ _____
       5. $(K \cdot R) \supset P$ _____
       6. $\sim(K \cdot R)$ _____
       7. $\sim K \cdot \sim R$ _____
       8. $\sim R \cdot \sim K$ _____
       9. $\sim R$ _____

(2)   1. $C \supset (\sim L \supset Q)$
      2. $L \supset \sim C$
      3. $\sim Q$ $/ \sim C$
      4. $(C \cdot \sim L) \supset Q$ _____
      5. $\sim(C \cdot \sim L)$ _____
      6. $\sim C \vee \sim\sim L$ _____
      7. $\sim C \vee L$ _____
      8. $C \supset L$ _____

9. $C \supset {\sim}C$ _____

10. ${\sim}C \vee {\sim}C$ _____

11. ${\sim}C$ _____

(3)   1. $(E \supset A) \cdot (F \supset A)$

      2. $E \vee G$

      3. $F \vee {\sim}G$ / A

      4. ${\sim}E \supset G$ _____

      5. ${\sim}F \supset {\sim}G$ _____

      6. $G \supset F$ _____

      7. ${\sim}E \supset F$ _____

      8. ${\sim}{\sim}E \vee F$ _____

      9. $E \vee F$ _____

    10. $A \vee A$ _____

    11. A _____

(4)   1. $(F \cdot H) \supset N$

      2. $F \vee S$

      3. H / N \vee S

      4. $(H \cdot F) \supset N$ _____

      5. $H \supset (F \supset N)$ _____

      6. $F \supset N$ _____

      7. ${\sim}N \supset {\sim}F$ _____

      8. ${\sim}F \supset S$ _____

      9. ${\sim}N \supset S$ _____

    10. ${\sim}{\sim}N \vee S$ _____

    11. $N \vee S$ _____

(5)   1. $T \supset (H \cdot J)$

      2. $(H \vee N) \supset T$ / T \equiv H

      3. ${\sim}T \vee (H \cdot J)$ _____

      4. $({\sim}T \vee H) \cdot ({\sim}T \vee J)$ _____

      5. ${\sim}T \vee H$ _____

      6. $T \supset H$ _____

      7. ${\sim}(H \vee N) \vee T$ _____

      8. $({\sim}H \cdot {\sim}N) \vee T$ _____

      9. $({\sim}H \vee T) \cdot ({\sim}N \vee T)$ _____

    10. ${\sim}H \vee T$ _____

    11. $H \supset T$ _____

    12. $(T \supset H) \cdot (H \supset T)$ _____

    13. $T \equiv H$ _____

II. Use the eighteen rules of inference to derive the conclusions of the following symbolized arguments:

★(1) 1. $(J \cdot R) \supset H$

      2. $(R \supset H) \supset M$

      3. ${\sim}(P \vee {\sim}J)$ / M \cdot {\sim}P

(2)   1. $(B \supset G) \cdot (F \supset N)$

      2. ${\sim}(G \cdot N)$ / ${\sim}(B \cdot F)$

(3) 1. T $/ S \supset T$

(4) 1. $\sim(U \cdot W) \supset X$
    2. $U \supset \sim U$ $/ \sim(U \vee \sim X)$

★(5) 1. $(O \supset C) \cdot (\sim S \supset \sim D)$
    2. $(E \supset D) \cdot (\sim E \supset \sim C)$ $/ O \supset S$

(6) 1. $T \supset R$
    2. $T \supset \sim R$ $/ \sim T$

(7) 1. $M \supset (U \supset H)$
    2. $(H \vee \sim U) \supset F$ $/ M \supset F$

(8) 1. $S \vee \sim N$
    2. $\sim S \vee Q$ $/ N \supset Q$

(9) 1. $\sim R \vee P$
    2. $R \vee \sim P$ $/ R \equiv P$

★(10) 1. $J \supset (G \supset L)$ $/ G \supset (J \supset L)$

(11) 1. $\sim B \supset H$
    2. $\sim D \supset H$
    3. $\sim(B \cdot D)$ $/ H$

(12) 1. $S \supset (L \cdot M)$
    2. $M \supset (L \supset R)$ $/ S \supset R$

(13) 1. $(I \supset E) \supset C$
    2. $C \supset \sim C$ $/ I$

(14) 1. $F \supset (A \cdot K)$
    2. $G \supset (\sim A \cdot \sim K)$
    3. $F \vee G$ $/ A \equiv K$

★(15) 1. $T \supset G$
    2. $S \supset G$ $/ (T \vee S) \supset G$

(16) 1. $Q \supset (W \cdot D)$ $/ Q \supset W$

(17) 1. $H \supset U$ $/ H \supset (U \vee T)$

(18) 1. $P \supset (\sim E \supset B)$
    2. $\sim(B \vee E)$ $/ \sim P$

(19) 1. $I \vee (N \cdot F)$
    2. $I \supset F$ $/ F$

★(20) 1. $(G \supset J) \supset (H \supset Q)$
    2. $J \cdot \sim Q$ $/ \sim H$

(21) 1. $T \supset \sim(A \supset N)$
    2. $T \vee N$ $/ T \equiv \sim N$

(22) 1. $(O \supset R) \supset S$
    2. $(P \supset R) \supset \sim S$ $/ \sim R$

(23) 1. $(D \supset E) \supset (E \supset D)$
    2. $(D \equiv E) \supset \sim(G \cdot \sim H)$
    3. $E \cdot G$ $/ G \cdot H$

(24) 1. $(L \lor P) \supset U$
    2. $(M \supset U) \supset I$
    3. P $/ I$

★(25) 1. $(S \lor T) \supset (S \supset \sim T)$
    2. $(S \supset \sim T) \supset (T \supset K)$
    3. $S \lor T$ $/ S \lor K$

(26) 1. $A \equiv W$
    2. $\sim A \lor \sim W$
    3. $R \supset A$ $/ \sim(W \lor R)$

(27) 1. $G \equiv M$
    2. $G \lor M$
    3. $G \supset (M \supset T)$ $/ T$

(28) 1. $H \equiv I$
    2. $H \supset (I \supset F)$
    3. $\sim(H \lor I) \supset F$ $/ F$

(29) 1. $O \supset (Q \cdot N)$
    2. $(N \lor E) \supset S$ $/ O \supset S$

★(30) 1. $P \supset A$
    2. $Q \supset B$ $/ (P \lor Q) \supset (A \lor B)$

III. Translate the following arguments into symbolic form and use the eighteen rules of inference to derive the conclusion of each:

★1. If Ramsey extorted the funds, then Hamilton lied on the witness stand. It is not the case that both Hamilton lied on the witness stand and Murphy was not in town on the date of the crime. Therefore, if Ramsey extorted the funds, then Murphy was in town on the date of the crime. (R, H, M)

2. Kendall will not be convicted of extortion only if Edwards and Ashton refuse to testify. Ashton will not refuse to testify. Therefore, Kendall will be convicted of extortion. (K, E, A)

3. Phillips did not libel the plaintiff. Therefore, if Phillips did libel the plaintiff, then Bryant will argue for a fair settlement. (P, B)

4. Norris was intoxicated at the time of his arrest only if Jordan is guilty of entrapment. Therefore, if both Norris and Conway were intoxicated at the time of their arrest, then Jordan is guilty of entrapment. (N, J, C)

★5. If either Garrison or Rogers filed a fraudulent tax return, then Taylor will call for an investigation. Therefore, if Garrison filed a fraudulent tax return, then Taylor will call for an investigation. (G, R, T)

6. Both Foster and Owens conspired with the defendant only if Stirling is on the payroll. Foster did conspire with the defendant. Therefore, Owens conspired with the defendant only if Stirling is on the payroll. (F, O, S)

7. Bennett will be indicted only if Evans turns State's evidence. Furthermore, Bennett will be indicted only if Dillon turns State's evidence. Therefore, if Bennett is indicted, both Evans and Dillon will turn State's evidence. (*B, E, D*)

8. Either Townsend set the hotel fire, or Navarro was not on guard duty at the time and Hoffman sabotaged the sprinklers. If Navarro was on guard duty at the time, then Townsend did not set the hotel fire. Therefore, Navarro was not on guard duty at the time. (*T, N, H*)

9. If Jensen witnessed the murder, then if Bradley can be extradited, then Daniels will be convicted. Therefore, if Daniels is not convicted, then if Bradley can be extradited, then Jensen did not witness the murder. (*J, B, D*)

★10. Porter and Manning will be found liable for damages if and only if Goodman sues. It is not the case that either Goodman will sue or Porter will not be found liable for damages. Therefore, Manning will not be found liable for damages. (*P, M, G*)

7.5 CONDITIONAL PROOF

Conditional proof is a method for obtaining a line in a proof sequence (either the conclusion or some intermediate line) that frequently offers the advantage of being both shorter and simpler to use than the conventional method. Moreover, there are a number of arguments having conclusions that cannot be derived by the conventional method, so some form of conditional proof must be used on them. While in theory the method of conditional proof can be used to derive any line in a proof sequence, in practice it is usually reserved for obtaining lines that are expressed in the form of conditional statements. The method consists in assuming the antecedent of the required conditional statement on one line, deriving the consequent on a subsequent line, and then "discharging" this sequence of lines in a conditional statement that exactly replicates the one that was to be obtained.

Any argument whose conclusion is a conditional statement is an immediate candidate for conditional proof. Consider the following example:

1. $A \supset (B \cdot C)$
2. $(B \vee D) \supset E$ / $A \supset E$

Using the conventional method to derive the conclusion of this argument would require a proof having at least twelve lines, and the precise strategy to be followed in constructing it might not be immediately obvious. Nevertheless, we need only give cursory inspection to the argument to see that the conclusion does indeed follow from the premises.

The conclusion states that if we have A, we then have E. Let us suppose, for a moment, that we do have A. We could then obtain $B \cdot C$ from the first premise via *modus ponens*. Simplifying this expression we could obtain B, and from this we could get $B \vee D$ via addition. E would then follow from the second premise via *modus ponens*. In other words, if we assume that we have A, we can get E. But this is exactly what the conclusion says; in other words, we have just proved that the conclusion follows from the premises.

The method of conditional proof consists of incorporating this simple thought process into the body of a proof sequence. A conditional proof for this argument requires only eight lines and is substantially simpler than a proof constructed by the conventional method:

$$
\begin{array}{lll}
1. & A \supset (B \cdot C) & \\
2. & (B \vee D) \supset E & \quad / \ A \supset E \\
\quad 3. & A & \text{CP} \\
\quad 4. & B \cdot C & 1, 3, \text{MP} \\
\quad 5. & B & 4, \text{Simp} \\
\quad 6. & B \vee D & 5, \text{Add} \\
\quad 7. & E & 2, 6, \text{MP} \\
8. & A \supset E & 3\text{--}7, \text{CP}
\end{array}
$$

Lines 3 through 7 are indented to indicate their hypothetical character: they all depend on the assumption introduced in line 3 via "CP" (conditional proof). These lines, which constitute the conditional proof sequence, tell us that if we assume A (line 3), we can obtain E (line 7). In line 8 the conditional sequence is discharged in the conditional statement $A \supset E$, which simply reiterates the result of the conditional sequence. Since line 8 is not hypothetical, it is written adjacent to the original margin, under lines 1 and 2.

The first step in constructing a conditional proof is to decide what should be assumed on the first line of the conditional sequence. While any statement whatsoever *can* be assumed on this line, only the right statement will lead to the desired result. The clue is always provided by the conditional statement to be obtained in the end. The antecedent of this statement is what must be assumed. For example, if the statement to be obtained is $(K \cdot L) \supset M$, then $K \cdot L$ should be assumed on the first line. This line is always indented and tagged with the designation "CP." Once the initial assumption has been made, the second step is to obtain the consequent of the desired conditional statement at the end of the conditional sequence. To do this, we simply apply the ordinary rules of inference to any previous line in the proof (including the assumed line), writing the result directly below the assumed line. The third and final step is to discharge the conditional sequence in a conditional statement. The antecedent of this conditional statement is whatever appears on the first line of the conditional sequence, and the consequent is whatever appears on the last line. For example, if $A \lor B$ is on the first line and $C \cdot D$ is on the last, the sequence is discharged by $(A \lor B) \supset (C \cdot D)$. This discharging line is always written adjacent to the original margin and is tagged with the designation "CP" together with the numerals corresponding to the first and last lines of the sequence.

I suggested earlier that conditional proof can be used to obtain a line other than the conclusion of an argument. The following proof, which illustrates this fact, incorporates two conditional sequences, one after the other, within the scope of a single conventional proof:

1.	$G \supset (H \cdot I)$	
2.	$J \supset (K \cdot L)$	
3.	$G \lor J$	$/ \ H \lor K$
4.	G	CP
5.	$H \cdot I$	1, 4, MP
6.	H	5, Simp
7.	$G \supset H$	4–6, CP
8.	J	CP
9.	$K \cdot L$	2, 8, MP
10.	K	9, Simp
11.	$J \supset K$	8–10, CP
12.	$(G \supset H) \cdot (J \supset K)$	7, 11, Conj
13.	$H \lor K$	3, 12, CD

The first conditional proof sequence gives us $G \supset H$, and the second $J \supset K$. These two lines are then conjoined and used together with line 3 to set up a constructive dilemma, from which the conclusion is obtained.

This proof sequence provides a convenient opportunity to introduce an important rule governing conditional proof. The rule states that after a conditional proof sequence has been discharged, no line in the sequence may be used as a reason for a subsequent line in the proof. If, for example, line 5 in the above proof were used as a reason in support of line 9 or line 12, this rule would be violated, and the corresponding inference would be invalid. Once the conditional sequence is discharged, it is sealed off from the remaining part of the proof. The logic behind this rule is easy to understand. The lines in a conditional sequence are hypothetical in that they depend on the assumption stated in the first line. Because no mere assumption can provide any genuine support for anything, neither can any line that depends on such an assumption. When a conditional sequence is discharged, the assumption upon which it rests is expressed as the antecedent of a conditional statement. This conditional statement *can* be used to support subsequent lines because it makes no claim that its antecedent is true. The conditional statement merely asserts that *if* its antecedent is true, then its consequent is true, and this, of course, is what has been established by the conditional sequence from which it is obtained.

Just as a conditional sequence can be used within the scope of a conventional proof to obtain a desired statement form, one conditional sequence can be used within the scope of another to obtain a desired statement form. The following proof provides an example:

$$
\begin{array}{lll}
1. & L \supset [M \supset (N \lor O)] & \\
2. & M \supset \sim N & \quad / L \supset (\sim M \lor O) \\
\quad 3. & L & \quad \text{CP} \\
\quad 4. & M \supset (N \lor O) & \quad 1, 3, \text{MP} \\
\qquad 5. & M & \quad \text{CP} \\
\qquad 6. & N \lor O & \quad 4, 5, \text{MP} \\
\qquad 7. & \sim N & \quad 2, 5, \text{MP} \\
\qquad 8. & O & \quad 6, 7, \text{DS} \\
\quad 9. & M \supset O & \quad 5\text{-}8, \text{CP} \\
\quad 10. & \sim M \lor O & \quad 9, \text{Impl} \\
11. & L \supset (\sim M \lor O) & \quad 3\text{-}10, \text{CP}
\end{array}
$$

The rule introduced in connection with the previous example applies unchanged to examples of this sort. No line in the sequence 5–8 could be used to support any line subsequent to line 9, and no line in the sequence 3–10 could be used to support any line subsequent to line 11. Line 3 or 4 could, of course, be used to support any line in the sequence 5–8.

One final reminder regarding conditional proof is that every conditional proof must be discharged. It is absolutely improper to end a proof on an indented line. If this rule is ignored, any conclusion one chooses can be derived from any set of premises. The following invalid proof illustrates this mistake:

$$
\begin{array}{lll}
1. & P & \quad / Q \supset R \\
\quad 2. & \sim Q & \quad \text{CP} \\
\quad 3. & \sim Q \lor R & \quad 2, \text{Add} \\
\quad 4. & Q \supset R & \quad 2, \text{Impl}
\end{array}
$$

EXERCISE 7.5

I. Use conditional proof and the eighteen rules of inference to derive the conclusions of the following symbolized arguments. Having done so, attempt to derive the conclusions without using conditional proof.

★(1) 1. $N \supset O$
    2. $N \supset P$ / $N \supset (O \cdot P)$

(2) 1. $F \supset E$
    2. $(F \cdot E) \supset R$ / $F \supset R$

(3) 1. $G \supset T$
    2. $(T \lor S) \supset K$ / $G \supset K$

(4) 1. $(G \lor H) \supset (S \cdot T)$
    2. $(T \lor U) \supset (C \cdot D)$ $/ G \supset C$

★(5) 1. $A \supset \sim(A \lor E)$ $/ A \supset F$

(6) 1. $J \supset (K \supset L)$
    2. $J \supset (M \supset L)$
    3. $\sim L$ $/ J \supset \sim(K \lor M)$

(7) 1. $M \lor (N \cdot O)$ $/ \sim N \supset M$

(8) 1. $P \supset (Q \lor R)$
    2. $(P \supset R) \supset (S \cdot T)$
    3. $Q \supset R$ $/ T$

(9) 1. $H \supset (I \supset N)$
    2. $(H \supset \sim I) \supset (M \lor N)$
    3. $\sim N$ $/ M$

★(10) 1. $C \supset (A \cdot D)$
     2. $B \supset (A \cdot E)$ $/ (C \lor B) \supset A$

(11) 1. $M \supset (K \supset L)$
     2. $(L \lor N) \supset J$ $/ M \supset (K \supset J)$

(12) 1. $F \supset (G \cdot H)$ $/ (A \supset F) \supset (A \supset H)$

(13) 1. $R \supset B$
     2. $R \supset (B \supset F)$
     3. $B \supset (F \supset H)$ $/ R \supset H$

(14) 1. $(F \cdot G) \equiv H$
     2. $F \supset G$ $/ F \equiv H$

★(15) 1. $C \supset (D \lor \sim E)$
     2. $E \supset (D \supset F)$ $/ C \supset (E \supset F)$

(16) 1. $Q \supset (R \supset S)$
     2. $Q \supset (T \supset \sim U)$
     3. $U \supset (R \lor T)$ $/ Q \supset (U \supset S)$

(17) 1. $N \supset (O \cdot P)$
     2. $Q \supset (R \cdot S)$ $/ (P \supset Q) \supset (N \supset S)$

(18) 1. $E \supset (F \supset G)$
     2. $H \supset (G \supset I)$
     3. $(F \supset I) \supset (J \lor \sim H)$ $/ (E \cdot H) \supset J$

(19) 1. $P \supset [(L \lor M) \supset (N \cdot O)]$
     2. $(O \lor T) \supset W$ $/ P \supset (M \supset W)$

★(20) 1. $A \supset [B \supset (C \cdot \sim D)]$
     2. $(B \lor E) \supset (D \lor E)$ $/ (A \cdot B) \supset (C \cdot E)$

II. Translate the following arguments into symbolic form. Then use conditional proof and the eighteen rules of inference to derive the conclusion of each. Having done so, attempt to derive the conclusion without using conditional proof.

★1. If Michigan goes Democratic, then Wisconsin will go Republican. Furthermore, if Georgia goes Democratic, Alabama will go Republican. Therefore, if Michigan and Georgia go Democratic, then Wisconsin and Alabama will go Republican. (M, W, G, A)

2. If Kentucky promotes coal mining, then if Texas curtails oil drilling, then New Mexico will promote natural gas exploration. If Texas curtails oil drilling, then if New Mexico promotes natural gas exploration, then Colorado will implement oil shale processing. Therefore, if Kentucky promotes coal mining, then if Texas curtails oil drilling, then Colorado will implement oil shale processing. (K, T, N, C)

3. Nebraska will expand wheat production only if South Dakota does. If both Nebraska and South Dakota expand wheat production, then Missouri will reduce corn production. If both Illinois and Missouri reduce corn production, then Ohio will expand soybean production. Therefore, if Nebraska expands wheat production, then if Illinois reduces corn production, then Ohio will expand soybean production. (N, S, M, I, O)

4. California will subsidize its lettuce growers if and only if Oregon's giving a tax break to its sugar beet growers implies that Washington will advertise its apples. If Idaho promotes its potatoes, then both Arizona and California will subsidize their lettuce growers. Oregon will give a tax break to its sugar beet growers. Therefore, Washington will advertise its apples unless Idaho does not promote its potatoes. (C, O, W, I, A)

5. If Connecticut reduces taxes, then Massachusetts will increase public employee salaries. Furthermore, if either New Hampshire or Rhode Island reduces welfare expenditures, then Vermont will increase expenditures for highways. Therefore, if Massachusetts increases public employee salaries only if New Hampshire reduces welfare expenditures, then Connecticut will reduce taxes only if Vermont increases expenditures for highways. (C, M, N, R, V)

7.6 INDIRECT PROOF

Indirect proof is a variety of conditional proof that can be used on any argument to derive either the conclusion or some intermediate line leading to the conclusion. It consists in assuming the negation of the statement form to be obtained, using this assumption to derive a contradiction, and then concluding that the original assumption is false. This last step, of course, establishes the truth of the statement form to be obtained. The following proof sequence uses indirect proof to derive the conclusion:

```
 1. (A v B) ⊃ (C • D)
 2. C ⊃ ~D              / ~A
       3. A             IP
       4. A v B         3, Add
       5. C • D         1, 4, MP
       6. C             5, Simp
       7. ~D            2, 6, MP
       8. D             5, Com, Simp
       9. D • ~D        7, 8, Conj
10.  ~A                 3-9, IP
```

The indirect proof sequence (lines 3–9) begins by assuming the negation of the conclusion. This assumption leads to a contradiction in line 9. Since any assumption that leads to a contradiction is false, the conditional sequence is discharged (line 10) by asserting the negation of the assumption made in line 3. This line is then tagged with the designation "IP" (indirect proof) together with the numerals indicating the scope of the indirect sequence from which it is obtained.

Indirect proof can also be used to derive an intermediate line leading to the conclusion. Example:

```
 1. E ⊃ [(F v G) ⊃ (H • J)]
 2. E • ~(J v K)          / ~(F v K)
 3. E                     2, Simp
 4. (F v G) ⊃ (H • J)     1, 3, MP
 5. ~(J v K)              2, Com, Simp
 6. ~J • ~K               5, DM
       7. F               IP
       8. F v G           7, Add
       9. H • J           4, 8, MP
      10. J               9, Com, Simp
      11. ~J              6, Simp
      12. J • ~J          10, 11, Conj
13.  ~F                   7-12, IP
14.  ~K                   6, Com, Simp
15.  ~F • ~K              13, 14, Conj
16.  ~(F v K)             15, DM
```

The indirect proof sequence begins with the assumption of F (line 7), leads to a contradiction (line 12), and is discharged (line 13) by asserting the negation of the assumption.

As with conditional proof, when an indirect proof sequence is discharged, no line in the sequence may be used as a justification for a subsequent line in the proof. In reference to the above proof, this means that none of the lines 7–12 could be used as a justification for any of the lines 14–16. Occasionally, this rule requires certain priorities in the derivation of lines. For example, for the purpose of deriving the contradiction, lines 5 and 6 could have been included as part of the indirect sequence. But this would not have been advisable because line 6 is needed as a justification for line 14, which lies outside the indirect sequence. If lines 5 and 6 had been included within the indirect sequence, they would have had to be repeated after the sequence had been discharged to allow ~K to be obtained on a line outside the sequence.

Just as a conditional sequence may be constructed within the scope of another conditional sequence, so a conditional sequence can be constructed within the scope of an indirect sequence, and, conversely, an indirect sequence may be constructed within the scope of either a conditional sequence or another indirect sequence. The next example illustrates the use of an indirect sequence within the scope of a conditional sequence:

1.	$L \supset [\sim M \supset (N \cdot O)]$	
2.	$\sim N \cdot P$	$/ L \supset (M \cdot P)$
3.	L	CP
4.	$\sim M \supset (N \cdot O)$	1, 3, MP
5.	$\sim M$	IP
6.	$N \cdot O$	4, 5, MP
7.	N	6, Simp
8.	$\sim N$	2, Simp
9.	$N \cdot \sim N$	7, 8, Conj
10.	$\sim \sim M$	5–9, IP
11.	M	10, DN
12.	P	2, Com, Simp
13.	$M \cdot P$	11, 12, Conj
14.	$L \supset (M \cdot P)$	3–13, CP

The indirect sequence (lines 5–9) is discharged (line 10) by asserting the negation of the assumption made in line 5. Technically, the double negation step (line 11) is required, but it could be incorporated into line 10. The conditional sequence (lines 3–13) is discharged (line 14) in the conditional statement that has the first line of the sequence as its antecedent and the last line as its consequent.

Indirect proof provides a convenient way for proving the validity of an argument having a tautology for its conclusion. In fact, the only way in which the conclusion of such an argument can be derived (assuming the premises of the argument are not self-contradictory) is through either conditional or indirect proof.

For the following argument, indirect proof is the easier of the two:

1.	S	$/ T \vee \sim T$
2.	$\sim(T \vee \sim T)$	IP
3.	$\sim T \cdot \sim \sim T$	2, DM
4.	$\sim \sim(T \vee \sim T)$	2–3, IP
5.	$T \vee \sim T$	4, DN

Here is another example of an argument having a tautology as its conclusion. In this case, since the conclusion is a conditional statement, conditional proof is the easier alternative:

1. S $/ \ T \supset T$
    2. T CP
    3. $T \lor T$ 2, Add
    4. T 3, Taut
5. $T \supset T$ 2–4, CP

I mentioned earlier that indirect proof is really a variety of conditional proof. This fact may be illustrated by returning to the first example presented in this section. In the proof that follows, conditional proof—not indirect proof—is used to obtain the conclusion:

1. $(A \lor B) \supset (C \cdot D)$
2. $C \supset {\sim}D$ $/ \ {\sim}A$
    3. A CP
    4. $A \lor B$ 3, Add
    5. $C \cdot D$ 1, 4, MP
    6. C 5, Simp
    7. ${\sim}D$ 2, 6, MP
    8. D 5, Com, Simp
    9. $D \lor {\sim}A$ 8, Add
    10. ${\sim}A$ 7, 9, DS
11. $A \supset {\sim}A$ 3–10, CP
12. ${\sim}A \lor {\sim}A$ 11, Impl
13. ${\sim}A$ 12, Taut

This example illustrates how a conditional proof can be used to derive the conclusion of *any* argument, whether or not the conclusion is a conditional statement. Simply begin by assuming the negation of the conclusion, derive contradictory statements on separate lines, and use these lines to set up a disjunctive syllogism yielding the negation of the assumption as the last line of the conditional sequence. Then, discharge the sequence and use tautology to obtain the negation of the assumption outside the sequence.

Indirect proof is a variety of conditional proof in that it amounts to a modification of the way in which the indented sequence is discharged, resulting in an overall shortening of the proof for many arguments. The indirect proof for the argument above is repeated below, with the requisite changes noted in the margin:

1. $(A \lor B) \supset (C \cdot D)$
2. $C \supset {\sim}D$ $/ \ {\sim}A$
    3. A (IP)   changed
    4. $A \lor B$ 3, Add

5. $C \cdot D$	1, 4, MP
6. C	5, Simp
7. $\sim D$	2, 6, MP
8. D	5, Com, Simp
9. $D \cdot \sim D$	7, 8, Conj ⎫
10. $\sim A$	3–9, IP ⎬ changed ⎭

The reminder at the end of the previous section regarding conditional proof pertains to indirect proof as well: It is essential that every indirect proof be discharged. No proof can be ended on an indented line. If this rule is ignored, indirect proof, like conditional proof, can produce any conclusion whatsoever. The following invalid proof illustrates such a mistake:

1. P		$/ Q$
2. Q	IP	
3. $Q \lor Q$	2, Add	
4. Q	3, Taut	

EXERCISE 7.6

I. Use either indirect proof or conditional proof (or both) and the eighteen rules of inference to derive the conclusions of the following symbolized arguments. Having done so, attempt to derive the conclusions without using indirect proof or conditional proof.

★(1) 1. $(S \lor T) \supset \sim S$ $/ \sim S$

(2) 1. $(K \supset K) \supset R$
     2. $(R \lor M) \supset N$ $/ N$

(3) 1. $(C \cdot D) \supset E$
     2. $(D \cdot E) \supset F$ $/ (C \cdot D) \supset F$

(4) 1. $H \supset (L \supset K)$
     2. $L \supset (K \supset \sim L)$ $/ \sim H \lor \sim L$

★(5) 1. $S \supset (T \lor \sim U)$
     2. $U \supset (\sim T \lor R)$
     3. $(S \cdot U) \supset \sim R$ $/ \sim S \lor \sim U$

(6) 1. $\sim A \supset (B \cdot C)$
     2. $D \supset \sim C$ $/ D \supset A$

(7) 1. $(E \lor F) \supset (C \cdot D)$
     2. $(D \lor G) \supset H$
     3. $E \lor G$ $/ H$

(8) 1. $\sim M \supset (N \cdot O)$
     2. $N \supset P$
     3. $O \supset \sim P$ $/ M$

(9) 1. $(R \lor S) \supset T$
2. $(P \lor Q) \supset T$
3. $R \lor P$ / T

★(10) 1. K / $S \supset (T \supset S)$

(11) 1. $(A \lor B) \supset C$
2. $(\sim A \lor D) \supset E$ / $C \lor E$

(12) 1. $(K \lor L) \supset (M \cdot N)$
2. $(N \lor O) \supset (P \cdot \sim K)$ / $\sim K$

(13) 1. $[C \supset (D \supset C)] \supset E$ / E

(14) 1. F / $(G \supset H) \lor (\sim G \supset J)$

★(15) 1. $B \supset (K \cdot M)$
2. $(B \cdot M) \supset (P \equiv \sim P)$ / $\sim B$

(16) 1. $(N \lor O) \supset (C \cdot D)$
2. $(D \lor K) \supset (P \lor \sim C)$
3. $(P \lor G) \supset \sim(N \cdot D)$ / $\sim N$

(17) 1. $(R \cdot S) \equiv (G \cdot H)$
2. $R \supset S$
3. $H \supset G$ / $R \equiv H$

(18) 1. $K \supset [(M \lor N) \supset (P \cdot Q)]$
2. $L \supset [(Q \lor R) \supset (S \cdot \sim N)]$ / $(K \cdot L) \supset \sim N$

(19) 1. $A \supset [(N \lor \sim N) \supset (S \lor T)]$
2. $T \supset \sim(F \lor \sim F)$ / $A \supset S$

★(20) 1. $F \supset [(C \supset C) \supset G]$
2. $G \supset \{[H \supset (E \supset H)] \supset (K \cdot \sim K)\}$ / $\sim F$

II. Translate the following arguments into symbolic form. Then use indirect proof and the eighteen rules of inference to derive the conclusion of each. Having done so, attempt to derive the conclusion without using indirect proof.

★1. Mercury and Venus have a high surface temperature only if Uranus (but not Neptune) has violent dust storms. Venus has a high surface temperature only if Neptune has violent dust storms. Therefore, either Mercury or Venus does not have a high surface temperature. (M, V, U, N)

2. If either Neptune or Uranus has rings, then both Saturn and Jupiter do, too. If either Saturn or Mars has rings, then if Jupiter has rings, then Neptune does not. Therefore, Neptune does not have rings. (N, U, S, J)

3. If Pluto has an iron core, then if Earth has a magnetic field then so does Mercury. If Pluto has an iron core, then Earth has a magnetic field. Furthermore, if Venus has an atmosphere, then either Pluto has

an iron core or Mercury has a magnetic field. Therefore, Mercury has a magnetic field unless Venus does not have an atmosphere. (*P*, *E*, *M*, *V*)

4. If Jupiter has volcanoes only if Saturn does, then Neptune has a satellite. Furthermore, if Saturn has volcanoes only if Jupiter does, then Neptune has a satellite. Therefore, Neptune has a satellite. (*J*, *S*, *N*)

5. Both Mars and Jupiter have craters unless Neptune does. If Neptune has craters, then Jupiter does. Therefore, Mars has craters only if Jupiter does. (*M*, *J*, *N*)

7.7 PROVING LOGICAL TRUTHS

Both conditional and indirect proof can be used to establish the truth of a tautology (logical truth). Tautological statements can be treated as if they were the conclusions of arguments having no premises. Such a procedure is suggested by the fact that any argument having a tautology for its conclusion is valid regardless of what its premises are. As we saw in the previous section, the proof for such an argument does not use the premises at all but derives the conclusion as the exclusive consequence of either a conditional or indirect sequence. Using this strategy for logical truths, we write the statement to be proved as if it were the conclusion of an argument, and we indent the first line in the proof and tag it as being the beginning of either a conditional or indirect sequence. In the end, this sequence is appropriately discharged to yield the desired statement form.

Tautologies expressed in the form of conditional statements are most easily proved via a conditional sequence. The following example utilizes two such sequences, one within the scope of the other:

$$/ \ P \supset (Q \supset P)$$

1. P	CP
2. Q	CP
3. $P \lor P$	1, Add
4. P	3, Taut
5. $Q \supset P$	2–4, CP
6. $P \supset (Q \supset P)$	1–5, CP

Notice that line 6 restores the proof to the original margin—the first line is indented.

Here is a proof of the same statement using an indirect proof. The indirect sequence begins, as usual, with the negation of the statement to be proved:

/ $P \supset (Q \supset P)$
1. $\sim[P \supset (Q \supset P)]$ IP
2. $\sim[\sim P \lor (\sim Q \lor P)]$ 1, Impl
3. $P \cdot \sim(\sim Q \lor P)$ 2, DM, DN
4. $P \cdot (Q \cdot \sim P)$ 3, DM, DN
5. $(P \cdot \sim P) \cdot Q$ 4, Com, Assoc
6. $P \cdot \sim P$ 5, Simp
7. $\sim\sim[P \supset (Q \supset P)]$ 1–6, IP
8. $P \supset (Q \supset P)$ 7, DN

More complex conditional statements are proved by merely extending the technique used in the first proof above. In the proof that follows, notice how each conditional sequence begins by asserting the antecedent of the conditional statement to be obtained:

/ $[P \supset (Q \supset R)] \supset [(P \supset Q) \supset (P \supset R)]$
1. $P \supset (Q \supset R)$ CP
2. $P \supset Q$ CP
3. P CP
4. $Q \supset R$ 1, 3, MP
5. Q 2, 3, MP
6. R 4, 5, MP
7. $P \supset R$ 3–6, CP
8. $(P \supset Q) \supset (P \supset R)$ 2–7, CP
9. $[P \supset (Q \supset R)] \supset [(P \supset Q) \supset (P \supset R)]$ 1–8, CP

Tautologies expressed as equivalences are usually proved using two conditional sequences, one after the other. Example:

/ $P \equiv [P \cdot (Q \supset P)]$
1. P CP
2. $P \lor \sim Q$ 1, Add
3. $\sim Q \lor P$ 2, Com
4. $Q \supset P$ 3, Impl
5. $P \cdot (Q \supset P)$ 1, 4, Conj
6. $P \supset [P \cdot (Q \supset P)]$ 1–5, CP
7. $P \cdot (Q \supset P)$ CP
8. P 7, Simp
9. $[P \cdot (Q \supset P)] \supset P$ 7–8, CP
10. $P \equiv [P \cdot (Q \supset P)]$ 6, 9, Conj, Equiv

EXERCISE 7.7

Use conditional proof or indirect proof and the eighteen rules of inference to establish the truth of the following tautologies:

★1. $P \supset [(P \supset Q) \supset Q]$

2. $(\sim P \supset Q) \lor (P \supset R)$

3. $P \equiv [P \vee (Q \cdot P)]$

4. $(P \supset Q) \supset [(P \cdot R) \supset (Q \cdot R)]$

★5. $(P \vee \sim Q) \supset [(\sim P \vee R) \supset (Q \supset R)]$

6. $P \equiv [P \cdot (Q \vee \sim Q)]$

7. $(P \supset Q) \vee (\sim Q \supset P)$

8. $(P \supset Q) \equiv [P \supset (P \cdot Q)]$

9. $[(P \supset Q) \cdot (P \supset R)] \supset [P \supset (Q \cdot R)]$

★10. $[\sim(P \cdot \sim Q) \cdot Q] \supset \sim P$

11. $(P \supset Q) \vee (Q \supset P)$

12. $[P \supset (Q \supset R)] \equiv [Q \supset (P \supset R)]$

13. $(P \supset Q) \supset [(P \supset \sim Q) \supset \sim P]$

14. $[(P \supset Q) \supset R] \supset [(R \supset \sim R) \supset P]$

★15. $(\sim P \vee Q) \supset [(P \vee \sim Q) \supset (P \equiv Q)]$

16. $\sim[(P \supset \sim P) \cdot (\sim P \supset P)]$

17. $P \supset [(Q \cdot \sim Q) \supset R]$

18. $[(P \cdot Q) \vee R] \supset [(\sim R \vee Q) \supset (P \supset Q)]$

19. $P \equiv [P \vee (Q \cdot \sim Q)]$

★20. $P \supset [Q \equiv (P \supset Q)]$

8

PREDICATE LOGIC

8.1 SYMBOLS AND TRANSLATION

Techniques were developed in earlier chapters for evaluating two basically different kinds of arguments. The chapter on categorical syllogisms dealt with arguments such as the following:

All horses are four-legged creatures.
No birds are four-legged creatures.
Therefore, no birds are horses.

In such arguments the fundamental components are *terms,* and the validity of the argument depends on the arrangement of the terms within the premises and conclusion.

The chapter on propositional logic, on the other hand, dealt with arguments such as this:

If the control rods fail, then the reactor will run wild and the core will melt. If the core melts, radiation will be released into the atmosphere. Therefore, if the control rods fail, radiation will be released into the atmosphere.

In such arguments the fundamental components are not terms but *statements.* The validity of these arguments depends not on the arrangement of the terms within the statements but on the arrangement of the statements themselves as atomic units.

Not all arguments, however, can be assigned to one or the other of

PREDICATE LOGIC

these two groups. There is a third type that is a kind of hybrid, sharing features in common with both categorical syllogisms and propositional arguments. Consider, for example, the following:

> Cats and dogs bite if they are either frightened or harassed.
> Therefore, cats bite if they are frightened.

The validity of this argument depends both on the arrangement of the terms and on the arrangement of the statements. Accordingly, neither syllogistic logic nor propositional logic alone is sufficient to establish its validity. What is needed is a third kind of logic that combines the distinctive features of syllogistic logic and propositional logic. This third kind is called **predicate logic.**

The fundamental component in predicate logic is the **predicate,** symbolized by upper-case letters ($A, B, C, \ldots X, Y, Z$). Here are some examples of bare predicates:

English predicate	Symbolic predicate
——is a rabbit	R__
——is gigantic	G__
——is a doctor	D__
——is helpless	H__

The blank space immediately following the predicate letter is not part of the predicate; rather, it indicates the place for some lower-case letter that will represent the subject of the statement. Depending on what lower-case letter is used, and on the additional symbolism involved, symbolic predicates may be used to translate three distinct kinds of statements: singular statements, universal statements, and particular statements.

A **singular statement,** you may recall from Section 4.8, is a statement that makes an assertion about a specifically named person, place, thing, or time. Translating a singular statement involves writing a lower-case letter corresponding to the subject of the statement to the immediate right of the upper-case letter corresponding to the predicate. The letters that are allocated to serve as names of individuals are the first twenty-three letters of the alphabet ($a, b, c, \ldots u, v, w$). These letters are called **individual constants.** Here are some examples of translated statements:

Statement	Symbolic translation
Socrates is mortal.	Ms
Tokyo is populous.	Pt
The *Sun-Times* is a newspaper.	Ns
King Lear is not a fairytale.	$\sim Fk$
Berlioz was not a German.	$\sim Gb$

Compound arrangements of singular statements may be translated by using the familiar connectives of propositional logic. Here are some examples:

Statement	Symbolic translation
If Paris is beautiful, then Andre told the truth.	$Bp \supset Ta$
Irene is either a doctor or a lawyer.	$Di \lor Li$
Senator Wilkins will be elected only if he campaigns.	$Ew \supset Cw$
General Motors will prosper if either Ford is crippled by a strike or Chrysler declares bankruptcy.	$(Cf \lor Dc) \supset Pg$
Indianapolis gets rain if and only if Chicago and Milwaukee get snow.	$Ri \equiv (Sc \cdot Sm)$

A **universal statement** is a statement that makes an assertion about every member of its subject class. Such statements are either affirmative or negative, depending on whether the statement affirms or denies that the members of the subject class are members of the predicate class. The key to translating universal statements is provided by the Boolean interpretation of these statements (see Section 4.5):

Statement form	Boolean interpretation
All S are P.	If anything is an S, then it is a P.
No S are P.	If anything is an S, then it is not a P.

According to the Boolean interpretation, universal statements are translated as conditionals. Now that we have a symbol (the horseshoe "$\supset$") to translate conditional statements, we may use it to translate universal statements. What is still needed, however, is a symbol to indicate that universal statements make an assertion about *every* member of the S class. This symbol, which we introduce now, is called the **universal quantifier** and is formed by placing a lower-case letter in parentheses, thus: (x), which is translated as "for any x." The letters that are allocated for forming the universal quantifier are the last three letters of the alphabet (x, y, z). These letters are called **individual variables.**

The symbol for implication and the universal quantifier are combined to translate universal statements as follows:

Statement form	Symbolic translation	Verbal meaning
All S are P.	$(x)(Sx \supset Px)$	For any x, if x is an S, then x is a P.
No S are P.	$(x)(Sx \supset {\sim}Px)$	For any x, if x is an S, then x is not a P.

An individual variable differs from an individual constant in that it can stand for any item at random in the universe. Accordingly, the expression (x)(Sx ⊃ Px) means "If anything is an S, then it is a P," and (x) (Sx ⊃ ~Px) means "If anything is an S, then it is not a P." The fact that these expressions are equivalent to the Boolean interpretation of universal statements may be seen by recalling how the Boolean interpretation is represented by Venn diagrams (see Section 4.6). The Venn diagrams corresponding to the two universal statement forms are as follows:

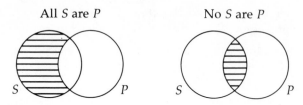

Where shading designates emptiness, the diagram on the left asserts that if anything is in the S circle, it is also in the P circle, and the one on the right asserts that if anything is in the S circle, it is not in the P circle. This is exactly what is asserted by the symbolic expressions above. These symbolic expressions may therefore be taken as being exactly synonymous with the Boolean interpretation of universal statements.

A possible source of confusion at this point concerns the fact that both S and P in the symbolic expressions are predicates, whereas in the original statement forms S is the subject and P is the predicate. Any problem in this regard vanishes, however, once one understands what happens when universal statements are converted into conditionals. When so converted, S becomes the predicate of the antecedent and P becomes the predicate of the consequent. In other words, in the conditional "If anything is an S, then it is a P," both S and P are predicates. Thus, using predicate symbolism to translate universal statements leads to no difficulties. When translating these statements, the point to remember is simply this: The subject of the original statement is represented by a capital letter in the antecedent, and the predicate by a capital letter in the consequent. Here are some examples:

Statement	Symbolic translation
All skyscrapers are tall.	(x)(Sx ⊃ Tx)
No frogs are birds.	(x)(Fx ⊃ ~Bx)
All ambassadors are statesmen.	(x)(Ax ⊃ Sx)
No diamonds are rubies.	(x)(Dx ⊃ ~Rx)

In these examples, the expressions Sx ⊃ Tx, Fx ⊃ ~Bx, and so on are called **statement functions.** The first one may be read "If *it* is an S, then *it* is a T," where "it" designates any random item in the universe. Similarly, the second one may be read, "if *it* is an *F*, then *it* is not a *B*." Statement functions, by themselves, are mere patterns for statements. They differ from complete statements in that they make no definite assertion about any item in the universe. Accordingly, they have no truth value. The variables that occur in statement functions are called **free variables** because they are not bound by any quantifier. In contrast, the variables that occur in statements are called **bound variables.**

In using quantifiers to translate statements, we adopt a convention similar to the one adopted for the negation symbol. That is: the quantifier governs only the expression immediately following it. For example, in the statement $(x)(Ax \supset Bx)$ the universal quantifier governs the entire statement function in parentheses—namely, $Ax \supset Bx$. But in the expression $(x) Ax \supset Bx$, the universal quantifier governs only the statement function Ax. The same convention is adopted for the existential quantifier, which will be introduced presently.

Particular statements are statements that make an assertion about one or more unnamed members of the subject class. As with universal statements, particular statements are either affirmative or negative, depending on whether the statement affirms or denies that members of the subject class are members of the predicate class. Also, as with universal statements, the key to translating particular statements is provided by the Boolean interpretation:

Statement form	Boolean interpretation
Some *S* are *P*.	At least one thing is an *S* and it is also a *P*.
Some *S* are not *P*.	At least one thing is an *S* and it is not a *P*.

In other words, particular statements are translated as conjunctions. Since we are already familiar with the symbol for conjunction (the dot), the only additional symbol that we need in order to translate these statements is a symbol for existence. This is provided by the **existential quantifier,** formed by placing a variable to the right of a backward "E" in parentheses, thus: $(\exists x)$. This expression is translated "there exists an x such that." The existential quantifier is combined with the symbol for conjunction to translate particular statements as follows:

Statement form	Symbolic translation	Verbal meaning
Soe *S* are *P*.	$(\exists x)(Sx \cdot Px)$	There exists an x such that x is an *S* and x is a *P*.
Some *S* are not *P*.	$(\exists x)(Sx \cdot {\sim}Px)$	There exists an x such that x is an *S* and x is not a *P*.

PREDICATE LOGIC

As in the symbolic expression of universal statements, the letter x is an individual variable, which can stand for any item in the universe. Accordingly, the expression $(\exists x)(Sx \cdot Px)$ means "Something exists that is both an S and a P," and $(\exists x)(Sx \cdot \sim Px)$ means "Something exists that is an S and not a P." To see the equivalence of these expressions with the Boolean interpretation of particular statements, it is again useful to recall how these statements are represented by Venn diagrams:

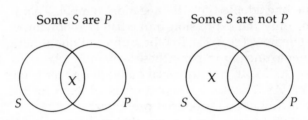

Some S are P Some S are not P

Where the "X" designates at least one existing item, the diagram on the left asserts that something exists that is both an S and a P, and the one on the right asserts that something exists that is an S and not a P. In other words, these diagrams assert exactly the same thing as the symbolic expressions above. These symbolic expressions, therefore, exactly express the Boolean interpretation of particular statements. Here are some examples:

Statement	Symbolic translation
Some men are paupers.	$(\exists x)(Mx \cdot Px)$
Some diseases are not contagious.	$(\exists x)(Dx \cdot \sim Cx)$
Some jobs are boring.	$(\exists x)(Jx \cdot Bx)$
Some vehicles are not motorcycles.	$(\exists x)(Vx \cdot \sim Mx)$

The general rule to follow in translating statements in predicate logic is always to make an effort to understand the meaning of the statement to be translated. If the statement makes an assertion about every member of its subject class, a universal quantifier should be used to translate it; but if it makes an assertion about only one or more members of this class, an existential quantifier should be used.

Many of the principles developed in syllogistic logic (see Section 4.8) may be carried over into predicate logic. Specifically, it should be understood that statements beginning with the words *only* and *none but* are exclusive propositions. When these statements are translated, the term occurring first in the original statement becomes the consequent in the symbolic expression, and the term occurring second becomes the antecedent. One of the few differences in this respect between predicate logic and syllogistic logic concerns singular statements. In syllogistic logic singular statements are translated as universals, while in predicate logic, as we have seen, they are translated in a unique way. Examples:

Statement	Symbolic translation
Sea lions are mammals.	$(x)(Sx \supset Mx)$
Sea lions live in these caves.	$(\exists x)(Sx \cdot Lx)$
Egomaniacs are not pleasant companions.	$(x)(Ex \supset {\sim}Px)$
A few egomaniacs did not arrive on time.	$(\exists x)(Ex \cdot {\sim}Ax)$
Only close friends were invited to the wedding.	$(x)(Ix \supset Cx)$
None but citizens are eligible to vote.	$(x)(Ex \supset Cx)$
It is not the case that every Girl Scout sells cookies.	${\sim}(x)(Gx \supset Sx)$ or $(\exists x)(Gx \cdot {\sim}Sx)$
Not a single psychologist attended the convention.	${\sim}(\exists x)(Px \cdot Ax)$ or $(x)(Px \supset {\sim}Ax)$

The last two examples illustrate the fact that a particular statement is equivalent to a negated universal, and vice versa. The first of these is equivalent to "Some Girl Scouts do not sell cookies" and the second to "No psychologists attended the convention." Actually, any quantified statement can be translated using either a universal or existential quantifier, provided that one of them is negated. The equivalence of these two forms of expression will be analyzed further in Section 8.3.

More complex statements may be translated by following the basic rules just presented. Examples:

Statement	Symbolic translation
1. Only snakes and lizards thrive in the desert.	$(x)[Tx \supset (Sx \lor Lx)]$
2. Oranges and lemons are citrus fruits.	$(x)[(Ox \lor Lx) \supset Cx]$
3. Ripe apples are crunchy and delicious.	$(x)[(Rx \cdot Ax) \supset (Cx \cdot Dx)]$
4. Azaleas bloom if and only if they are fertilized.	$(x)[Ax \supset (Bx \equiv Fx)]$

5. Peaches are edible unless $(x)[Px \supset (\sim Rx \supset Ex)]$
   they are rotten.   or
                                   $(x)[Px \supset (Ex \lor Rx)]$

6. Cats and dogs bite if they $(x) \{(Cx \lor Dx) \supset [(Fx \lor Hx) \supset Bx]\}$
   are frightened or harassed.

Notice that the first example is translated in terms of the disjunction $Sx \lor Lx$ even though the English statement reads "snakes *and* lizards." If the translation were rendered as $(x)[Tx \supset (Sx \cdot Lx)]$ it would mean that anything that thrives in the desert is both a snake and a lizard (at the same time). And this is surely *not* what is meant. For the same reason, the second example is translated in terms of the disjunction $Ox \lor Lx$ even though the English reads "oranges *and* lemons." If the statement were translated $(x)[(Ox \cdot Lx) \supset Cx]$, it would mean that anything that is simultaneously an orange and a lemon (and there are none of these) is a citrus fruit. The same principle is used in translating the sixth example, which, incidentally, reads "If anything is a cat or a dog, then if it is frightened or harassed, it bites." The third example employs the conjunction $Rx \cdot Ax$ to translate ripe apples. This, of course, is correct, because such a thing is both ripe and an apple at the same time. The fifth example illustrates the fact that "unless" may be translated as either "if not" or "or."

The connectives of propositional logic can be used to form compound arrangements of universal and particular statements, just as they can be used to form compound arrangements of singular statements. Here are some examples:

Statement	Symbolic translation
If Elizabeth is a historian, then some women are historians.	$He \supset (\exists x)(Wx \cdot Hx)$
If some cellists are music directors, then some orchestras are properly led.	$(\exists x)(Cx \cdot Mx) \supset (\exists x)(Ox \cdot Px)$
Either everything is alive or Bergson's theory is not correct.	$(x)Ax \lor \sim Cb$
All novels are interesting if and only if some Steinbeck novels are not romances.	$(x)(Nx \supset Ix) \equiv (\exists x)[(Nx \cdot Sx) \cdot \sim Rx)]$
Green avocados are never purchased unless all the ripe ones are expensive.	$(x)[(Gx \cdot Ax) \supset \sim Px] \lor (x)[(Rx \cdot Ax) \supset Ex]$

A CONCISE INTRODUCTION TO LOGIC

In translating statements into the symbolism of predicate logic, the usual procedure is to translate universal statements as conditionals preceded by a universal quantifier and to translate particular statements as conjunctions preceded by an existential quantifier. There are exceptions to this procedure, however. Whenever a statement is made about literally everything in the universe, the statement is translated in terms of a single predicate preceded by a universal quantifier. For example, the statement "Everything is made of matter" is translated $(x)Mx$, where Mx means "x is made of matter." Similarly, whenever it is asserted that a certain thing simply exists, the statement is translated in terms of a single predicate preceded by an existential quantifier. For example, the statement "An acorn exists" is translated $(\exists x)Ax$.

It is interesting to note what happens to ordinary universal and particular statements when they are translated using the wrong quantifier. Let us consider the false statement "No cats are animals." This is correctly translated $(x)(Cx \supset {\sim}Ax)$. If, however, it were translated $(\exists x)(Cx \supset {\sim}Ax)$, the symbolic statement would turn out to be true. This may be seen as follows. $(\exists x)(Cx \supset {\sim}Ax)$ is equivalent via material implication to $(\exists x)({\sim}Cx \vee {\sim}Ax)$, which in turn is equivalent via De-Morgan's Rule to $(\exists x){\sim}(Cx \cdot Ax)$. The latter statement, however, merely asserts that something exists that is not both a cat and an animal—for example, a dog—which is true. Again, consider the true statement "Some cats are animals." This is correctly translated $(\exists x)(Cx \cdot Ax)$. If, however, it were translated $(x)(Cx \cdot Ax)$, the symbolic statement would assert that everything in the universe is both a cat and an animal, which is clearly false. Thus, as these examples illustrate, it is imperative that the two quantifiers not be confused with each other.

One final observation needs to be made. It was mentioned earlier that the letters x, y, and z are reserved for use as variables for translating universal and particular statements. In accord with this convention, the other twenty-three lower-case letters (a, b, c, ... u, v, w) may be used as names for translating singular statements. Thus, for example, "Albert is a scientist" is translated Sa. But a question naturally arises with statements such as "Xerxes was a king." Should this statement be translated Kx? The answer is no. Some other letter, for example the second letter in the name, should be selected instead of x. Maintaining this alphabetical convention will help us avoid mistakes in the next section when we use natural deduction to derive the conclusions of arguments.

EXERCISE 8.1

Translate the following statements into symbolic form. Avoid negation signs preceding quantifiers. The predicate letters are given in parentheses.

★1. Elaine is a chemist. (C)

2. All maples are trees. (M, T)

3. Some grapes are sour. (G, S)

4. No novels are biographies. (N, B)

5. Some holidays are not relaxing. (H, R)

★6. If Gertrude is correct, then the Taj Mahal is made of marble. (C, M)

7. Gertrude is not correct only if the Taj Mahal is made of granite. (C, G)

8. A thoroughbred is a horse. (T, H)

9. A thoroughbred won the race. (T, W)

★10. Not all mushrooms are edible. (M, E)

11. Not any horsechestnuts are edible. (H, E)

12. A few guests arrived late. (G, A)

13. None but gentlemen prefer blondes. (G, P)

14. The only musicians that are available are trombonists. (M, A, T)

★15. Only talented musicians perform in the symphony. (T, M, P)

16. Any well-made car runs smoothly. (W, C, R)

17. Not every foreign car runs smoothly. (F, C, R)

18. A good violin is rare and expensive. (G, V, R, E)

19. Violins and cellos are stringed instruments. (V, C, S, I)

★20. A room with a view is available. (R, V, A)

21. A room with a view is expensive. (R, V, E)

22. Some French restaurants are exclusive. (F, R, E)

23. Some French cafes are not recommended. (F, C, R)

24. Taylor is guilty if and only if all the witnesses committed perjury. (G, W, C)

★25. If any witnesses told the truth, then either Parsons or Harris is guilty. (W, T, G)

26. If all mysteries are interesting, then *Rebecca* is interesting. (M, I)

27. If there are any interesting mysteries, then *Rebecca* is interesting. (M, I)

28. Skaters and dancers are energetic individuals. (S, D, E, I)

29. Swiss watches are not expensive unless they are made of gold. (S, W, E, M)

★30. If all the buildings in Manhattan are skyscrapers, then the Chrysler building is a skyscraper. (B, M, S)

A CONCISE INTRODUCTION TO LOGIC

31. Experienced mechanics are well paid only if all the inexperienced ones are lazy. (*E, M, W, L*)

32. Balcony seats are never chosen unless all the orchestra seats are taken. (*B, S, C, O, T*)

33. Some employees will get raises if and only if some managers are overly generous. (*E, R, M, O*)

34. The physicists and astronomers at the symposium are listed in the program if they either chair a meeting or read a paper. (*P, A, S, L, C, R*)

★35. If the scientists and technicians are conscientious and exacting, then some of the mission directors will be either pleased or delighted. (*S, T, C, E, M, P, D*)

8.2 REMOVING AND INTRODUCING QUANTIFIERS

The chief reason for using truth functional connectives (implication, conjunction, and so on) in translating statements into the symbolism of predicate logic is to allow for the application of the eighteen rules of inference to derive the conclusion of arguments via natural deduction. Since, however, the first eight of these rules are applicable only to whole lines in an argument, as long as the quantifier is attached to a line these rules of inference cannot be applied. To provide for their application, four additional rules are required to remove quantifiers at the beginning of a proof sequence and to introduce them, when needed, at the end of the sequence. These four rules are called universal instantiation, universal generalization, existential instantiation, and existential generalization. The first two are used to remove and introduce universal quantifiers, respectively, and the second two to remove and introduce existential quantifiers.

Let us first consider **universal instantiation.** As an illustration of the need for this rule, consider the following argument:

> All economists are social scientists.
> Milton Friedman is an economist.
> Therefore, Milton Friedman is a social scientist.

This argument, which is clearly valid, is symbolized as follows:

> 1. $(x)(Ex \supset Sx)$
> 2. Em / Sm

As the argument now stands, none of the first eight rules of inference can be applied; as a result, there is no way in which the two premises can be combined to obtain the conclusion. However, if the first premise could be used to obtain a line that reads *Em* ⊃ *Sm*, this statement could be combined with the second premise to yield the conclusion via *modus ponens*. Universal instantiation serves exactly this purpose.

The first premise states that for any item *x* in the universe, if that item is an *E*, then it is an *S*. But since Milton Friedman is himself an item in the universe, the first premise implies that if Milton Friedman is an *E*, then Milton Friedman is an *S*. A line stating exactly this can be obtained by universal instantiation (UI). In other words, universal instantiation provides us with an *instance* of the universal statement (x) $(Ex ⊃ Sx)$. In the completed proof, which follows, the *m* in line 3 is called the **instantial letter**:

> 1. $(x)(Ex ⊃ Sx)$
> 2. Em / Sm
> 3. $Em ⊃ Sm$ 1, UI
> 4. Sm 2, 3, MP

At this point the question might arise as to why *modus ponens* is applicable to lines 2 and 3. In Chapter 7 we applied *modus ponens* to lines of the form $p ⊃ q$, but are we justified in applying it to a line that reads *Em* ⊃ *Sm*? The answer is yes, because *Em* and *Sm* are simply alternate ways of symbolizing atomic statements. As so understood, these symbols do not differ in any material way from the *p* and *q* of propositional logic.

Let us now consider **universal generalization**. The need for this rule may be illustrated through reference to the following argument:

> All psychiatrists are doctors.
> All doctors are college graduates.
> Therefore, all psychiatrists are college graduates.

This valid argument is symbolized as follows:

> 1. $(x)(Px ⊃ Dx)$
> 2. $(x)(Dx ⊃ Cx)$ / $(x)(Px ⊃ Cx)$

Once universal instantiation is applied to the two premises, we will have lines that can be used to set up a hypothetical syllogism. But then we will have to reintroduce a universal quantifier to obtain the conclusion as written. This final step is obtained by universal generalization (UG). The justification for such a step lies in the fact that both premises are universal statements. The first states that if *anything* is a *P*, then it is a *D*, and the second states that if *anything* is a *D*, then it is a *C*. We may therefore conclude that if *anything* is a *P*, then it is a *C*. But because of the complete generality of this reasoning process, there is a special way in which we must perform the universal instantiation step. Instead of selecting a *specifically named* instance, as we did in the previous example, we must select a *variable* that can range over every instance in the universe. The variables at our disposal, you may recall from the previous section, are x, y, and z. Let us select y. The completed proof is as follows:

1. $(x)(Px \supset Dx)$
2. $(x)(Dx \supset Cx)$ / $(x)(Px \supset Cx)$
3. $Py \supset Dy$ 1, UI
4. $Dy \supset Cy$ 2, UI
5. $Py \supset Cy$ 3, 4, HS
6. $(x)(Px \supset Cx)$ 5, UG

As was noted earlier, the expression $Py \supset Dy$ in line 3 is called a *statement function*. It may be read, "If *it* is a P, then *it* is a D." Similarly, line 4 may be read, "If *it* is a D, then *it* is a C." In these lines "it" can stand for any item at random in the universe. Accordingly, line 5 may be read, "If any item in the universe is a P, then that item is a C." Line 6 is simply another way of expressing line 5.

As the two previous examples illustrate, we have two ways of performing universal instantiation. On the one hand, we may instantiate with respect to a *constant*, such as a or b, and on the other, with respect to a *variable*, such as x or y. The exact way in which this operation is to be performed depends on the kind of result intended. If we want some part of a universal statement to match a singular statement on another line, as in the first example, we instantiate with respect to a constant. But if, at the end of the proof, we want to perform universal generalization over some part of the statement we are instantiating, then we *must* instantiate by using a variable. This latter point leads to an important restriction governing universal generalization, namely, that we cannot perform this operation when the instantial letter is a constant. Consider the following *erroneous* proof sequence:

1. Ta
2. $(x)Tx$ 1, UG (invalid)

If Ta means "Albert is a thief," then on the basis of this information, we have concluded (line 2) that everything in the universe is a thief. Clearly, such an inference is invalid. This illustrates the fact that universal generalization can be performed only when the instantial letter (in this case a) is a variable.

The need for **existential generalization** can be illustrated through the following argument:

> All chemists are scientists.
> Linus Pauling is a chemist.
> Therefore, there is at least one scientist.

This argument is symbolized as follows:

    1. $(x)(Cx \supset Sx)$
    2. Cp / $(\exists x)Sx$

If we instantiate the first line with respect to p, we can obtain Sp via *modus ponens*. But if it is true that Linus Pauling is a scientist, then it certainly follows that there is at least one scientist (namely, Pauling). This last step is accomplished by existential generalization (EG). The proof is as follows:

    1. $(x)(Cx \supset Sx)$
    2. Cp / $(\exists x)Sx$
    3. $Cp \supset Sp$ 1, UI
    4. Sp 2, 3, MP
    5. $(\exists x)Sx$ 4, EG

There are no restrictions on existential generalization, and the operation can be performed when the instantial letter is either a constant (as above) or a variable. As an instance of the latter, consider the following sequence:

    1. $(x)(Px \supset Qx)$
    2. $(x) Px$ / $(\exists x)Qx$
    3. $Py \supset Qy$ 1, UI
    4. Py 2, UI
    5. Qy 3, 4, MP
    6. $(\exists x) Qx$ 5, EG

Line 5 states that everything in the universe is a Q. From this, the much weaker conclusion follows (line 6) that *something* is a Q. If you should wonder how an existential conclusion can be drawn from particular premises, the answer is that predicate logic assumes that at least one thing exists in the universe. Hence, line 2, which asserts that everything in the universe is a P, entails that at least one thing is a P. Without this assumption, universal instantiation in line 4 would not be possible.

    The need for **existential instantiation** can be illustrated through the following argument:

    All attorneys are college graduates.
    Some attorneys are golfers.
    Therefore, some golfers are college graduates.

The symbolic formulation is as follows:

    1. $(x)(Ax \supset Cx)$
    2. $(\exists x)(Ax \cdot Gx)$ / $(\exists x)(Gx \cdot Cx)$

If both quantifiers can be removed, the conclusion can be obtained via simplification, *modus ponens,* and conjunction. The universal quantifier can be removed by universal instantiation, but to remove the existential quantifier we need existential instantiation (EI). Line 2 states that there is *something* that is both an A and a G. Existential instantiation consists in giving this something a *name,* for example, "David." We will call this name an "existential name" because it is obtained through existential instantiation. The completed proof is as follows:

1. $(x)(Ax \supset Cx)$
2. $(\exists x)(Ax \cdot Gx)$ / $(\exists x)(Gx \cdot Cx)$
3. $Ad \cdot Gd$ 2, EI
4. $Ad \supset Cd$ 1, UI
5. Ad 3, Simp
6. Cd 4, 5, MP
7. Gd 3, Com, Simp
8. $Gd \cdot Cd$ 6, 7, Conj
9. $(\exists x)(Gx \cdot Cx)$ 8, EG

Examination of this proof reveals an immediate restriction that must be placed on existential instantiation. The name that we have assigned to the particular something in line 2 that is both an A and a G is a hypothetical name. It would be a mistake to conclude that this something really has that name. Accordingly, we must introduce a restriction that prevents us from ending the proof with some line that includes the letter d. If, for example, the proof were ended at line 8, we would be concluding that the something that is a G and a C really does have the name d. This, of course, would not be legitimate, because d is an arbitrary name introduced into the proof for mere convenience. To prevent such a mistake, we require that the name selected for existential instantiation not appear to the right of the slanted line adjacent to the last premise that indicates the conclusion to be obtained. Since the last line in the proof must be identical to this line, such a restriction prevents us from ending the proof with a line that contains the existential name.

Further examination of this proof indicates another important restriction on existential instantiation. Notice that the line involving existential instantiation is listed before the line involving universal instantiation. There is a reason for this. If the order were reversed, the existential instantiation step would rest upon the illicit assumption that the something that is both an A and a G has the *same* name as the name used in the earlier universal instantiation step. In other words, it would involve the assumption that the something that is both an A and a G is the very same something named in the line $Ad \supset Cd$. Of course, no such assumption is legitimate. To keep this mistake from happening, we introduce the restriction that the name introduced by existential instantiation be a new name not occurring earlier in the proof sequence.

The following defective proof illustrates what can happen if this restriction is violated:

1. $(\exists x)(Fx \cdot Ax)$
2. $(\exists x)(Fx \cdot Ox)$ / $(\exists x)(Ax \cdot Ox)$
3. $Fb \cdot Ab$ 1, EI
4. $Fb \cdot Ob$ 2, EI (invalid)
5. Ab 3, Com, Simp
6. Ob 4, Com, Simp
7. $Ab \cdot Ob$ 5, 6, Conj
8. $(\exists x)(Ax \cdot Ox)$ 7, EG

To see that this proof is indeed defective, let F stand for fruits, A for apples, and O for oranges. The argument that results is:

Some fruits are apples.
Some fruits are oranges.
Therefore, some apples are oranges.

Since the premises are true and the conclusion false, the argument is clearly invalid. The defect in the proof occurs on line 4. This line asserts that the something that is both an F and an O is the very same something that is both an F and an A. In other words, the restriction that the name introduced by existential instantiation be a new name not occurring earlier in the proof is violated.

The first restriction on existential instantiation requires that the existential name not occur in the line that indicates the conclusion to be obtained, and the second restriction requires that this name be a new name that has not occurred earlier in the proof. These two restrictions can easily be combined into a single restriction that requires that the name introduced by existential instantiation be a new name that has not occurred *anywhere* in the proof, including the line adjacent to the last premise that indicates the conclusion to be obtained.

One further restriction that affects all four of these rules of inference requires that the rules be applied only to *whole lines* in a proof. The following sequence illustrates a violation of this restriction:

1. $(x)Px \supset (x)Qx$
2. $Py \supset Qy$ 1, UI (invalid)

In line 2 universal instantiation is applied to both the antecedent and consequent of the first line. To obtain line 2 validly the first line would have to read $(x)(Px \supset Qx)$. With this final restriction in mind, the four new rules of inference may now be summarized. In the formulation that follows, the symbol $\mathscr{F} x$ represents any **statement function**—that is, any symbolic arrangement containing individual variables, such as $Ax \supset Bx$, $Cy \supset (Dy \vee Ey)$, or $Gz \cdot Hz$. And the symbol $\mathscr{F} a$ represents any **statement;** that is, any symbolic arrangement containing individual constants (or names), such as $Ac \supset Bc$, $Cm \supset (Dm \lor Em)$, or $Gw \cdot Hw$:

1. Universal instantiation (UI):

$$\frac{(x)\mathfrak{F} x}{\mathfrak{F} y} \qquad \frac{(x)\mathfrak{F} x}{\mathfrak{F} a}$$

2. Universal generalization (UG):

$$\frac{\mathfrak{F} y}{(x)\mathfrak{F} x} \qquad \text{not} \atop \text{allowed:} \qquad \frac{\mathfrak{F} a}{(x)\mathfrak{F} x}$$

3. Existential instantiation (EI):

$$\frac{(\exists x)\mathfrak{F} x}{\mathfrak{F} a} \qquad \text{not} \atop \text{allowed:} \qquad \frac{(\exists x)\mathfrak{F} x}{\mathfrak{F} y}$$

Restriction: The existential name a must be a new name that has not occurred earlier in the proof.

4. Existential generalization (EG):

$$\frac{\mathfrak{F} a}{(\exists x)\mathfrak{F} x} \qquad \frac{\mathfrak{F} y}{(\exists x)\mathfrak{F} x}$$

The *not allowed* version of universal generalization recalls the already familiar fact that generalization is not possible when the instantial letter is a constant. In other words, the mere fact that the individual a is an $\mathfrak{F}$ is not sufficient to allow us to conclude that everything in the universe is an $\mathfrak{F}$. At present this is the only restriction needed for universal generalization. In Sections 8.4 and 8.6, however, two additional restrictions will be introduced. The *not allowed* version of existential instantiation merely recalls the fact that this operation is a naming process. Because variables (x, y, and z) are not names, they cannot be used as instantial letters in existential instantiation.

Let us now investigate some applications of these rules. Consider the following proof:

1. $(x)(Hx \supset Ix)$
2. $(x)(Ix \supset Hx)$ / $(x)(Hx \equiv Ix)$
3. $Hx \supset Ix$ 1, UI
4. $Ix \supset Hx$ 2, UI
5. $(Hx \supset Ix) \cdot (Ix \supset Hx)$ 3, 4, Conj
6. $Hx \equiv Ix$ 5, Equiv
7. $(x)(Hx \equiv Ix)$ 6, UG

Because we want to perform universal generalization on the last line of the proof, we instantiate in lines 3 and 4 using a variable, not a constant. Notice that the variable selected is the same letter that occurs in lines 1 and 2. While a new letter (y or z) *could* have been selected, this is never necessary in such a step. It *is* necessary, however, since we want to combine lines 3 and 4, that the *same* variable be selected in obtaining these lines.

Another example:

1. $(x)[(Ax \lor Bx) \supset Cx]$
2. $(\exists x)Ax$ $/ (\exists x)Cx$
3. Am 2, EI
4. $(Am \lor Bm) \supset Cm$ 1, UI
5. $Am \lor Bm$ 3, Add
6. Cm 4, 5, MP
7. $(\exists x)Cx$ 6, EG

In conformity with the restriction on existential instantiation, the EI step is performed *before* the UI step. The same letter is then selected in the UI step as was used in the EI step. In line 5, Bm is joined disjunctively via addition to Am. This rule applies in predicate logic in basically the same way that it does in propositional logic. Any statement or statement function we choose can be joined disjunctively to a given line.

Another example:

1. $(\exists x)Kx \supset (x)(Lx \supset Mx)$
2. $Kc \cdot Lc$ $/ Mc$
3. Kc 2, Simp
4. $(\exists x)Kx$ 3, EG
5. $(x)(Lx \supset Mx)$ 1, 4, MP
6. $Lc \supset Mc$ 5, UI
7. Lc 2, Com, Simp
8. Mc 6, 7, MP

Since the instantiation (and generalization) rules must be applied to whole lines, it is impossible to instantiate line 1. The only strategy that can be followed is to use some other line to obtain the antecedent of this line and then obtain the consequent via *modus ponens.* Once the consequent is obtained (line 5), it is instantiated using the same letter that appears in line 2.

The following example incorporates all four of the instantiation and generalization rules:

1. $(x)(Px \supset Qx) \supset (\exists x)(Rx \cdot Sx)$
2. $(x)(Px \supset Sx) \cdot (x)(Sx \supset Qx)$ $/ (\exists x)Sx$
3. $(x)(Px \supset Sx)$ 2, Simp
4. $(x)(Sx \supset Qx)$ 2, Com, Simp
5. $Py \supset Sy$ 3, UI
6. $Sy \supset Qy$ 4, UI
7. $Py \supset Qy$ 5, 6, HS
8. $(x)(Px \supset Qx)$ 7, UG
9. $(\exists x)(Rx \cdot Sx)$ 1, 8 MP

10. $Ra \cdot Sa$	9, EI
11. Sa	10, Com, Simp
12. $(\exists x)Sx$	11, EG

As with the previous example, line 1 cannot be instantiated. To instantiate the two conjuncts in line 2, they must first be separated (lines 3 and 4). Because UG is to be used in line 8, lines 3 and 4 are instantiated using a variable. On the other hand, a constant is used to instantiate line 9 because the statement in question is a particular statement.

Another example:

1. $[(\exists x)Ax \cdot (\exists x)Bx] \supset Cj$	
2. $(\exists x)(Ax \cdot Dx)$	
3. $(\exists x)(Bx \cdot Ex)$	$/\ Cj$
4. $Am \cdot Dm$	2, EI
5. $Bn \cdot En$	3, EI
6. Am	4, Simp
7. Bn	5, Simp
8. $(\exists x)Ax$	6, EG
9. $(\exists x)Bx$	7, EG
10. $(\exists x)Ax \cdot (\exists x)Bx$	8, 9, Conj
11. Cj	1, 10, MP

When line 2 is instantiated (line 4), a letter other than j, which appears in line 1, is selected. Then, when line 3 is instantiated (line 5), another new letter is selected. The conclusion is obtained, as in earlier examples, via *modus ponens* by obtaining the antecedent of line 1.

The following examples illustrate *invalid* or *improper* applications of the instantiation and generalization rules:

1. $Fb \cdot Gb$	
2. $(\exists x)(Fx \cdot Gb)$	1, EG (improper—every instance of b must be replaced with x)

1. $(x)Fx \supset Ga$	
2. $Fx \supset Ga$	1, UI (invalid—instantiation can be applied only to whole lines)

1. $(x)Fx \supset (x)Gy$	
2. $Fx \supset Gx$	1, UI (invalid—instantiation can be applied only to whole lines)

1. Fc	
2. $(\exists x)Gx$	
3. Gc	2, EI (invalid—c appears in line 1)

1. $Fm \supset Gm$	
2. $(x)(Fx \supset Gx)$	1, UG (invalid—the instantial letter must be a variable; m is a constant.)

1. $(\exists x)\ Fx$
2. $(\exists x)\ Gx$
3. Fe 1, EI
4. Ge 2, EI   (invalid—e appears in line 3)

1. $Fs \cdot Gs$
2. $(\exists x)\ Fx \cdot Gs$ 1, EG   (improper—generalization can be
                                          applied only to whole lines)

1. $\sim(x)Fx$ 1, UI   (invalid—lines involving negated
2. $\sim Fy$ quantifiers cannot be instantiated;
                                     see Section 8.3)

EXERCISE 8.2

I. Use the eighteen rules of inference to derive the conclusions of the following symbolized arguments. Do not use either conditional proof or indirect proof.

★(1) 1. $(x)(Ax \supset Bx)$
     2. $(x)(Bx \supset Cx)$ / $(x)(Ax \supset Cx)$

 (2) 1. $(x)(Bx \supset Cx)$
     2. $(\exists x)(Ax \cdot Bx)$ / $(\exists x)(Ax \cdot Cx)$

 (3) 1. $(x)(Ax \supset Bx)$
     2. $\sim Bm$ / $(\exists x)\sim Ax$

 (4) 1. $(x)[Ax \supset (Bx \lor Cx)]$
     2. $Ag \cdot \sim Bg$ / Cg

★(5) 1. $(x)\,[(Ax \lor Bx) \supset Cx]$
     2. $(\exists y)(Ay \cdot Dy)$ / $(\exists y)\ Cy$

 (6) 1. $(x)\,[Jx \supset (Kx \cdot Lx)]$
     2. $(\exists y)\sim Ky$ / $(\exists z)\sim Jz$

 (7) 1. $(x)[Ax \supset (Bx \lor Cx)]$
     2. $(\exists x)(Ax \cdot \sim Cx)$ / $(\exists x)\ Bx$

 (8) 1. $(x)(Ax \supset Bx)$
     2. $Am \cdot An$ / $Bm \cdot Bn$

 (9) 1. $(x)(Ax \supset Bx)$
     2. $Am \lor An$ / $Bm \lor Bn$

★(10) 1. $(x)(Bx \lor Ax)$
      2. $(x)(Bx \supset Ax)$ / $(x)\ Ax$

(11) 1. $(x)[(Ax \cdot Bx) \supset Cx]$
     2. $(\exists x)(Bx \cdot \sim Cx)$ / $(\exists x)\sim Ax$

(12) 1. $(\exists x)\ Ax \supset (x)(Bx \supset Cx)$
     2. $Am \cdot Bm$ / Cm

(13) 1. $(\exists x)\ Ax \supset (x)\ Bx$

2. $(\exists x) Cx \supset (\exists x) Dx$
3. $An \cdot Cn$ / $(\exists x)(Bx \cdot Dx)$

(14) 1. $(\exists x) Ax \supset (x)(Cx \supset Bx)$
    2. $(\exists x)(Ax \lor Bx)$
    3. $(x)(Bx \supset Ax)$ / $(x)(Cx \supset Ax)$

★(15) 1. $(\exists x) Ax \supset (x)(Bx \supset Cx)$
    2. $(\exists x) Dx \supset (\exists x) \sim Cx$
    3. $(\exists x)(Ax \cdot Dx)$ / $(\exists x) \sim Bx$

II. Translate the following arguments into symbolic form. Then use the eighteen rules of inference to derive the conclusion of each. Do not use conditional or indirect proof.

★1. Oranges are sweet. Also, oranges are fragrant. Therefore, oranges are sweet and fragrant. (O, S, F)

2. Tomatoes are vegetables. Therefore, the tomatoes in the garden are vegetables. (T, V, G)

3. Apples and pears grow on trees. Therefore, apples grow on trees. (A, P, G)

4. Carrots are vegetables and peaches are fruit. Furthermore, there are carrots and peaches in the garden. Therefore, there are vegetables and fruit in the garden. (C, V, P, F, G)

★5. Beans and peas are legumes. There are no legumes in the garden. Therefore, there are no beans in the garden. (B, P, L, G)

6. There are some cucumbers in the garden. If there are any cucumbers, there are some pumpkins in the garden. All pumpkins are vegetables. Therefore, there are some vegetables in the garden. (C, G, P, V)

7. All gardeners are industrious. Furthermore, anyone industrious is respected. Therefore, since Arthur and Catherine are gardeners, it follows that they are respected. (G, I, R)

8. Some huckleberries are ripe. Furthermore, some boysenberries are sweet. If there are any huckleberries, then the boysenberries are edible if they are sweet. Therefore, some boysenberries are edible. (H, R, B, S, E)

9. If there are any ripe watermelons, then the caretakers performed well. Furthermore, if there are any large watermelons, then whoever performed well will get a bonus. There are some large, ripe watermelons. Therefore, the caretakers will get a bonus. (R, W, C, P, L, B)

★10. If the artichokes in the kitchen are ripe, then the guests will be surprised. Furthermore, if the artichokes in the kitchen are flavorful, then the guests will be pleased. The artichokes in the kitchen are ripe and flavorful. Therefore, the guests will be surprised and pleased. (A, K, R, G, S, F, P)

8.3 CHANGE OF QUANTIFIER RULES

The rules of inference developed thus far are not sufficient to derive the conclusion of every argument in predicate logic. For instance, consider the following:

$$\sim(\exists x)(Px \cdot \sim Qx)$$
$$\underline{\sim(x)(\sim Rx \lor Qx)}$$
$$(\exists x)\sim Px$$

Both premises have negation signs preceding the quantifiers. As long as these negation signs remain, neither statement can be instantiated; and if these statements cannot be instantiated, the conclusion cannot be derived. What is needed is a set of rules that will allow us to remove the negation signs. These rules, which we will proceed to develop now, are called **change of quantifier rules.**

For the purpose of introducing these rules, it is convenient to use the square of opposition in modern logic (see Sections 4.5 and 4.7):

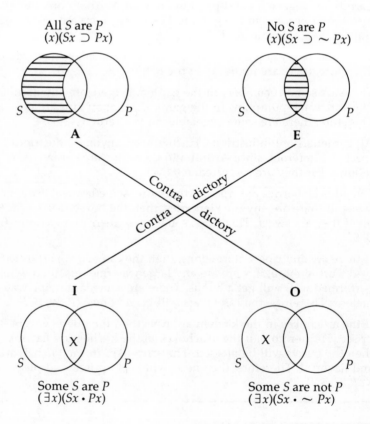

All S are P
$(x)(Sx \supset Px)$

No S are P
$(x)(Sx \supset \sim Px)$

A

E

Contra dictory

Contra dictory

I

O

Some S are P
$(\exists x)(Sx \cdot Px)$

Some S are not P
$(\exists x)(Sx \cdot \sim Px)$

The four types of statements—universal affirmative, universal negative, particular affirmative, and particular negative—are identified respectively by the letters **A, E, I,** and **O** (see Section 4.2). The Venn diagrams illustrate the contradictory relationship prevailing between **A** and **O** on the one hand and between **I** and **E** on the other.

In these diagrams, shading an area indicates that the area in question is empty, and placing an "X" in an area indicates that the area contains at least one member. For the **A** statement, the left-hand portion of the S circle is empty, and for the **O** statement the corresponding area is not empty. Clearly, these two statements contradict each other. Similarly, for the **E** statement the overlapping portion of the diagram is empty, and for the **I** statement it is not empty.

Now, since any statement is logically equivalent to the negation of its contradictory, it follows that the **A** statement is logically equivalent to the negation of the **O**, the **I** is logically equivalent to the negation of the **E**, and so on. Let us consider the first of these equivalences:

$$(x)(Sx \supset Px) \equiv \sim(\exists x)(Sx \cdot \sim Px)$$
$$\equiv \sim(\exists x)\sim(\sim Sx \vee Px) \text{ by DN \& DM}$$
$$\equiv \sim(\exists x)\sim(Sx \supset Px) \text{ by Impl}$$

We begin by setting the **A** statement equivalent to the negation of the **O** statement and then proceed to rearrange the components of the **O** statement using double negation, DeMorgan's Rule, and the rule of material implication. Such a procedure is quite legitimate because these rules are rules of equivalence; they apply to parts of lines as well as to whole lines. It is therefore not necessary to remove the existential quantifiers to perform these operations. In the end we arrive at the equivalence

$$(x)(Sx \supset Px) \equiv \sim(\exists x)\sim(Sx \supset Px)$$

Notice that the statement functions in these expressions are identical. This fact allows us to conclude that a universal quantifier may be replaced by an existential quantifier if and only if a negation sign is introduced immediately before and after the new quantifier.

Similar results are obtained by setting the negation of the **A** statement equivalent to the **O** statement:

$$\sim(x)(Sx \supset Px) \equiv (\exists x)(Sx \cdot \sim Px)$$
$$\equiv (\exists x)\sim(\sim Sx \vee Px) \text{ by DN \& DM}$$
$$\equiv (\exists x)\sim(Sx \supset Px) \text{ by Impl}$$

By setting the **I** statement equivalent to the negation of the **E** statement we obtain:

$$(\exists x)(Sx \cdot Px) \equiv \sim(x)(Sx \supset \sim Px)$$
$$\equiv \sim(x)(\sim Sx \vee \sim Px) \text{ by Impl}$$
$$\equiv \sim(x)\sim(Sx \cdot Px) \text{ by DM}$$

And finally, by setting the negation of the **I** statment equivalent to the **E** statement, we have:

$$\sim(\exists x)(Sx \cdot Px) \equiv (x)(Sx \supset \sim Px)$$
$$\equiv (x)(\sim Sx \vee \sim Px) \text{ by Impl}$$
$$\equiv (x)\sim(Sx \cdot Px) \text{ by DM}$$

These equivalences demonstrate that negated and non-negated quantifiers may be replaced by their correlative if and only if negation signs are appropriately introduced or deleted before and after the new quantifier. If we let $\mathfrak{F}x$ represent any statement function, we may abbreviate these results as follows:

$$(x)\mathfrak{F}x \equiv \sim(\exists x)\sim \mathfrak{F}x$$
$$\sim(x)\mathfrak{F}x \equiv (\exists x) \sim \mathfrak{F}x$$
$$(\exists x)\mathfrak{F}x \equiv \sim(x)\sim \mathfrak{F}x$$
$$\sim(\exists x)\mathfrak{F}x \equiv (x)\sim \mathfrak{F}x$$

These are the change of quantifier rules (CQ). Since they are stated as logical equivalences, they apply to parts of lines as well as to whole lines. They can be summarized into a single rule that reads:

> One type of quantifier can be replaced by the other type if and only if immediately before and after the new quantifier:
> 1. Negation signs that were present earlier are deleted.
> 2. Negation signs that were not present earlier are introduced.

At this point we might question whether statements of the form $(x)Px$ and $(\exists x)Qx$ fall under this rule, since they are not in the same form as the more typical universal and particular statements. The answer is that they do indeed fall under this rule. The statement that everything in the universe is a P, symbolized $(x)Px$, is simply a shortened form of $(x)(Ux \supset Px)$, where Ux means "x is in the universe," and the statement that something in the universe is a Q, symbolized $(\exists x)Qx$, is simply another way of writing $(\exists x)(Ux \cdot Qx)$. Since everything whatsoever is a thing in the universe, the expression Ux is always true. As a result, $(x)(Ux \supset Px)$ reduces to $(x)Px$, and $(\exists x)(Ux \cdot Qx)$ reduces to $(\exists x)Qx$.

Let us now turn to some applications of the change of quantifier rule. Consider first the argument mentioned at the beginning of this section. The proof is as follows:

1. $\sim(\exists x)(Px \cdot \sim Qx)$
2. $\sim(x)(\sim Rx \vee Qx)$ / $(\exists x)\sim Px$
3. $(x)\sim(Px \cdot \sim Qx)$ 1, CQ
4. $(\exists x)\sim(\sim Rx \vee Qx)$ 2, CQ
5. $\sim(\sim Ra \vee Qa)$ 4, EI
6. $\sim(Pa \cdot \sim Qa)$ 3, UI
7. $Ra \cdot \sim Qa$ 5, DM, DN
8. $\sim Pa \vee Qa$ 6, DM, DN
9. $\sim Qa$ 7, Com, Simp
10. $\sim Pa$ 8, 9, Com, DS
11. $(\exists x)\sim Px$ 10, EG

Before either line 1 or line 2 can be instantiated, the negation signs preceding the quantifiers must be removed. In accordance with the change of quantifier rule, negation signs are introduced immediately after the new quantifiers in the expressions on lines 3 and 4.
    Another example:

1. $(\exists x)(Hx \cdot Gx) \supset (x)Ix$
2. $\sim Im$ / $(x)(Hx \supset \sim Gx)$
3. $(\exists x)\sim Ix$ 2, EG
4. $\sim(x)Ix$ 3, CQ
5. $\sim(\exists x)(Hx \cdot Gx)$ 1, 4, MT
6. $(x)\sim(Hx \cdot Gx)$ 5, CQ
7. $(x)(\sim Hx \vee \sim Gx)$ 6, DM
8. $(x)(Hx \supset \sim Gx)$ 7, Impl

The statement that m is not an I (line 2) intuitively implies that not everything is an I (line 4); but existential generalization and change of quantifier are needed to get the desired result. Notice that lines 7 and 8 are obtained via DeMorgan's rule and the rule of material implication, even though the quantifier is still attached. Since these rules are rules of logical equivalence, they apply to parts of lines as well as to whole lines. The following example illustrates the same point with respect to the change of quantifier rules:

1. $(\exists x)Jx \supset \sim(\exists x)Kx$
2. $(x)\sim Kx \supset (x)\sim Lx$ / $(\exists x)Jx \supset \sim(\exists x)Lx$
3. $(\exists x)Jx \supset (x)\sim Kx$ 1, CQ
4. $(\exists x)Jx \supset (x)\sim Lx$ 2, 3, HS
5. $(\exists x)Jx \supset \sim(\exists x)Lx$ 4, CQ

The change of quantifier rule is applied to only the consequent of line 1, yielding line 3. Similarly, the change of quantifier rule is then applied to only the consequent of line 4, yielding line 5.

PREDICATE LOGIC   **321**

EXERCISE 8.3

I. Use the change of quantifier rule together with the eighteen rules of inference to derive the conclusions of the following symbolized arguments. Do not use either conditional proof or indirect proof.

★(1) 1. $(x)Ax \supset (\exists x)Bx$
2. $(x) \sim Bx$ / $(\exists x) \sim Ax$

(2) 1. $(\exists x) \sim Ax \lor (\exists x) \sim Bx$
2. $(x)Bx$ / $\sim (x)Ax$

(3) 1. $\sim (\exists x)Ax$ / $(x)(Ax \supset Bx)$

(4) 1. $(\exists x)Ax \lor (\exists x)(Bx \cdot Cx)$
2. $\sim (\exists x)Bx$ / $(\exists x)Ax$

★(5) 1. $(x)(Ax \cdot Bx) \lor (x)(Cx \cdot Dx)$
2. $\sim (x)Dx$ / $(x)Bx$

(6) 1. $(\exists x) \sim Ax \supset (x)(Bx \supset Cx)$
2. $\sim (x)(Ax \lor Cx)$ / $\sim (x)Bx$

(7) 1. $(x)(Ax \supset Bx)$
2. $\sim (x)Cx \lor (x)Ax$
3. $\sim (x)Bx$ / $(\exists x) \sim Cx$

(8) 1. $(x)Ax \supset (\exists x) \sim Bx$
2. $\sim (x)Bx \supset (\exists x) \sim Cx$ / $(x)Cx \supset (\exists x) \sim Ax$

(9) 1. $(\exists x)(Ax \lor Bx) \supset (x)Cx$
2. $(\exists x) \sim Cx$ / $\sim (\exists x)Ax$

★(10) 1. $\sim (\exists x)(Ax \cdot \sim Bx)$
2. $\sim (\exists x)(Bx \cdot \sim Cx)$ / $(x)(Ax \supset Cx)$

(11) 1. $\sim (\exists x)(Ax \cdot \sim Bx)$
2. $\sim (\exists x)(Ax \cdot \sim Cx)$ / $(x)[Ax \supset (Bx \cdot Cx)]$

(12) 1. $(x)[(Ax \cdot Bx) \supset Cx]$
2. $\sim (x)(Ax \supset Cx)$ / $\sim (x)Bx$

(13) 1. $(x)(Ax \cdot \sim Bx) \supset (\exists x)Cx$
2. $\sim (\exists x)(Cx \lor Bx)$ / $\sim (x)Ax$

(14) 1. $(\exists x) \sim Ax \supset (x) \sim Bx$
2. $(\exists x) \sim Ax \supset (\exists x)Bx$
3. $(x)(Ax \supset Cx)$ / $(x)Cx$

★(15) 1. $\sim (\exists x)(Ax \lor Bx)$
2. $(\exists x)Cx \supset (\exists x)Ax$
3. $(\exists x)Dx \supset (\exists x)Bx$ / $\sim (\exists x)(Cx \lor Dx)$

II. Translate the following arguments into symbolic form. Then use the change of quantifier rule and the eighteen rules of inference to derive the conclusion of each. Do not use either conditional proof or indirect proof.

★1. If all the physicians are either hematologists or neurologists, then there are no cardiologists. But Dr. Frank is a cardiologist. Therefore, some physicians are not neurologists. (P, H, N, C)

2. Either Dr. Adams is an internist or all the pathologists are internists. But it is not the case that there are any internists. Therefore, Dr. Adams is not a pathologist. (I, P)

3. If some surgeons are allergists, then some psychiatrists are radiologists. But no psychiatrists are radiologists. Therefore, no surgeons are allergists. (S, A, P, R)

4. Either some general practitioners are pediatricians or some surgeons are endocrinologists. But it is not the case that there are any endocrinologists. Therefore, there are some pediatricians. (G, P, S, E)

★5. All physicians who did not attend medical school are incompetent. It is not the case, however, that some physicians are incompetent. Therefore, all physicians have attended medical school. (P, A, I)

6. It is not the case that some internists are not physicians. Furthermore, it is not the case that some physicians are not doctors of medicine. Therefore, all internists are doctors of medicine. (I, P, D)

7. All pathologists are specialists and all internists are generalists. Therefore, since it is not the case that some specialists are generalists, it is not the case that some pathologists are internists. (P, S, I, G)

8. If some obstetricians are not gynecologists, then some hematologists are radiologists. But it is not the case that there are any hematologists or gynecologists. Therefore, it is not the case that there are any obstetricians. (O, G, H, R)

9. All poorly trained allergists and dermatologists are untrustworthy specialists. It is not the case, however, that some specialists are untrustworthy. Therefore, it is not the case that some dermatologists are poorly trained. (P, A, D, U, S)

★10. It is not the case that some physicians are either on the golf course or in the hospital. All of the neurologists are physicians in the hospital. Either some physicians are cardiologists or some physicians are neurologists. Therefore, some cardiologists are not on the golf course. (P, G, H, N, C)

8.4 CONDITIONAL AND INDIRECT PROOF

Many arguments with conclusions that are either difficult or impossible to derive by the conventional method can be handled with ease by using either conditional or indirect proof. The use of these techniques on arguments in predicate logic is basically the same as it is on arguments in propositional logic. Arguments having conclusions expressed in the form of conditional statements or disjunctions (which can be converted into conditional statements) are immediate candidates for conditional proof. For these arguments, the usual strategy is to assume the antecedent of the conditional statement to be obtained as the first line of an indented sequence, to derive the consequent as the last line, and to discharge the conditional sequence in a conditional statement that exactly matches the one to be obtained. Here is an example of such a proof:

1. $(x)(Hx \supset Ix)$ / $(\exists x)Hx \supset (\exists x)Ix$
2. $(\exists x)Hx$ CP
3. Ha 2, EI
4. $Ha \supset Ia$ 1, UI
5. Ia 3, 4, HS
6. $(\exists x)Ix$ 5, EG
7. $(\exists x)Hx \supset (\exists x)Ix$ 2–6, CP

In this argument the antecedent of the conclusion is a complete statement consisting of a statement function, Hx, preceded by a quantifier. This complete statement is assumed as the first line in the conditional sequence. The instantiation and generalization rules are used within an indented sequence (both conditional and indirect) in basically the same way as they are in a conventional sequence. When the consequent of the conclusion is obtained, the conditional sequence is completed, and it is then discharged in a conditional statement having the first line of the sequence as its antecedent and the last line as its consequent.

The next example differs from the previous one in that the antecedent of the conclusion is a statement function, not a complete statement. With arguments such as this, only the statement function is assumed as the first line in the conditional sequence. The quantifier is added after the sequence is discharged.

1. $(x)[(Ax \lor Bx) \supset Cx]$ / $(x)(Ax \supset Cx)$
2. Ax CP
3. $Ax \lor Bx$ 2, Add
4. $(Ax \lor Bx) \supset Cx$ 1, UI
5. Cx 3, 4, MP
6. $Ax \supset Cx$ 2–5, CP
7. $(x)(Ax \supset Cx)$ 6, UG

This example leads to an important restriction on the use of universal generalization. You may recall that the x in line 2 of this proof is called a *free variable* because it is not governed by any quantifier. (In contrast, the x's in lines 1 and 7 are called *bound variables*.) The restriction is as follows:

UG: $\dfrac{\mathfrak{I}y}{(x)\mathfrak{I}x}$ *Restriction:*   UG must not be used within the scope of an indented sequence if the instantial variable occurs free in the first line of that sequence.

The above proof does not violate this restriction because UG is not used within the scope of the indented sequence at all. It is used only after the sequence has been discharged, which is perfectly acceptable. If, on the other hand, UG had been applied to line 5 to produce a statement reading $(x)Cx$, the restriction would have been violated because the instantial variable x occurs free in the first line of the sequence.

To understand why this restriction is necessary, consider the following *defective* proof:

1. $(x)Rx \supset (x)Sx$ / $(x) (Rx \supset Sx)$
    2. Rx CP
    3. $(x)Rx$ 2, UG (invalid)
    4. $(x)Sx$ 1, 3, MP
    5. Sx 4, UI
6. $Rx \supset Sx$ 2–5, CP
7. $(x)(Rx \supset Sx)$ 6, UG

If Rx means "x is a rabbit" and Sx means "x is a snake," then the premise translates "If everything in the universe is a rabbit, then everything in the universe is a snake." This statement is *true* because the antecedent is false; that is, it is *not* the case that everything in the universe is a rabbit. The conclusion, on the other hand, is *false*, because it asserts that all rabbits are snakes. The argument is therefore invalid. If the restriction on UG had been obeyed, UG would not have been used on line 3 and, as a result, the illicit conclusion would not have been obtained.

It is interesting to see what happens when the premise and the conclusion of this defective argument are switched. The proof, which is perfectly legitimate, is as follows:

1. $(x)(Rx \supset Sx)$ / $(x)Rx \supset (x)Sx$
    2. $(x)Rx$ CP
    3. Rx 2, UI
    4. $Rx \supset Sx$ 1, UI
    5. Sx 3, 4, HS
    6. $(x)Sx$ 5, UG
7. $(x)Rx \supset (x)Sx$ 2–6, CP

Notice in this proof that UG *is* used within the scope of a conditional sequence, but the restriction is not violated because the instantial variable x is not free on the first line of the sequence.

Let us now consider some examples of *indirect* proof. We begin an indirect sequence by assuming the negation of the statement to be obtained. When a contradiction is derived, the indirect sequence is discharged by asserting the denial of the original assumption. In the examples that follow, the negation of the conclusion is assumed as the first line of the sequence, and the change of quantifier rule is then used to eliminate the negation sign. When the resulting statement is then instantiated, a new letter, m, is selected that has not appeared anywhere in a previous line. The same letter is then selected for the universal instantiation of line 1:

1. $(x)[(Px \supset Px) \supset (Qx \supset Rx)]$ / $(x)(Qx \supset Rx)$
2. $\sim (x)(Qx \supset Rx)$ IP
3. $(\exists x)\sim(Qx \supset Rx)$ 2, CQ
4. $\sim(Qm \supset Rm)$ 3, EI
5. $(Pm \supset Pm) \supset (Qm \supset Rm)$ 1, UI
6. $\sim(Pm \supset Pm)$ 4, 5, MT
7. $\sim(\sim Pm \vee Pm)$ 6, Impl
8. $Pm \cdot \sim Pm$ 7, DM, DN
9. $\sim\sim(x)(Qx \supset Rx)$ 2–8, IP
10. $(x)(Qx \supset Rx)$ 9, DN

The next example has a particular statement for its conclusion:

1. $(\exists x)Ax \vee (\exists x)Fx$
2. $(x)(Ax \supset Fx)$ / $(\exists x)Fx$
3. $\sim(\exists x)Fx$ IP
4. $(\exists x)Ax$ 1, 3, Com, DS
5. Ac 4, EI
6. $Ac \supset Fc$ 2, UI
7. Fc 5, 6, MP
8. $(x)\sim Fx$ 3, CQ
9. $\sim Fc$ 8, UI
10. $Fc \cdot \sim Fc$ 7, 9, Conj
11. $(\exists x)Fx$ 3–10, IP, DN

Since indirect proof sequences are indented, they are subject to the same restriction on universal generalization as conditional sequences. The following proof, which is similar to the previous one, violates this restriction because the instantial variable x is free in the first line of the sequence. The violation (line 4) allows a universal statement to be drawn for the conclusion, whereas only a particular statement (as above) is legitimate:

1. $(\exists x)Ax \vee (\exists x)Fx$
2. $(x)(Ax \supset Fx)$ / $(x)Fx$
3. $\sim Fx$ IP
4. $(x)\sim Fx$ 3, UG (invalid)
5. $\sim(\exists x)Fx$ 4, CQ
6. $(\exists x)Ax$ 1, 5, Com, DS
7. Ac 6, EI

8. $Ac \supset Fc$	2, UI
9. Fc	7, 8, MP
10. $\sim Fc$	4, UI
11. $Fc \cdot \sim Fc$	9–10, Conj
12. Fx	3–11, IP, DN
13. $(x)Fx$	12, UG

To see that this argument is indeed invalid, let Ax stand for "x is an apple" and Fx for "x is a fruit." The first premise then reads "Either an apple exists or a fruit exists" (which is true), and the second premise reads "All apples are fruits" (which is also true). The conclusion, however, reads "Everything in the universe is a fruit"; and this, of course, is false.

As in propositional logic, conditional and indirect sequences in predicate logic may include each other. The following proof uses an indirect sequence within the scope of a conditional sequence.

1. $(x)[(Px \vee Qx) \supset (Rx \cdot Sx)]$	/ $(\exists x)(Px \vee Sx) \supset (\exists x)Sx$
2. $(\exists x)(Px \vee Sx)$	CP
3. $\sim(\exists x)Sx$	IP
4. $(x)\sim Sx$	3, CQ
5. $Pa \vee Sa$	2, EI
6. $\sim Sa$	4, UI
7. Pa	5, 6, Com, DS
8. $Pa \vee Qa$	7, Add
9. $(Pa \vee Qa) \supset (Ra \cdot Sa)$	1, UI
10. $Ra \cdot Sa$	8, 9, MP
11. Sa	10, Com, Simp
12. $Sa \cdot \sim Sa$	6, 11, Conj
13. $(\exists x)Sx$	3–12, IP, DN
14. $(\exists x)(Px \vee Sx) \supset (\exists x)Sx$	2–13, CP

The conditional sequence begins, as usual, by assuming the antecedent of the conditional statement to be obtained. The objective, then, is to obtain the consequent. This is accomplished by the indirect sequence, which begins with the negation of the consequent and ends (line 12) with a contradiction.

EXERCISE 8.4

I. Use either indirect proof or conditional proof to derive the conclusions of the following symbolized arguments:

★(1) 1. $(x)(Ax \supset Bx)$
2. $(x)(Ax \supset Cx)$ / $(x)[Ax \supset (Bx \cdot Cx)]$

(2) 1. $(\exists x)Ax \supset (\exists x)(Bx \cdot Cx)$
2. $(\exists x)(Cx \vee Dx) \supset (x)Ex$ / $(x)(Ax \supset Ex)$

(3) 1. $(\exists x)Ax \supset (\exists x)(Bx \cdot Cx)$
2. $\sim(\exists x)Cx$ / $(x)\sim Ax$

(4) 1. $(x)(Ax \supset Cx)$
2. $(\exists x)Cx \supset (\exists x)(Bx \cdot Dx)$ / $(\exists x)Ax \supset (\exists x)Bx$

★(5) 1. $(x)(Ax \supset Bx)$
2. $(x)[(Ax \cdot Bx) \supset Cx]$ / $(x)(Ax \supset Cx)$

(6) 1. $(\exists x)Ax \supset (x)Bx$
2. $An \supset \sim Bn$ / $\sim An$

(7) 1. $(x)[(Ax \lor Bx) \supset Cx]$
2. $(x)[(Cx \lor Dx) \supset Ex]$ / $(x)(Ax \supset Ex)$

(8) 1. $(\exists x)(Ax \lor Bx) \supset \sim(\exists x)Ax$ / $(x)\sim Ax$

(9) 1. $(x)(Ax \supset Bx)$
2. $(x)(Cx \supset Dx)$ / $(\exists x)(Ax \lor Cx) \supset (\exists x)(Bx \lor Dx)$

★(10) 1. $(x)(Ax \supset Bx)$
2. $Am \lor An$ / $(\exists x)Bx$

(11) 1. $(x)[(Ax \lor Bx) \supset Cx]$
2. $(x)[(Cx \lor Dx) \supset \sim Ax]$ / $(x)\sim Ax$

(12) 1. $(\exists x)Ax \supset (x)(Bx \supset Cx)$
2. $(\exists x)Dx \supset (x)\sim Cx$ / $(x)[(Ax \cdot Dx) \supset \sim Bx]$

(13) 1. $(\exists x)Ax \supset (x)(Bx \supset Cx)$
2. $(\exists x)Dx \supset (\exists x)Bx$ / $(\exists x)(Ax \cdot Dx) \supset (\exists x)Cx$

(14) 1. $(\exists x)Ax \lor (\exists x)(Bx \cdot Cx)$
2. $(x)(Ax \supset Cx)$ / $(\exists x)Cx$

★(15) 1. $(\exists x)Ax \supset (\exists x)(Bx \cdot Cx)$
2. $(\exists x)Cx \supset (x)(Dx \cdot Ex)$ / $(x)(Ax \supset Ex)$

(16) 1. $(x)[(Ax \lor Bx) \supset Cx]$
2. $(\exists x)(\sim Ax \lor Dx) \supset (x)Ex$ / $(x)Cx \lor (x)Ex$

(17) 1. $(x)Ax \equiv (\exists x)(Bx \cdot Cx)$
2. $(x)(Cx \supset Bx)$ / $(x)Ax \equiv (\exists x)Cx$

(18) 1. $(x)(Ax \equiv Bx)$
2. $(x)[Ax \supset (Bx \supset Cx)]$
3. $(\exists x)Ax \lor (\exists x)Bx$ / $(\exists x)Cx$

(19) 1. $(x)[Bx \supset (Cx \cdot Dx)]$ / $(x)(Ax \supset Bx) \supset (x)(Ax \supset Dx)$

★(20) 1. $(x)[Ax \supset (Bx \cdot Cx)]$
2. $(x)[Dx \supset (Ex \cdot Fx)]$ / $(x)(Cx \supset Dx) \supset (x)(Ax \supset Fx)$

(21) 1. $(\exists x)(Ax \lor Bx)$
2. $(\exists x)Ax \supset (x)(Cx \supset Bx)$
3. $(\exists x)Cx$ / $(\exists x)Bx$

II. Translate the following arguments into symbolic form. Then use conditional or indirect proof to derive the conclusion of each.

★1. All ambassadors are wealthy. Furthermore, all Republicans are clever. Therefore, all Republican ambassadors are clever and wealthy. (*A, W, R, C*)

2. All senators are well liked. Also, if there are any well-liked senators, then O'Brien is a voter. Therefore, if there are any senators, then O'Brien is a voter. (*S, W, V*)

3. If all judges are wise, then some attorneys are rewarded. Furthermore, if there are any judges who are not wise, then some attorneys are rewarded. Therefore, some attorneys are rewarded. (*J, W, A, R*)

4. All secretaries and undersecretaries are intelligent and cautious. All those who are cautious or vigilant are restrained and austere. Therefore, all secretaries are austere. (*S, U, I, C, V, R, A*)

★5. All ambassadors are diplomats. Furthermore, all experienced ambassadors are cautious, and all cautious diplomats have foresight. Therefore, all experienced ambassadors have foresight. (*A, D, E, C, F*)

6. If there are any senators, then some employees are well paid. If there is anyone who is either an employee or a volunteer, then there are some legislative assistants. Either there are some volunteers or there are some senators. Therefore, there are some legislative assistants. (*S, E, W, V, L*)

7. If there are any counsels, then all ambassadors are satisfied diplomats. If no counsels are ambassadors, then some diplomats are satisfied. Therefore, some diplomats are satisfied. (*C, A, S, D*)

8. If there are any voters, then all politicians are astute. If there are any politicians, then whoever is astute is clever. Therefore, if there are any voters, then all politicians are clever. (*V, P, A, C*)

9. Either no senators are present or no representatives are present. Furthermore, either some senators are present or no women are present. Therefore, none of the representatives who are present are women. (*S, P, R, W*)

★10. Either some governors are present or some ambassadors are present. If anyone is present, then some ambassadors are clever diplomats. Therefore, some diplomats are clever. (*G, P, A, C, D*)

8.5 PROVING INVALIDITY

In a valid deductive argument the conclusion follows *necessarily* from the premises. This means that for such an argument the link between premises and conclusion is independent of the actual arrangement of things in the world. If an argument is valid, it remains valid irrespective of whether the sun rises in the east or whether World War III starts tomorrow. Accordingly, if the premises of a valid argument are assumed true, the conclusion must be true, no matter what happens. Conversely, if, under a certain assumption, the premises of an argument are true and the conclusion false, the argument is invalid. In other words, if we can imagine an arrangement of things in the world that causes the premises to be true and the conclusion false, the argument is invalid. The method that we are about to describe for proving the invalidity of arguments in predicate logic rests upon this basic insight.

To see how this method works, it is important to understand what happens to the meaning of universal and particular statements when we imagine the universe to be changed in certain ways. To this end, let us imagine that the universe contains only one thing instead of the billions of things that it actually contains. Let us name that one thing "Abigail." The statement "Everything in the universe is perfect" is then equivalent to "Abigail is perfect" (because Abigail is all that there is), and the statement "Something in the universe is perfect" is also equivalent to "Abigail is perfect" (because Abigail is that "something"). In symbols, we have:

$$(x)Px \equiv Pa$$
$$(\exists x)Px \equiv Pa$$

Proceeding, if we imagine that the universe contains exactly two things—let us name them "Abigail" and "Beatrice"—the statement "Everything in the universe is perfect" is equivalent to "Abigail is perfect *and* Beatrice is perfect." Conversely, the statement "Something in the universe is perfect" is equivalent to "Abigail is perfect *or* Beatrice is perfect" (because *some* means *at least one*). In other words, the universal statement is equivalent to a *conjunction* of singular statements, and the particular statement is equivalent to a *disjunction* of singular statements. In symbols:

$$(x)Px \equiv (Pa \cdot Pb)$$
$$(\exists x)Px \equiv (Pa \vee Pb)$$

If the universe is increased to three—let us call the new member "Charmaine"—we have:

$$(x)Px \equiv (Pa \cdot Pb \cdot Pc)$$
$$(\exists x)Px \equiv (Pa \vee Pb \vee Pc)$$

This equivalence continues indefinitely as more and more members are added to the universe.

Extending this treatment to the more typical kinds of universal and particular statements, we have, for a universe of three:

$$(x)(Px \supset Qx) \equiv [(Pa \supset Qa) \cdot (Pb \supset Qb) \cdot (Pc \supset Qc)]$$
$$(\exists x)(Px \cdot Qx) \equiv [(Pa \cdot Qa) \vee (Pb \cdot Qb) \vee (Pc \cdot Qc)]$$

A CONCISE INTRODUCTION TO LOGIC

For expressions involving combinations of quantified statements, each of the component statements is translated separately and the resulting statement groups are linked together by means of the connective appearing in the original statement. Here are two examples for a universe of three:

$$[(x)Px \supset (\exists x)Qx] \equiv [(Pa \cdot Pb \cdot Pc) \supset (Qa \vee Qb \vee Qc)]$$
$$[(x)(Px \supset Qx) \vee (\exists x)(Rx \cdot Sx)] \equiv \{[(Pa \supset Qa) \cdot (Pb \supset Qb) \cdot (Pc \supset Qc)]$$
$$\vee [(Ra \cdot Sa) \vee (Rb \cdot Sb) \vee (Rc \cdot Sc)]\}$$

The method for proving an argument invalid consists in translating the premises and conclusion into singular statements, as per the above examples, and then testing the result with an indirect truth table (see Section 6.6). First a universe of one is tried. If it is possible for the premises to be true and the conclusion false in this universe, the argument is immediately identified as invalid. If, on the other hand, a contradiction results from this assumption, a universe of two is then tried. If, in this second universe, it is possible for the premises to be true and the conclusion false, the argument is invalid. If not, a universe of three is tried, and so on.

Consider the following argument:

$$(x)(Gx \supset Hx)$$
$$(\exists x)Hx \qquad / (\exists x)Gx$$

For a universe having one member—call this member "Abigail"—the argument translates into:

$$Ga \supset Ha$$
$$Ha \qquad / Ga$$

Testing with an indirect truth table, we have

$Ga \supset Ha$	/	Ha	//	Ga
F T T		T		F

Because it is possible for the premises to be true and the conclusion false, the argument is invalid.

Another example:

$$(x) (Jx \supset Kx)$$
$$(\exists x)Jx \qquad / (x)Kx$$

For a universe having one member, the indirect truth table is as follows:

$$Ja \supset Ka \quad / \quad Ja \quad // \quad Ka$$
$$\text{T } \cancel{\text{T}} \text{ F} \qquad \quad \text{T} \qquad \quad \text{F}$$

Since it is impossible for the premises to be true and the conclusion false for this universe, we try a universe having two members, a and b:

$$(Ja \supset Ka) \cdot (Jb \supset Kb) \quad / \quad Ja \vee Jb \quad // \quad Ka \cdot Kb$$
$$\text{T T} \quad \text{T T F T} \quad \text{F} \qquad \text{T T F} \qquad \text{T F F}$$

Since it is possible for the premises to be true and the conclusion false for this universe, the argument is invalid.

Here is an example involving compound statements:

$$(\exists x)Hx \supset (x)(Fx \supset Gx)$$
$$(\exists x)Fx \quad / \ (\exists x)Hx \supset (x)Gx$$

The indirect truth table for a universe having one member is as follows:

$$Ha \supset (Fa \supset Ga) \quad / \quad Fa \quad // \quad Ha \supset Ga$$
$$\text{T } \cancel{\text{T}} \text{ T F F} \qquad \quad \text{T} \qquad \text{T F F}$$

A contradiction results, so we try a universe having two members. The resulting indirect truth table, which follows, proves the argument invalid:

$$(Ha \vee Hb) \supset [(Fa \supset Ga) \cdot (Fb \supset Gb)] \ / \ Fa \vee Fb \ // \ (Ha \vee Hb) \supset (Ga \vee Gb)$$
$$\text{T} \quad \text{T} \quad \text{T T T T F T} \quad \text{F} \qquad \text{T T F} \qquad \text{T} \quad \text{F T F F}$$

The next example involves singular statements:

$$(\exists x)Mx \cdot (\exists x)Nx$$
$$Md \quad /Nd$$

The second premise asserts that something named d is an M. For this argument, the assumption that the universe contains only one member entails that this one member is named d. Here is the indirect truth table for such a universe:

$$Md \cdot Nd \quad / \quad Md \quad // \quad Nd$$
$$\text{T } \cancel{\text{T}} \text{ F} \qquad \quad \text{T} \qquad \quad \text{F}$$

When the universe is expanded to include two members, we are free to give any name we wish to the second member. Let us call it e. The resulting indirect truth table, which follows, shows that the argument is invalid. Notice that the second premise and the conclusion remain the same:

A CONCISE INTRODUCTION TO LOGIC

$$(Md \vee Me) \cdot (Nd \vee Ne) \quad / \quad Md \quad // \quad Nd$$
$$\text{T T} \quad \text{T F T T} \qquad \text{T} \qquad \text{F}$$

The basic concept behind this method of proving invalidity rests on the fact that a valid argument is valid in all possible universes. Consequently, if an argument fails in a universe consisting of one, two, or any number of members, it is invalid.

While this method is primarily intended for proving arguments invalid, theoretically it can also be used to prove arguments valid. Several years ago a theorem was proved to the effect that an argument that does not fail in a universe of 2^n members, where n designates the number of different predicates, is valid.* According to this theorem, establishing the validity of an argument containing two different predicates requires a universe having four members, establishing the validity of an argument containing three different predicates requires a universe having eight members, and so on. For most arguments, however, a universe having four members is unwieldy at best, and a universe having eight members approaches the impossible (although a computer could handle it easily). Thus, while this method is usually quite convenient for proving invalidity, its usefulness in establishing validity is impeded by certain practical limitations.

EXERCISE 8.5

I. Prove that the following symbolized arguments are invalid:

★(1) 1. $(x)(Ax \supset Bx)$
    2. $(x)(Ax \supset Cx)$ / $(x)(Bx \supset Cx)$

(2) 1. $(x)(Ax \vee Bx)$
    2. $\sim An$ / $(x)Bx$

(3) 1. $(\exists x)Ax \vee (\exists x)Bx$
    2. $(\exists x)Ax$ / $(\exists x)Bx$

(4) 1. $(x)(Ax \supset Bx)$
    2. $(\exists x)Ax$ / $(x)Bx$

★(5) 1. $(x)[Ax \supset (Bx \vee Cx)]$
    2. $(\exists x)Ax$ / $(\exists x)Bx$

(6) 1. $(\exists x)Ax$
    2. $(\exists x)Bx$ / $(\exists x)(Ax \cdot Bx)$

(7) 1. $(x)(Ax \supset Bx)$
    2. $(\exists x)Bx \supset (\exists x)Cx$ / $(x)(Ax \supset Cx)$

---

*See Wilhelm Ackermann, *Solvable Cases of the Decision Problem* (Amsterdam: North-Holland Publishing Co., 1954), Chapter 4. This theorem, incidentally, holds only for monadic predicates.

(8) 1. $(\exists x)(Ax \cdot Bx) \equiv (\exists x)Cx$
    2. $(x)(Ax \supset Bx)$ / $(x)Ax \equiv (\exists x)Cx$

(9) 1. $(\exists x)(Ax \cdot \sim Bx)$
    2. $(\exists x)(Bx \cdot \sim Ax)$ / $(x)(Ax \vee Bx)$

★(10) 1. $(\exists x)(Ax \cdot Bx)$
      2. $(\exists x)(\sim Ax \cdot \sim Bx)$ / $(x)(Ax \equiv Bx)$

II. Translate the following arguments into symbolic form. Then prove that each is invalid.

★1. Violinists who play well are accomplished musicians. There are some violinists in the orchestra. Therefore, some musicians are accomplished. (*V, P, A, M, O*)

2. Pianists and harpsichordists are meticulous. Rudoff Serkin is a pianist. Therefore, everyone is meticulous. (*P, H, M*)

3. If there are any oboists, there are some bassoonists. If there are any clarinetists, there are some flutists. Amelia is both an oboist and a clarinetist. Therefore, some bassoonists are flutists. (*O, B, C, F*)

4. All tympanists are haughty. If some tympanists are haughty, then some percussionists are overbearing. Therefore, all tympanists are overbearing. (*T, H, P, O*)

5. All cellists and violinists are members of the string section. Some violinists are not cellists. Also, some cellists are not violinists. Therefore, everyone is a member of the string section. (*C, V, M*)

8.6 RELATIONAL PREDICATES AND OVERLAPPING QUANTIFIERS

Even the logical machinery developed thus far is not adequate for deriving the conclusions of a number of arguments. Consider, for example, the following:

> All dogs are animals. Therefore, whoever owns a dog owns an animal.
>
> If there are any butterflies, then if all butterflies are free, they are free. There are butterflies in the garden. Therefore, if all butterflies are free, something in the garden is free.

The first argument involves a relation—the relation of ownership—and we have yet to see how relations can be dealt with. The second argument, while not involving any relations, involves a quantifier that overlaps another quantifier. In this section the apparatus of predicate logic will be extended to cover examples such as these.

Relations (that is **relational predicates**) come in varying degrees of complexity, depending on the number of individuals related. The simplest, called *binary* (or *dyadic*) relations, establish a connection between two individuals. Some examples are the relation of being taller than, as expressed in the statement "Steve is taller than David," and the relation of being a friend, as expressed in "Sylvia is a friend of Olivia." *Trinary* (or *triadic*) relations establish a connection between three individuals. For example, the relation of being between, as in "St. Louis is between Chicago and New Orleans," and the relation of reading something to someone, as in "George read *Othello* to Madeline." *Quaternary* (or *tetradic*) relations link four individuals together—for example, the relation of reading something to someone at a certain time, as in "George read *Othello* to Madeline on Thursday." The complexity increases until we have what are called *n-ary* (or *n-adic*) relations, which link n things together. In this section we will restrict our attention to binary relations.

Relations are symbolized like other predicates except that two lower-case letters, representing the two related individuals, are written to the immediate right of the upper-case letter representing the relation. Here are some examples of relational statements involving specifically named individuals:

Statement	Symbolic translation
Anthony is married to Cynthia.	*Mac*
Deborah loves physics.	*Ldp*
The Sears Tower is taller than the Empire State Building.	*Tse*
Donald is the father of Jim.	*Fdj*

Notice that the order in which the lower-case letters are listed often makes a difference. If the third statement were translated *Tes,* the symbolic statement would read "The Empire State Building is taller than the Sears Tower," which is false. Quantifiers are attached to relational predicates in the same way they are to ordinary predicates. Some examples of relational statements involving quantifiers are as follows:

Statement	Symbolic translation
Thomas knows everything.	$(x)Ktx$
Thomas knows something.	$(\exists x)Ktx$
Everything is different from everything.	$(x)(y)Dxy$

Something is different from something.	$(\exists x)(\exists y)Dxy$
Everything is different from something (or other).	$(x)(\exists y)Dxy$
Something is different from everything.	$(\exists x)(y)Dxy$

The last four statements involve **overlapping quantifiers.** We may read these symbols as follows:

$(x)(y)$	For all x and for all y . . .
$(\exists x)(\exists y)$	There exists an x such that there exists a y such that . . .
$(x)(\exists y)$	For all x there exists a y such that . . .
$(\exists x)(y)$	There exists an x such that for all y . . .

Applying this phraseology to the last statement above, for example, we have "There exists an x such that for all y, x is different from y"—which is simply another way of saying "Something is different from everything."

When two quantifiers of the same sort appear adjacent to each other, the order in which they are listed is not significant. In other words, the statement $(x)(y)Dxy$ is logically equivalent to $(y)(x)Dxy$, and $(\exists x)(\exists y)Dxy$ is logically equivalent to $(\exists y)(\exists x)Dxy$. A little reflection on the meaning of these statements should justify this equivalence. But when different quantifiers appear adjacent to each other, the order *does* make a difference, at least when the statement function involves a relation. Accordingly, $(x)(\exists y)Dxy$ is not logically equivalent to $(\exists y)(x)Dxy$. This fact can be seen more clearly in terms of a different example. If Lxy means "x loves y" and we imagine the universe restricted to persons, then $(x)(\exists y)Lxy$ means "Everyone loves someone (or other)," while $(\exists y)(x)Lxy$ means "There is someone who loves everyone." Clearly these two statements are not equivalent.

Relational predicates can be combined with ordinary predicates to translate statements having varying degrees of complexity. In the examples that follow, Px means "x is a person." The meaning of the other predicates should be clear from the context:

1. Any heavyweight can defeat any lightweight.
   $(x)[Hx \supset (y)(Ly \supset Dxy)]$

2. Some heavyweights can defeat any lightweight.
   $(\exists x)[Hx \cdot (y)(Ly \supset Dxy)]$

3. No heavyweight can defeat every lightweight.
$(x)[Hx \supset (\exists y)(Ly \cdot \sim Dxy)]$
   or
$\sim(\exists x)[Hx \cdot (y)(Ly \supset Dxy)]$

4. Everyone cares for someone (or other).
$(x)[Px \supset (\exists y)(Py \cdot Cxy)]$

5. Someone does not care for anyone.
$(\exists x)[Px \cdot (y)(Py \supset \sim Cxy)]$

6. Anyone who cares for someone is cared for himself.
$(x)\{[Px \cdot (\exists y)(Py \cdot Cxy)] \supset (\exists z)(Pz \cdot Czx)\}$

7. Not everyone respects himself.
$(\exists x)(Px \cdot \sim Rxx)$
   or
$\sim(x)(Px \supset Rxx)$

8. Anyone who does not respect himself is not respected by anyone.
$(x)[(Px \cdot \sim Rxx) \supset (y)(Py \supset \sim Ryx)]$

The same general rule applies in translating these statements as applies in translating any other statement in predicate logic: Universal quantifiers go with implications and existential quantifiers go with conjunctions. Every one of the symbolic expressions above follows this rule. For example, in the first statement, both quantifiers are universal and both connectives are implications. In the second statement, the main quantifier is existential and the subordinate quantifier universal; accordingly, the main connective is a conjunction and the subordinate connective is an implication. Among these statements, number 6 is the most complex. The symbolic translation of this statement reads, "For all x, if x is a person and there exists a y such that y is a person and x cares for y, then there exists a z such that z is a person and z cares for x." Upon reflection it should be clear that this is simply another way of expressing the original English statement.

Another important rule to keep in mind when translating statements of this kind is that every variable must be bound by some quantifier. If a variable is left dangling outside the scope of its intended quantifier, the translation is meaningless. For example, if the second statement were translated $(\exists x)Hx \cdot (y)(Ly \supset Dxy)$, then the x in Dxy would not be bound by the existential quantifier. As a result, the translation would be meaningless. To correct it, brackets must be inserted that provide for the existential quantifier to range over Dxy.

The same techniques used to translate these eight statements are also used to translate certain statements involving ordinary predicates throughout. Consider the following:

If anything is good and all good things are safe, then it is safe.

$$(x)\{[Gx \cdot (y)(Gy \supset Sy)] \supset Sx\}$$

If anything is good and some good things are dangerous, then it is dangerous.

$$(x)\{[Gx \cdot (\exists x)(Gy \cdot Dy)] \supset Dx\}$$

Since the "it" at the end of these statements refers to one of the "good" things mentioned at the beginning, the quantifier that binds the x in Gx must also bind the x in Sx and Dx. The set of braces in the symbolic expressions ensures this.

Another point to notice regarding statements such as these is that the quantified expression inside the brackets is expressed in terms of a *new* variable. This procedure is essential to avoid ambiguity. If instead of y, x had been used, the variable in this expression would be bound by two different quantifiers at the same time.

In other statements, the one or more individuals mentioned at the end are *not* necessarily the same ones mentioned at the beginning. In such cases the quantifier that binds the individuals at the beginning should *not* bind those at the end. Compare the next pair of statements with those we have just considered.

If anything is good and all good things are safe, then something is safe.

$$[(\exists x)Gx \cdot (y)(Gy \supset Sy)] \supset (\exists z)Sz$$

If anything is good and some good things are dangerous, then something is dangerous.

$$[(\exists x)Gx \cdot (\exists y)(Gy \cdot Dy)] \supset (\exists z)Dz$$

In these cases the "something" at the end is not necessarily one of the "good" things mentioned at the beginning. Accordingly, the quantifier that binds the x in Gx does *not* range all the way to the end of the statement. Furthermore, the quantifier in question is now an *existential* quantifier. In the previous pair of statements the quantifier had to be universal because it ranged over the main connective, which was an implication. In the new pair, however, no quantifier ranges over the implication symbol. As a result, the sense of these statements has shifted to mean "If *something* is good . . ."

I should point out here that although a different variable is used to express each of the three different components in the pair of statements above, this is not required. Because no quantifier ranges over any other quantifier, it would be perfectly appropriate to use the same variable throughout.

The next pair of statements involve relational predicates. Like the previous pair, no single quantifier ranges over the entire statement because the individuals mentioned at the end are not necessarily the same ones mentioned at the beginning:

If everyone helps himself, then everyone will be helped.

$$(x)(Px \supset Hxx) \supset (x)[(Px \supset (\exists y)Hyx)]$$

If someone helps himself, then someone will be helped.

$$(\exists x)(Px \cdot Hxx) \supset (\exists x)(\exists y)(Px \cdot Hyx)$$

Let us now see how the various quantifier rules apply to overlapping quantifiers. The change of quantifier rule is applied in basically the same way as it is with single quantifiers. The following short sequence illustrates its application:

1. $\sim(x)(\exists y)Pxy$
2. $(\exists x)\sim(\exists y)Pxy$ 1, CQ
3. $(\exists x)(y)\sim Pxy$ 2, CQ

As the negation sign is moved past a quantifier, the quantifier in question is switched for its correlative. With the exception of a restriction on universal generalization, which we will introduce presently, the instantiation and generalization rules are also used in basically the same way as they are with single quantifiers. Example:

1. $(\exists x)(\exists y)Pxy$
2. $(\exists y)Pay$ 1, EI
3. Pab 2, EI
4. $(\exists x)Pxb$ 3, EG
5. $(\exists y)(\exists x)Pxy$ 4, EG

With each successive instantiation the outermost quantifier drops off. Generalization restores the quantifiers in the reverse order.

This proof demonstrates our earlier observation that the order of the quantifiers is not significant when the same kind of quantifier is used throughout. We also observed that the order does make a difference when different quantifiers appear together. Accordingly, the statement $(x)(\exists y)Pxy$ is not logically equivalent to $(\exists y)(x)Pxy$. As the instantiation and generalization rules now stand, however, it is quite possible, with a proof similar to the one above, to establish the logical equivalence of these two expressions. Therefore, to keep this from happening we now introduce a new restriction on universal generalization:

UG: $\dfrac{\mathfrak{F}y}{(x)\mathfrak{F}x}$ *Restriction:*   UG must not be used if $\mathfrak{F}y$ contains an existential name and y is free in the line where that name is introduced.

To see how this restriction applies, let us attempt to deduce $(\exists y)(x)Pxy$ from $(x)(\exists y)Pxy$:

1. $(x)(\exists y)Pxy$
2. $(\exists y)Pxy$ 1, UI
3. Pxa 2, EI
4. $(x)Pxa$ 3, UG (invalid)
5. $(\exists y)(x)Pxy$ 4, EG

The proof fails on line 4 because $\mathfrak{I}y$ (that is, Pxa) contains a name introduced by existential instantiation (namely, a), and x is free in line 3 where that name is introduced. Our new restriction is required precisely to prevent this kind of proof sequence from occurring. The reasonableness of the restriction may be seen once it is realized what happens in this proof. Line 1 asserts that for every x in the universe there exists some y that has relation P to it. This does not mean that there is one *single* thing that is related to every x but that each x has, perhaps, a *different* thing related to it. On line 2 we select one of these x's at random, and on line 3 we give the name a to the thing related to it. Then on line 4 we draw the conclusion that everything in the universe has relation P to a. But this, as we just saw, is precisely what line 1 does *not* say. Line 4, therefore, is fallacious.

In summary, we now have two restrictions on universal generalization. The first concerns only conditional and indirect sequences and prevents UG from occurring within the scope of such a sequence when the instantial variable is free in the first line. The second restriction concerns only arguments involving overlapping quantifiers. With these two restrictions in hand, we may now proceed to illustrate the use of natural deduction in arguments involving relational predicates and overlapping quantifiers. The example that follows does not include any relational predicates, but it does involve overlapping quantifiers.:

1. $(\exists x)Ax \supset (\exists x)Bx$ / $(\exists y)(x)(Ax \supset By)$
2. Ax CP
3. $(\exists x)Ax$ 2, EG
4. $(\exists x)Bx$ 1, 3, MP
5. Bc 4, EI
6. $Ax \supset Bc$ 2-5, CP
7. $(x)(Ax \supset Bc)$ 6, UG
8. $(\exists y)(x)(Ax \supset By)$ 7, EG

Conditional and indirect proof are used in the same way with relational predicates and overlapping quantifiers as they are with ordinary predicates and nonoverlapping quantifiers. The conditional proof above begins, as usual, by assuming the antecedent of the conclusion. When line 7 is reached, we must be careful that neither of the restrictions against universal generalization is violated. While the instantial variable x is free in the first line of the conditional sequence, line 7 does not lie within that sequence, so the first restriction is obeyed. And while line 7 does include the existential name c, x is not free in line 5 where that name is introduced. Thus, the second restriction is obeyed as well.

The next proof involves a relational predicate. The proof shows that while $(x)(\exists y)Dxy$ is not *equivalent* to $(\exists y)(x)Dxy$, it can be deduced from that statement:

1. $(\exists y)(x)Dxy$ / $(x)(\exists y)Dxy$
2. $(x)Dxm$ 1, EI
3. Dxm 2, UI
4. $(\exists y)Dxy$ 3, EG
5. $(x)(\exists y)Dxy$ 4, UG

The next example concludes with a line in which an individual is related to itself. Since there are no restrictions on universal instantiation, the procedure leading up to this line is perfectly legitimate. Notice in line 4 that tautology is used with relational predicates in the same way that it is with ordinary predicates:

1. $(\exists y)(x)(Exy \lor Eyx)$ / $(\exists z)Ezz$
2. $(x)(Exa \lor Eax)$ 1, EI
3. $Eaa \lor Eaa$ 2, UI
4. Eaa 3, Taut
5. $(\exists z)Ezz$ 4, EG

Sometimes the order in which instantiation steps are performed is critical. The following proof provides an example:

1. $(x)(\exists y)(Fxy \supset Gxy)$
2. $(\exists x)(y)Fxy$ / $(\exists x)(\exists y)Gxy$
3. $(y)Fmy$ 2, EI
4. $(\exists y)(Fmy \supset Gmy)$ 1, UI
5. $Fmo \supset Gmo$ 4, EI
6. Fmo 3, UI
7. Gmo 5, 6, MP
8. $(\exists y)Gmy$ 7, EG
9. $(\exists x)(\exists y)Gxy$ 8, EG

Line 2 must be instantiated before line 1 because the step introduces a new existential name. For the same reason, line 4 must be instantiated before line 3.

The next proof involves an indirect sequence. Such sequences often make use of the change of quantifier rule, as this proof illustrates:

1. $(\exists x)(\exists y)(Jxy \lor Kxy) \supset (\exists x)Lx$
2. $(x)(y)(Lx \supset {\sim}Ly)$ / $(x)(y){\sim}Jxy$
   3. ${\sim}(x)(y){\sim}Jxy$ IP
   4. $(\exists x){\sim}(y){\sim}Jxy$ 3, CQ
   5. $(\exists x)(\exists y)Jxy$ 3, CQ, DN
   6. $(\exists y)Jmy$ 5, EI
   7. Jmn 6, EI
   8. $Jmn \lor Kmn$ 7, Add
   9. $(\exists y)(Jmy \lor Kmy)$ 8, EG
  10. $(\exists x)(\exists y)(Jxy \lor Kxy)$ 9, EG
  11. $(\exists x)Lx$ 1, 10, MP
  12. Lo 11, EI
  13. $(y)(Lo \supset {\sim}Ly)$ 2, UI
  14. $Lo \supset {\sim}Lo$ 13, UI
  15. ${\sim}Lo$ 12, 14, MP
  16. $Lo \cdot {\sim}Lo$ 12, 15, Conj
17. $(x)(y){\sim}Jxy$ 3–16, IP, DN

Because line 1 cannot be instantiated, the only strategy is to obtain the antecedent of the conditional with the aim of obtaining the consequent via *modus ponens*. This is accomplished on line 10 via indirect proof. Notice on line 8 that addition is used with relational predicates in the same way that it is with ordinary predicates.

A final word of caution is called for regarding universal instantiation and the two generalization rules. First, when UI is used to introduce variables into a proof, it is important that these variables end up free and that they not be captured in the process by other quantifiers. The following examples illustrate both correct and incorrect applications of this rule:

1. $(x)(\exists y)Pxy$
2. $(\exists y)Pyy$ 1, UI   (invalid—the instantial variable y has been captured by the existential quantifier)

1. $(x)(\exists y)Pxy$
2. $(\exists y)Pxy$ 1, UI   (valid—the instantial variable x is free)

1. $(x)(\exists y)Pxy$
2. $(\exists y)Pzy$ 1, UI   (valid—the instantial variable z is free)

An analogous caution applies to the two generalization rules. When either UG or EG is used to introduce quantifiers, it is important that the quantifiers capture only the variables they are intended to capture. They must not capture variables that are already bound by other quantifiers, and they must not capture other free variables in the statement function. The following examples illustrate both correct and incorrect applications of these rules:

1. $(\exists x)Pxy$
2. $(x)(\exists x)Pxx$ 1, UG (invalid—the variable x is now bound by two quantifiers)

1. $(\exists x)Pxy$
2. $(\exists x)(\exists x)Pxx$ 1, EG (invalid—the variable x is now bound by two quantifiers)

1. $(\exists x)Pxy$
2. $(\exists y)(\exists x)Pxy$ 1, EG (valid)

1. $(x)(\exists y)Lxy$
2. $(\exists y)Lxy$ 1, UI
3. Lxa 2, EI
4. $(\exists x)Lxx$ 3, EG (invalid—the quantifier has captured the x immediately adjacent to the L)

1. $(x)(\exists y)Lxy$
2. $(\exists y)Lxy$ 1, UI
3. Lxa 2, EI
4. $(\exists z)Lxz$ 3, EG (valid—the x remains free)

1. $(x)(y)Kxy$
2 $(y)Kxy$ 1, UI
3. Kxx 2, UI
4. $(x)Kxx$ 3, UG (valid)

To see that the fourth example is indeed invalid, let Lxy stand for "x is larger than y," and let the variables range over the real numbers. The statement $(x)(\exists y)Lxy$ then means that there is no smallest number—which is true. But the statement $(\exists x)Lxx$ means that there is a number that is larger than itself—which is false.

EXERCISE 8.6

I. Translate the following statements into symbolic form:

★1. Charmaine read *Paradise Lost*. (Rxy: x read y)

2. Whoever reads *Paradise Lost* is educated. (Rxy: x reads y; Ex: x is educated)

3. James is a friend of either Ellen or Connie. (Fxy: x is a friend of y)

4. If James has any friends, then Marlene is one of them. (Fxy: x is a friend of y)

★5. Dr. Jordan teaches only geniuses. (*Txy*: *x* teaches y; *Gx*: *x* is a genius)

6. Dr. Nelson teaches a few morons. (*Txy*: *x* teaches *y*; *Mx*: *x* is a moron)

7. Every person can sell something or other. (*Px*: *x* is a person; *Sxy*: *x* can sell *y*)

8. Some people cannot sell anything.

9. No person can sell everything.

★10. Some people can sell anything.

11. The Royal Hotel serves only good drinks. (*Sxy*: *x* serves *y*; *Gx*: *x* is good; *Dx*: *x* is a drink)

12. The Clark Corporation advertises everything it produces. (*Axy*: *x* advertises *y*; *Pxy*: *x* produces *y*)

13. Peterson can drive some of the cars in the lot. (*Dxy*: *x* can drive *y*; *Cx*: *x* is a car; *Lx*: *x* is in the lot)

14. Jones can drive any car in the lot.

★15. Sylvia invited only her friends. (*Ixy*: *x* invited *y*; *Fxy*: *x* is a friend of *y*)

16. Christopher invited some of his friends.

17. Some people break everything they touch. (*Px*: *x* is a person; *Bxy*: *x* breaks *y*; *Txy*: *x* touches *y*)

18. Some people speak to whoever speaks to them. (*Px*: *x* is a person; *Sxy*: *x* speaks to *y*)

19. Every person admires some people he or she meets. (*Px*: *x* is a person; *Axy*: *x* admires *y*; *Mxy*: *x* meets *y*)

★20. Some people admire every person they meet.

21. Some policemen arrest only traffic violators. (*Px*: *x* is a policeman; *Axy*: *x* arrests *y*; *Tx*: *x* is a traffic violator)

22. Some policemen arrest every traffic violator they see. (*Px*: *x* is a policeman; *Axy*: *x* arrests *y*; *Tx*: *x* is a traffic violator; *Sxy*: *x* sees *y*)

23. If there are any cheaters, then some cheaters will be punished. (*Cx*: *x* is a cheater; *Px*: *x* will be punished)

24. If there are any cheaters, then if all the referees are vigilant they will be punished. (*Cx*: *x* is a cheater; *Rx*: *x* is a referee; *Vx*: *x* is vigilant; *Px*: *x* will be punished)

★25. Every lawyer will represent a wealthy client. (*Lx*: *x* is a lawyer; *Rxy*: *x* will represent *y*; *Wx*: *x* is wealthy; *Cx*: *x* is a client)

26. Some lawyers will represent any person who will not represent himself. (*Lx*: *x* is a lawyer; *Px*: *x* is a person; *Rxy*: *x* represents *y*)

27. Some children in the third grade can read any of the books in the library. (*Cx*: *x* is a child; *Tx*: *x* is in the third grade; *Rxy*: *x* can read *y*; *Bx*: *x* is a book; *Lx*: *x* is in the library)

28. All children in the fourth grade can read any of the books in the library.

29. If there are any safe drivers, then if none of the trucks break down they will be hired. (*Sx*: *x* is safe; *Dx*: *x* is a driver; *Tx*: *x* is a truck; *Bx*: *x* breaks down; *Hx*: *x* will be hired)

★30. If there are any safe drivers, then some safe drivers will be hired.

II. Derive the conclusion of the following symbolized arguments. Use conditional proof or indirect proof as needed.

★(1) 1. $(x)[Ax \supset (y)Bxy]$
2. Am / $(y)Bmy$

(2) 1. $(x)[Ax \supset (y)(By \supset Cxy)]$
2. $Am \cdot Bn$ /Cmn

(3) 1. $(\exists x)[Ax \cdot (y)(By \supset Cxy)]$
2. $(\exists x)Ax \supset Bj$ / $(\exists x)Cxj$

(4) 1. $(x)(\exists y)(Ax \supset By)$ / $(x)Ax \supset (\exists y)By$

★(5) 1. $(\exists x)Ax \supset (\exists y)By$ / $(\exists y)(x)(Ax \supset By)$

(6) 1. $(x)(y)(Ax \supset By)$
2. $(x)(\exists y)(Ax \supset Cy)$ / $(x)(\exists y)[Ax \supset (By \cdot Cy)]$

(7) 1. $(\exists x)[Ax \cdot (y)(Ay \supset Bxy)]$ / $(\exists x)Bxx$

(8) 1. $(\exists x)[Ax \cdot (y)(By \supset Cxy)]$
2. $(x)(\exists y)(Ax \supset By)$ / $(\exists x)(\exists y)Cxy$

(9) 1. $(\exists x)(y)(Axy \supset Bxy)$
2. $(x)(\exists y)\sim Bxy$ / $\sim(x)(y)Axy$

★(10) 1. $(x)(\exists y)Axy \supset (x)(\exists y)Bxy$
2. $(\exists x)(y)\sim Bxy$ / $(\exists x)(y)\sim Axy$

(11) 1. $(\exists x)\{Ax \cdot [(\exists y)By \supset Cx]\}$
2. $(x)(Ax \supset Bx)$ / $(\exists x)Cx$

(12) 1. $(\exists x)(y)[(Ay \cdot By) \supset Cxy]$
2. $(y)(Ay \supset By)$ / $(y)[Ay \supset (\exists x)Cxy]$

(13) 1. $(\exists x)\{Ax \cdot (y)[(By \lor Cy) \supset Dxy]\}$
2. $(\exists x)Ax \supset (\exists y)By$ / $(\exists x)(\exists y)Dxy$

(14) 1. $(x)\{Ax \supset [(\exists y)(By \cdot Cy) \supset Dx]\}$
2. $(x)(Bx \supset Cx)$ / $(x)[Ax \supset (Bx \supset Dx)]$

★(15) 1. $(\exists x)(y)(Ayx \supset \sim Axy)$ / $\sim(x)Axx$

(16) 1. $(x)(\exists y)(Ax \cdot By)$ / $(\exists y)(x)(Ax \cdot By)$

(17) 1. $(x)(\exists y)(Ax \lor By)$ / $(\exists y)(x)(Ax \lor By)$

(18) 1. $(x)[Ax \supset (\exists y)(By \cdot Cxy)]$
    2. $(\exists x)[Ax \cdot (y)(By \supset Dxy)]$ / $(\exists x)(\exists y)(Cxy \cdot Dxy)$

(19) 1. $(x)(\exists y)Axy \lor (x)(y)Bxy$
    2. $(x)(\exists y)(Cx \supset \sim Bxy)$ / $(x)(\exists y)(Cx \supset Axy)$

★(20) 1. $(x)(y)[Axy \supset (Bx \cdot Cy)]$
    2. $(x)(y)[(Bx \lor Dy) \supset \sim Axy]$ / $\sim(\exists x)(\exists y)Axy$

III. Translate the following arguments into symbolic form. Then derive the conclusion of each, using conditional proof or indirect proof when needed.

★1. Any professional can outplay any amateur. Jones is a professional but he cannot outplay Meyers. Therefore, Meyers is not an amateur. (*Px*: *x* is a professional; *Ax*: *x* is an amateur; *Oxy*: *x* can outplay *y*)

2. Whoever is a friend of either Michael or Paul will receive a gift. If Michael has any friends, then Eileen is one of them. Therefore, if Ann is a friend of Michael, then Eileen will receive a gift. (*Fxy*: *x* is a friend of *y*; *Rx*: *x* will receive a gift)

3. A horse is an animal. Therefore, whoever owns a horse owns an animal. (*Hx*: *x* is a horse; *Ax*: *x* is an animal; *Oxy*: *x* owns *y*)

4. O'Brien is a person. Furthermore, O'Brien is smarter than any person in the class. Since no person is smarter than himself, it follows that O'Brien is not in the class. (*Px*: *x* is a person; *Sxy*: *x* is smarter than *y*; *Cx*: *x* is in the class)

★5. If there are any honest politicians, then if all the ballots are counted they will be reelected. Some honest politicans will not be reelected. Therefore, some ballots will not be counted. (*Hx*: *x* is honest; *Px*: *x* is a politician; *Bx*: *x* is a ballot; *Cx*: *x* is counted; *Rx*: *x* will be reelected)

6. Dr. Rogers can cure any person who cannot cure himself. Dr. Rogers is a person. Therefore, Dr. Rogers can cure himself. (*Px*: *x* is a person; *Cxy*: *x* can cure *y*)

7. Some people are friends of every person they know. Every person knows someone (or other). Therefore, at least one person is a friend of someone. (*Px*: *x* is a person; *Fxy*: *x* is a friend of *y*; *Kxy*: *x* knows *y*)

8. If there are any policemen, then if there are any robbers, then they will arrest them. If any robbers are arrested by policemen, they will go to jail. There are some policemen and Macky is a robber. Therefore, Macky will go to jail. (*Px*: *x* is a policeman; *Rx*: *x* is a robber; *Axy*: *x* arrests *y*; *Jx*: *x* will go to jail)

9. If anything is missing, then some person stole it. If anything is damaged, then some person broke it. Something is either missing or damaged. Therefore, some person either stole something or broke

something. (*Mx*: *x* is missing; *Px*: *x* is a person; *Sxy*: *x* stole *y*; *Dx*: *x* is damaged; *Bxy*: *x* broke *y*)

★10. If there are any instructors, then if at least one classroom is available they will be effective. If there are either any textbooks or workbooks, there will be instructors and classrooms. Furthermore, if there are any classrooms, they will be available. Therefore, if there are any textbooks, then some instructors will be effective. (*Ix*: *x* is an instructor; *Cx*: *x* is a classroom; *Ax*: *x* is available; *Ex*: *x* is effective; *Tx*: *x* is a textbook; *Wx*: *x* is a workbook)

9
INDUCTION

Unlike deductive logic, the logic of induction offers no neat, harmonious system of ideas agreed upon by all logicians. Rather, it consists of several independently developed areas of thought about which there is little agreement. The sections in this chapter touch upon four such areas. The first section deals with causality and John Stuart Mill's methods for discovering causal connections, the second with probability, the third with statistical methods of reasoning, and the fourth with hypotheses. Because these four sections are basically independent of one another, they can be read in any order. Furthermore, the material presented is only slightly dependent on ideas developed earlier in this book. In addition to material from Chapter 1, which is presupposed by all four sections, Sections 9.1 and 9.2 presuppose only a few ideas from Chapter 6, and Section 9.3 extends the material developed in Chapter 3.

9.1 CAUSALITY AND MILL'S METHODS

A knowledge of causal connections plays a prominent role in our effort to control the environment in which we live. We insulate our homes because we know insulation will prevent heat loss, we vaccinate our children because we know vaccination will protect them from smallpox and diphtheria, we practice the piano and violin because we know that by doing so we may become proficient on these instruments, and we cook our meat and fish because we know that doing so will make them edible.

When the word "cause" is used in ordinary English, however, it is seriously affected by ambiguity. For example, when we say that sprinkling water on the flowers will cause them to grow, we mean that water is required for growth, not that water alone will do the job—sunshine and the proper temperature are also required. On the other hand, when we say that taking a swim on a hot summer day will cause us to cool off, we mean that the dip by itself *will* do the job; but we understand that other things will work just as well, such as taking a cold shower, entering an air-conditioned room, and so on.

To clear up this ambiguity affecting the meaning of "cause," it is useful to adopt the language of sufficient and necessary conditions. When we say that electrocution is a cause of death, we mean "cause" in the sense of *sufficient* condition. Electrocution is sufficient to produce death; but there are other methods equally effective, such as poisoning, drowning, and shooting. On the other hand, when we say that the presence of clouds is a cause of rain, we mean "cause" in the sense of *necessary* condition. Without clouds, rain cannot occur, but clouds alone are not sufficient. Certain combinations of pressure and temperature are also required.

Sometimes "cause" is used in the sense of necessary *and* sufficient condition, as when we say that the action of a force causes a body to accelerate or that an increase in voltage causes an increase in electrical current. For a body to accelerate, nothing more and nothing less is required than for it to be acted on by a net force; and for an electrical current to increase through a resistive circuit, nothing more and nothing less is required than an increase in voltage.

Thus, as these examples illustrate, the word "cause" can have any one of three different meanings:

1. Sufficient condition.
2. Necessary condition.
3. Sufficient and necessary condition.

Sometimes the context provides an immediate clue to the sense in which "cause" is being used. If we are trying to *prevent* a certain phenomenon from happening, we usually search for a cause that is a necessary condition, and if we are trying to *produce* a certain phenomenon we usually search for a cause that is a sufficient condition. For example, in attempting to prevent the occurrence of smog around cities, scientists try to isolate a necessary condition or group of necessary conditions that, if removed, will eliminate the smog. And in their effort to produce an abundant harvest, farmers search for a sufficient condition that, given sunshine and rainfall, will increase crop growth.

Another point that should be understood is that whenever an event occurs, at least *one* sufficient condition is present and *all* the necessary conditions are present. The conjunction of the necessary conditions *is* the sufficient condition that actually produces the event. For example, the necessary conditions for lighting a match are heat (produced by striking) and oxygen. Combining these two necessary conditions gives the sufficient condition. In other words, striking the match in the presence of oxygen is sufficient to ignite it. In cases where the sufficient condition is also a necessary condition, there is only one necessary condition, which is identical with the sufficient condition.

In Chapter 6 we saw that statements expressed in terms of sufficient and necessary conditions could be translated as conditional statements:

A is a sufficient condition for *B*:	$A \supset B$
A is a necessary condition for *B*:	$B \supset A$

From these translations we see that if *A* is a sufficient condition for *B*, then *B* is a necessary condition for *A*; conversely, if *A* is a necessary condition for *B*, then *B* is a sufficient condition for *A*. In addition, by the transposition rule, $(p \supset q) \equiv (\sim q \supset \sim p)$, we see that the following pairs of statements are equivalent:

The absence of *A* is a sufficient condition for the absence of *B*:	$\sim A \supset \sim B$
B is a sufficient condition for *A*:	$B \supset A$
The absence of *A* is a necessary condition for the absence of *B*:	$\sim B \supset \sim A$
B is a necessary condition for *A*:	$A \supset B$

By the truth functional rule for conditional statements, we also know that $A \supset B$ is false if and only if *A* is true and *B* is false, and that $B \supset A$ is false if and only if *B* is true and *A* is false. From this we can obtain the following translations:

A is not a sufficient condition for *B*:	$A \cdot \sim B$
A is not a necessary condition for *B*:	$B \cdot \sim A$

In other words, if *A* is present when *B* is absent, then *A* is not sufficient to produce *B*; and if *B* is present when *A* is absent, then *A* is not necessary for the occurrence of *B*. These concepts will be useful in understanding and applying Mill's methods for induction, to which we now turn.

In his *System of Logic*, the nineteenth-century philosopher John Stuart

Mill compiled five methods for identifying causal connections between events. These he called the method of agreement, the method of difference, the joint method of agreement and difference, the method of residues, and the method of concomitant variation. In the years that have elapsed since the publication of this work, the five methods have received a good deal of philosophical criticism. Today most logicians agree that the methods fall short of the claims made for them by Mill, but the fact nevertheless remains that the methods function implicitly in many of the inductive inferences we make in everyday life. The presentation that follows differs from Mill's in that Mill did not distinguish the various senses of "cause" to which the methods pertain. When "cause" in the sense of necessary condition is distinguished from "cause" in the sense of sufficient condition, the method of agreement breaks down into two methods, here called the direct method of agreement and the inverse method of agreement. Combining these two methods yields a third method, the double method of agreement. Additional variations are possible, but I have chosen to ignore them in this text.

Direct Method of Agreement

The **direct method of agreement** is a method for identifying a causal connection between an effect and a necessary condition. The method consists in recognizing some single factor that is present in a number of different occurrences in which the effect is also present. This single factor, which is the one way that all the occurrences agree, is taken to be the cause. Here is an example:

> After eating lunch at the same restaurant, five individuals
> became ill with hepatitis. Inspectors from the Health Depart-
> ment learned that while the five individuals had eaten
> different foods, they all had had tomatoes in their salad. Fur-
> thermore, this was the only food that all five had eaten. The
> inspectors concluded that the disease had been transmitted by
> the tomatoes.

To see how the argument contained in this example identifies a cause in the sense of a necessary condition, it is helpful to present the evidence in the form of a table. Where $A, B, C, \ldots G$ designate the various foods eaten, with B standing for tomatoes, and the five occurrences designate the five individuals, the table is as follows (an asterisk means that a certain condition is present and a dash means it is absent:

Table 1

Occurrence	Possible necessary condition							Phenomenon (hepatitis)
	A	*B*	*C*	*D*	*E*	*F*	*G*	
1	*	*	–	*	*	–	*	*
2	*	*	*	–	*	*	–	*
3	*	*	*	*	–	*	*	*
4	–	*	*	*	*	–	*	*
5	*	*	–	*	*	*	–	*

Occurrence 1 asserts that the designated individual ate the foods represented by the letters *A*, *B*, *D*, *E*, and *G* and avoided foods *C* and *F*. Occurrence 2 asserts that the designated individual ate foods *A*, *B*, *C*, *E*, and *F* and avoided *D* and *G*, and so on. The application of the direct method of agreement consists in systematically eliminating as many of the possible necessary conditions as the evidence allows, leaving in the end (it is hoped) only a single candidate as the cause of the phenomenon. The principle used in accomplishing this elimination was stated earlier:

> *X* is not a necessary condition for *Y* if *X* is absent when *Y* is present.

Beginning with occurrence 1 we eliminate *C* and *F*. These conditions are absent when the phenomenon is present, so they are not necessary for the occurrence of the phenomenon. Occurrence 2 eliminates *D* and *G*, occurrence 3 eliminates *E*, occurrence 4 eliminates *A* and *F* (again), and occurrence 5 eliminates *C* (again) and *G* (again). This leaves only *B* as a possible necessary condition. The conclusion is therefore warranted that the tomatoes (condition *B*) were the cause of the hepatitis.

This conclusion follows only probably, for two reasons. First, it is quite possible that some important condition was overlooked. For example, if the eating utensils were contaminated, the hepatitis might have been transmitted through them and not through the tomatoes. Second, if *more than one* of the foods had been contaminated, the disease might have been transmitted through a combination of foods, in which case, once again, the tomatoes might not have been involved. Thus, the strength of the argument depends on the nonoccurrence of these two possibilities.

Another important point to understand is that the conclusion applies directly to only the five occurrences listed and not to everyone who ate in the restaurant. The conclusion does not say that all patrons who did not eat tomatoes would not get hepatitis. It is quite possible that some food other than those listed was also contaminated, in which case only if they did not eat *that* food as well as the tomatoes could the other patrons be assured that they would not become ill. But if, among all the foods in the restaurant, only the tomatoes were contaminated, the conclusion would extend to the other patrons as well. This point serves to illustrate the fact that a conclusion derived via the method of agreement has limited generality. The conclusion applies directly to only those occurrences listed, and only indirectly, through a second inductive inference, to others. Obviously, the more occasions listed and the larger the number of possible conditions, the more general the conclusion.

Basically, what the conclusion says is that condition B, the tomatoes, is a highly suspect factor and that if investigators want to track down the source of the hepatitis, this is where they should begin. It does not say that the tomatoes were the only source of the disease for all those who ate in the restaurant or, least of all, for those who ate in other restaurants. And certainly it does not say that anyone who had eaten the tomatoes would have contracted the disease. Many people are relatively immune to hepatitis and do not get the disease even if they eat contaminated food.

An example of an actual use of the direct method of agreement is provided by the discovery of the beneficial effects of fluoride on teeth. It was noticed several years ago that people in certain communities were favored with especially healthy teeth. In researching the various factors these communities shared in common, scientists discovered that all had a high level of natural fluoride in their water supply. The scientists concluded from this evidence that fluoride causes teeth to be healthy and free of cavities.

Inverse Method of Agreement

Whereas the direct method of agreement identifies a connection between an effect and a *necessary* condition, the **inverse method of agreement** identifies a connection between an effect and a *sufficient* condition. The method consists in recognizing some single factor that is absent from a number of occurrences in which the effect is also absent. This factor is taken to be the cause of the phenomenon. Here is an example:

> After conducting a study on the work force at a certain factory, industrial engineers found that five workers performed their tasks with less efficiency than others doing the same kind of work. A list was made of the various factors that were present and absent in the employment conditions of these five employees. It was discovered that among eight likely candidates, only one factor was missing for all five: participation in a profit sharing program. The conclusion was therefore drawn that profit sharing causes workers to be efficient.

The conclusion of the argument asserts, in regard to the five workers, that profit sharing is a sufficient condition for efficiency. In other words, if these five workers began to participate in profit sharing, they would be expected to become efficient. To see how this conclusion follows, we may represent the evidence in a table similar to the one used previously. The letters A, B, C, . . . H designate the eight likely candidates for a sufficient condition, with B standing for profit sharing, and the five occurrences designate the five individuals. Notice in Table 2 that the phenomenon is absent in every occurrence, whereas in Table 1 it was present:

Table 2

Occurrence	Possible sufficient conditions								Phenomenon (efficiency)
	A	**B**	**C**	**D**	**E**	**F**	**G**	**H**	
1	–	–	–	–	*	–	*	–	–
2	*	–	–	–	–	*	–	–	–
3	–	–	*	–	–	–	–	–	–
4	*	–	–	–	–	–	–	*	–
5	–	–	–	*	–	–	*	–	–

As with the direct method of agreement, we begin by attempting to eliminate as many of the possible conditions as the evidence allows; but here we use the rule for *sufficient* conditions:

> X is not a sufficient condition for Y if X is present when Y is absent.

Occurrence 1 eliminates conditions E and G. They are present when the phenomenon is absent, so they cannot be sufficient to produce the phenomenon. Similarly, occurrence 2 eliminates A and F, occurrence 3 eliminates C, occurrence 4 eliminates A (again) and H, and occurrence 5 eliminates D and G (again). Condition B (profit sharing) is the only candidate that remains, and so it is taken to be the cause of the phenomenon.

As with our first example, this conclusion follows only probably, for two reasons. First, there is no assurance that all the important conditions have been identified, and second, there is no assurance that the phenomenon is not caused by two or more factors acting in conjunction. If, for example, a sixth worker had turned up who was inefficient at doing the same task but who did participate in profit sharing, then candidate B would be eliminated, and the engineers would have to renew their search for relevant conditions. And if, for example, the combined occurrence of conditions A and C provided a sufficient condition for the phenomenon, this combination of conditions could be the sought-after cause, and not B at all.

As with the example treated in the direct method, the conclusion of this argument pertains directly only to the five people mentioned in the occurrences and only indirectly to others. Getting the five workers to participate in profit sharing might well stimulate efficiency, but it is less likely that it would work for everyone in the factory, and less likely still that it would work for all employees in all factories. As additional occurrences are added to the picture, an increasing number of possible conditions must be taken into account. These additional conditions may have a significant impact on the conclusion drawn in the end.

The sense of the conclusion drawn in this example is that the engineers should give paramount consideration to the factor of profit sharing if they want to increase the efficiency of the five workers. But the conclusion does not state that profit sharing is the only thing that might work. Condition B is identified as a sufficient, not a necessary condition. Thus, other solutions, such as higher pay or more frequent coffee breaks, might accomplish the same purpose.

Double Method of Agreement

The direct method of agreement may be combined with the inverse method to obtain the **double method of agreement.** This method may be used to identify causes that are both necessary and sufficient conditions. Researchers often use this method to determine the effectiveness of drugs on groups of people or animals. Example:

> Eight inhabitants of a South Pacific island contracted a rare form of plague. Hearing about it, a doctor flew to the island with a serum that was thought to be a cure. When the doctor arrived, only four of the infected inhabitants would accept the serum, but all eight had previously been treated with various native remedies. After a short time the four who received the serum recovered while the other four did not. Among those who recovered, no single native remedy had been given to all; and among those who did not recover, every native remedy had been given to at least one. The doctor concluded that the serum was a cure for the disease.

To see that this evidence suggests that the serum is a cure in the sense of a necessary and sufficient condition, we may once again present it in the form of a table. Conditions A, B, C, D, and E stand for the native remedies, and condition F for the serum. The eight occurrences stand for the infected inhabitants, with the first four designating those who recovered and the second four, those who did not. Table 3 reflects the doctor's findings regarding the remedies given to each native:

Table 3

Occurrence	Possible sufficient or necessary conditions						Phenomenon (cure)
	A	*B*	*C*	*D*	*E*	*F*	
1	*	*	−	*	*	*	*
2	*	−	*	*	−	*	*
3	−	*	−	*	*	*	*
4	*	−	*	−	*	*	*
5	−	*	−	*	−	−	−
6	−	*	−	*	*	−	−
7	*	−	−	−	−	−	−
8	−	−	*	−	*	−	−

To evaluate these findings we combine the techniques of the direct and inverse methods of agreement. When the phenomenon is present, we attempt to eliminate possible necessary conditions; when it is absent, we attempt to eliminate possible sufficient conditions. Occurrences 1, 2, 3, and 4 eliminate *A*, *B*, *C*, *D*, and *E* as necessary conditions, because they are absent when the phenomenon is present, and occurrences 5, 6, 7, and 8 eliminate *A*, *B*, *C*, *D*, and *E* as sufficient conditions because they are present when the phenomenon is absent. This leaves condition *F* as the sole candidate for either a necessary or sufficient condition. Thus, the conclusion is warranted that *F* is the cause of the phenomenon in the sense of a necessary and sufficient condition.

This conclusion should be interpreted as applying directly to the natives on the island and to hold for others only through a subsequent inductive generalization. While it is highly probable that the serum cured the natives on the island, it is somewhat less probable that it would cure *anyone* having that disease. But even as restricted to the natives, the conclusion is at best probable. As with the direct and inverse methods of agreement, it is quite possible that some relevant condition was overlooked (such as something mistakenly injected along with the serum), or that more than one of the candidates listed is a sufficient condition and that a combination of these candidates provides a necessary condition. The strength of the argument depends on the nonoccurrence of these possibilities.

Method of Difference

The **method of difference** identifies a sufficient condition among the possible candidates present in a specific occurrence. The method consists in finding one single factor that is present in that specific occurrence but absent in a similar occurrence in which the phenomenon is absent. This single factor, which is the one way in which the two occurrences differ, is taken to be the cause of the phenomenon. The method of difference is sometimes called the laboratory method because it is used by researchers to discover causal connections under carefully controlled conditions. Here is an example:

> Two identical white mice in a controlled experiment were given identical amounts of four different foods. In addition, one of the mice was fed a certain drug. A short time later the mouse that was fed the drug became nervous and agitated. The researchers concluded that the drug caused the nervousness.

The conclusion rests upon the supposition that the only relevant differentiating factor between the two mice is the drug. As with the previous methods, the procedure depends upon the elimination of the other factors as possible sufficient conditions. In Table 4, A, B, C, and D stand for the different foods, and E for the drug. Occurrence 1 represents the mouse that was given the drug:

Table 4

Occurrence	Possible sufficient conditions					Phenomenon (nervousness)
	A	B	C	D	E	
1	*	*	*	*	*	*
2	*	*	*	*	−	−

Occurrence 2 eliminates A, B, C, and D as possible sufficient conditions because they are present when the phenomenon is absent. This leaves E as the one remaining candidate.

The method of difference differs from the inverse method of agreement, which also identifies sufficient conditions, in that the conclusion yielded by the method of difference is less general. In this method the conclusion applies directly only to the specific occurrence in which the phenomenon is present, whereas in the inverse method of agreement it applies to all the occurrences listed. However, the conclusion yielded by the method of difference may often be extended to cover other occurrences as well. The white mice used in biological experiments are, for all practical purposes, genetically identical. Thus, what produces nervousness in one will probably produce nervousness in the others. But without some such basis of similarity, generalizing the results of this method to cover additional occurrences would not be legitimate.

The conclusion yielded by the method of difference is probabilistic, however, even for the one occurrence to which it directly pertains. The problem is that it is impossible for two occurrences to be literally identical in every respect but one. The mere fact that the two occurrences occupy different regions of space, that one is closer to the wall than the other, amounts to a difference. Such differences may be insignificant, but therein lies the possibility for error. It is not at all obvious how insignificant differences should be distinguished from significant ones. Furthermore, it is impossible to make an exhaustive list of all the possible conditions; but without such a list there is no assurance that significant conditions have not been overlooked.

The objective of the method of difference is to identify a sufficient condition among those that are *present* in a specific occurrence. Sometimes, however, the absence of a factor may count as something positive that must be taken into account. Here is an example:

> Two identical white mice in a controlled experiment were fed identical diets. In addition, both were given vitamins A, B, and C. One of the mice was also given vitamin D while the other was not. The mouse that was not fed vitamin D developed rickets, but the other one did not. The researchers concluded that the lack of vitamin D caused the rickets.

To represent these findings adequately in a table we must include the negations of the conditions as well as their affirmative expressions. Then the absence of condition D (vitamin D) can be represented by the presence of $\sim D$:

Table 5

Occurrence	Possible sufficient conditions								Phenomenon (rickets)
	A	*B*	*C*	*D*	$\sim A$	$\sim B$	$\sim C$	$\sim D$	
1	*	*	*	–	–	–	–	*	*
2	*	*	*	*	–	–	–	–	–

Now, since the method of difference is concerned with identifying a sufficient condition among those possible conditions that are *present* in occurrence 1, D, $\sim A$, $\sim B$, and $\sim C$ are immediately eliminated. Among those that remain, occurrence 2 eliminates A, B, and C, because they are present when the phenomenon is absent. This leaves $\sim D$ as the sole remaining candidate. In other words, the absence of vitamin D is the cause of the rickets in occurrence 1. This may otherwise be expressed by saying that the *presence* of vitamin D is a *necessary* condition for health in occurrence 1.

The method of difference may also be used, for example, by a farmer who fertilizes part of a field of corn but does not fertilize the other part. If the fertilized part turns out to be noticeably fuller and healthier, the farmer may conclude that the improvement has been caused by the fertilizer. Another situation in which this method can be used is in cooking. A cook may leave some ingredient out of one batch of biscuits to test the results. If that batch turns out hard and crunchy, the cook may attribute the difference to the absence of that ingredient.

A CONCISE INTRODUCTION TO LOGIC

Joint Method of Agreement and Difference

The **joint method** results from combining the method of difference with the direct method of agreement. Because the method of difference identifies a sufficient condition that is present in one specific occurrence, and the direct method of agreement identifies a necessary condition, the joint method can be used to identify a sufficient and necessary condition that is present in one specific occurrence. Here is an example:

> George, who exercised regularly, took vitamins, and got plenty of rest, contracted a rare disease. Doctors administered an antibiotic and the disease cleared up. Convinced that the cure was caused by either the exercise, the vitamins, the rest, or the antibiotics, the doctors searched for analogous cases. Of the two that were found, one got no exercise, took no vitamins, and got little rest. He was given the same antibiotic and was cured. The other person, who did the same things George did, was given no antibiotic and was not cured. The doctors concluded that George was cured by the antibiotic.

The conclusion suggests that the antibiotic caused the cure in the sense of a necessary and sufficient condition. This is illustrated in Table 6, where A, B, C, and D stand for exercise, vitamins, rest, and the antibiotic, respectively. Occurrence 1 represents George; occurrences 2 and 3 represent the analogous cases.

Table 6

Occurrence	Possible conditions				Phenomenon (cure)
	A	B	C	D	
1	*	*	*	*	*
2	–	–	–	*	*
3	*	*	*	–	–

The direct method of agreement is applied to occurrence 2, eliminating A, B, and C as necessary conditions because they are absent when the phenomenon is present. Then the method of difference is applied to occurrence 3, eliminating A, B, and C as sufficient conditions because they are present when the phenomenon is absent. The one remaining condition, D, is thus the sufficient and necessary condition for the phenomenon.

The joint method is similar to the double method of agreement in that it identifies conditions that are both necessary and sufficient. But the conclusion provided by the double method is more general in that it pertains directly to all the occurrences listed. The joint method, like the method of difference, yields a conclusion that pertains directly only to the one specific occurrence. In the above argument the conclusion asserts that the antibiotic is what cured *George;* the question is open as to whether it would cure others as well. But given some basis of similarity between George and other individuals, the conclusion might be extended by a subsequent inductive generalization.

The joint method differs from the method of difference in that it is sometimes simpler to apply. The method of difference requires strict controls to ensure that the two occurrences are identical in every important respect except one. In the joint method this need for strict control is relaxed in favor of additional occurrences that identify the sufficient condition as also being necessary.

The conclusion yielded by the joint method is only probable because, as with the method of difference, a relevant condition may have been overlooked. If, for example, George had taken some other medicine together with the antibiotic, the conclusion that the antibiotic cured him would be less probable.

Before turning to the last two methods, let us reiterate the pair of principles that have provided the basis for the five methods we have seen thus far:

1. X is not a necessary condition for Y if X is absent when Y is present.
2. X is not a sufficient condition for Y if X is present when Y is absent.

Understanding the use of these two principles is more important than remembering the peculiarities of the various methods to which they pertain.

Method of Residues

This method and the one that follows are used to identify a causal connection between two conditions without regard for the specific kind of connection. Both methods may be used to identify conditions that are sufficient, necessary, or both sufficient and necessary. The **method of residues** consists in separating from a group of causally connected conditions and phenomena those strands of causal connection that are already known, leaving the required causal connection as the "residue." The method may be diagramed as follows:

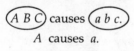

A causes a.

B causes b.

Therefore, C causes c.

When the facts that A causes a and B causes b are subtracted from the compound causal connection, the fact that C causes c remains as the residue. Here is an example:

> After occupying his new house Mr. Smith found it drafty. He traced the source of the draft to three conditions: a broken window in the garage, a crack under the front door, and a broken damper in the fireplace. When the window was replaced he noticed an improvement, and a further improvement when weather stripping was installed on the door. He concluded that the draft that remained was caused by the broken damper in the fireplace.

The conclusion follows only probably because it is quite possible that a fourth source of the draft was overlooked. Here is another example:

> After realizing a loss of $100,000 a department store's chief accountant could suggest only three causes: an excessive number of clerks, increases in utility rates, and damage to merchandise caused by a flood. These expenses were estimated at $25,000, $30,000, and $10,000, respectively. Since no other ordinary sources could be found, the accountant attributed the remaining $35,000 to shoplifting.

Because the estimates might have been incorrect and because additional sources of financial loss might have been overlooked, the conclusion is only probable.

Some procedures that, at least on the face of it, appear to utilize the method of residues come closer to being deductive than inductive. A case in point is the procedure used to determine the weight of the cargo carried by a truck. First, the empty truck is put on a scale and the weight recorded. Then the truck is loaded and the truck together with the cargo is put on the same scale. The weight of the cargo is the difference between the two weights. If, to this procedure, we add the rather unproblematic assumptions that weight is an additive property, that the scale is accurate, that the scale operator reads the indicator properly, that the truck is not altered in the loading process, and a few others, the conclusion about the weight of the cargo follows deductively.

To distinguish deductive from inductive uses of the method of residues, one must take the intention of the arguer into account. If the intent is to argue necessarily, the use made of this method is deductive; but if the intent is to argue probabilistically, the use is inductive.

Method of Concomitant Variation

The **method of concomitant variation** identifies a causal connection between two conditions by matching variations in one condition with variations in another. According to one formulation, increases are matched with increases and decreases with decreases. Where plus and minus signs indicate increase and decrease, this formulation of the method may be diagramed as follows:

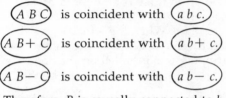

Therefore, B is causally connected to b.

The second formulation of the method matches increases with decreases and decreases with increases. It may be diagramed as follows:

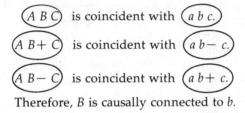

Therefore, B is causally connected to b.

In both cases the conclusion asserts that either B causes b, b causes B, or B and b have a common cause. If B happens before b, then, of course, the second alternative is eliminated, and if b happens before B, then the first alternative is eliminated.

The method of concomitant variation is useful when it is impossible for a condition to be either wholly present or wholly absent, as was required for the use of the first five methods. Many conditions are of this sort—for example, the temperature of the ocean, the price of gold, the incidence of crime, the size of a mountain glacier, a person's blood pressure, and so on. If some kind of correlation can be detected between variations in conditions such as these, the method of concomitant variation asserts that the two are causally connected. Example:

> In attempting to diagnose Mrs. Thompson's high blood pressure, doctors discovered a correlation between fluctuations in blood pressure and certain brain waves. As the blood pressure increased and decreased, so did the intensity of the brain waves. The doctors concluded that the two conditions were causally related.

Whether the changes in blood pressure caused the changes in the intensity of the brain waves or vice versa, or whether the two had a common cause, would have to be determined by further investigation. But the fact that the two were causally connected in some way follows with a high degree of probability. The conclusion is not absolutely certain, however, because the fluctuations could have been merely coincidental.

The blood pressure example illustrates the first formulation of the method. Here is an example of the second formulation:

> Researchers have discovered a correlation between changes in the national divorce rate and fluctuations in the gross national product. As the GNP increases, the divorce rate decreases, and when the GNP sags, the divorce rate goes up. The researchers have concluded that the two phenomena are causally connected.

In this case an even stronger conclusion could probably be drawn— namely, that decreases in the GNP cause increases in the divorce rate, and not conversely. That changes in economic prosperity should affect the divorce rate is quite plausible, but the converse is less so.

At this point we should note that the existence of a mere correlation between two phenomena is never sufficient to identify a causal connection. In addition, the causal connection suggested by the correlation must at least make sense. Consider the following example:

> After an in-depth study researchers discovered a correlation between the price of pork belly futures on the Chicago Mercantile Exchange and earthquake activity in Japan. As the number and intensity of the quakes increased, the future prices also increased, and vice versa. The researchers concluded that the two phenomena were causally connected.

The argument is clearly weak. Because it is virtually inconceivable that either phenomenon could cause a change in the other, or that changes in both could have a common cause, it is most likely that the correlation is purely coincidental.

When used correctly, the method of concomitant variation can yield conclusions that are highly probable. It has been used successfully in the past to help establish the existence of causal connections between such phenomena as smoking and lung cancer, nuclear radiation and leukemia, and alcohol consumption and cirrhosis of the liver.

EXERCISE 9.1

I. Identify the kind of causality intended by the following statements. Is the cause a sufficient condition, necessary condition, or both sufficient and necessary condition?

★1. Throwing a brick through a window will cause the window to break.

2. Heating an iron rod causes it to expand.

3. Releasing the shutter of a camera causes an image to appear on the film.

4. Slashing an inflated automobile tire with a knife will cause it to go flat.

★5. Pulling the trigger of a gun causes it to fire.

6. Wetting blue litmus paper with an acid causes it to turn red.

7. Pouring water on a wood fire will cause it to be extinguished.

8. Eating contaminated food will cause one to become ill.

9. Stretching a spring causes it to exert an opposing force.

★10. Flipping the wall switch to the "up" position causes the overhead lights to go on.

II. Identify the method of reasoning used and the kind of causality intended in the following reports of argumentation:

★1. To determine the effectiveness of an oil additive, a testing firm purchased two identical automobiles and drove each a distance of 30,000 miles, using the same kind of gasoline, the same kind of oil, and the same driver. The oil in one engine included the additive, whereas the oil in the other did not. At the end of the test the engines of both cars were dismantled, and it was found that the engine that used the additive had less wear. The testing firm concluded that the oil additive caused the reduced wear.

2. An eighth-grade teacher had six pupils who read very poorly. These pupils came from different sized families, had different social and economic backgrounds, and attended different schools in the primary grades. The single factor they shared in common was the lack of any phonics instruction in the first grade. The teacher concluded that phonics causes children to be good readers.

3. An administrator for the Internal Revenue Service noticed that tax revenues for a certain year were substantially less than anticipated. Part of the deficiency could be attributed to the fact that productivity was down as a result of a recession, and another part to spiraling interest rates that led to higher than usual write-offs. Unable to account for the remaining deficiency, the administrator attributed it to increased cheating by the taxpayers.

4. The repair manager for a manufacturer of home computers noticed that a large number of units were being returned for repairs. These units had been produced in different years and were sold in different cities to different kinds of customers. The only noticeable common factor was the fact that all of the units had been shipped from coastal areas. Since coastal areas have a higher salt content in the air, the repair manager concluded that salty air from the sea caused the breakdowns.

★5. A manufacturer of fishing lures conducted a test on a new bass plug it had developed. The plug was given to four of a group of eight fishermen, and these fishermen then tried their luck in different locations in a lake using different kinds of poles, reels, lures, and techniques. At the end of the day, all of the fishermen who had used the new plug had caught fish, whereas none of those who had used other lures had caught anything. The manufacturer concluded that the new bass plug caused the fish to bite.

6. During the first storm of the season, Mrs. Johnson's telephone stopped working. After the weather dried up the phone began working again. Since no one at the phone company had been alerted to the problem, Mrs. Johnson concluded that the breakdown was caused by dampness in the lines.

7. From a comparison of statistics a criminologist detected a correlation between fluctuations in the employment rate and crimes of theft. As the employment rate increased, the theft rate decreased, and vice versa. The criminologist concluded that unemployment causes an increase in crimes of theft.

8. A patient developed an allergic reaction to an unknown substance. Doctors instructed the patient to eliminate certain foods from her diet; after she had done so, the reaction disappeared. She was then told to gradually add the foods back into her diet. When the patient began to use milk products, the allergic reaction reappeared. The doctors concluded that the reaction was caused by milk products.

9. A psychiatrist had six adult women patients who were unable to sustain meaningful relationships with men. The patients came from different walks of life, were of varying ages, and had different religious and economic backgrounds. The only factor they shared in common was the lack of a male parent figure during their early childhood. The psychiatrist concluded that the presence of a male parent figure causes the ability in women to sustain meaningful relationships with men.

★10. A metallurgist added six different substances in various combinations to ten samples of molten aluminum for the purpose of producing aluminum alloys. Later she found that the five samples that contained silicon were resistant to corrosion, whereas the five that contained no silicon were not resistant. The metallurgist concluded that silicon causes aluminum to be resistant to corrosion.

11. A doctor had five patients suffering from an unusual form of cancer. The only factor common to all five was the fact that all were employed by a chemical company that produced a certain defoliant for use by the military. The doctor concluded that the defoliant chemical caused the cancer.

12. After moving to a new home in a distant city, a housewife noticed that her clothes came out of the washing machine noticeably cleaner

than before. Part of the cleaning she attributed to the soap and part to the machine, both of which were the same as she had used in her previous home. Unable to identify any other factor, she decided that the improvement must be because the water in the new location was softer than it was in the old location.

13. A television set got an excellent picture in the front room of a home, but when the set was moved to other rooms, the picture greatly deteriorated. Since everything except the location appeared to be the same, the homeowner concluded that the location of the front room was the cause of the superior picture.

14. A health worker discovered a correlation between the weekly suicide rate and the index levels of the major stock exchanges. As stock prices increased, the suicide rate decreased, and as stock prices fell, the suicide rate increased. The health worker concluded that the price of stocks is a factor in why people commit suicide.

★15. Two of Mr. Andrews' rose bushes became infested with aphids. Mr. Andrews proceeded to spray one of the bushes with malathion but left the other bush untouched. Within three days the aphids disappeared from the bush that was sprayed, but they continued to thrive on the other bush. Mr. Andrews concluded that malathion killed the aphids on the bush that was sprayed.

III. Identify the cause suggested by the information presented in the following tables. Is the cause a sufficient condition, a necessary condition, or both a sufficient and necessary condition? What method is used?

★1.

Occurrence	Possible conditions					Phenomenon
	A	*B*	*C*	*D*	*E*	
1	–	*	–	–	*	–
2	–	–	*	–	–	–
3	–	*	*	–	–	–
4	–	–	–	–	*	–
5	–	*	–	*	–	–

2.

Occurrence	Possible conditions					Phenomenon
	A	*B*	*C*	*D*	*E*	
1	*	–	*	*	*	*
2	*	*	*	*	–	*
3	*	–	*	*	*	*
4	*	*	–	*	*	*
5	–	*	*	*	–	*

3.

Occurrence	Possible conditions					Phenomenon
	A	B	C	D	E	
1	*	*	*	*	*	*
2	*	–	*	*	*	–

4.

Occurrence	Possible conditions						Phenomenon
	A	B	C	D	E	F	
1	*	–	–	*	–	–	–
2	–	*	*	*	–	–	*
3	*	–	*	*	*	–	*
4	–	*	–	–	–	*	–
5	*	–	–	–	*	–	–
6	*	*	*	–	*	–	*

★5.

Occurrence	Possible conditions					Phenomenon
	A	B	C	D	E	
1	*	*	*	*	*	*
2	–	*	*	*	*	–
3	*	–	–	–	–	*

6.

Occurrence	Possible conditions						Phenomenon
	A	B	C	~A	~B	~C	
1	*	*	–	–	–	*	*
2	–	*	*	*	–	–	–
3	*	–	*	–	*	–	–

7.

Occurrence	Possible conditions					Phenomenon
	A	B	C	D	E	
1	*	*	*	*	–	*
2	–	–	*	–	*	*
3	*	–	–	–	*	–
4	–	*	–	*	*	*
5	*	*	–	–	–	–
6	–	*	*	–	–	–

8.

Occurrence	Possible conditions					Phenomenon
	A	B	C	D	E	
1	–	–	*	–	*	–
2	–	*	*	–	*	*
3	*	*	–	*	*	*
4	–	*	–	–	*	–
5	*	–	*	*	–	–
6	*	*	*	–	–	*

IV. Prepare tables for arguments 1, 2, 4, 5, and 8 in Part II. Use your imagination to supplement the information given on the possible conditions.

9.2 PROBABILITY

Probability is a topic that is central to the question of induction, but like causality, it has different meanings. Consider the following statements:

> The probability of picking a spade from a full deck of cards is one-fourth.
>
> The probability that a 20-year-old man will live to age 75 is .63.
>
> There is a high probability that Margaret and Peter will get married.

In each statement the word "probability" is used in a different sense. This difference stems from the fact that a different procedure is used in each case to determine or estimate the probability. To determine the probability of picking a spade from a deck of cards, a purely mathematical procedure is used. Given that there are fifty-two cards in a deck and thirteen are spades, 13 is divided by 52 to obtain one-fourth. A different procedure is used to determine the probability that a 20-year-old man will live to age 75. For this, one must sample a large number of 20-year-old men and count the number that live 55 more years. Yet a different procedure is used to determine the probability that Margaret and Peter will get married. This probability can only be estimated roughly, and doing so requires that we become acquainted with Margaret and Peter and with how they feel toward each other and toward marriage. These three procedures give rise to three distinct theories about probability: the classical theory, the relative frequency theory, and the subjectivist theory.

The **classical theory** traces its origin to the work of the seventeenth-century mathematicians Blaise Pascal and Pierre de Fermat in determining the betting odds for a game of chance. The theory is otherwise called the *a priori* theory of probability because the computations are made independently of any sensory observation of actual events. According to the classical theory, the probability of an event A is given by the formula

$$P(A) = \frac{f}{n}$$

where f is the number of favorable outcomes and n is the number of possible outcomes. For example, in computing the probability of drawing an ace from a poker deck, the number of favorable outcomes is four (because there are four aces) and the number of possible outcomes is fifty-two (because there are fifty-two cards in the deck). Thus, the probability of that event is 4/52 or 1/13 (or .077).

Two assumptions are involved in computing probabilities according to the classical theory: (1) that all possible outcomes are taken into account, and (2) that all possible outcomes are equally probable. In the card example the first assumption entails that only the fifty-two ordinary outcomes are possible. In other words, it is assumed that the cards will not suddenly self-destruct or reproduce, that the printing will not suddenly vanish, and so on. The second assumption, which is otherwise called the **principle of indifference,** entails that there is an equal likelihood of selecting any card. In other words, it is assumed that the cards are stacked evenly, that none are glued together, and so on.

Whenever these two assumptions can be made about the occurrence of an event, the classical theory can be used to compute its probability. Here are some additional examples:

P(a fair coin turning up heads) $= 1/2$
P(drawing a face card) $= 12/52 = 3/13$
P(a single die coming up "3") $= 1/6$
P(a single die coming up "even") $= 3/6 = 1/2$

Strictly speaking, of course, the two assumptions underlying the classical theory are never perfectly reflected in any actual situation. Every coin is slightly off balance, as is every pair of dice. As a result, the probabilities of the various outcomes are never exactly equal. Similarly, the outcomes are never strictly confined to the normal ones entailed by the first assumption. When tossing a coin, there is always the possibility that the coin will land on edge, and in rolling dice there is the analogous possibility that one of them might break in half. These outcomes may not be possible in the *practical* sense, but they are *logically* possible in that they do not involve any contradiction. Because these outcomes are so unusual, however, it is reasonable to think that for all practical purposes the two assumptions hold and that therefore the classical theory is applicable.

There are many events, however, for which the two assumptions required by the classical theory obviously do not hold. For example, in attempting to determine the probability of a 60-year-old woman dying of a heart attack within ten years, it would be virtually impossible to take account of all the possible outcomes. She might die of cancer, pneumonia, or an especially virulent case of the flu. She might be incapacitated by a car accident, or she might move to Florida and buy a house on the beach. Furthermore, none of these outcomes is equally probable in comparison with the others. To compute the probability of events such as these we need the relative frequency theory of probability.

The **relative frequency theory** originated with the use of mortality tables by life insurance companies in the eighteenth century. In contrast with the classical theory, which rests upon a priori computations, the relative frequency theory depends on actual observations of the frequency with which certain events happen. The probability of an event A is given by the formula

$$P(A) = \frac{f_O}{n_O}$$

where f_O is the number of *observed* favorable outcomes and n_O is the total number of *observed* outcomes. For example, to determine the probability that a 50-year-old man will live five more years, a sample of 1,000 50-year-old men could be observed. If 968 were alive five years later, the probability that the man in question will live an additional five years is 968/1000 or .968.

Similarly, if one wanted to determine the probability that a certain irregularly shaped pyramid with different colored sides would, when rolled, come to rest with the green side down, the pyramid could be rolled 1,000 times. If it came to rest with its green side down 327 times, the probability of this event happening would be computed to be .327.

The relative frequency method can also be used to compute the probability of the kinds of events that conform to the requirements of the classical theory. For example, the probability of a coin coming up heads could be determined by tossing the coin 100 times and counting the heads. If, after this many tosses, 46 heads have been recorded, one might assign a probability of .46 to this event. This leads us to an important point about the relative frequency theory: the results hold true only in the long run. It might be necessary to toss the coin 1,000 or even 10,000 times to get a close approximation. After 10,000 tosses one would expect to count close to 5,000 heads. If in fact only 4,623 heads have been recorded, one would probably be justified in concluding that the coin is off balance or that something was irregular in the way it had been tossed.

Strictly speaking, neither the classical method nor the relative frequency method can assign a probability to individual events. From the standpoint of these approaches only certain *kinds* or *classes* of events have probabilities. But many events in the actual world are unique, one-of-a-kind happenings—for example, Margaret's marrying Peter or Native Prancer's winning the fourth race at Churchill Downs. To interpret the probability of these events we turn to the subjectivist theory.

The **subjectivist theory** interprets the meaning of probability in terms of the beliefs of individual people. Although such beliefs are vague and nebulous, they may be given quantitative interpretation through the odds that a person would accept on a bet. For example, if a person believes that a certain horse will win a race and he or she is willing to give 7 to 4 odds on that event happening, this means that he or she has assigned a probability of 7/(7+4) or 7/11 to that event. This procedure is unproblematic as long as the person is consistent in giving odds on the same event *not* happening. If, for example, 7 to 4 odds are given that an event will happen and 5 to 4 odds that it will not happen, the individual who gives these odds will inevitably lose. If 7 to 4 odds are given that an event *will* happen, no better than 4 to 7 odds can be given that the same event will *not* happen.

One of the difficulties surrounding the subjectivist theory is that one and the same event can be said to have different probabilities, depending on the willingness of different people to give different odds. If probabilities are taken to be genuine attributes of events, this would seem to be a serious problem. The problem might be avoided, though, either by interpreting probabilities as attributes of beliefs or by taking the average of the various individual probabilities as *the* probability of the event.

The three theories discussed thus far, the classical theory, the relative frequency theory, and the subjectivist theory, provide separate procedures for assigning a probability to an event (or class of events). Sometimes one theory is more readily applicable, sometimes another. But once individual events have been given a probability, the groundwork has been laid for computing the probabilities of compound arrangements of events. This is done by means of what is called the **probability calculus.** In this respect the probability calculus functions analogously to the set of truth functional rules in propositional logic. Just as the truth functional rules allow us to compute the truth values of molecular propositions from the individual truth values of the atomic components, the rules of the probability calculus allow us to compute the probability of compound events from the individual probabilities of the events.

Two preliminary rules of the probability calculus are (1) the probability of an event that must necessarily happen is taken to be 1, and (2) the probability of an event that necessarily cannot happen is taken to be 0. For example, the event consisting of it either raining or not raining (at the same time and place) has probability 1, and the event consisting of it both raining and not raining (at the same time and place) has proba-

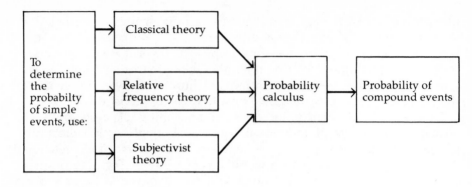

bility 0. These events correspond to statements that are tautological and self-contradictory, respectively. Contingent events, on the other hand, have probabilities greater than 0 but less than 1. For example, the probability that the Dow Jones Industrial Averages will end a certain week at least five points higher than the previous week would usually be around 1/2, the probability that the polar ice cap will melt next year is very close to 0, and the probability that a traffic accident will occur somewhere tomorrow is very close to 1. Let us now consider five additional rules of the probability calculus.

1. Restricted Conjunction Rule

The **restricted conjunction rule** is used to compute the probability of two events occurring together when the events are *independent* of one another. Events are said to be independent when the occurrence of one has no effect on the occurrence of the other. Examples include tossing two coins, drawing two cards from a deck when the first is replaced before the second is drawn, and playing two sequential games of poker or roulette. The probability of two such events A and B occurring together is given by the formula

$$P(A \text{ and } B) = P(A) \times P(B)$$

For example, the probability of tossing two heads on a single throw of two coins is

$$P(H_1 \text{ and } H_2) = 1/2 \times 1/2 = 1/4$$

This result may be checked very easily by listing all the possible outcomes and comparing that number with the number of favorable outcomes:

Coin 1	Coin 2
H	H
H	T
T	H
T	T

Only one of the four possible outcomes shows both coins turning up heads.

Similarly, we may compute the probability of rolling two sixes with a pair of dice:

$$P(S_1 \text{ and } S_2) = 1/6 \times 1/6 = 1/36$$

Again, we may check the results by listing all the possible outcomes:

1-1	2-1	3-1	4-1	5-1	6-1
1-2	2-2	3-2	4-2	5-2	6-2
1-3	2-3	3-3	4-3	5-3	6-3
1-4	2-4	3-4	4-4	5-4	6-4
1-5	2-5	3-5	4-5	5-5	6-5
1-6	2-6	3-6	4-6	5-6	6-6

Since only one of the thirty-six possible outcomes shows two sixes together, the probability of this event is 1/36.

2. General Conjunction Rule

The **general conjunction rule** is used to compute the probability of two events occurring together whether or not the events are independent. When the events are independent, the general conjunction rule reduces to the restricted conjunction rule. Some examples of events that are not independent (that is, that are *dependent*) are drawing two cards from a deck when the first card drawn is not replaced, and selecting two or more seats on an airplane. After the first card is drawn, the number of cards available for the second draw is reduced, and after one of the seats is taken on the plane, the number of seats remaining for subsequent choices is reduced. In other words, in both cases the second event is dependent on the first. The formula for computing the probability of two such events occurring together is

$$P(A \text{ and } B) = P(A) \times P(B \text{ given } A)$$

The expression $P(B$ given $A)$ is the probability that B will occur on the assumption that A has already occurred. Let us suppose, for example, that A and B designate the events of drawing two kings from a deck when the first card is not replaced before the second is drawn. If event A

occurs, then only three kings remain, and the deck is also reduced to fifty-one cards. Thus, $P(B$ given $A)$ is $3/51$. Since the probability of event A is $4/52$, the probability of both events happening is the product of these two fractions, or $12/2652$ ($= 1/221$).

For another illustration, consider an urn containing five red balls, six green balls, and seven yellow balls. The probability of drawing two red balls (without replacement) is computed as follows:

$$P(R_1 \text{ and } R_2) = 5/18 \times 4/17 = 20/306 = 10/153$$

If a red ball is selected on the first draw, this leaves four red balls from a total of seventeen. Thus, the probability of drawing a second red ball if one has already been drawn is $4/17$.

For another example, consider the same urn with the same contents, but let us compute the probability of drawing first a green ball and then a yellow ball (without replacement):

$$P(G \text{ and } Y) = 6/18 \times 7/17 = 42/306 = 7/51$$

If a green ball is selected on the first draw, this affects the selection of a yellow ball on the second draw only to the extent of reducing the total number of balls to seventeen.

3. Restricted Disjunction Rule

The **restricted disjunction rule** is used to compute the probability of either of two events occurring when the events are *mutually exclusive—* that is, when they cannot both occur. Examples of such events include picking either an ace or a king from a deck of cards on a single draw or rolling either a six or a one on a single roll of a die. The probability is given by the formula

$$P(A \text{ or } B) = P(A) + P(B)$$

For example, the probability of drawing either a king or a queen (of any suit) from a deck of cards on a single draw is

$$P(K \text{ or } Q) = 4/52 + 4/52 = 8/52 = 2/13$$

For another example, consider an urn containing six black balls, four white balls, and two red balls. The probability of selecting either a black or red ball on a single draw is

$$P(B \text{ or } R) = 6/12 + 2/12 = 8/12 = 2/3$$

When the event in question is one that must *necessarily* occur, the

A CONCISE INTRODUCTION TO LOGIC

probability is, of course, 1. Thus, the probability of obtaining either heads or tails on a single toss of a coin is

$$P(H \text{ or } T) = 1/2 + 1/2 = 1$$

The restricted disjunction rule may be combined with the restricted conjunction rule to compute the probability of getting either a five or a six on each of two consecutive rolls of a single die:

$$
\begin{aligned}
P[(F \text{ or } S)_1 \text{ and } (F \text{ or } S)_2] &= P(F \text{ or } S)_1 \times P(F \text{ or } S)_2 \\
&= (1/6 + 1/6) \times (1/6 + 1/6) \\
&= 1/3 \times 1/3 \\
&= 1/9
\end{aligned}
$$

Since getting a five and getting a six on a single die are mutually exclusive events, $P(F \text{ or } S)_1$ is evaluated using the restricted disjunction rule. The same is true of $P(F \text{ or } S)_2$. Then, since rolling a die is an independent event, the conjunction of the two disjunctive events is evaluated by the restricted conjunction rule.

4. General Disjunction Rule

The **general disjunction rule** is used to compute the probability of either of two events whether or not they are mutually exclusive. The rule holds for any two events, but since its application is simplified when the events are independent, we will confine our attention to events of this kind. Examples of independent events that are not mutually exclusive include obtaining at least one head on two tosses of a coin, drawing at least one king from a deck on two draws when the first card is replaced before the second card is drawn, and getting at least one six when rolling a pair of dice. The formula for computing the probability of either of two such events is

$$P(A \text{ or } B) = P(A) + P(B) - P(A \text{ and } B)$$

If the events are independent, $P(A \text{ and } B)$ is computed using the restricted conjunction rule, and the general disjunction formula reduces to

$$P(A \text{ or } B) = P(A) + P(B) - [P(A) \times P(B)]$$

The general disjunction rule may be proved as follows. When A and B are nonexclusive, A occurs either with or without B, and B occurs either with or without A. Thus

$$
\begin{aligned}
P(A) &= P(A \text{ and } B) + P(A \text{ and not-}B) \\
P(B) &= P(B \text{ and } A) + P(B \text{ and not-}A)
\end{aligned}
$$

But *A* or *B* occurs in exactly three possible ways: *A* and not-*B*, *B* and not-*A*, and *A* and *B*. Thus

$$P(A \text{ or } B) = P(A \text{ and not-}B) + P(B \text{ and not-}A) + P(A \text{ and } B)$$

Thus, when $P(A \text{ and } B)$ is subtracted from $P(A) + P(B)$, the difference is equal to $P(A \text{ or } B)$. [Note: $P(A \text{ and } B) = P(B \text{ and } A)$.]

For an example of the use of the general disjunction rule let us consider the probability of getting heads on either of two tosses of a coin. We have

$$
\begin{aligned}
P(H_1 \text{ or } H_2) &= 1/2 + 1/2 - (1/2 \times 1/2) \\
&= 1 - 1/4 \\
&= 3/4
\end{aligned}
$$

For another example, consider the probability of getting at least one six when rolling a pair of dice. The computation is

$$
\begin{aligned}
P(S_1 \text{ or } S_2) &= 1/6 + 1/6 - (1/6 \times 1/6) \\
&= 2/6 - 1/36 \\
&= 11/36
\end{aligned}
$$

The general disjunction rule may be combined with the restricted disjunction rule to compute the probability of getting either a three or a five when rolling a pair of dice. This is the probability of getting either a three or a five on the first die or either a three or a five on the second:

$$
\begin{aligned}
P[(T \text{ or } F)_1 \text{ or } (T \text{ or } F)_2] &= P(T \text{ or } F)_1 + P(T \text{ or } F)_2 \\
&\quad -[P(T \text{ or } F)_1 \times P(T \text{ or } F)_2] \\
&= (1/6 + 1/6) + (1/6 + 1/6) \\
&\quad - [(1/6 + 1/6) \times (1/6 + 1/6)] \\
&= 2/6 + 2/6 - 4/36 \\
&= 20/36 \\
&= 5/9
\end{aligned}
$$

Since getting a three or a five on a single throw is an exclusive event, $P(T \text{ or } F)_1$ is equal to the sum of the separate probabilities. The same is true for $P(T \text{ or } F)_2$.

The general disjunction rule may be combined with the general conjunction rule to compute the probability of drawing first a red ball and then a black ball on pairs of draws from either of two urns (without replacement). Suppose that the first urn contains two red balls, two black balls, and one green ball, and that the second urn contains three red balls, one black ball, and one white ball. The probability, giving two draws per urn, is

A CONCISE INTRODUCTION TO LOGIC

$P[(R \text{ and } B)_1 \text{ or } (R \text{ and } B)_2]$
$$= P(R \text{ and } B)_1 + P(R \text{ and } B)_2 - [P(R \text{ and } B)_1 \times P(R \text{ and } B)_2]$$
$$= (2/5 \times 2/4) + (3/5 \times 1/4) - [(2/5 \times 2/4) \times (3/5 \times 1/4)]$$
$$= 4/20 + 3/20 - (4/20 \times 3/20)$$
$$= 7/20 - 12/400$$
$$= 8/25$$

5. Negation Rule

The **negation rule** is useful for computing the probability of an event when the probability of the event *not* happening is either known or easily computed. The formula is as follows:

$$P(A) = 1 - P(\text{not-}A)$$

The formula can be proved very easily. By the restricted disjunction rule the probability of A or not-A is

$$P(A \text{ or not-}A) = P(A) + P(\text{not-}A)$$

But since A or not-A happens necessarily, $P(A \text{ or not-}A) = 1$. Thus

$$1 = P(A) + P(\text{not-}A)$$

Rearranging the terms in this equation gives us the negation rule. For an example of the use of this rule, consider the probability of getting heads at least once on two tosses of a coin. The probability of the event *not* happening, which is the probability of getting tails on both tosses, is immediately computed by the restricted conjunction rule to be $1/4$. Then, applying the negation rule

$$P(H_1 \text{ or } H_2) = 1 - 1/4$$
$$= 3/4$$

The negation rule may also be used to compute the probabilities of disjunctive events that are *dependent*. In presenting the general disjunction rule we confined our attention to *independent* events. Let us suppose we are given an urn containing two black balls and three white balls. To compute the probability of getting at least one black ball on two draws (without replacement), we first compute the probability of the event not happening. This event consists in drawing two white balls, which, by the general conjunction rule, has the probability

$$P(W_1 \text{ and } W_2) = 3/5 \times 2/4 = 6/20$$

Now, applying the negation rule, the probability of getting at least one black ball on two draws is

$$P(B_1 \text{ or } B_2) = 1 - 6/20$$
$$= 14/20$$
$$= 7/10$$

For an example that is only slightly more complex, consider an urn containing two white, two black, and two red balls. To compute the probability of getting either a white or black ball on two draws (without replacement) we first compute the probability of the event not happening. This is the probability of getting red balls on both draws, which is

$$P(R_1 \text{ and } R_2) = 2/6 \times 1/5 = 2/30 = 1/15$$

Now, by the negation rule the probability of drawing either a white or black ball is

$$P(W \text{ or } B) = 1 - 1/15$$
$$= 14/15$$

All of the examples considered thus far have used the classical theory to determine the probability of the component events. But as was mentioned earlier, the probability calculus can also be used in conjunction with the relative frequency theory and the subjectivist theory. If we apply the relative frequency theory to the mortality tables used by insurance companies, we find that the probability of a 25-year-old man living an additional 40 years is .82, and the probability of a 25-year-old woman living the same number of years is .88. To compute the probability of two such people living that long we use the restricted conjunction rule and obtain .82 $\times$ .88 = .72. For the probability that either of these people would live that long, we use the general disjunction rule and obtain

$$.82 + .88 - (.82 \times .88) = .98$$

Let us suppose that these two people are married and both would give 9 to 1 odds on their staying married for 40 years. This translates into a probability of $9/(9+1)$ or .9. Using the restricted conjunction rule, the probability of this event happening is the product of the latter figure and the probability of their both living that long, or .65.

For an example involving the subjectivist theory, if the Dallas Cowboys are given 7 to 5 odds at winning the NFC championship, and the Pittsburgh Steelers are given 3 to 2 odds at winning the AFC championship, the probability that at least one of these teams will win is computed using the general disjunction rule. The odds translate respectively into probabilities of $7/12$ and $3/5$, and so the probability of the disjunction is $7/12 + 3/5 - (7/12 \times 3/5) = 5/6$. The probability that the two teams will meet in the Superbowl (that both will win their conference championship) is, by the restricted conjunction rule, $7/12 \times 3/5 =$

21/60, or 7/20. The probability that neither will play in the Superbowl is, by the negation rule, $1 - 5/6 = 1/6$.

The probability calculus can also be used to evaluate the strength of inductive arguments. Consider the following argument:

> The Dallas Cowboys are given 7 to 5 odds on winning the NFC championship. The Pittsburgh Steelers are given 3 to 2 odds on winning the AFC championship. Therefore, probably the Cowboys and the Steelers will meet in the Superbowl.

On the assumption that the premises are true, that is, on the assumption that the odds are reported correctly, the conclusion follows with a probability of 7/20 or .35. Thus, the argument is not particularly strong. But if the odds given in the premises should increase, the strength of the argument would increase proportionately. The premises of the following argument give different odds:

> The Dallas Cowboys are given 7 to 2 odds on winning the NFC championship. The Pittsburgh Steelers are given 8 to 3 odds on winning the AFC championship. Therefore, probably the Cowboys and the Steelers will meet in the Superbowl.

In this argument, if the premises are assumed true, the conclusion follows with probability $7/9 \times 8/11 = 56/99$, or .57. Thus, the argument is at least moderately strong.

Lest this procedure be misinterpreted, however, it is important to recall a point raised in Chapter 1. The strength of an inductive argument depends not merely upon whether the conclusion is probably true but upon whether the conclusion follows probably from the premises. As a result, to evaluate the strength of an inductive argument it is not sufficient merely to know the probability of the conclusion on the assumption that the premises are true. One must also know whether the probability of the conclusion rests upon the evidence given in the premises. If the probability of the conclusion does not rest on this evidence, the argument is weak regardless of whether the conclusion is probably true. The following argument is a case in point:

> All dogs are animals.
> Therefore, probably a traffic accident will occur somewhere tomorrow.

The conclusion of this argument is probably true independently of the premises, so the argument is weak.

In this connection the analogy between deductive and inductive arguments breaks down. As we saw in Chapter 6, any argument having a conclusion that is necessarily true is deductively valid regardless of the content of its premises. But any inductive argument having a probably true conclusion is not strong unless the probability of the conclusion rests upon the evidence given in the premises.

A final comment is in order about the material covered in this section. Probability is one of those subjects about which there is little agreement in philosophical circles. There are philosophers who defend each of the theories we have discussed as providing the only acceptable approach, and there are numerous views regarding the fine points of each. In addition, some philosophers argue that there are certain uses of "probability" that none of these theories can interpret. The statement "There is high probability that Einstein's theory of relativity is correct" may be a case in point. In any event, the various theories about the meaning of probability, as well as the details of the probability calculus, are highly complex subjects, and the brief account given here has done little more than scratch the surface.

EXERCISE 9.2

I. Simple events.

★1. What is the probability of rolling a five on a single roll of a die?

2. From a sample of 9,750 Ajax trucks, 273 developed transmission problems within the first two years of operation. What is the probability that an Ajax truck will develop transmission problems within the first two years?

3. If the standard odds are 8 to 5 that the Chargers will beat the Lions, what is the probability that this event will happen?

4. From a sample of 7,335 75-year-old women, 6,260 lived an additional 5 years. What is the probability that a 75-year-old woman will live to age 80?

★5. What is the probability of picking a black jack from a poker deck (without jokers) on a single draw?

6. If the standard odds are 6 to 11 that the Red Sox will beat the Tigers, what is the probability that this event will happen?

7. Given an urn containing three red balls, four green balls, and five yellow balls, what is the probability of drawing a red ball on a single draw?

II. Compound events.

★1. What is the probability of getting either a six or a one from a single roll of a die?

2. What is the probability of getting heads on three successive tosses of a coin?

3. What is the probability of drawing either a king or a queen from a poker deck (no jokers) on a single draw?

4. What is the probability of drawing two aces from a poker deck in two draws:
   a. If the first card is replaced before the second is drawn?
   b. If the first card is not replaced before the second is drawn?

★5. What is the probability of drawing at least one ace from a poker deck on two draws if the first card is replaced before the second is drawn?

6. What is the probability of getting at least one head on three tosses of a coin?

7. What is the probability of getting at least one six on three rolls of a die?

8. If a pair of dice are rolled, what is the probability that the points add up to:
   a. 5?
   b. 6?
   c. 7?

9. Given two urns, one containing two red, three green, and four yellow balls, the other containing four red, two green, and three yellow balls, if a single ball is drawn from each urn, what is the probability that:
   a. Both are red?
   b. At least one is green?
   c. One is red, the other yellow?
   d. At least one is either red or yellow?
   e. Both are the same color?

★10. Given an urn containing three red, four green, and five yellow balls, if two balls are drawn from the urn (without replacement), what is the probability that:
   a. Both are red?
   b. One is green, the other yellow?
   c. One is either red or green?
   d. At least one is green?
   e. Both have the same color?

11. What is the probability of drawing either an ace or a king (or both) on three draws (without replacement) from a poker deck? (Hint: Use the negation rule.)

12. What is the probability of drawing an ace and a king on three draws (without replacement) from a poker deck? (Hint: Use the negation rule.)

13. The probability of a 20-year-old man living to age 70 is .74, and the probability of a 20-year-old woman living to the same age is .82. If a recently married couple, both age 20, give 8 to 1 odds on their staying married for 50 years, what is the probability that:

a. At least one will live to age 70?

b. They will celebrate their golden wedding anniversary?

14. Assign a numerical value to the strength of the following argument: The odds are 5 to 3 that the Indians will win the American League pennant and 7 to 5 that the Cardinals will win the National League pennant. Therefore, the Indians and the Cardinals will probably meet in the World Series.

★15. Assign a numerical value to the strength of the following argument: The Wilson family has four children. Therefore, at least two of the children were probably born on the same day of the week.

9.3 STATISTICAL REASONING

In our day-to-day experience all of us encounter arguments that rest on statistical evidence. An especially prolific source of such arguments is the advertising industry. We are constantly told that we ought to smoke a certain brand of cigarettes because it has 20 percent less tar, buy a certain kind of car because it gets 5 percent better gas mileage, and use a certain cold remedy because it is recommended by four out of five physicians. But the advertising industry is not the only source. We often read in the newspapers that some union is asking an increase in pay because its members earn less than the average or that a certain region is threatened with floods because rainfall has been more than the average.

To evaluate such arguments, we must be able to interpret the statistics upon which they rest, but doing so is not always easy. Statements expressing averages and percentages are often ambiguous and can mean any number of things, depending on how the average or percentage is computed. These difficulties are compounded by the fact that statistics provide a highly convenient way for people to deceive one another. Such deceptions can be effective even though they fall short of being outright lies. Thus, to evaluate arguments based on statistics one must be familiar not only with the ambiguities that occur in the language but with the devices that unscrupulous individuals use to deceive others.

This section touches on five areas that are frequent sources of such ambiguity and deception: problems in sampling, the meaning of "average," the importance of dispersion in a sample, the use of graphs and pictograms, and the use of percentages for the purpose of comparison. By becoming acquainted with these topics and with some of the misuses that occur, we are better able to determine whether a conclusion follows probably from a set of statistical premises.

Samples

Much of the statistical evidence presented in support of inductively drawn conclusions is gathered from analyzing samples. When a sample is found to possess a certain characteristic, it is argued that the group as a whole (the population) possesses that characteristic. For example, if we wanted to know the opinion of the student body at a certain university about whether the Selective Service System should reinstate the draft, we could take a poll of 10 percent of the students. If the results of the poll showed that 80 percent of those sampled were opposed to the draft, we might draw the conclusion that 80 percent of the entire student body was opposed. Such an argument would be classified as an inductive generalization.

The problem that arises with the use of samples has to do with whether the sample is representative of the population. Samples that are not representative are said to be **biased.** Depending on what the population consists of, whether machine parts or human beings, different considerations enter into determining whether a sample is biased. These considerations include (1) whether the sample is randomly selected, (2) the size of the sample, and (3) psychological factors.

A sample is *random* if and only if every member of the population has an equal chance of being selected. The requirement that a sample be randomly selected applies to practically all samples, but sometimes it can be taken for granted. For example, when a physician draws a blood sample to test for blood sugar, there is no need to take a little bit from the finger, a little from the arm, and a little from the leg. Because blood is a circulating fluid, it can be assumed that it is homogenous in regard to blood sugar.

The randomness requirement must be given more attention when the population consists of discrete units. Suppose, for example, that a quality control engineer for a manufacturing firm needed to determine whether the components on a certain conveyor belt were within specifications. To do so, let us suppose the engineer removed every tenth component for measurement. The sample obtained by such a procedure would not be random if the components were not randomly arranged on the conveyor belt. As a result of some malfunction in the manufacturing process it is quite possible that every tenth component turned out perfect and the rest imperfect. If the engineer happened to select only the perfect ones, the sample would be biased. A selection procedure that would be more likely to insure a random sample would be to roll a pair of dice and remove every component corresponding to a roll of ten. Since the outcome of a roll of dice is a random event, the selection would also be random. Such a procedure would be more likely to include defective components that turn up at regular intervals.

The randomness requirement presents even greater problems when the population consists of human beings. Suppose, for example, that a public opinion poll is to be conducted on the question of excess corporate profits. It would hardly do to ask such a question randomly of the people encountered on Wall Street in New York City. Such a sample would almost certainly be biased in favor of the corporations. A less biased sample could be obtained by randomly selecting phone numbers from the telephone directory, but even this procedure would not yield a completely random sample. Among other things, the time of day in which a call is placed influences the kind of responses obtained. Most people who are employed full time are not available during the day, and even if calls are made at night, approximately 25 percent of the population have unlisted numbers.

A poll conducted by mail based on the addresses listed in the city directory would also yield a fairly random sample, but this method, too, has shortcomings. Many apartment dwellers are not listed, and others move before the directory is printed. Furthermore, none of those who live in rural areas are listed. In short, it is both difficult and expensive to conduct a large-scale public opinion poll that succeeds in obtaining responses from anything approximating a random sample of individuals.

A classic case of a poll that turned out to be biased in spite of a good deal of effort and expense was conducted by *Literary Digest* magazine to predict the outcome of the 1936 presidential election. The sample consisted of a large number of the magazine's subscribers together with a number of others selected from the telephone directory. Because four similar polls had picked the winner in previous years, the results of this poll were highly respected. As it turned out, however, the Republican candidate, Alf Landon, got a significant majority in the poll, but Franklin D. Roosevelt won the election by a landslide. The incorrect prediction is explained by the fact that 1936 occurred in the middle of the Depression, at a time when many people could afford neither a telephone nor a subscription to the *Digest*. These were the people who were overlooked in the poll, and they were also the ones who voted for Roosevelt.

Size is also an important factor in determining whether a sample is representative. Given that a sample is randomly selected, the larger the sample, the more closely it replicates the population. In statistics, this degree of closeness is expressed in terms of **sampling error**. The sampling error is the difference between the frequency with which some characteristic occurs in the sample and the frequency with which the same characteristic occurs in the population. If, for example, a poll were taken of a labor union and 60 percent of the members sampled expressed their intention to vote for Smith for president but in fact only 55 percent of the whole union intended to vote for Smith, the sampling error would be 5 percent. If a larger sample were taken, the error would be less.

Just how large a sample should be is a function of the size of the population and of the degree of sampling error that can be tolerated. For a sampling error of, say, 5 percent, a population of 10,000 would require a larger sample than would a population of 100. However, the ratio is not linear. The sample for the larger population need not be 100 times as large as the one for the smaller population to obtain the same precision. When the population is very large, the size of the sample needed to ensure a certain precision levels off to a constant figure. Studies based on the Gallup poll show that a random sample of 400 will yield results of plus or minus 5 percent whether the population is 100,000 or 100 million. Additional figures for large populations are given in Table 7[*]:

Table 7 Sample Size and Sampling Error

Numbers of interviews	Margin of error (in percentage points)
4,000	±2
1,500	±3
1,000	±4
750	±4
600	±5
400	±6
200	±8
100	±11

As the table indicates, reducing the sampling error below 5 percent requires rather substantial increases in the size of the sample. The cost of obtaining large samples may not justify an increase in precision. The table also points up the importance of randomness. The sample in the 1936 *Literary Digest* poll was based on 2 million responses, yet the sampling error was huge because the sample was not randomly selected.

Statements of sampling error are often conspicuously absent from surveys used to support advertising claims. Marketers of products such as patent medicines have been known to take a number of rather small samples until they obtain one that gives the "right" result. For example, twenty polls of twenty-five people might be taken inquiring about the preferred brand of aspirin. Even though the samples might be randomly selected, one will eventually be found in which twenty of the twenty-five respondents indicate their preference for alpha brand aspirin. Having found such a sample, the marketing firm proceeds to promote this brand as the one preferred by four out of five of those sampled. The results of the other samples are, of course, discarded, and no mention is made of sampling error.

Psychological factors can also have a bearing on whether the sample is representative. When the population consists of inanimate objects, such as cans of soup or machine parts, psychological factors are usually irrelevant, but they can play a significant role when the population consists of human beings. If the people composing the sample think that they

---

[*]From Charles W. Roll Jr. and Albert H. Cantril, *Polls: Their Use and Misuse in Politics* (New York: Basic Books, 1972), p. 72.

will gain or lose something by the kind of answer they give, it is to be expected that their involvement will affect the outcome. For example, if the residents of a neighborhood were to be surveyed for annual income with the purpose of determining whether the neighborhood should be ranked among the fashionable areas in the city, it would be expected that the residents would exaggerate their answers. But if the purpose of the study were to determine whether the neighborhood could afford a special levy that would increase property taxes, one might expect the incomes to be underestimated.

The kind of question asked can also have a psychological bearing. Questions such as "How often do you brush your teeth?" and "How many books do you read in a year?" can be expected to generate responses that overestimate the truth, while "How many times have you been intoxicated?" and "How many extramarital affairs have you had?" would probably receive answers that underestimate the truth. Similar exaggerations can result from the way a question is phrased. For example, "Do you favor a reduction in welfare benefits as a response to rampant cheating?" would be expected to receive more affirmative answers than simply "Do you favor a reduction in welfare benefits?"

Another source of psychological influence is the personal interaction between the surveyor and the respondent. Suppose, for example, that a door-to-door survey were taken to determine how many people believe in God or attend church on Sunday. If the survey were conducted by priests and ministers dressed in clerical garb, one might expect a larger number of affirmative answers than if the survey were taken by non-clerics. The simple fact is that many people like to give answers that please the questioner.

To prevent this kind of interaction from affecting the outcome, scientific studies are often conducted under "double blind" conditions in which neither the surveyor nor the respondent knows what the "right" answer is. For example, in a double blind study to determine the effectiveness of a drug, bottles containing the drug would be mixed with other bottles containing a placebo (sugar tablet). The contents of each bottle would be matched with a code number on the label, and neither the person distributing the bottles nor the person recording the responses would know what the code is. Under these conditions the persons conducting the study would not be able to influence, by some smile or gesture, the response of the persons to whom the drugs are given.

Most of the statistical evidence encountered in ordinary experience contains no reference to such factors as randomness, sampling error, or the conditions under which the sample was taken. In the absence of such information, the person faced with evaluating the evidence must use his or her best judgment. If either the organization conducting the study or the persons composing the sample have something to gain by the kind of answer that is given, the results of the survey should be regarded as suspect. And if the questions that are asked concern topics that would naturally elicit distorted answers, the results should probably be rejected. In either event, the mere fact that a study *appears* scientific or is expressed in mathematical language should never intimidate a person into accepting the results. Numbers and scientific terminology are no substitute for an unbiased sample.

The Meaning of "Average"

In statistics the word "average" is used in three different senses: mean, median, and mode. In evaluating arguments and inferences that rest upon averages, it is often important to know in precisely what sense the word is being used.

The **mean** value of a set of data is the arithmetical average. It is computed by dividing the sum of the individual values by the number of data in the set. Suppose, for example, that we are given Table 8 listing the ages of a group of people:

Table 8	
Number of people	Age
1	16
4	17
1	18
2	19
3	23

To compute the mean age, we divide the sum of the individual ages by the number of people:

$$\text{mean age} = \frac{(1 \times 16) + (4 \times 17) + (1 \times 18) + (2 \times 19) + (3 \times 23)}{11}$$

$$= 19$$

The **median** of a set of data is the middle point when the data are arranged in ascending order. In other words, the median is the point at which there are an equal number of data above and below. In Table 8 the median age is 18 because there are five people above this age and five below.

The **mode** is the value that occurs with the greatest frequency. Here the mode is 17, because there are four people with that age and fewer people with any other age.

In this example, the mean, median, and mode, while different from one another, are all fairly close together. The problem for induction occurs when there is a great disparity between these values. This sometimes occurs in the case of salaries. Consider, for example, Table 9, which reports the salaries of a hypothetical architectural firm:

Table 9

Capacity	Number of personnel	Salary
president	1	$140,000
senior architect	2	80,000
junior architect	2	66,000
senior engineer	1	35,000←mean
junior engineer	4	32,000
senior draftsman	1	20,000←median
junior draftsman	10	12,000←mode

Since there are twenty-one employees and a total of $735,000 is paid in salaries, the mean salary is $735,000/21, or $35,000. The median salary is $20,000 because ten employees earn less than this and ten earn more, and the mode, which is the salary that occurs most frequently, is $12,000. Each of these figures represents the "average" salary of the firm, but in different senses. Depending on the purpose for which the average is used, different figures might be cited as the basis for an argument.

For example, if the senior engineer were to request a raise in salary, the president could respond that his or her salary is already well above the average (in the sense of median and mode) and that therefore that person does not deserve a raise. If the junior draftsmen were to make the same request, the president could respond that they are presently earning the firm's average salary (in the sense of mode), and that for draftsmen to be earning the average salary is excellent. Finally, if someone from outside the firm were to make the allegation that the firm pays subsistence-level wages, the president could respond that the average salary of the firm is a hefty $35,000. All of the president's responses would be true, but if the reader or listener is not sophisticated enough to distinguish the various senses of "average," he or she might be persuaded by the arguments.

In some situations, the mode is the most useful average. Suppose, for example, that you are in the market for a three-bedroom house. Suppose further that a real estate agent assures you that the houses in a certain complex have an average of three bedrooms and that therefore you will certainly want to see them. If the salesman has used "average" in the sense of mean, it is possible that half the houses in the complex are four-bedroom, the other half are two-bedroom, and there are no three-bedroom houses at all. A similar result is possible if the salesman has used average in the sense of median. The only sense of average that would be useful for your purposes is mode: If the modal average is three bed-rooms, there are more three-bedroom houses than any other kind.

On other occasions a mean average is the most useful. Suppose, for example, that you have taken a job as a pilot on a plane that has nine passenger seats and a maximum carrying capacity of 1,350 pounds (in addition to yourself). Suppose further that you have arranged to fly a group of nine passengers over the Grand Canyon and that you must determine whether their combined weight is within the required limit. If a representative of the group tells you that the average weight of the passengers is 150 pounds, this by itself tells you nothing. If he means average in the sense of median, it could be the case that the four heavier passengers weigh 200 pounds and the four lighter ones weigh 145, for a combined weight of 1,530 pounds. Similarly, if the passenger represen-tative means average in the sense of mode, it could be that two pas-sengers weigh 150 pounds and that the others have varying weights in excess of 200 pounds, for a combined weight of over 1,700 pounds. Only if the representative means average in the sense of mean do you know that the combined weight of the passengers is 9×150 or 1,350 pounds.

Finally, sometimes a median average is the most meaningful. Sup-pose, for example, that you are a manufacturer of a product that appeals to an age group under 35. To increase sales you decide to run an ad in a national magazine, but you want some assurance that the ad will be read by the right age group. If the advertising director of a magazine tells you that the average age of the magazine's readers is 35, you know virtually nothing. If the director means average in the sense of mean, it could be that 90 percent of the readership is over 35 and that the re-maining 10 percent bring the average down to 35. Similarly, if the direc-tor means average in the sense of mode, it could be that 3 percent of the readership are exactly 35 and that the remaining 97 percent have ages ranging from 35 to 85. Only if the director means average in the sense of median do you know that half the readership is 35 or less.

As these examples illustrate, the sense of average used often makes an important difference. There is one group of data, however, for which the three senses always have identical values. This is the group of data that corresponds to random phenomena. Examples include the height of adult men or women, the velocity of the wind in a certain area, the useful life of a certain kind of light bulb or automobile tire, the weekly sales of a certain kind of toothpaste or shampoo, and the results of any random sample. Data that correspond to these phenomena usually con-form quite closely to what is called the **normal probability distribution,** whose curve has the shape of a bell (see Figure 1).

As the curve indicates, the number of instances tapers off to zero when the data reach maximum and minimum values, and it reaches a high point when the data have middle values. Mean, median, and mode occur together at the high point on the curve. This point indicates an

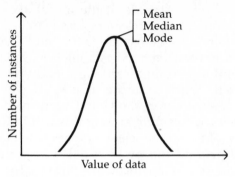

Figure 1

average in the sense of mode because it is the point at which the most instances are recorded. It is a median point because the data are random, so the number of instances greater than the high point equals the number of instances less than the high point. And this same point is a mean because the values of the data under the right-hand part exceed the median value to the same extent that the values under the left-hand part are less than the median value. An example of the use of this curve will be given in connection with dispersion.

Dispersion

The **dispersion** of a set of data refers to how spread out the data are in regard to numerical value. Suppose, for example, that wind velocity measurements are taken over a period of several months in the middle of the ocean. Suppose further that the wind blows constantly at this particular point, never dropping below 30 mph but never exceeding 60 mph. The dispersion of the data in this case would be rather slight, and, assuming that the data conform to the normal probability distribution, the curve would be relatively high and narrow, as in Figure 2:

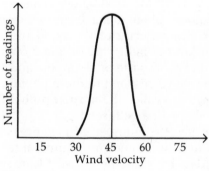

Figure 2

A CONCISE INTRODUCTION TO LOGIC

This curve indicates that all the velocity readings occur within the rather narrow range of 30 to 60 mph, for an average velocity of 45 mph.

If, on the other hand, the same number of velocity measurements are taken at a different point, where the wind occasionally stops completely but at other times reaches a maximum of 90 mph, the dispersion of the data would be much greater. Assuming that the data conform to the normal probability distribution, the curve would be flatter and lower, as in Figure 3:

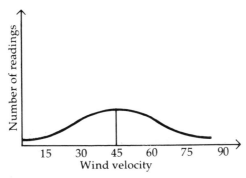

Figure 3

In both cases the average velocity in the sense of mean, median, and mode is 45 mph, but the difference in dispersion indicates that the situations are clearly different.

In statistics dispersion is expressed in terms of such parameters as range, variance, and standard deviation. The **range** of a set of data is the difference between the largest and the smallest values. Thus, in the first case the range is 30 and in the second case it is 90. The **variance** and **standard deviation,** on the other hand, measure how far the data vary or deviate from the mean value. (The standard deviation is defined as the square root of the variance.) In the two curves we have presented, the first has a relatively small variance and standard deviation in comparison with the second.

Information about the dispersion of a set of data is important in drawing inductive inferences because it supplements information about averages. Sometimes statements about averages are virtually useless without some additional statement about the dispersion, which, if ignored, can produce disastrous consequences. Suppose, for example, that after living for many years in an intemperate climate, you decide to relocate in an area that has a more ideal mean temperature. Upon discovering that the annual mean temperature of Oklahoma City is 60°F you decide to move there, only to find that you roast in the summer and freeze in the winter. Unfortunately, you had ignored the fact that Oklahoma City has a temperature *range* of 130°, extending from a record low of −17° to a record high of 113°. In contrast, San Nicholas Island, off the coast of

California, has a mean temperature of 61° but a range of only 40 degrees, extending from 47° in the winter to 87° in the summer. The temperature ranges for these two locations are approximated in Figure 4*:

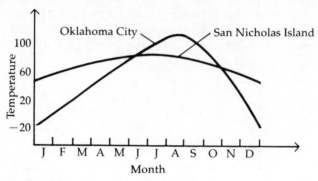

Figure 4

For another example, suppose that you are 25 years old and are planning an ocean cruise. Your primary concern in selecting a tour is that there be plenty of people on the ship within your age group. The manager of Holiday Tours sets your mind at rest when he assures you that the mean age of the voyagers departing on the Holiday Prince for a cruise of the Caribbean is 25. You select that cruise, and after departing you find to your dismay that the voyagers are primarily comprised of two groups, one ranging in age from 1 to 10, the other from 40 to 50. Together they balance out for a mean age of 25. This situation is depicted in Figure 5:

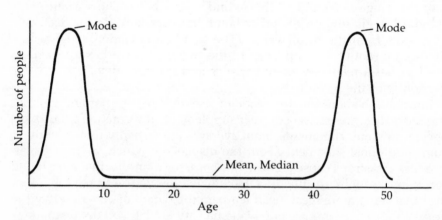

Figure 5

*This example is taken from Darrell Huff, *How To Lie with Statistics* (New York: W. W. Norton, 1954), p. 52.

The curve has two modes and is thus described as bimodal. In this case if you had known either the average age in the sense of mode or the dispersion, you would not have signed up for the cruise.

For a final example, suppose that you decide to put your life savings into a business that designs and manufactures women's clothing. As corporation president you decide to save money by restricting production to clothes that fit the average woman. Because the average size in the sense of mean, median, and mode is 12, you decide to make only size 12 clothing. Unfortunately, you later discover that while size 12 is indeed the average, 95 percent of women fall outside this range, as Figure 6 shows:

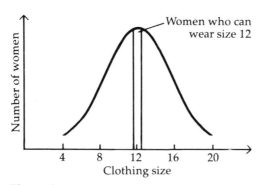

Figure 6

Again, if you had taken into account the dispersion of the data, you would not have made this mistake.

Graphs and Pictograms

Graphs provide a highly convenient and informative way to represent statistical data, but they are also susceptible to misuse and misinterpretation. Here we will confine our attention to some of the typical ways in which graphs are misused.

First of all, if a graph is to represent an actual situation, it is essential that both the vertical and horizontal axes be scaled. Suppose, for example, that the profit level of a corporation is represented by a graph such as Figure 7. Such a graph is practically meaningless because it fails to show how much the profits increased over what period of time. If the curve represents a 10 percent increase over 20 years, then, of course, the picture is not very bright. Although they convey practically no information, graphs of this kind are used quite often in advertising. A manufacturer of vitamins, for example, might print such a graph on the label of the bottle to suggest that a person's energy level is supposed to increase dramatically after taking the tablets. Such ads frequently make an impression because they look scientific, and the viewer rarely bothers to

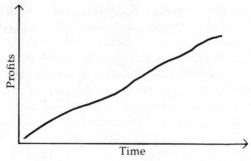

Figure 7

check whether the axes are scaled or precisely what the curve is supposed to signify.

A graph that more appropriately represents corporate profits is represented in Figure 8 (the corporation is fictitious):

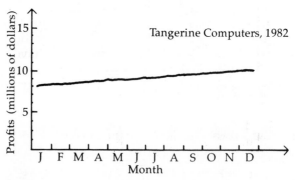

Figure 8

Inspection of the graph reveals that between January and December profits rose from $8 to $10 million, which represents a respectable 25 percent increase. This increase can be made to *appear* even more impressive by chopping off the bottom of the graph, as shown in Figure 9:

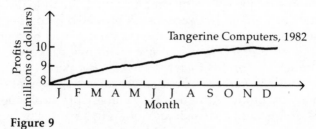

Figure 9

Strictly speaking, the new graph accurately represents the increase because the scale on the vertical axis indicates that the profits increased 25 percent. But the increase *looks* more impressive because the curve now

A CONCISE INTRODUCTION TO LOGIC

stretches from the bottom of the graph to the top. This same effect can be exaggerated by altering the scale on the vertical axis while leaving the horizontal scale as is:

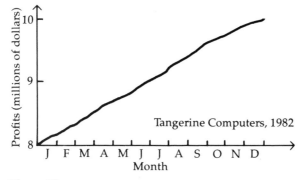

Figure 10

Again, strictly speaking, the graph accurately represents the facts, but if the viewer fails to notice what has been done to the vertical scale, he or she is liable to derive the impression that the profits have increased by something like a thousand percent.

The same strategy can be used with bar graphs. The graphs in Figure 11 compare sales volume for two consecutive years, but the one on the right conveys the message more dramatically:

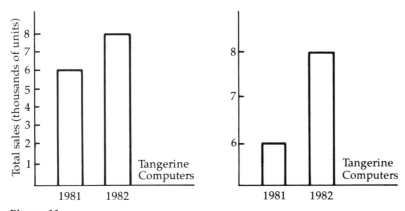

Figure 11

Of course, if the sales volume has decreased, the corporate directors would probably want to minimize the difference, in which case the design on the left is preferable.

An even greater illusion can be created with the use of pictograms. A **pictogram** is a diagram that compares two situations through drawings that differ either in size or in the number of entities depicted. Consider

Figure 12, which illustrates the increase in the amount of oil consumed in the United States between 1960 and 1978:

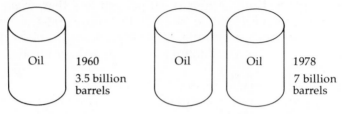

Figure 12

This pictogram accurately represents the facts because it unequivocally shows that the amount doubled between the years represented. But the effect is not especially dramatic. The increase in consumption can be exaggerated by representing the 1978 level with an oil barrel twice as tall:

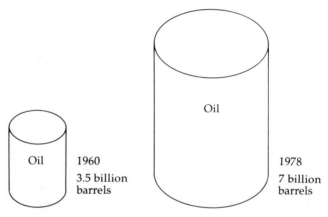

Figure 13

Even though the actual consumption is stated adjacent to each drawing, this pictogram creates the illusion that consumption has much more than doubled. While the drawing on the right is exactly twice as high as the one on the left, it is also twice as wide. Thus, it occupies four times as much room on the page. Furthermore, when the viewer's three-dimensional judgment is called into play, the barrel on the right is perceived as having eight times the volume of the one on the left. Thus, when the third dimension is taken into account, the increase in consumption is exaggerated by 400 percent.

Percentages

The use of percentages to compare two or more situations or quantities is another source of illusion in statistics. A favorite of advertisers is to make claims such as "Zesty Cola has 20 percent fewer calories" or "The new Zipmobile has 15 percent more trunk space." These claims are virtually meaningless. The question is, 20 percent less than *what*, and 15 percent more than *what*? If the basis of the comparison is not mentioned, the claim tells us nothing. Yet such claims are often effective because they leave one with the impression that the product is in some way superior.

Another strategy sometimes used by governments and businesses involves playing sleight-of-hand tricks with the base of the percentages. Suppose, for example, that you are a university president involved with a funding drive to increase the university's endowment. Suppose further that the endowment presently stands at $15 million and that the objective is to increase it to $20 million. To guarantee the success of the drive, you engage the services of a professional fund-raising organization. At the end of the alotted time the organization has increased the endowment to $16 million. They justify their effort by stating that, since $16 of the $20 million has been raised, the drive was 80 percent successful ($16/20 \times 100\%$).

In fact, of course, the drive was nowhere near that successful. The objective was not to raise $20 million, but only $5 million, and of that amount only $1 million has actually been raised. Thus, at best the drive was only 20 percent successful. Even this figure is probably exaggerated, though, because $1 million might have been raised without any special drive. The trick played by the fund-raising organization consisted in switching the numbers by which the percentage was to be computed.

This same trick, incidentally, was allegedly used by Joseph Stalin to justify the success of his first five-year plan.* Among other things, the original plan called for an increase in steel output from 4.2 million tons to 10.3 million. After five years the actual output rose to 5.9 million, whereupon Stalin announced that the plan was 57 percent successful ($5.9/10.3 \times 100\%$). The correct percentage, of course, is much less. The plan called for an increase of 6.1 million tons and the actual increase was only 1.7 million. Thus, at best, the plan was only 28 percent successful.

Similar devices have been used by employers on their unsuspecting employees. When business is bad, an employer may argue that salaries must be reduced by 20 percent. Later, when business improves, salaries will be raised by 20 percent, thus restoring them to their original level. Such an argument, of course, is fallacious. If a person earns $10 per hour and that person's salary is reduced by 20 percent, the adjusted salary is $8. If that figure is later increased by 20 percent, the final salary is $9.60. The problem, of course, stems from the fact that a different base is used

---

*Stephen K. Campbell, *Flaws and Fallacies in Statistical Thinking* (Englewood Cliffs, N.J.: Prentice-Hall, 1974) p. 8. The original reference is to Eugene Lyons' *Workers' Paradise Lost.*

for the two percentages. The fallacy committed by such arguments is a variety of equivocation. Percentages are relative terms, and they mean different things in different contexts.

A different kind of fallacy occurs when a person attempts to add percentages as if they were cardinal numbers. Suppose, for example, that a baker increases the price of a loaf of bread by 50 percent. To justify the increase the baker argues that it was necessitated by rising costs: the price of flour increased by 10 percent, the cost of labor by 20 percent, utility rates went up 10 percent, and the cost of the lease on the building increased 10 percent. This adds up to a 50 percent increase. Again, the argument is fallacious. If *everything* had increased by 20 percent, this would justify only a 20 percent increase in the price of bread. As it is, the justified increase is less than that. The fallacy committed by such arguments would probably be best classified as a case of missing the point (*ignoratio elenchi*). The arguer has failed to grasp the significance of his own premises.

Statistical variations of the suppressed evidence fallacy are also quite common. One variety consists in drawing a conclusion from a comparison of two different things or situations. For example, persons running for political office sometimes cite figures indicating that crime in the community has increased by, let us say, 20 percent during the past three or four years. What is needed, they conclude, is an all-out war on crime. But they fail to mention the fact that the population in the community has also increased by 20 percent during the same period. The number of crimes per capita, therefore, has not changed. Another example of the same fallacy is provided by the ridiculous argument that 90 percent more traffic accidents occur in clear weather than in foggy weather and that therefore it is 90 percent more dangerous to drive in clear than in foggy weather. The arguer ignores the fact that the vast percentage of vehicle miles are driven in clear weather, which accounts for the greater number of accidents.

A similar misuse of percentages is committed by businesses and corporations that, for whatever reason, want to make it appear that they have earned less profits than they actually have. The technique consists in expressing profits as a percentage of sales volume instead of as a percentage of investment. For example, during a certain year a corporation might have a total sales volume of $100 million, a total investment of $10 million, and a profit of $5 million. If profits are expressed as a percentage of investment, they amount to a hefty 50 percent; but as a percentage of sales they are only 5 percent. To appreciate the fallacy in this procedure, consider the case of the jewelry merchant who buys one piece of jewelry each morning for $9 and sells it in the evening for $10. At the end of the year the total sales volume is $3650, the total investment $9, and the total profit $365. Profits as a percentage of sales amount to only 10 percent, but as a percentage of investment they exceed 4000 percent.

EXERCISE 9.3

I. Criticize the following arguments in light of the material presented in this section:

★1. To test the algae content in a lake, a biologist took a sample of the water at one end. The algae in the sample registered 5 micrograms per liter. Therefore, the algae in the lake at that time registered 5 micrograms per liter.

2. To estimate public support for a new municipality-funded convention center, researchers surveyed 100 homeowners in one of the city's fashionable neighborhoods. They found that 89 percent of those sampled were enthusiastic about the project. Therefore, we may conclude that 89 percent of the city's residents favor the convention center.

3. A quality-control inspector for a food-processing firm needed assurance that the cans of fruit in a production run were filled to capacity. He opened every tenth box in the warehouse and removed the can in the left front corner of each box. He found that all of these cans were filled to capacity. Therefore, it is probable that all of the cans in the production run were filled to capacity.

4. When a random sample of 600 voters was taken on the eve of the presidential election, it was found that 51 percent of those sampled intended to vote for the Democrat and 49 percent for the Republican. Therefore, the Democrat will probably win.

★5. To determine the public's attitude toward TV soap operas, 1,000 people were contacted by telephone between 8 A.M. and 5 P.M. on week days. The numbers were selected randomly from the phone directories of cities across the nation. The researchers reported that 43 percent of the respondents said that they were avid viewers. From this we may conclude that 43 percent of the public watches TV soap operas.

6. To predict the results of a U.S. Senate race in New York State, two polls were taken. One was based on a random sample of 750 voters, the other on a random sample of 1,500 voters. Since the second sample was twice as large as the first, the results of the second poll were twice as accurate as the first.

7. In a survey conducted by the manufacturers of Ultrasheen toothpaste, 65 percent of the dentists randomly sampled preferred that brand over all others. Clearly Ultrasheen is the brand preferred by most dentists.

INDUCTION

8. To determine the percentage of adult Americans who have never read the U.S. Constitution, surveyors put this question to a random sample of 1,500 adults. Only 13 percent gave negative answers. Therefore, since the sampling error for such a sample is 3 percent, we may conclude that no more than 16 percent of American adults have not read the Constitution.

9. To determine the percentage of patients who follow the advice of their personal physician, researchers asked 200 randomly chosen physicians to put the question to their patients. Of the 4,000 patients surveyed, 98 percent replied that they did indeed follow their doctor's advice. We may therefore conclude that at least 95 percent of the patients across the nation follow the advice of their personal physician.

★10. Janet Ryan can afford to pay no more than $15 for a birthday gift for her 8-year-old daughter. Since the average price of a toy at General Toy Company is $15, Janet can expect to find an excellent selection of toys within her price range at that store.

11. Anthony Valardi, who owns a fish market, pays $2 per pound to fishermen for silver salmon. A certain fisherman certifies that the average size of the salmon in his catch of the day is 10 pounds, and that the catch numbers 100 salmon. Mr. Valardi is therefore justified in paying the fisherman $2,000 for the whole catch.

12. Pamela intends to go shopping for a new pair of shoes. She wears size 8. Since the average size of the shoes carried by the Bon Marche is size 8, Pamela can expect to find an excellent selection of shoes in her size at that store.

13. Tim Cassidy, who works for a construction company, is told to load a pile of rocks onto a truck. The rocks are randomly sized, and the average piece weighs 50 pounds. Thus, Tim should have no trouble loading the rocks by hand.

14. The average IQ (in the sense of mean, median, and mode) of the students in Dr. Jacob's symbolic logic class is 120. Thus, none of the students should have any trouble mastering the subject matter.

★15. An insecticide manufacturer prints the following graph on the side of its spray cans:

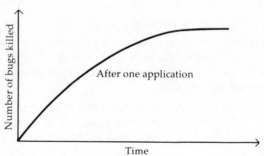

A CONCISE INTRODUCTION TO LOGIC

Obviously, the insecticide is highly effective at killing bugs, and it keeps working for a long time.

16. A corporation's sales for two consecutive years are represented in a bar graph. Since the bar for the later year is twice as high as the one for the previous year, it follows that sales for the later year were double those for the previous year.

17. Forced to make cutbacks, the president of a manufacturing firm reduced certain costs as follows: Advertising by 4 percent, transportation by 5 percent, materials by 2 percent, and employee benefits by 3 percent. The president thus succeeded in reducing total costs by 14 percent.

18. During a certain year, a grocery store chain had total sales of $100 million, and profits of $10 million. The profits thus amounted to a modest 10 percent for that year.

19. There were 40 percent more traffic accidents in 1980 than there were in 1950. Therefore, it was 40 percent more dangerous to drive a car in 1980 than it was in 1950.

★20. An efficiency expert was hired to increase the productivity of a manufacturing firm and was given three months to accomplish the task. At the end of the period the productivity had increased from 1500 units per week to 1700. Since the goal was 2000 units per week, the effort of the efficiency expert was 85 percent successful (1700/2000).

II. Determine the average in the sense of mean, median, and mode for the following distributions of weight and salary:

1. Number of people	Weight
2	150
4	160
3	170
1	180
1	190
1	200
1	220
2	230

2. Number of people	Salary
1	$95,000
2	85,000
1	70,000
3	40,000
1	30,000
2	20,000
5	15,000

III. Answer "true" or "false" to the following statements:

1. If a sample is very large, it need not be randomly selected.

2. If a population is randomly arranged, a sample obtained by selecting every tenth member would be a random sample.

3. If a sample is randomly selected, the larger the sample is the more closely it replicates the population.

4. To ensure the same precision, a population of 1 million would require a much larger random sample than would a population of 100,000.

5. In general, if sample A is twice as large as sample B, then the sampling error for A is one-half that for B.

6. When a sample consists of human beings, the purpose for which the sample is taken can affect the outcome.

7. The personal interaction between a surveyor and a respondent can affect the outcome of a survey.

8. The mean value of a set of data is the value that occurs with the greatest frequency.

9. The median value of a set of data is the middle point when the data are arranged in ascending order.

10. The modal value of a set of data is the arithmetical average.

11. If one needed to know whether a sizable portion of a group were above or below a certain level, the most useful sense of average would be mode.

12. Data reflecting the results of a random sample conform fairly closely to the normal probability distribution.

13. If a set of data conform to the normal probability distribution, then the mean, median, and mode have the same value.

14. The range, variance, and standard deviation are measurements of dispersion.

15. Statements about averages often present an incomplete picture without information about the dispersion.

16. Data reflecting the size of full-grown horses would exhibit greater dispersion than data reflecting the size of full-grown dogs.

17. The visual impression made by graphs can be exaggerated by changing one of the scales while leaving the other unchanged.

18. Data reflecting a 100 percent increase in housing construction could be accurately represented by a pictogram of two houses, one twice as high as the other.

19. If a certain quantity is increased by 10 percent and later decreased by 10 percent, the quantity is restored to what it was originally.

20. Expressing profits as a percentage of sales volume presents an honest picture of the earnings of a corporation.

9.4 HYPOTHETICAL REASONING

All inductive arguments proceed from the known to the unknown. For example, we might see storm clouds gathering overhead and predict that it will rain, or we might drive past a signboard advertising a new bank in town and conclude that the town really does have a new bank. We can see the rain clouds and the signboard, and our reasoning leads us beyond these to the storm in the future and the bank in some distant part of town.

Sometimes, though, the available evidence does not immediately suggest what lies ahead, beyond, or beneath the surface. For example, if we should turn the key in the ignition of our car and hear the engine crank but fail to start, we might not be able to reason directly to the unknown cause. If we know anything at all about the workings of an automobile, we might begin to wonder: Could it be the spark plugs? The carburetor? The fuel pump? The ignition coil? The distributor? The evidence by itself, the fact that the engine cranks but does not start, is not sufficient to provide the answer. To fill the gap, our creative imagination supplements the evidence by suggesting possible approaches to the problem. These possible approaches are **hypotheses,** and the reasoning process used to produce them is **hypothetical reasoning.**

Hypothetical reasoning is used by nearly all of us in our day-to-day experience. The television repairman constructs hypotheses to determine why the picture appears unclear after all the ordinary solutions have been tried without success, the motorist on the freeway or turnpike reasons hypothetically to determine why the traffic is backed up bumper-to-bumper even though it is not yet rush hour, the physician hypothesizes about the cause of a disease prior to prescribing medicine, the teacher hypothesizes about the best way to present a complicated subject in the classroom, and the prosecuting attorney suggests hypotheses to the jury in arguing about the motive for a crime. In all of these cases the evidence is not sufficient to indicate exactly what is going on, what lies behind the scene, or what approach to take, so hypotheses are constructed to make sense of the situation and to direct future action.

Hypothetical reasoning is used most explicitly in philosophical and scientific inquiry. Every scientific theory can be viewed as a hypothesis for unifying and rationalizing events in nature. The Ptolemaic and Copernican theories about the sun and planets, Dalton's atomic theory, Darwin's theory of evolution, and Einstein's theory of relativity are all hypotheses for making sense of the data of observation. The problem for the scientist is that the underlying structure of nature is hidden from view, and the data of observation by themselves are not sufficient to reveal this structure. In response, the scientist constructs hypotheses that provide ways of conceptualizing the data and that suggest specific questions to be answered through the design of controlled experiments.

Analogously, every philosophical system can be viewed as a grand hypothesis for interpreting the content of experience. Plato's theory of forms, Aristotle's theory of substance, Leibniz's monads, and Kant's theory about the mind are all hypotheses aimed at illuminating various aspects of experience. Just as the structure of nature is hidden from the scientist, the meaning of experience is hidden from the philosopher, and ordinary common sense will not provide the answer. In response, the philosopher constructs hypotheses that can be used to shed light on the content of experience and to provide suggestions for further analysis.

Whether it is applied in philosophy, science, or ordinary life, the hypothetical method involves four basic stages:

1. Occurrence of a problem.
2. Formulating a hypothesis.
3. Drawing implications from the hypothesis.
4. Testing the implications.

These four stages may be illustrated through the procedure used by a detective in solving a crime. Suppose that a woman has been murdered in her apartment. Initially, everything in the apartment is a potential clue: the empty wine glasses in the sink, the small container of cocaine on the coffee table, the automobile key found on the carpet, the strand of blonde hair removed from the couch, and so on. To introduce an element of rationality into the situation, the detective formulates a hypothesis—let us say the hypothesis that the key found on the carpet fits the murderer's car.

From this hypothesis a number of implications can be drawn. Suppose that the key is the kind that fits only late-model Cadillacs. It follows that the murderer drives a late-model Cadillac. Furthermore, if the key is the only one the murderer owns, it follows that the car may be parked nearby. A third implication is that the murderer's name may be on record at the local Cadillac dealership. To test these implications, the detective conducts a search of the streets in the vicinity and contacts the local Cadillac dealer for the names of recent buyers.

This example illustrates three additional points about hypotheses. The first is that a hypothesis is not *derived* from the evidence to which it pertains but rather is *added* to the evidence by the investigator. A hypothesis is a free creation of the mind used to structure the evidence and unveil the pattern that lies beneath the surface. It may be that the detective's hypothesis is completely false. Perhaps the key fits a car that was lent to the victim for the weekend. Any number of other possibilities are conceivable.

The second point is that a hypothesis directs the search for evidence. Without a hypothesis for guidance, all facts are equally relevant. The mineral content of moon rocks and the temperature in the Sahara would be as relevant as the cars parked on the street outside the apartment. The hypothesis tells the investigator what to look for and what to ignore.

The third point concerns the proof of hypotheses. Let us suppose that the detective finds a late-model Cadillac parked outside the apartment building and that the key fits the ignition. Such a discovery might lend credibility to the hypothesis, but it would not in any sense prove it. Concluding that a hypothesis is proven true by the discovery that one of its implications is true amounts to committing the fallacy of affirming the consequent (see Section 6.4). Where H stands for a hypothesis and I for an implication, such an argument has the invalid form

$$H \supset I$$
$$\underline{I}$$
$$H$$

Let us suppose, on the other hand, that the murderer turns himself or herself in to the police and that the only car the murderer owns or drives is a Ford. Such a fact would prove the hypothesis false because it would falsify the implication that the murderer drives a Cadillac. The argument form involved in such an inference is *modus tollens:*

$$H \supset I$$
$$\underline{\sim I}$$
$$\sim H$$

For the hypothesis to be proved true, the car that the key fits would have to be found and the owner would have to confess to the crime.

Some of the clearest illustrations of the hypothetical method of reasoning can be found in scientific discoveries. Four examples are the discovery of radium by Pierre and Marie Curie; the discovery of the planet Neptune by Adams, Leverrier, and Galle; the discovery of atmospheric pressure by Torricelli; and Pasteur's research concerning the spontaneous generation of life. Following is a consideration of each of these examples with special attention to the four stages of hypothetical inquiry.

Radium

In 1896 the French physicist Henri Becquerel discovered that crystals containing uranium had the power to expose photographic plates. He found that when these crystals were placed on top of an unexposed plate and left for a certain time, dark blotches appeared in their place when the plate was developed. Becquerel concluded that the crystals emitted certain rays that penetrated the opaque covering of the plates and reacted with the photosensitive material underneath. Further investigation showed that these rays were not as strong as x-rays, which could be used to photograph bone structure, and so Becquerel's interest in them lapsed.

A year later Marie Curie revived the question when she adopted it as the topic of her doctoral research at the University of Paris. In place of Becquerel's photographic plates she substituted an electrometer, which was better suited to measuring the intensity of the rays, and she proceeded to conduct various experiments with pure uranium to determine the source of the rays that the metal emitted. When none of these experiments proved fruitful, she shifted her attention to the question of whether other metals or minerals emitted the same kind of rays as uranium. She tested hundreds of metals, compounds, and ores, but the only one that proved interesting was pitchblende, a certain ore of uranium. Because pitchblende contained uranium, she anticipated that it would emit rays; but because it also contained a number of impurities, she expected the rays to be weaker than they were for pure uranium. Instead, they turned out to be stronger. This problem caught Madame Curie's attention and provided the focus for her research in the months ahead.

In response to the problem, Madame Curie formulated the hypothesis that the impurities in the pitchblende somehow triggered the uranium to increase the emission of rays. One implication of this hypothesis was that mixing pure uranium with the kinds of impurities found in pitchblende would cause an increase in the emission of rays. To test this implication, Curie diluted pure uranium with various elements and measured the strength of the rays. The results were always the same: the emissions were always less than they were for pure uranium. Because of these results, she abandoned the hypothesis.

Madame Curie then formulated a second hypothesis: The intensified emissions were caused directly by some impurity in the pitchblende. The only other element besides uranium that was known to emit rays, however, was thorium, and the pitchblende that had been tested contained no thorium. Thus, an immediate implication of the hypothesis was that the increased rays were caused by an unknown element. A second implication was that this element could be separated from the pitchblende through a process of refinement. At this point Marie Curie was joined by her husband, Pierre, and they began a combined effort to isolate the unknown element.

Because the element was present in only the most minute quantities, separating a measurable amount from the other impurities required a great deal of effort. The Curies began by grinding up some pitchblende and dissolving it in acid. Finally, after numerous stages of filtration and the addition of other chemicals, they obtained a pinch of white powder. By weight, this material was found to be 900 times more radioactive than pure uranium, but since the primary component in the powder was barium, the unknown element still had not been isolated.

Rather than continue with additional stages of refinement, the Curies decided to attempt a spectographic analysis of the powder. Such analysis, they hoped, would reveal the characteristic spectrum line of the unknown element. This proposal, which amounted to a third implication of the hypothesis, was put to the test. When the powder was burned in a spectrometer, a line appeared in the ultraviolet range that was different from that for any other element. From the combined evidence of the spectrum line and the intense radiation the Curies announced in 1898 the discovery of a new element, which they called radium. After more processing and refinement, enough of the material was finally obtained to determine the atomic weight.

Neptune

In 1781 the planet Uranus was discovered by William Herschel, but the production of a table giving the motion of the new planet had to wait until the gravitational interaction between Uranus, Jupiter, and Saturn had been worked out mathematically. The latter task was accomplished by Pierre Laplace in his *Mechanique Celeste*, and in 1820 Alexis Bouvard used this work to construct tables for all three planets. These tables predicted the orbital motions of Jupiter and Saturn very accurately, but within a few years Uranus was found to have deviated from its predicted path. A problem thus emerged: Why did the tables work for Jupiter and Saturn but not for Uranus?

In response to this problem a number of astronomers entertained the hypothesis that an eighth planet existed beyond the orbit of Uranus and that the gravitational interaction between these two planets caused Uranus to deviate from its predicted position. It was not until 1843, however, that John Couch Adams, a recent graduate of Cambridge, undertook the task of working out the mathematical implications of this hypothesis. After two years' work Adams produced a table of motions and orbital elements that predicted the location of the hypothetical planet, and his computations were so accurate that if anyone with a telescope had bothered to look, they would have found the new planet within two degrees of its predicted position. Unfortunately, no one looked for it.

At about the same time that Adams completed his work on the problem, the French astronomer U. J. J. Leverrier, working independently of Adams, reported a similar set of motions and orbital elements to the French Academy of Science. The close agreement between Adams's and

Leverrier's predictions prompted a search for the planet; but because a rather broad section of sky was swept, the planet was missed.

Finally, Leverrier sent a copy of his figures to Johann Galle at the Berlin Observatory, where a set of star charts was being prepared. It was suggested that the region corresponding to Leverrier's computations be observed and the results matched against the charts. This was done, and a small starlike object was found that was not on the charts. The next night the same object was sighted, and it was found to have moved. The new planet was thus identified. It was named Neptune after most astronomers outside France objected to the original suggestion that it be called Leverrier.

Atmospheric Pressure

The principle that nature abhors a vacuum, originated by Aristotle, was used for centuries to explain the fact that in emptying a keg of wine an opening had to be made at the top as well as at the bottom. Because nature would not allow a vacuum to be created inside the keg, the wine would not drain from the bottom until air was let in at the top. It was thought that this principle held universally for all applications involving a vacuum, but in the sixteenth century it was found that suction pumps used to drain water from mine shafts would not work if the pump was situated over 30 feet above the water level. This caused people to wonder whether nature's abhorrence of a vacuum, while holding true for kegs of wine, had certain limits for pumps.

In 1630 Giovanni Baliani of Genoa discovered a similar limitation in regard to siphons. When he attempted to siphon water from a reservoir over a 60-foot hill, he found that the siphon would not work. When the siphon was completely filled with water and the stoppers were removed from both ends, a vacuum seemed to be created in the uppermost parts of the pipe.

These findings were communicated to Gasparo Berti in Rome, who, around 1641, attempted to determine more scientifically whether a vacuum could actually be created. Berti designed an apparatus consisting of a spherical glass vessel attached to a pipe about 40 feet long. The apparatus was affixed upright to the side of a tower, and after the valve at the lower end of the pipe was closed, water was poured through the upper opening in the glass vessel. When both the pipe and the glass vessel were completely filled, the opening in the vessel was sealed and the valve at the lower end of the pipe was opened. Immediately water rushed from the bottom of the pipe, creating a vacuum in the glass vessel. This experiment crystalized a problem that had been developing for a number of years: If nature abhorred a vacuum, how did it happen that it tolerated the creation of one in the glass vessel? Furthermore, why did it happen, when the experiment was repeated, that the water always descended to the same level in the pipe?

The results of Berti's experiment were communicated to Evangelista Torricelli in Florence, who was at that time Galileo's assistant. Galileo himself thought that the water was supported in the pipe by the power of the vacuum, but after Galileo's death in 1642, Torricelli formulated his own hypothesis: The water was supported in the pipe by the pressure of the atmosphere. Torricelli reasoned that we live "at the bottom of an ocean of air" and that the pressure of the air pushing against the bottom of the pipe supported the water at a certain height in the pipe. A point of equilibrium was reached, he thought, when the weight of the water remaining in the pipe equalled the weight of the air pushing down from above.

From this hypothesis Torricelli derived several implications. One was that the pressure of the atmosphere would support a column of mercury about 29 inches high in a tube sealed at the top. This followed from the fact that the atmosphere supports a column of water 33 feet high, that mercury is 13.6 times as dense as water, and that $33/13.6 \times 12$ inches = 29 inches. A second implication was that such a tube filled with mercury could be used to measure fluctuations in atmospheric pressure. This second implication won Torricelli the credit for formulating the theory of the barometer. Finally, Torricelli reasoned that if such a device were conveyed to a place where the air was more rarefied, such as on a mountaintop, the column of mercury would descend.

The first of these implications was tested by Torricelli's associate, Vincenzo Viviani. Viviani obtained a 4-foot section of glass tube sealed at one end, enough mercury to completely fill it, and a dish to hold more mercury. After pouring the mercury into the tube Viviani placed his thumb over the open end, inverted the tube, and placed the open end in the dish of mercury. After he released his thumb he watched the column of mercury descend to about 29 inches above the level of mercury in the dish. Thus was created the first barometer. Its successful use in measuring atmospheric pressure came later.

The test of Torricelli's third implication was taken up in 1647 by the French philosopher Blaise Pascal. Having received word of Torricelli's experiments with the barometer, Pascal constructed one for himself. He readily became convinced of the correctness of Torricelli's hypothesis, and to demonstrate its correctness in opposition to the vacuum principle, he requested that his brother-in-law, F. Perier, convey a barometer to the top of the Puy de Dôme, one of the highest mountains in Auvergne. A year later Perier was able to fulfill this request. He began the experiment by setting up two barometers in the monastery at the foot of the mountain. After noting that both columns of mercury rose to an identical height, he disassembled one of the barometers and instructed one of the friars to check the mercury level in the other throughout the day. Then Perier, accompanied by a group of witnesses, set off up the mountain with the other barometer. Upon reaching the summit, he assembled the second barometer and discovered to the amazement of all that the mercury level was more than 3 inches lower than it had been at the foot of the mountain. As a double check the barometer was taken apart and reassembled at five different spots on the summit. Each time the results were the same.

At the midpoint of his descent Perier reassembled the barometer once again. He found that the mercury level was about midway between where it was at the bottom and at the top of the mountain. Finally, upon returning to the monastery, the friar who had been watching the barometer there was questioned about what he had observed. He reported that the mercury level had not changed since early that morning when the group had departed. Pascal announced the results of this experiment to the educated world, and the announcement succeeded in abolishing the principle that nature abhors a vacuum.

Spontaneous Generation

The theory of spontaneous generation holds that living beings arise spontaneously from lifeless matter. The roots of the theory extend into ancient times. Aristotle held that worms, the larvae of bees and wasps, ticks, fireflies, and other insects developed continually from the morning dew and from dry wood and hair. He also held that crabs and various molluscs developed from moist soil and decaying slime. Extensions of this theory prevailed throughout the Middle Ages and well into modern times. In the seventeenth century it was widely held that frogs were produced from the slime of marshes and eels from river water, and the physician Van Helmont thought that mice were produced from the action of human sweat on kernels of wheat. All one needed to do, according to Van Helmont, was toss a dirty shirt into a container of wheat, and in 21 days the container would be teaming with mice. Even Descartes and Newton accepted the theory of spontaneous generation. Descartes held that various plants and insects originated in moist earth exposed to sunlight, and Newton thought that plants were produced from emanations from the tails of comets.

The first systematic effort to abolish the belief in spontaneous generation was made by the Italian physician Francesco Redi. In response to the commonly held idea that worms were spontaneously generated in rotting meat, Redi hypothesized that the worms were caused by flies. An immediate implication was that if flies were kept away from the meat, the worms would not develop. To test this hypothesis Redi cut up a piece of meat and put part of it in sealed glass flasks and the other part in flasks open to the air. Flies were attracted to the open flasks, and in a

A CONCISE INTRODUCTION TO LOGIC

short time worms appeared; but no worms developed in the flasks that were sealed.

When Redi published his findings in 1668, they had an immediate impact on the theory of spontaneous generation. Within a few years, though, the microscope came into common use, and it was discovered that even though meat sealed in glass containers produced no worms, it did produce countless microorganisms. The theory of spontaneous generation was thus reawakened on the microbial level.

By the middle of the nineteenth century the theory had received considerable refinement. It was thought that spontaneous generation resulted from the direct action of oxygen on lifeless organic nutrients. Oxygen was thought to be essential to the process because the technique of canning fruits and vegetables had come into practice, and it was known that boiling fruits and vegetables and sealing them in the absence of oxygen would cause them to be preserved. If they were left exposed to the air, however, microbes would develop in a short time.

One of the defenders of spontaneous generation at that time was the Englishman John Needham, an amateur biologist. Needham conducted an experiment in which flagons containing oxygen and a vegetable solution were buried in hot coals. The coals would have been expected to kill any life in the solution, but several days later the flagons were opened and the contents were found to be alive with microbes. Needham concluded that the oxygen acting alone on the nutrient solution caused the generation of the microbes. In response to this experiment, Lazzaro Spallanzani, an Italian physiologist, conducted a similar experiment. To ensure that the nutrient solution was lifeless he boiled it for an hour. Later no microbes could be found. To this Needham objected that in boiling the solution for a full hour Spallanzani had destroyed its "vegetative force." In addition, Needham argued, he had polluted the small amount of oxygen in the containers by the fumes and heat. Thus, it was no wonder that microbes were not spontaneously generated.

To settle the issue once and for all, the French Academy of Science offered a prize for an experimental endeavor that would shed light on the question of spontaneous generation. This challenge succeeded in drawing Louis Pasteur into the controversy. Spontaneous generation presented a special problem for Pasteur because of his previous work with fermentation. He had discovered that fermentations, such as those involved in the production of wine and beer, required yeast; and yeast, as he also discovered, was a living organism. In view of these findings Pasteur adopted the hypothesis that life comes only from life. An immediate implication was that for life forms to develop in a sterile nutrient solution, they must first be introduced into the solution from the outside.

It was well known that life forms did indeed develop in sterile nutrient solutions exposed to the air. To account for this Pasteur adopted the second hypothesis that life forms are carried by dust particles in the air. To test this second hypothesis Pasteur took a wad of cotton and drew air through it, trapping dust particles in the fibers. Then he washed the cotton in a mixture of alcohol and examined drops of the fluid under a microscope. He discovered microbes in the fluid.

Returning to his first hypothesis, Pasteur prepared a nutrient solution and boiled it in a narrow-necked flask. As the solution boiled, the air in the neck of the flask was forced out by water vapor, and as it cooled the water vapor was slowly replaced by sterilized air drawn through a heated platinum tube. The neck of the flask was then closed off with a flame and blowpipe. The contents of the flask thus consisted of a sterilized nutrient solution and unpolluted sterilized air—all that was supposedly needed for the production of life. With the passage of time, however, no life developed in the flask. This experiment posed a serious threat to the theory of spontaneous generation.

Pasteur now posed the hypothesis that sterile nutrient solutions exposed to the air normally developed life forms precisely because these forms were deposited by dust particles. To test this third hypothesis Pasteur reopened the flask containing the nutrient solution, and, using a special arrangement of tubes that insured that only sterilized air would contact the solution, he deposited a piece of cotton in which dust particles had been trapped. The flask was then resealed, and in due course microbes developed in the solution. This experiment proved not only that dust particles were responsible for the life but that the "vegetative force" of the nutrient solution had not been destroyed by boiling, as Needham was prone to claim.

Pasteur anticipated one further objection from the proponents of spontaneous generation: Perhaps the capacity of oxygen to generate life was destroyed by drawing it through a heated tube. To dispel any such notions Pasteur devised yet another experiment. He boiled a nutrient solution in a flask with a long, narrow gooseneck. As the solution boiled, the air was forced out, and as it cooled, the air returned very slowly through the long neck, trapping the dust particles on the moist inside surface. No microbes developed in the solution. Then, after a prolonged wait, Pasteur sealed the flask and shook it vigorously, dislodging the particles that had settled in the neck. In a short time the solution was alive with microbes.

When Pasteur reported these experiments to the Academy of Science in 1860, he was awarded the prize that had been offered a year earlier. The experiments dealt a mortal blow to the theory of spontaneous generation, and although the theory was not abandoned immediately, by 1900 it had very little support.

The Proof of Hypotheses

The four instances of hypothetical reasoning in science that we have investigated illustrate the use of two different kinds of hypotheses. The hypotheses involved in the discovery of Neptune and radium are sometimes called **empirical hypotheses,** and those relating to atmospheric pressure and spontaneous generation are sometimes called **theoretical hypotheses.** Empirical hypotheses concern the production of some thing or the occurrence of some event that can be observed. When radium had finally been obtained as a pure metal it was something that could be seen directly, and when Neptune was finally sighted through the telescope, it, too, had been observed. Theoretical hypotheses, on the other hand, concern how something should be conceptualized. When Galileo observed the water level rising in a suction pump, he conceived it as being *sucked* up by the vacuum. When Torricelli observed it, however, he conceived it as being *pushed* up by the atmosphere. Similarly, when Needham observed life emerging in a sterile nutrient solution, he conceived it as being spontaneously generated by the action of oxygen. But when Pasteur observed it, he conceived it as being implanted there by dust particles in the air.

The distinction between empirical and theoretical hypotheses has certain difficulties, which we will turn to shortly, but it sheds some light on the problem of the verification or confirmation of hypotheses. Empirical hypotheses are for all practical purposes *proved* when the thing or event hypothesized is observed. Today practically all of us would agree that the hypotheses relating to radium and Neptune have been established. Theoretical hypotheses, on the other hand, are never proved but are only *confirmed* to varying degrees. The greater the number of implications that are found to be correct, the more certain we can be of the hypothesis. If an implication is found to be incorrect, however, a theoretical hypothesis can be *disproved.* For example, if it should happen some day that life is produced in a test tube from inorganic materials, Pasteur's hypothesis that life comes only from life might be considered to be disproved.

The problem with the distinction between empirical and theoretical hypotheses is that observation is theory-dependent. Consider, for example, a man and a woman watching a sunrise. The man happens to believe that the sun travels around the earth, as Ptolemy held, and the woman that the earth travels around the sun, as Copernicus and Galileo contended. As the sun rises, the man thinks that he sees the sun moving upward, while the woman thinks she sees the earth turning. The point is that all of us have a tendency to see what we think is out there to be seen. As a result, it is sometimes difficult to say when something has or has not been observed.

In regard to the discovery of Neptune, the unknown planet was observed two times in 1795 by J. J. Lalande, 51 years before it was "discovered" by Adams, Leverrier, and Galle. Lalande noted that his observations of the position of the small starlike object were discordant, so he rejected one as erroneous. But he thought he was observing a *star*, so he received no credit for discovering a *planet*. Analogous remarks extend to Galle's observations of the *planet* Neptune in 1846. If Leverrier's computations had been erroneous, Galle might have seen what was really a comet. Thus, if we can never be sure that we really see what we think we see, is it ever possible for a hypothesis to be actually proved? Perhaps it is better to interpret the proof of empirical hypotheses as a high degree of confirmation.

Conversely, with theoretical hypotheses, would we want to say that Torricelli's hypothesis relating to atmospheric pressure has *not* been proved? Granted, we cannot observe atmospheric pressure directly, but might we not say that we observe it *instrumentally?* If barometers can be regarded as extensions of our sense organs, Torricelli's hypothesis has been proved. Another example is provided by Copernicus' hypothesis that the earth and planets move around the sun, instead of the sun and planets around the earth, as Ptolemy hypothesized. Can we consider this theoretical hypothesis to be proved? If a motion picture camera were sent outside the solar system and pictures were taken supporting the Copernican hypothesis, would we say that these pictures constituted proof? We probably would. Thus, while the distinction between theoretical and empirical hypotheses is useful, it is more a distinction in degree than in kind.

The Tentative Acceptance of Hypotheses

A certain amount of time is required for a hypothesis to be proved or disproved. The hypotheses relating to the discovery of radium and Neptune required more than a year to prove. Theoretical hypotheses in science often take much longer, and theoretical hypotheses in philosophy may never be confirmed to the satisfaction of the majority of philosophers. During the period that intervenes between the proposal of a hypothesis and its proof, confirmation, or disproof, the question arises as to its tentative acceptability. Four criteria that bear upon this question are (1) adequacy, (2) internal coherence, (3) external consistency, and (4) fruitfulness.

A hypothesis is **adequate** to the extent that it fits the facts it is intended to unify or explain. A hypothesis is said to "fit" the facts when each fact can be interpreted as an instance of some idea or term in the hypothesis. For example, before the Neptune hypothesis was confirmed, every fluctuation in the position of Uranus could be interpreted as an instance of gravitational interaction with an unknown planet. Similarly, before Torricelli's hypothesis was confirmed, the fact that water would rise only 30 feet in suction pumps and siphons could be interpreted as an instance of equilibrium between the pressure of the water and the pressure of the atmosphere.

A hypothesis is inadequate to the extent that facts exist that the hypothesis cannot account for. The principle that nature abhors a vacuum was inadequate to explain the fact that water would rise no more than 30 feet in suction pumps and siphons. Nothing in the hypothesis could account for this fact. Similarly, Needham's hypothesis that life is generated by the direct action of oxygen on nutrient solutions was inadequate to account for the fact that life would not develop in Pasteur's flask containing a sterilized nutrient solution and sterilized oxygen.

In scientific hypotheses a second kind of adequacy is the *accuracy* with which a hypothesis accounts for the data. If one hypothesis accounts for a set of data with greater accuracy than another, then that hypothesis is more adequate than the other. For example, Kepler's hypothesis that the orbits of the planets were elipses rather than circles, as Copernicus had hypothesized, accounted for the position of the planets with greater accuracy than the Copernican hypothesis. Similarly, Einstein's theory of relativity accounted for the precise time of certain eclipses with greater accuracy than Newton's theory. For these reasons Kepler's and Einstein's theories were more adequate than the competing theories.

A hypothesis is **internally coherent** to the extent that its component ideas are rationally interconnected. The purpose of a hypothesis is to unify and interconnect a set of data and by so doing to *explain* the data. Obviously, if the hypothesis itself is not internally connected, there is no way that it can interconnect the data. After the mathematical details of the Neptune hypothesis had been worked out by Adams and Leverrier, it exhibited a great deal of internal coherence. The hypothesis showed how all the fluctuations in the position of Uranus could be rationally linked in terms of the gravitational interaction of an eighth planet. Similarly, Torricelli's hypothesis showed how the various fluid levels could be rationally interconnected in terms of the equilibrium of pressures. Internal coherence is responsible for the features of elegance and simplicity that often attract scientists to a hypothesis.

An example of incoherence in science is provided by the theoretical interpretation of light, electricity, and magnetism that prevailed during the first half of the nineteenth century. During that period each of these phenomena was understood separately, but the interconnections between them were unknown. Toward the end of the century the English physicist James Clerk Maxwell showed how these three phenomena were interconnected in terms of his theory of the electromagnetic field. Maxwell's theory was thus more coherent than the ones that preceded

Similarly, in philosophy, Spinoza's metaphysical theory is more internally coherent than Descartes's. Descartes postulated the existence of two kinds of substance to account for the data of experience. He introduced extended, material substance to explain the data of the visible world, and nonextended, immaterial substance to explain the phenomena of the invisible world, including the existence and activity of the human soul. But Descartes failed to show how the two kinds of substance were interconnected. In the wake of this disconnection there arose the famous mind-body problem, according to which no account could be given of how the human body acted on the mind through the process of sensation or how the mind acted on the body through the exercise of free choice. Spinoza, on the other hand, postulated only one substance to account for everything. Spinoza's theory is thus more internally coherent than Descartes's.

A hypothesis is **externally consistent** when it does not disagree with other, well-confirmed hypotheses. Adams's and Leverrier's hypothesis of an eighth planet was perfectly consistent with the nineteenth-century theory of the solar system, and it was rendered even more attractive by the fact that the seventh planet, Uranus, had been discovered only a few years earlier. Similarly, Marie Curie's hypothesis of the existence of a new element was consistent with Mendeleev's periodic table and with the general hypothesis that elements could emit penetrating rays. In 1890 Mendeleev's table had certain gaps that were expected to be filled in by the discovery of new elements, and two ray-emitting elements, thorium and uranium, had already been discovered.

The fact that a hypothesis is inconsistent with other, well-confirmed hypotheses does not, however, immediately condemn it to obscurity. It often happens that a new hypothesis arises in the face of another, well-confirmed hypothesis and that the two hypotheses compete for acceptance in the future. Which hypothesis will win is determined by an appeal to the other three criteria. For example, Torricelli's hypothesis was inconsistent with the ancient hypothesis that nature abhors a vacuum, and Pasteur's hypothesis was inconsistent with the equally ancient hypothesis of spontaneous generation. In the end, the newer hypotheses won out because they were more adequate, coherent, or fruitful than their competitors. For the same reason the Copernican hypothesis eventually triumphed over the Ptolemaic, the theory of oxidation won out over the old phlogiston theory, and Einstein's theory of relativity won out over Newton's theory.

A hypothesis is **fruitful** to the extent that it suggests new ideas for future analysis and confirmation. Torricelli's hypothesis suggested the design of an instrument for measuring fluctuations in the pressure of the atmosphere. Similarly, Pasteur's hypothesis suggested changes in the procedures used to maintain sterile conditions in hospitals. After these changes were implemented, the death rate from surgical operations decreased dramatically. The procedure of pasteurization, used to preserve milk, was another outgrowth of the hypothesis that life comes only from life.

Newton's theory of universal gravitation is an example of a hypothesis that proved especially fruitful. It was originated to solve the problem of falling bodies, but it also explained such things as the ebb and flow of the tides, the orbital motion of the moon and planets, and the fluctuations in planetary motion caused by a planet's interaction with other planets. Einstein's theory of relativity is another example. It was originated to account for certain features of Maxwell's theory of electricity and magnetism, but it succeeded, 40 years later, in ushering in the atomic age.

The factors of coherence and fruitfulness together account for the overall rationality and explanatory power of a hypothesis. Suppose, for example, that someone formulated the hypothesis that the water level in suction devices is maintained by the action of demons instead of by atmospheric pressure. Such a hypothesis would be neither coherent nor fruitful. It would not be coherent because it would not explain why the maximum water level in these devices is consistently about 30 feet, why the mercury level in barometers is much less, and why the mercury level in a barometer decreases when the instrument is carried to the top of a mountain. Do the demons decide to maintain these levels by free choice or according to some plan? Because there is no answer to this question, the hypothesis exhibits internal disconnectedness, which leaves it open to the charge of being irrational. As for the fourth criterion, the demon hypothesis is unfruitful because it suggests no new ideas that experimenters can put to the test. The hypothesis that nature abhors a vacuum is hardly any more fruitful, which accounts in part for why it was so suddenly abandoned in favor of Torricelli's hypothesis—it simply did not lead anywhere.

In summary, for any hypothesis to receive tentative acceptance it must cover the facts it is intended to interpret and it must rationally interconnect these facts—in other words, it must be adequate and coherent. After that, it helps if the hypothesis does not conflict with other, well-confirmed hypotheses. Finally, it is important that a hypothesis capture the imagination of the community to which it is posed. This it does by being fruitful—by suggesting interesting ideas and experiments to which members of the community can direct their attention in the years ahead.

EXERCISE 9.4

I. For the four scientific discoveries presented in this section identify the problem, the hypotheses that were formulated, the implications that were drawn, and the test procedure that was used.

II. Write a short paper (3–5 pages) on one of the following scientific events. Discuss the problem, one or more hypotheses that were formulated, the implications that were drawn, and the test procedures that were used. Then evaluate the hypothesis in terms of adequacy, internal coherence, external consistency, and fruitfulness.

1. Isaac Newton: corpuscular theory of light.

2. Christian Huygens: wave theory of light.

3. Johannes Kepler: orbit of Mars.

4. Nicolaus Copernicus: theory of the solar system.

5. Count von Rumford: theory of heat.

6. Charles Darwin: theory of natural selection.

7. John Dalton: theory of atoms.

8. William Harvey: circulation of the blood.

9. Louis Pasteur: theory of vaccination.

10. J. J. Thomson: discovery of the electron.

11. Andre Marie Ampere: discovery of the electromagnet.

12. Niels Bohr: structure of the atom.

13. Alexander Fleming: discovery of penicillin.

14. Henri Becquerel: radioactivity of uranium.

15. Dmitri Mendeleev and Clemens Winkler: discovery of germanium.

16. Amedeo Avogadro: Avogadro's law.

17. Johann Balmer: theory of the spectograph.

18. Alfred Wegener: theory of continental drift.

19. James Watson and Francis Crick: structure of the DNA molecule.

20. John Bardeen: theory of superconductivity.

21. Albert Einstein: theory of Brownian motion.

22. Edwin Hubble: recession of the galaxies.

23. Jean Baptiste Lamarck: inheritance of acquired characteristics.

III. Write a short paper (2–3 pages) analyzing one or more of the hypotheses formulated by Sherlock Holmes in one of the stories by Arthur Conan Doyle. Include a discussion of the problem, the hypothesis, the implications that were drawn, and the test procedures.

IV. Answer "true" or "false" to the following statements:

1. Hypothetical reasoning is useful when the evidence by itself does not provide the solution to the problem.

2. Hypotheses are derived directly from the evidence.

3. Hypotheses serve the purpose of directing the search for additional evidence.

4. If the implications of a hypothesis are true, then we may conclude that the hypothesis is true.

5. If an implication of a hypothesis is false, then we may conclude that the hypothesis is false, at least in part.

6. In the episode pertaining to the discovery of radium, all of the hypotheses turned out to be true.

7. In the Neptune episode, Adams and Leverrier deserve the credit for working out the implications of the hypothesis.

8. Torricelli's hypothesis was consistent with the hypothesis that nature abhors a vacuum.

9. In Pasteur's day, the theory of spontaneous generation held that life was produced by the direct action of oxygen on organic nutrients.

10. The hypotheses relating to the discoveries of radium and Neptune may be classified as empirical hypotheses.

11. Torricelli's and Pasteur's hypotheses may be classified as theoretical hypotheses.

12. Theoretical hypotheses concern how something should be conceptualized.

13. The problem with the distinction between empirical and theoretical hypotheses is that observation is dependent on theory.

14. The adequacy of a hypothesis has to do with how well the ideas or terms in the hypothesis are rationally interconnected.

15. The coherence of a hypothesis has to do with how well the hypothesis fits the facts.

16. If a hypothesis is not externally consistent, then it must be discarded.

17. A hypothesis is fruitful to the extent that it suggests new ideas for future analysis and confirmation.

18. If a theory is incoherent, it is deficient in rationality.

19. The theoretical interpretations of light, electricity, and magnetism during the first part of the nineteenth century illustrate a condition of inadequacy.

20. If a hypothesis gives rise to contradictory implications, it is incoherent.

ANSWERS TO SELECTED EXERCISES

Exercise 1.1
I.
1. P_1: Catherine's car has a dead battery.
    P_2: Catherine has no other means of transportation.
    C: Catherine most likely will not be going to the concert tonight.
5. P_1: No incompetent businessmen are corporate officers.
    P_2: All shareholders are incompetent businessmen.
    C: No shareholders are corporate officers.
10. P: Punishment, when speedy and specific, may suppress undesirable behavior, but it cannot teach or encourage desirable alternatives.
    C: It is crucial to use positive techniques to model and reinforce appropriate behavior that the person can use in place of the unacceptable response that has to be suppressed.
15. P: Every art and every inquiry, and similarly every action and pursuit, is thought to aim at some good.
    C: The good has rightly been declared to be that at which all things aim.
20. P: The denial or perversion of justice by the sentences of courts, as well as in any other manner, is with reason classed among the just causes of war.
    C: The federal judiciary ought to have cognizance of all causes in which the citizens of other countries are concerned.
25. P: To the owner of a commodity, every other commodity is, in regard to his own, a particular equivalent.
    C: The owner's own commodity is the universal equivalent for all the others.

Exercise 1.2
I.
1. Nonargument (explanation).
5. Argument (conclusion: Barbara can file a joint tax return for that year).
10. Nonargument (command).
15. Nonargument (statement of belief).
20. Argument (conclusion: Dachshunds are ideal dogs for small children).
25. Argument (conclusion: Words are slippery customers).
30. This passage is most likely an illustration. If an argument, the conclusion is: Almost all living things act to free themselves from harmful contacts.

Exercise 1.3
I.
1. Deductive.
5. Inductive (generalization).
10. Inductive (causal inference).
15. Deductive.
20. Deductive.

Exercise 1.4
I.
1. False premises, false conclusion, valid, unsound.
5. False premises, true conclusion, invalid, unsound.
II.
1. True premise, probably false conclusion, weak, uncogent.
5. False premise, probably true conclusion, weak, uncogent.
III.
1. Deductive, valid.
5. Deductive, valid.
10. Deductive, invalid.
15. Inductive, weak.
20. Deductive, invalid.

Exercise 1.5
I.
1. All *A* are *C*.   All mammals are animals.
   All *L* are *A*.   All dogs are mammals.
   All *C* are *L*.   All animals are dogs.

5. Some *E* are not *S*.   Some mammals are not dogs.
   Some *V* are not *S*.   Some animals are not dogs.
   Some *E* are not *V*.   Some mammals are not animals.

II.
1. If *C*, then *P*.   If George Washington was beheaded,
                                 then George Washington is dead.

   Not *C*.   George Washington was not beheaded.
   Not *P*.   George Washington is not dead.

Exercise 2.1
I.
4a. Plant, tree, conifer, spruce, Sitka spruce.

Exercise 2.3
I.
1. "Skyscraper" means the Empire State Building, Chrysler Building, Sears Tower, and so on.
III.
1. "Animal" means a horse, bear, fish, and so on.
V.
1. "Intersection" means crossing.
VI.
1. A person is a "genius" if and only if that person can earn a score of 140 on an IQ test.
VII.
1. "Drake" means a male duck.

Exercise 2.4
  1. Rule 2: too narrow.
  5. Rule 1: fails to state essential meaning (no reference is made to the purpose of a slide rule).
 10. Rule 5: obscure.
 15. Rule 7: fails to indicate context.
 20. Rule 6: affective terminology; perhaps also
     Rule 5: figurative language.
 25. Rule 1: fails to state the essential meaning (no reference is made to the essential features of a camera).
 30. Rule 2: both too broad and too narrow (brandy is also made from grapes; some wines are made from fruits other than grapes).

Exercise 3.2
I.
  1. Appeal to authority. It is unlikely that a concert pianist would be an expert on Martian craters.
  5. Appeal to force. The arguer is threatening the listener/reader.
 10. Appeal to the people—indirect approach. The appeal involves a bandwagon argument and an appeal to vanity.
 15. Accident. The rule stated in the first premise does not apply to price.
 20. Argument against the person, circumstantial. The arguer alleges that Noland cannot be objective because of his place of birth.
 25. Appeal to the people—indirect approach. The arguer appeals to the vanity of the listener/reader.

Exercise 3.3

I.
1. Amphiboly. What is happening in the supervisor's office? Is it the interviewing or the drilling?
5. Good argument.
10. Equivocation. "Good" is a relative word that means different things in different contexts.
15. Complex question. The arguer presumes that the listener did in fact lie on the witness stand.
20. Begging the question. The conclusion and the premise say the same thing in slightly different ways.
25. Division. The characteristic of being almost extinct is transferred from the class of condors to one of the members of this class.

III.
1. Accident. The rule stated in the first premise does not apply to the price of gold.
5. Appeal to pity. The arguer attempts to elicit pity from the listener/reader.
10. Appeal to force. The arguer threatens the listener/reader.
15. Argument against the person, circumstantial. The arguer alleges that Clark's arguments are defective because of the circumstance of his being a conscientious objector.
20. Accent. The arguer places verbal stress on the word "brother."
25. Complex question. The arguer presumes that it is in fact difficult for the reader/listener to reach a decision.
30. Appeal to authority. The three physicists are not experts in psychical research.
35. Appeal to ignorance. The arguer concludes something positive on the evidence that nothing has been proved.
40. Missing the point. The premise supports the conclusion that Miss Malone will be pleasant to look at, not that she will be capable and efficient.
45. Equivocation. Psychological forces and physical forces are probably quite different.

Exercise 3.4

I.
1. Straw man. The real issue is political unification, not whether the Protestants will be forced to become Catholic.

II.
1. The passage may contain two arguments. If so, the first argument is that Sands's death is without consequence because it was his own choice. Such an argument commits the fallacy of arguing beside the point. The second argument concludes that Sands and others should be punished. This argument commits a slippery slope and perhaps false analogy and suppressed evidence.
5. The terms "lunatic nation," "moron," and "madmen" suggest three arguments against the person, abusive. The comparison of Iraq with India may involve a false analogy.
10. Good argument or fallacy of composition? If the general staff were Nazis, does this imply that the army, navy, and air force were Nazi?
15. Tu quoque.
20. Complex question.
25. Good argument or false analogy? The argument depends on the analogy between a gun and a car.
30. In comparing John Kennedy's Bay of Pigs with Nixon's obstruction of justice, the argument commits a false analogy. The same is true of the comparison between Teddy Kennedy's cheating at Harvard and Nixon's obstruction of justice. The assertions that John Kennedy instigated the Vietnam War and that Teddy Kennedy "conspired" at Chappaquiddick may involve begging the question or suppressed evidence.

Exercise 4.1
1. *Quantifier:* some   *Copula:* are
   Subject term: pigs   *Predicate term:* wild animals

Exercise 4.2
I.
1. **E** proposition, universal, negative, both terms distributed.
II.
1. No pigs are greedy creatures.
III.
1. Some sandwiches are satisfying meals.
IV.
1. Some rabbits are not furry animals.

Exercise 4.3
I.
1. a. False.   5. a. Undetermined.
   b. True.   b. False.
   c. False.   c. Undetermined.
II.
1. Valid.   5. Valid.   10. Valid.
III.
1. Invalid, unsound.   5. Valid, sound.

Exercise 4.4
I.
1a. "All dreaded creatures are bores"—not logically equivalent.
2a. "No thieves are honest individuals"—logically equivalent.
3a. "All persons capable of being managers are educated people"—logically equiv-
    alent.
II.
1. Invalid; illicit conversion.   10. Invalid; illicit contraposition.
5. Valid; obversion.
III.
1. All non-*B* are *A*; true.   15. Conversion, undetermined.
5. Some *A* are non-*B*; true.   20. Subcontrary, true.
10. Some non-*A* are not non-*B*; true.
IV.
1. All artichokes are vegetables.
   Some artichokes are vegetables. (subalternation)
   Some vegetables are artichokes. (conversion)
5. No non-writers are editors.
   No editors are non-writers. (conversion)
   All editors are writers. (obversion)
   It is false that some editors are not writers. (contradiction)
10. It is false that some oysters are not fish.
    It is false that some oysters are non-fish. (obversion)
    It is false that all oysters are non-fish. (subalternation)
    It is false that all fish are non-oysters. (contraposition)

Exercise 4.5
1. Valid.   5. Invalid.   10. Valid.

Exercise 4.6
1.

    D   *P*

Exercise 4.7
II.
1. All *P* are non-*S*.   No *P* are *S*.

    P   *S*   *P*   *S*

423

5. Some non-*P* are not non-*S*.   Some *S* are not *P*.

Exercise 4.8
1. All prudent men are persons who shun tigers.
2. Some bores are not uneducated persons.

           or

    Some bores are educated persons.
10. All mice-killers are carnivores.
15. All people who do mischief are thoughtless people.
20. All lions are wild animals.
25. All places there is life are places there is hope.
30. All well-fed cats are contented cats.
35. All gamblers that can be trusted are gamblers that have an honest face.
40. All persons identical to me are persons who like strawberries.

           or

    All things identical to strawberries are things that I like.

Exercise 5.1
I.

1. All *P* are *R*.
   No *S* are *R*.
   No *S* are *P*.   **AEE-2**
             valid

5. Some *P* are *T*.
   No *T* are *H*.
   Some *H* are *P*.   **IEI-4**
             invalid

10. Some *G* are not *P*.
    All *B* are *G*.
    Some *B* are *P*.   **OAI-1**
              invalid

II.

1. Some *M* are not *P*.
   All *M* are *S*.
   No *S* are *P*.

5. All *P* are *M*.
   Some *S* are not *M*.
   Some *S* are not *P*.

10. Some *P* are not *M*.
    No *M* are *S*.
    All *S* are *P*.

Exercise 5.2
I.

1. All *C* are *B*.
   Some *B* are *S*.
   Some *S* are *C*.   **AII-4**
                                      invalid

5. No *C* are *S*.
   No *S* are *Q*.
   No *Q* are *C*.   **EEE-4**
                                      invalid

10. No *B* are *L*.
    Some *P* are not *L*.
    Some *P* are not *B*.   **EOO-2**
                                           invalid

II.

1.

5.

10.

Conclusion: No *S* are *P*.   *Conclusion:* Some *S* are *P*.   *Conclusion:* Some *S* are not *P*.

424

Exercise 5.3

I.

1. All *M* are *P*.
   All *M* are *S*.
   All *S* are *P*.

invalid; illicit minor

5. Some *M* are *P*.
   No *S* are *M*.
   Some *S* are not *P*.

invalid; illicit major

10. Some *M* are *P*.
    All *M* are *S*.
    Some *S* are not *P*.

invalid; illicit major

15. No *M* are *P*.
    All *M* are *S*.
    Some *S* are not *P*.

invalid (Boolean); existential
fallacy; valid if *M* exist.

20. No *M* are *P*.
    All *S* are *M*.
    Some *S* are not *P*.

invalid (Boolean); existential
fallacy; valid if *S* exist.

Exercise 5.4

1. Some non-*T* are *M*.   (convert, obvert)
   All non-*I* are non-*M*.
   Some *I* are *T*.   (contrapose)

   Some *M* are not *T*.
   All *M* are *I*.
   Some *I* are *T*.

invalid; drawing an affirmative
conclusion from a negative
premise

5. All non-*S* are non-*P*.   (contrapose)
   All *S* are *C*.
   No non-*C* are *P*.   (convert, obvert)

   All *P* are *S*.
   All *S* are *C*.
   All *P* are *C*.

valid; no rules broken

10. Some *S* are non-*E*.   (obvert)
    All non-*A* are non-*S*.
    Some *A* are not *E*.   (contrapose)

    Some *S* are not *E*.
    All *S* are *A*.
    Some *A* are not *E*.

valid; no rules broken

Exercise 5.5

1. All students who can pass this exam are good students.
   All students identical to Theresa are students who can pass this exam.
   All students identical to Theresa are good students.

   All *P* are *G*.
   All *T* are *P*.
   All *T* are *G*.

   valid; no rules broken

5. All places there is smoke are places there is fire.
   No places identical to the warehouse are places there is smoke.
   No places identical to the warehouse are places there is fire.

   All *S* are *F*.
   No *W* are *S*.
   No *W* are *F*.

   invalid; illicit major

10. All places there is live music on Saturdays are places there is dancing on
    Saturdays.
    All places identical to the Blue Fox Tavern are places there is live music on
    Saturdays.
    All places identical to the Blue Fox Tavern are places there is dancing on
    Saturdays.

    All *L* are *D*.
    All *B* are *L*.
    All *B* are *D*.

    valid; no rules broken

15. All profitable businesses are well-managed businesses.
    All businesses identical to the Alpha General Corporation are well-managed
    businesses.
    All businesses identical to the Alpha General Corporation are profitable busi-
    nesses.

    All *P* are *W*.
    All *A* are *W*.
    All *A* are *P*.

    invalid; undistributed middle

Exercise 5.6

I.
1. Premise missing: George is not intelligent.
5. Conclusion missing: Karen is a successful businesswoman.
10. Premise missing: Whenever the market is off every day for a month is not a
    good time to invest in stocks.
15. Premise missing: Marylou is a topless dancer.

II.
1. All students of mine are intelligent students.
   No students identical to George are intelligent students.
   No students identical to George are students of mine.

   All *M* are *I*.
   No *G* are *I*.
   No *G* are *M*.

   valid; no rules broken

426

5. All successful businesswomen are persons who dress stylishly.
   All persons identical to Karen are persons who dress stylishly.
   All persons identical to Karen are successful businesswomen.

All S are D.
All K are D.
All K are S.

invalid; undistributed middle

10. No times the market has been off for a month are good times to invest in stocks.
    All present times are times the market has been off for a month.
    No present times are good times to invest in stocks.

No M are G.
All P are M.
No P are G.

valid; no rules broken

15. No topless dancers are Campfire Girls.
    All persons identical to Marylou are topless dancers.
    No persons identical to Marylou are Campfire Girls.

No T are C.
All M are T.
No M are C.

valid; no rules broken

III.

1. All A are B.
   No B are C.
   Some D are C.
   Some D are not A.

No C are A.

Some D are not A.

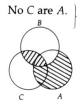

valid

5. All V are U.   (contraposed)
   All U are W.   (obverted)
   All V are Y.
   No X are W.
   No Y are X.   (obverted)

No X are W.
All U are W.
All V are U.
All V are Y.
No Y are X.

No U are X.

No V are X.

(no conclusion)

invalid

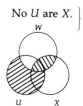

427

IV.
1. No ducks are waltzers.
   No officers are non-waltzers.   (obvert)
   All poultry of mine are ducks.
   No poultry of mine are officers.

   No *D* are *W*.
   All *O* are *W*.
   All *P* are *D*.
   No *P* are *O*.

All *O* are *W*. ⎫
No *D* are *W*. ⎭   No *D* are *O* ⎫
All *P* are *D*.
No *P* are *O*.

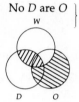

No *P* are *O*

5. All non-ripe fruits are non-wholesome fruits.   (contrapose)
   All apples identical to these are wholesome fruits.
   No fruits grown in the shade are ripe fruits.
   ―――
   All apples identical to these are apples not grown in the shade.   (obvert)

All *W* are *R*.   No *S* are *R*. ⎫
All *A* are *W*.   All *W* are *R*. ⎭   No *W* are *S*. ⎫
No *S* are *R*.   All *A* are *W*.
No *A* are *S*.   No *A* are *S*.

No *A* are *S*.

Exercise 6.1
 1. ~ *A*
 5. *E* ⊃ *F*
10. *A* · (*B* v *C*)
15. ~ (*E* v *F*) or ~ *E* · ~ *F*
20. *A* ⊃ (*B* v *C*)

25. (*C* · *D*) v ~ (*E* v *F*)
30. (*A* v *B*) · (*C* v *D*)
35. *A* · [*B* ⊃ (*C* v *D*)]
40. *A* ≡ *B*
45. (*B* ⊃ *A*) · [(*C* · *D*) ⊃ ~ (*E* ⊃ ~ *F*)]

Exercise 6.2
I.
 1. ~ *N*
   Ⓕ T
 5. *E* v ~ *N*
   FⒻF T

10. *N* ⊃ (*C* v *E*)
   T Ⓣ T T F
15. *N* · [*C* ⊃ (*W* v *E*)]
   TⒻT F F F F

II.
 1. *A* · *X*
   TⒻF
 5. *B* ⊃ ~ *Z*
   T Ⓣ T F

10. ~ (*A* · ~ *Z*)
   Ⓕ T T T F
15. (*Y* ⊃ *C*) · ~ (*B* ⊃ ~ *X*)
   F T T Ⓕ F T T T F

20. (*X* ⊃ *Z*) ⊃ [(*B* ≡ ~ *X*) · ~ (*C* v ~ *A*)]
   F T F Ⓕ T T T F F F T T F T
25. (*Z* ⊃ *C*) ⊃ {[(~ *X* ⊃ *B*) ⊃ (*C* ⊃ *Y*)] ≡ [(*Z* ⊃ *X*) ⊃ (~ *Y* ⊃ *Z*)]}
   F T T Ⓣ   T F T T F T F F T F T F F   T F F F

III.
 1. *A* v *P*
   TⓉ
 5. *P* ⊃ *B*
   ⓉT

10. (*P* ⊃ *A*) ≡ (*Q* ⊃ *B*)
   T T Ⓣ   T T
15. [*Q* ⊃ (*A* v *P*)] ≡ [(*Q* ⊃ *B*) ⊃ *Y*]
   T T T   Ⓕ   T T F F

Exercise 6.3

I.

1. $A \supset (A \supset A)$
```
T [T] T T T
F [T] F T F
```
tautologous

5. $(H \supset J) \equiv (H \cdot \sim J)$
```
T T T [F] T F F T
T T F [F] T T T F
F T T [F] F F F T
F T F [F] F F T F
```
self-contradictory

10. $[F \supset (T \supset X)] \equiv [(F \supset T) \supset X]$
```
T T T T T [T] T T T T T
T F T F F [T] T T T F F
T T F T T [T] T F F T T
T T F T F [T] T F F T F
F T T T T [T] F T T T T
F T T F F [F] F T T F F
F T F T T [T] F T F T T
F T F T F [F] F T F F F
```
contingent

15. $[(E \vee F) \cdot (G \vee H)] \equiv [(E \cdot G) \vee (F \cdot H)]$
```
T T T T T T T [T] T T T T T T T
T T T T T T F [T] T T T T T F F
T T T T F T T [T] T F F T T T T
T T T F F F F [T] T F F F T F F
T T F T T T T [T] T T T T F F T
T T F T T T F [T] T T T T F F F
T T F T T T T [F] T F F F F F T
T T F F F F F [T] T F F F F F F
F T T T T T T [T] F F T T T T T
F T T T T T F [F] F F F T F F F
F T T T F T T [T] F F F T T T T
F T T F F F F [T] F F F F T F F
F F F F T T T [T] F F T F F F T
F F F F T T F [T] F F F F F F F
F F F F F T T [T] F F F F F F T
F F F F F F F [T] F F F F F F F
```
contingent

II.

1. $\sim D \vee T$ $\sim (D \cdot \sim T)$
```
F T [T] T        [T] T F F T
F T [F] F        [F] T T T F
T F [T] T        [T] F F F T
T F [T] F        [T] F F T F
```
logically equivalent

5. $N \supset \sim P$ $N \cdot P$
```
T [F] F T        T [T] T
T [T] T F        T [F] F
F [T] F T        F [F] T
F [T] T F        F [F] F
```
contradictory

10. $H \cdot (J \vee K)$ $(J \cdot H) \vee (H \cdot K)$
```
T [T] T T T      T T T [T] T T T
T [T] T T F      T T T [T] T F F
T [T] F T T      F F T [T] T T T
T [F] F F F      F F T [T] T F F
F [F] T T T      T F F [F] F F T
F [F] T T F      T F F [F] F F F
F [F] F T T      F F F [F] F F T
F [F] F F F      F F F [F] F F F
```
logically equivalent

Exercise 6.4

I.

1. $M \supset A$
   $\underline{\sim A}$
   $\sim M$ MT

5. $\sim R \vee \sim H$
   $\underline{\sim R}$
   $\sim H$ invalid

10. $(M \supset A) \cdot (H \supset D)$
    $\underline{\sim M \cdot \sim H}$
    $\sim A \cdot \sim D$ invalid

15. $I \supset \sim P$
    $\underline{\sim P}$
    I AC

20. $(\sim R \supset \sim A) \cdot (F \supset A)$
    $\underline{A \vee \sim A}$
    $R \vee \sim F$ DD

II.

1. $(S \supset M) \cdot (\sim S \supset F)$
   $\underline{S \vee \sim S}$
   $M \vee F$ CD

Since the second premise is a tautology, it is impossible to escape between the horns. The two available strategies are therefore grasping by the horns and constructing a counterdilemma. Perhaps Melinda could take her books to the party and study there. Such an event would falsify the left-hand conjunct of the first premise, thus falsifying the entire premise. Here is a counterdilemma:

If Melinda spends the night studying, she will pass the test tomorrow; and, if she doesn't spend the night studying, she will go to the party. She will either spend the night studying or not studying. Therefore, she will either pass the test or go to the party.

5. $(S \supset F) \cdot (W \supset V)$
   $\underline{\sim F \vee \sim V}$
   $\sim S \vee \sim W$ DD

Since the second premise is not a tautology, it is at least possible to escape between the horns. Perhaps one could argue that flowers and vegetables could be planted on the same plot of land. It is probably easier, though, to grasp the dilemma by the horns. One could argue that, if flowers are planted, vegetables could be bought; and, if vegetables are planted, flowers could be bought. Constructing a counterdilemma is not recommended.

Exercise 6.5

I.

1. $A \supset B$ // $\sim A \supset \sim B$

```
A ⊃ B          ~ A ⊃ ~ B
T T T          F T T F T
T F F          F T T T F
F T T          T F F F T
F T F          T F T T F
invalid
```

5. $B \supset C$ / $D \supset C$ // $B \supset D$

```
B ⊃ C     D ⊃ C     B ⊃ D
T T T     T T T     T T T
T T T     F T T     T F F
T F F     T F F     T T T
T F F     F T F     T F F
F T T     T T T     F T T
F T T     F T T     F T F
F T F     T F F     F T T
F T F     F T F     F T F
invalid
```

10. $(C \supset D) \cdot (E \supset F)$ / $C \vee E$ // $D \vee F$

```
(C ⊃ D) • (E ⊃ F)  /  C v E  //  D v F
T T T   T T T T        T T T      T T T
T T T   F T F F        T T T      T T F
T T T   T F T T        T T F      T T T
T T T   T F T F        T T F      T T F
T F F   F T T T        T T T      F T T
T F F   F T F F        T T T      F F F
T F F   F F T T        T T F      F T T
T F F   F F T F        T T F      F F F
F T T   T T T T        F T T      T T T
F T T   F T F F        F T T      T T F
F T T   T F T T        F F F      T T T
F T T   T F T F        F F F      T T F
F T F   T T T T        F T T      F T T
F T F   F T F F        F T T      F F F
F T F   T F T T        F F F      F T T
F T F   T F T F        F F F      F F F
valid
```

II.

1. K ⊃ ~ K   //   ~ K

K ⊃ ~ K					~ K	
T	**F**	F	T		**F**	T
F	**T**	T	F		**T**	F

valid

5. ~ (K • L)   //   ~ K • ~ L

~ (K • L)					~ K • ~ L				
F	T	T	T		F	T	**F**	F	T
T	T	F	F		F	T	**F**	T	F
T	F	F	T		T	F	**F**	F	T
T	F	F	F		T	F	**T**	T	F

invalid

10. J ⊃ (K ⊃ L) / K ⊃ (J ⊃ L) / (J ∨ K) ⊃ L

J ⊃ (K ⊃ L)					K ⊃ (J ⊃ L)					(J ∨ K) ⊃ L				
T	**T**	T T T			T	**T**	T T T			T T T	**T**	T
T	**F**	T F F			T	**F**	T F F			T T T	**F**	F
T	**T**	F T T			F	**T**	T T T			T T F	**T**	T
T	**T**	F T F			F	**T**	T F F			T T F	**F**	F
F	**T**	T T T			T	**T**	F T T			F T T	**T**	T
F	**T**	T F F			T	**T**	F T T			F T T	**T**	F
F	**T**	F T T			F	**T**	F T T			F F F	**T**	T
F	**T**	F T F			F	**T**	F T F			F F F	**T**	F

invalid

15. L ⊃ M / M ⊃ N / N ⊃ L // L ∨ N

L ⊃ M			M ⊃ N			N ⊃ L			L ∨ N		
T	**T**	T	T	**T**	T	T	**T**	T	T	**T**	T
T	**T**	T	T	**F**	F	F	**T**	T	T	**T**	F
T	**F**	F	F	**T**	T	T	**T**	T	T	**T'**	T
T	**F**	F	F	**T**	F	F	**T**	T	T	**T**	F
F	**T**	T	T	**T**	T	T	**F**	F	F	**T**	T
F	**T**	T	T	**F**	F	F	**T**	F	F	**F**	F
F	**T**	F	F	**T**	T	T	**F**	F	F	**T**	T
F	**T**	F	F	**T**	F	F	**T**	F	F	**F**	F

invalid

20. W ⊃ X / X ⊃ W / X ⊃ Y / Y ⊃ X // W ≡ Y

W ⊃ X			X ⊃ W	X ⊃ Y		Y ⊃ X	W ≡ Y		
T	**T**	T	**T**	**T**	T	**T**		**T**	
T	**T**	T	**T**	**F**	F	**T**		**F**	
T	**F**	F	**T**	**T**	T	**F**		**T**	
T	**F**	F	**T**	**T**	F	**F**		**F**	
F	**T**	T	**F**	**T**	T	**T**		**F**	
F	**T**	T	**F**	**T**	T	**F**		**T**	
F	**T**	F	**T**	**T**	T	**F**		**F**	
F	**T**	F	**T**	**T**	F	**T**		**T**	

valid

Exercise 6.6

1. B ≡ C   //   ~ C ⊃ ~ B

B ≡ C			~ C ⊃ ~ B				
T	**T**	F	T	F	F	F	T

valid

5. W ⊃ (X ⊃ Y) / X ⊃ (Y ⊃ Z) // W ⊃ (X ⊃ Z)

W ⊃ (X ⊃ Y)					X ⊃ (Y ⊃ Z)					W ⊃ (X ⊃ Z)				
T	**T**	T	T	T	T	**T**	T	F	F	T	**F**	T	F	F

valid

10. F ⊃ G / ~ H ∨ I / (G ∨ I) ⊃ J / ~ J // ~ (F ∨ H)

F ⊃ G			~ H ∨ I				(G ∨ I) ⊃ J					~ J		~ (F ∨ H)			
T	**T**	F	T	F	T	F	F	F	F	T	F	**T**	F	**F**	T	T	F

valid

15. N ∨ ~ O / P ∨ O / P ⊃ Q / (N ∨ Q) ⊃ (R • S) /

N ∨ ~ O				P ∨ O			P ⊃ Q			(N ∨ Q) ⊃ (R • S)						
T	**T**	F	T	T	**T**		**T**			T	**T**	**T**	T T T			
F	**T**	T	F	T	**T**	F	**T**	T	T	F	**T**	**T**	T T T T			

S ⊃ (R ⊃ T) / O ⊃ (T ⊃ U) // U

S ⊃ (R ⊃ T)					O ⊃ (T ⊃ U)					U	
T	**T**	T	T	T	T	**T**	T	F	F	F	
T	**T**	T	T	T	F	**T**	T	F	F	F	

invalid

431

Exercise 7.1

I.

(1) 1. $J \supset (K \supset L)$
    2. $L \vee J$
    3. $\sim L$ / $\sim K$
    4. J 2, 3, DS
    5. $K \supset L$ 1, 4, MP
    6. $\sim K$ 3, 5, MT

II.

(1) 1. $F \vee (D \supset T)$
    2. $\sim F$
    3. D / T
    4. $D \supset T$ 1, 2, DS
    5. T 3, 4, MP

(5) 1. $\sim S \supset D$
    2. $\sim S \vee (\sim D \supset K)$
    3. $\sim D$ / K
    4. $\sim \sim S$ 1, 3, MT
    5. $\sim D \supset K$ 2, 4, DS
    6. K 3, 5, MP

(10) 1. $(L \equiv N) \supset C$
    2. $(L \equiv N) \vee (P \supset \sim E)$
    3. $\sim E \supset C$
    4. $\sim C$ / $\sim P$
    5. $\sim (L \equiv N)$ 1, 4, MT
    6. $P \supset \sim E$ 2, 5, DS
    7. $\sim \sim E$ 3, 4, MT
    8. $\sim P$ 6, 7, MT

(15) 1. $\sim N \supset [(B \supset D) \supset (N \vee \sim E)]$
    2. $(B \supset E) \supset \sim N$
    3. $B \supset D$
    4. $D \supset E$ / $\sim E$
    5. $B \supset E$ 3, 4, HS
    6. $\sim N$ 2, 5, MP
    7. $(B \supset D) \supset (N \vee \sim E)$ 1, 6, MP
    8. $N \vee \sim E$ 3, 7, MP
    9. $\sim E$ 6, 8, DS

III.

(1) 1. $P \supset (C \vee R)$
    2. P
    3. $\sim C$ / R
    4. $C \vee R$ 1, 2, MP
    5. R 3, 4, DS

(5) 1. $C \vee (D \supset P)$
    2. $\sim B \vee (P \supset \sim A)$
    3. $\sim C$
    4. $\sim \sim B$ / $D \supset \sim A$
    5. $D \supset P$ 1, 3, DS
    6. $P \supset \sim A$ 2, 4, DS
    7. $D \supset \sim A$ 5, 6, HS

(10) 1. $\sim T \supset [T \vee (R \supset B)]$
    2. $T \supset (I \cdot \sim A)$
    3. $\sim (I \cdot \sim A)$
    4. $\sim B$ / $\sim R$
    5. $\sim T$ 2, 3, MT
    6. $T \vee (R \supset B)$ 1, 5, MP
    7. $R \supset B$ 5, 6, DS
    8. $\sim R$ 4, 7, MT

Exercise 7.2

I.

(1) 1. $(\sim M \cdot \sim N) \supset [(\sim M \vee H) \supset (K \cdot L)]$
    2. $\sim M \cdot (C \supset D)$
    3. $\sim N \cdot (F \equiv G)$ / $K \cdot \sim N$
    4. $\sim M$ 2, Simp
    5. $\sim N$ 3, Simp
    6. $\sim M \cdot \sim N$ 4, 5, Conj
    7. $(\sim M \vee H) \supset (K \cdot L)$ 1, 6, MP
    8. $\sim M \vee H$ 4, Add
    9. $K \cdot L$ 7, 8, MP
    10. K 9, Simp
    11. $K \cdot \sim N$ 5, 11, Conj

II.

(1) 1. $\sim M \supset Q$
    2. $R \supset \sim T$
    3. $\sim M \vee R$ / $Q \vee \sim T$
    4. $(\sim M \supset Q) \cdot (R \supset \sim T)$ 1, 2, Conj
    5. $Q \vee \sim T$ 3, 4, CD

432

(5) 1. $(\sim F \vee X) \supset (P \vee T)$
   2. $F \supset P$
   3. $\sim P$ / T
   4. $\sim F$ 2, 3, MT
   5. $\sim F \vee X$ 4, Add
   6. $P \vee T$ 1, 5, MP
   7. T 3, 6, DS

(15) 1. $(M \vee N) \supset (F \supset G)$
   2. $D \supset \sim C$
   3. $\sim C \supset B$
   4. $M \cdot H$
   5. $D \vee F$ / B \vee G
   6. $D \supset B$ 2, 3, HS
   7. M 4, Simp
   8. $M \vee N$ 7, Add
   9. $F \supset G$ 1, 8, MP
   10. $(D \supset B) \cdot (F \supset G)$ 6, 9, Conj
   11. $B \vee G$ 5, 10, CD

(10) 1. $(P \supset R) \supset (M \supset P)$
   2. $(P \vee M) \supset (P \supset R)$
   3. $P \vee M$ / R \vee P
   4. $P \supset R$ 2, 3, MP
   5. $M \supset P$ 1, 4, MP
   6. $(P \supset R) \cdot (M \supset P)$ 4, 5, Conj
   7. $R \vee P$ 3, 6, CD

(20) 1. $(W \cdot X) \supset (Q \vee R)$
   2. $(S \vee F) \supset (Q \vee W)$
   3. $(S \vee G) \supset (\sim Q \supset X)$
   4. $Q \vee S$
   5. $\sim Q \cdot H$ / R
   6. $\sim Q$ 5, Simp
   7. S 4, 6, DS
   8. $S \vee F$ 7, Add
   9. $Q \vee W$ 2, 8, MP
   10. W 6, 9, DS
   11. $S \vee G$ 7, Add
   12. $\sim Q \supset X$ 3, 11, MP
   13. X 6, 12, MP
   14. $W \cdot X$ 10, 13, Conj
   15. $Q \vee R$ 1, 14, MP
   16. R 6, 15, DS

III.

(1) 1. $F \supset (D \cdot C)$
   2. $F \cdot V$ / D \vee G
   3. F 2, Simp
   4. $D \cdot C$ 1, 3, MP
   5. D 4, Simp
   6. $D \vee G$ 5, Add

(5) 1. $C \supset [(S \vee F) \supset D]$
   2. $(C \vee R) \supset \sim D$
   3. C / \sim (S \vee F)
   4. $C \vee R$ 3, Add
   5. $\sim D$ 2, 4, MP
   6. $(S \vee F) \supset D$ 1, 3, MP
   7. $\sim (S \vee F)$ 5, 6, MT

(10) 1. $H \cdot (T \vee D)$
   2. $(H \cdot V) \supset (H \supset F)$
   3. $V \cdot \sim D$ / F
   4. H 1, Simp
   5. V 3, Simp
   6. $H \cdot V$ 4, 5, Conj
   7. $H \supset F$ 2, 6, MP
   8. F 4, 7, MP

Exercise 7.3
I.

(1) 1. $(J \vee F) \vee M$
   2. $(J \vee M) \supset \sim P$
   3. $\sim F$ / \sim (F \vee P)
   4. $(F \vee J) \vee M$ 1, Com
   5. $F \vee (J \vee M)$ 4, Assoc
   6. $J \vee M$ 3, 5, DS
   7. $\sim P$ 2, 6, MP
   8. $\sim F \cdot \sim P$ 3, 7, Conj
   9. $\sim (F \vee P)$ 8, DM

II.

(1) 1. $(\sim M \supset P) \cdot (\sim N \supset Q)$
   2. $\sim (M \cdot N)$ / P \vee Q
   3. $\sim M \vee \sim N$ 2, DM
   4. $P \vee Q$ 1, 3, CD

(5) 1. $Q \vee (L \vee C)$
   2. $\sim C$ / L \vee Q
   3. $(Q \vee L) \vee C$ 1, Assoc
   4. $C \vee (Q \vee L)$ 3, Com
   5. $Q \vee L$ 2, 4, DS
   6. $L \vee Q$ 5, Com

(10) 1. $(G \cdot H) \lor (M \cdot G)$
    2. $G \supset (T \cdot A)$ / A
    3. $(G \cdot H) \lor (G \cdot M)$ 1, Com
    4. $G \cdot (H \lor M)$ 3, Dist
    5. G 4, Simp
    6. $T \cdot A$ 2, 5, MP
    7. $A \cdot T$ 6, Com
    8. A 7, Simp

(15) 1. $E \supset \sim B$
    2. $U \supset \sim C$
    3. $\sim (\sim E \cdot \sim U)$ / $\sim(B \cdot C)$
    4. $(E \supset \sim B) \cdot (U \supset \sim C)$ 1, 2, Conj
    5. $\sim\sim E \lor \sim\sim U$ 3, DM
    6. $E \lor U$ 5, DN
    7. $\sim B \lor \sim C$ 4, 6, CD
    8. $\sim (B \cdot C)$ 7, DM

(20) 1. $(\sim M \lor E) \supset (S \supset U)$
    2. $(\sim Q \lor E) \supset (U \supset H)$
    3. $\sim (M \lor Q)$ / $S \supset H$
    4. $\sim M \cdot \sim Q$ 3, DM
    5. $\sim M$ 4, Simp
    6. $\sim M \lor E$ 5, Add
    7. $S \supset U$ 1, 6, MP
    8. $\sim Q \cdot \sim M$ 4, Com
    9. $\sim Q$ 8, Simp
    10. $\sim Q \lor E$ 9, Add
    11. $U \supset H$ 2, 10, MP
    12. $S \supset H$ 7, 11, HS

(25) 1. $(T \cdot K) \lor (C \cdot E)$
    2. $K \supset \sim E$
    3. $E \supset \sim C$ / $T \cdot K$
    4. $[(T \cdot K) \lor C] \cdot [(T \cdot K) \lor E]$ 1, Dist
    5. $[(T \lor C) \cdot (K \lor C)] \cdot [(T \lor E) \cdot (K \lor E)]$ 4, Com, Dist
    6. $K \lor E$ 5, Com, Assoc, Simp
    7. $(K \supset \sim E) \cdot (E \supset \sim C)$ 2, 3, Conj
    8. $\sim E \lor \sim C$ 6, 7, CD
    9. $\sim C \lor \sim E$ 8, Com
    10. $\sim(C \cdot E)$ 9, DM
    11. $(C \cdot E) \lor (T \cdot K)$ 1, Com
    12. $T \cdot K$ 10, 11, DS

III.

(1) 1. $(M \cdot P) \lor (M \cdot H)$
    2. $M \supset (J \cdot D)$ / $M \cdot D$
    3. $M \cdot (P \lor H)$ 1, Dist
    4. M 3, Simp
    5. $J \cdot D$ 2, 4, MP
    6. $D \cdot J$ 5, Com
    7. D 6, Simp
    8. $M \cdot D$ 4, 7, Conj

(5) 1. $(M \cdot B) \cdot U$
    2. $(U \cdot M) \supset \sim(B \cdot C)$ / $M \cdot \sim C$
    3. $U \cdot (M \cdot B)$ 1, Com
    4. U 3, Simp
    5. $M \cdot (B \cdot U)$ 1, Assoc
    6. M 5, Simp
    7. $U \cdot M$ 4, 6, Conj
    8. $\sim(B \cdot C)$ 2, 7, MP
    9. $\sim B \lor \sim C$ 8, DM
    10. $(B \cdot M) \cdot U$ 1, Com
    11. $B \cdot (M \cdot U)$ 10, Assoc
    12. B 11, Simp
    13. $\sim\sim B$ 12, DN
    14. $\sim C$ 9, 13, DS
    15. $M \cdot \sim C$ 6, 14, Conj

(10) 1. $B \lor (E \cdot V)$
    2. $B \lor (S \cdot P)$
    3. $\sim V \lor \sim P$ / B
    4. $(B \lor E) \cdot (B \lor V)$ 1, Dist
    5. $(B \lor S) \cdot (B \lor P)$ 2, Dist
    6. $(B \lor V) \cdot (B \lor E)$ 4, Com
    7. $B \lor V$ 6, Simp
    8. $(B \lor P) \cdot (B \lor S)$ 5, Com
    9. $B \lor P$ 8, Simp
    10. $(B \lor V) \cdot (B \lor P)$ 7, 9, Conj
    11. $B \lor (V \cdot P)$ 10, Dist
    12. $(V \cdot P) \lor B$ 11, Com
    13. $\sim(V \cdot P)$ 3, DM
    14. B 12, 13, DS

Exercise 7.4
I.
(1) 1. $K \equiv R$
    2. $K \supset (R \supset P)$
    3. $\sim P$ $/ \sim R$
    4. $(K \cdot R) \lor (\sim K \cdot \sim R)$ 1, Equiv
    5. $(K \cdot R) \supset P$ 2, Exp
    6. $\sim(K \cdot R)$ 3, 5, MT
    7. $\sim K \cdot \sim R$ 4, 6, DS
    8. $\sim R \cdot \sim K$ 7, Com
    9. $\sim R$ 8, Simp

II.
(1) 1. $(J \cdot R) \supset H$
    2. $(R \supset H) \supset M$
    3. $\sim(P \lor \sim J)$ $/ M \cdot \sim P$
    4. $J \supset (R \supset H)$ 1, Exp
    5. $J \supset M$ 2, 4, HS
    6. $\sim P \cdot J$ 3, DM, DN
    7. $\sim P$ 6, Simp
    8. J 6, Com, Simp
    9. M 5, 8, MP
   10. $M \cdot \sim P$ 7, 9, Conj

(5) 1. $(O \supset C) \cdot (\sim S \supset \sim D)$
    2. $(E \supset D) \cdot (\sim E \supset \sim C)$ $/ O \supset S$
    3. $O \supset C$ 1, Simp
    4. $\sim S \supset \sim D$ 1, Com, Simp
    5. $D \supset S$ 4, Trans
    6. $E \supset D$ 2, Simp
    7. $\sim E \supset \sim C$ 2, Com, Simp
    8. $C \supset E$ 7, Trans
    9. $O \supset E$ 3, 8, HS
   10. $O \supset D$ 6, 9, HS
   11. $O \supset S$ 5, 10, HS

(10) 1. $J \supset (G \supset L)$ $/ G \supset (J \supset L)$
     2. $(J \cdot G) \supset L$ 1, Exp
     3. $(G \cdot J) \supset L$ 2, Com
     4. $G \supset (J \supset L)$ 3, Exp

(15) 1. $T \supset G$
     2. $S \supset G$ $/ (T \lor S) \supset G$
     3. $\sim T \lor G$ 1, Impl
     4. $\sim S \lor G$ 2, Impl
     5. $(\sim T \lor G) \cdot (\sim S \lor G)$ 3, 4, Conj
     6. $(\sim T \cdot \sim S) \lor G$ 5, Com, Dist
     7. $\sim(T \lor S) \lor G$ 6, DM
     8. $(T \lor S) \supset G$ 7, Impl

(20) 1. $(G \supset J) \supset (H \supset Q)$
    2. $J \cdot \sim Q$ $/ \sim H$
    3. J 2, Simp
    4. $J \lor \sim G$ 3, Add
    5. $\sim G \lor J$ 4, Com
    6. $G \supset J$ 5, Impl
    7. $H \supset Q$ 1, 6, MP
    8. $\sim Q$ 2, Com, Simp
    9. $\sim H$ 7, 8, MT

(25) 1. $(S \lor T) \supset (S \supset \sim T)$
    2. $(S \supset \sim T) \supset (T \supset K)$
    3. $S \lor T$ $/ S \lor K$
    4. $S \supset \sim T$ 1, 3, MP
    5. $T \supset K$ 2, 4, MP
    6. $\sim S \supset T$ 3, Impl
    7. $\sim S \supset K$ 5, 6, HS
    8. $S \lor K$ 7, Impl

(30) 1. $P \supset A$
    2. $Q \supset B$ / $(P \lor Q) \supset (A \lor B)$
    3. $\sim P \lor A$ 1, Impl
    4. $\sim Q \lor B$ 2, Impl
    5. $(\sim P \lor A) \lor B$ 3, Add
    6. $(\sim Q \lor B) \lor A$ 4, Add
    7. $\sim P \lor (A \lor B)$ 5, Assoc
    8. $\sim Q \lor (A \lor B)$ 6, Assoc, Com
    9. $[\sim P \lor (A \lor B)] \cdot [\sim Q \lor (A \lor B)]$ 7, 8, Conj
  10. $(\sim P \cdot \sim Q) \lor (A \lor B)$ 9, Com, Dist
  11. $\sim(P \lor Q) \lor (A \lor B)$ 10, DM
  12. $(P \lor Q) \supset (A \lor B)$ 11, Impl

III.

(1) 1. $R \supset H$
    2. $\sim(H \cdot \sim M)$ / $R \supset M$
    3. $\sim H \lor M$ 2, DM, DN
    4. $H \supset M$ 3, Impl
    5. $R \supset M$ 1, 4, MP

(5) 1. $(G \lor R) \supset T$ / $G \supset T$
    2. $\sim(G \lor R) \lor T$ 1, Impl
    3. $(\sim G \cdot \sim R) \lor T$ 2, DM
    4. $(\sim G \lor T) \cdot (\sim R \lor T)$ 3, Com, Dist
    5. $\sim G \lor T$ 4, Simp
    6. $G \supset T$ 5, Impl

(10) 1. $(P \cdot M) \equiv G$
    2. $\sim(G \lor \sim P)$ / $\sim M$
    3. $[(P \cdot M) \supset G] \cdot [G \supset (P \cdot M)]$ 1, Equiv
    4. $(P \cdot M) \supset G$ 3, Simp
    5. $\sim G \cdot \sim\sim P$ 2, DM
    6. $\sim G$ 5, Simp
    7. $\sim(P \cdot M)$ 4, 6, MT
    8. $\sim P \lor \sim M$ 7, DM
    9. $\sim\sim P$ 5, Com, Simp
  10. $\sim M$ 8, 9, DS

Exercise 7.5
I.

(1) 1. $N \supset O$ (5) 1. $A \supset \sim(A \lor E)$ / $A \supset F$
    2. $N \supset P$ / $N \supset (O \cdot P)$ 2. A CP
      3. N CP   3. $\sim(A \lor E)$ 1, 2, MP
      4. O 1, 3, MP   4. $\sim A \cdot \sim E$ 3, DM
      5. P 2, 3, MP   5. $\sim A$ 4, Simp
      6. $O \cdot P$ 4, 5, Conj   6. $A \lor F$ 2, Add
    7. $N \supset (O \cdot P)$ 3–6, CP   7. F 5, 6, DS
                                      8. $A \supset F$ 2–7, CP

(10) 1. $C \supset (A \cdot D)$
    2. $B \supset (A \cdot E)$ / $(C \lor B) \supset A$
      3. $C \lor B$ CP
      4. $[C \supset (A \cdot D)] \cdot [B \supset (A \cdot E)]$ 1, 2, Conj
      5. $(A \cdot D) \lor (A \cdot E)$ 3, 4, CD
      6. $A \cdot (D \lor E)$ 5, Dist
      7. A 6, Simp
    8. $(C \lor B) \supset A$ 3–7, CP

(15) 1. $C \supset (D \lor \sim E)$
    2. $E \supset (D \supset F)$ / $C \supset (E \supset F)$
      3. C CP
        4. E CP
        5. $D \lor \sim E$ 1, 3, MP
        6. D 4, 5, Com, DN, DS
        7. $D \supset F$ 2, 4, MP
        8. F 6, 7, MP
      9. $E \supset F$ 4–8, CP
  10. $C \supset (E \supset F)$ 3–9, CP

(20) 1. $A \supset [B \supset (C \cdot \sim D)]$
    2. $(B \vee E) \supset (D \vee E)$ / $(A \cdot B) \supset (C \cdot E)$
        3. $A \cdot B$ CP
        4. A 3, Simp
        5. $B \supset (C \cdot \sim D)$ 1, 4, MP
        6. B 3, Com, Simp
        7. $C \cdot \sim D$ 5, 6, MP
        8. C 7, Simp
        9. $\sim D$ 7, Com, Simp
      10. $B \vee E$ 6, Add
      11. $D \vee E$ 2, 10, MP
      12. E 9, 11, DS
      13. $C \cdot E$ 8, 12, Conj
    14. $(A \cdot B) \supset (C \cdot E)$ 3–13, CP

II.
(1) 1. $M \supset W$
    2. $G \supset A$ / $(M \cdot G) \supset (W \cdot A)$
        3. $M \cdot G$ CP
        4. M 3, Simp
        5. G 3, Com, Simp
        6. W 1, 4, MP
        7. A 2, 5, MP
        8. $W \cdot A$ 6, 7, Conj
    9. $(M \cdot G) \supset (W \cdot A)$ 3–8, CP

Exercise 7.6
I.
(1) 1. $(S \vee T) \supset \sim S$ / $\sim S$
      2. S IP
      3. $S \vee T$ 2, Add
      4. $\sim S$ 1, 3, MP
      5. $S \cdot \sim S$ 2, 4, Conj
    6. $\sim S$ 2–5, IP
(10) 1. K / $S \supset (T \supset S)$
      2. S CP
      3. $S \vee \sim T$ 2, Add
      4. $\sim T \vee S$ 3, Com
      5. $T \supset S$ 4, Impl
    6. $S \supset (T \supset S)$ 2–5, CP

(5) 1. $S \supset (T \vee \sim U)$
    2. $U \supset (\sim T \vee R)$
    3. $(S \cdot U) \supset \sim R$ / $\sim S \vee \sim U$
      4. $\sim (\sim S \vee \sim U)$ IP
      5. $S \cdot U$ 4, DM, DN
      6. $\sim R$ 3, 5, MP
      7. S 5, Simp
      8. U 5, Com, Simp
      9. $T \vee \sim U$ 1, 7, MP
     10. $\sim T \vee R$ 2, 8, MP
     11. $\sim T$ 6, 10, Com, DS
     12. $\sim U$ 9, 11, DS
     13. $U \cdot \sim U$ 8, 12, Conj
    14. $\sim\sim(\sim S \vee \sim U)$ 4–13, IP
    15. $\sim S \vee \sim U$ 14, DN

(15) 1. $B \supset (K \cdot M)$
    2. $(B \cdot M) \supset (P \equiv \sim P)$ / $\sim B$
      3. B IP
      4. $K \cdot M$ 1, 3, MP
      5. M 4, Com, Simp
      6. $B \cdot M$ 3, 5, Conj
      7. $P \equiv \sim P$ 2, 6, MP
      8. $(P \cdot \sim P) \vee (\sim P \cdot \sim\sim P)$ 7, Equiv
      9. $(P \cdot \sim P) \vee (P \cdot \sim P)$ 8, Com, DN
     10. $P \cdot \sim P$ 9, Taut
    11. $\sim B$ 3–10, IP

(20) 1. $F \supset [(C \supset C) \supset G]$
    2. $G \supset \{[H \supset (E \supset H)] \supset (K \cdot \sim K)\}$ $/ \sim F$
       3. F IP
       4. $(C \supset C) \supset G$ 1, 3, MP
         5. C CP
         6. $C \vee C$ 5, Add
         7. C 6, Taut
       8. $C \supset C$ 5-7, CP
       9. G 4, 8, MP
      10. $[H \supset (E \supset H)] \supset (K \cdot \sim K)$ 2, 9, MP
        11. H CP
        12. $H \vee \sim E$ 11, Add
        13. $\sim E \vee H$ 12, Com
        14. $E \supset H$ 13, Impl
      15. $H \supset (E \supset H)$ 11-14, CP
      16. $K \cdot \sim K$ 10, 15, MP
   17. $\sim F$ 3-16, IP

II.
(1) 1. $(M \cdot V) \supset (U \cdot \sim N)$
    2. $V \supset N$ $/ \sim M \vee \sim V$
       3. $M \cdot V$ IP
       4. $U \cdot \sim N$ 1, 3, MP
       5. $\sim N$ 4, Com, Simp
       6. $\sim V$ 2, 5, MT
       7. V 3, Com, Simp
       8. $V \cdot \sim V$ 6, 7, Conj
   9. $\sim(M \cdot V)$ 3-8, IP
  10. $\sim M \vee \sim V$ 9, DM

Exercise 7.7
(1) / $P \supset [(P \supset Q) \supset Q]$
       1. P CP
        2. $P \supset Q$ CP
        3. Q 1, 2, MP
       4. $(P \supset Q) \supset Q$ 2-3, CP
     5. $P \supset [(P \supset Q) \supset Q]$ 1-4, CP
(5) / $(P \vee \sim Q) \supset [(\sim P \vee R) \supset (Q \supset R)]$
       1. $P \vee \sim Q$ CP
        2. $\sim P \vee R$ CP
        3. $\sim Q \vee P$ 1, Com
        4. $Q \supset P$ 3, Impl
        5. $P \supset R$ 2, Impl
        6. $Q \supset R$ 4, 5, HS
      7. $(\sim P \vee R) \supset (Q \supset R)$ 2-6, CP
     8. $(P \vee \sim Q) \supset [(\sim P \vee R) \supset (Q \supset R)]$ 1-7, CP
(10) / $[\sim(P \cdot \sim Q) \cdot \sim Q] \supset \sim P$
        1. $\sim(P \cdot \sim Q) \cdot \sim Q$ CP
        2. $\sim(P \cdot \sim Q)$ 1, Simp
        3. $\sim P \vee Q$ 2, DM, DN
        4. $\sim Q$ 1, Com, Simp
        5. $\sim P$ 3, 4, Com, DS
     6. $[\sim(P \cdot \sim Q) \cdot \sim Q] \supset \sim P$ 1-5, CP
(15) / $(\sim P \vee Q) \supset [(P \vee \sim Q) \supset (P \equiv Q)]$
       1. $\sim P \vee Q$ CP
       2. $P \vee \sim Q$ CP
       3. $P \supset Q$ 1, Impl
       4. $\sim Q \vee P$ 2, Com
       5. $Q \supset P$ 4, Impl
       6. $(P \supset Q) \cdot (Q \supset P)$ 3, 5, Conj
       7. $P \equiv Q$ 6, Equiv
      8. $(P \vee \sim Q) \supset (P \equiv Q)$ 2-7, CP
    9. $(\sim P \vee Q) \supset [(P \vee \sim Q) \supset (P \equiv Q)]$ 1-8, CP

(20) / $P \supset [Q \equiv (P \supset Q)]$

1. P	CP
2. Q	CP
3. $Q \lor \sim P$	2, Add
4. $\sim P \lor Q$	3, Com
5. $P \supset Q$	4, Impl
6. $Q \supset (P \supset Q)$	2-5, CP
7. $P \supset Q$	CP
8. Q	1, 7, MP
9. $(P \supset Q) \supset Q$	7-8, CP
10. $[Q \supset (P \supset Q)] \cdot [(P \supset Q) \supset Q]$	6, 9, Conj
11. $Q \equiv (P \supset Q)$	10, Equiv
12. $P \supset [Q \equiv (P \supset Q)]$	1-11, CP

Exercise 8.1

1. Ce

5. $(\exists x)(He \cdot \sim Rx)$

10. $(\exists x)(Mx \cdot \sim Ex)$

15. $(x)[(Mx \cdot Px) \supset Tx]$

20. $(\exists x)[(Rx \cdot Vx) \cdot Ax]$

25. $(\exists x)(Wx \cdot Tx) \supset (Gp \lor Gh)$

30. $(x)[(Bx \cdot Mx) \supset Sx] \supset Sc$

35. $(x)[(Sx \lor Tx) \supset (Cx \cdot Ex)] \supset (\exists x)[Mx \cdot (Px \lor Dx)]$

Exercise 8.2

I.

(1)
1. $(x)(Ax \supset Bx)$	
2. $(x)(Bx \supset Cx)$	/ $(x)(Ax \supset Cx)$
3. $Ax \supset Bx$	1, UI
4. $Bx \supset Cx$	2, UI
5. $Ax \supset Cx$	3, 4, HS
6. $(x)(Ax \supset Cx)$	5, UG

(5)
1. $(x)[(Ax \lor Bx) \supset Cx]$	
2. $(\exists y)(Ay \cdot Dy)$	/ $(\exists y)Cy$
3. $Am \cdot Dm$	2, EI
4. Am	3, Simp
5. $(Am \lor Bm) \supset Cm$	1, UI
6. $Am \lor Bm$	4, Add
7. Cm	5, 6, MP
8. $(\exists y)Cy$	7, EG

(10)
1. $(x)(Bx \lor Ax)$	
2. $(x)(Bx \supset Ax)$	/ $(x)Ax$
3. $Bx \lor Ax$	1, UI
4. $Bx \supset Ax$	2, UI
5. $Ax \lor Bx$	3, Com
6. $\sim Ax \supset Bx$	5, Impl
7. $\sim Ax \supset Ax$	4, 6, HS
8. $Ax \lor Ax$	7, Impl, DN
9. Ax	8, Taut
10. $(x)Ax$	9, UG

(15)
1. $(\exists x)Ax \supset (x)(Bx \supset Cx)$	
2. $(\exists x)Dx \supset (\exists x)\sim Cx$	
3. $(\exists x)(Ax \cdot Dx)$	/ $(\exists x) \sim Bx$
4. $Am \cdot Dm$	3, EI
5. Am	4, Simp
6. Dm	4, Com, Simp
7. $(\exists x)Ax$	5, EG
8. $(\exists x)Dx$	6, EG
9. $(x)(Bx \supset Cx)$	1, 7, MP
10. $(\exists x) \sim Cx$	2, 8, MP
11. $\sim Cn$	10, EI
12. $Bn \supset Cn$	9, UI
13. $\sim Bn$	11, 12, MT
14. $(\exists x) \sim Bx$	13, EG

II.

(1)
1. $(x)(Ox \supset Sx)$	
2. $(x)(Ox \supset Fx)$	/ $(x)[Ox \supset (Sx \cdot Fx)]$
3. $Ox \supset Sx$	1, UI
4. $Ox \supset Fx$	2, UI
5. $\sim Ox \lor Sx$	3, Impl
6. $\sim Ox \lor Fx$	4, Impl
7. $(\sim Ox \lor Sx) \cdot (\sim Ox \lor Fx)$	5, 6, Conj
8. $\sim Ox \lor (Sx \cdot Fx)$	7, Dist
9. $Ox \supset (Sx \cdot Fx)$	8, Impl
10. $(x)[Ox \supset (Sx \cdot Fx)]$	9, UG

(5) 1. $(x)[(Bx \lor Px) \supset Lx]$
   2. $(x)(Gx \supset \sim Lx)$ / $(x)(Gx \supset \sim Bx)$
   3. $(Bx \lor Px) \supset Lx$ 1, UI
   4. $Gx \supset \sim Lx$ 2, UI
   5. $\sim Lx \supset \sim(Bx \lor Px)$ 3, Trans
   6. $Gx \supset \sim(Bx \lor Px)$ 4, 5, HS
   7. $Gx \supset (\sim Bx \cdot \sim Px)$ 6, DM
   8. $\sim Gx \lor (\sim Bx \cdot \sim Px)$ 7, Impl
   9. $(\sim Gx \lor \sim Bx) \cdot (\sim Gx \lor \sim Px)$ 8, Dist
   10. $\sim Gx \lor \sim Bx$ 9, Simp
   11. $Gx \supset \sim Bx$ 10, Impl
   12. $(x)(Gx \supset \sim Bx)$ 11, UG

(10) 1. $(x)[(Ax \cdot Kx) \supset Rx] \supset (x)(Gx \supset Sx)$
   2. $(x)[(Ax \cdot Kx) \supset Fx] \supset (x)(Gx \supset Px)$
   3. $(x)[(Ax \cdot Kx) \supset (Rx \cdot Fx)]$ / $(x)[Gx \supset (Sx \cdot Px)]$
   4. $(Ax \cdot Kx) \supset (Rx \cdot Fx)$ 3, UI
   5. $\sim(Ax \cdot Kx) \lor (Rx \cdot Fx)$ 4, Impl
   6. $[\sim(Ax \cdot Kx) \lor Rx] \cdot [\sim(Ax \cdot Kx) \lor Fx]$ 5, Dist
   7. $\sim(Ax \cdot Kx) \lor Rx$ 6, Simp
   8. $\sim(Ax \cdot Kx) \lor Fx$ 6, Com, Simp
   9. $(Ax \cdot Kx) \supset Rx$ 7, Impl
   10. $(Ax \cdot Kx) \supset Fx$ 8, Impl
   11. $(x)(Ax \cdot Kx) \supset Rx$ 9, UG
   12. $(x)(Ax \cdot Kx) \supset Fx$ 10, UG
   13. $(x)(Gx \supset Sx)$ 1, 11, MP
   14. $(x)(Gx \supset Px)$ 2, 12, MP
   15. $Gx \supset Sx$ 13, UI
   16. $Gx \supset Px$ 14, UI
   17. $\sim Gx \lor Sx$ 15, Impl
   18. $\sim Gx \lor Px$ 16, Impl
   19. $(\sim Gx \lor Sx) \cdot (\sim Gx \lor Px)$ 17, 18, Conj
   20. $\sim Gx \lor (Sx \cdot Px)$ 19, Dist
   21. $Gx \supset (Sx \cdot Px)$ 20, Impl
   22. $(x)[Gx \supset (Sx \cdot Px)]$ 21, UG

Exercise 8.3

I.

(1) 1. $(x)Ax \supset (\exists x)Bx$
   2. $(x)\sim Bx$ / $(\exists x)\sim Ax$
   3. $\sim(\exists x)Bx$ 2, CQ
   4. $\sim(x)Ax$ 1, 3, MT
   5. $(\exists x)\sim Ax$ 4, CQ

(5) 1. $(x)(Ax \cdot Bx) \lor (x)(Cx \cdot Dx)$
   2. $\sim(x)Dx$ / $(x)Bx$
   3. $(\exists x)\sim Dx$ 2, CQ
   4. $\sim Dm$ 3, EI
   5. $\sim Dm \lor \sim Cm$ 4, Add
   6. $\sim Cm \lor \sim Dm$ 5, Com
   7. $\sim(Cm \cdot Dm)$ 6, DM
   8. $(\exists x)\sim(Cx \cdot Dx)$ 7, EG
   9. $\sim(x)(Cx \cdot Dx)$ 8, CQ
   10. $(x)(Ax \cdot Bx)$ 1, 9, Com, DS
   11. $Ax \cdot Bx$ 10, UI
   12. Bx 11, Com, Simp
   13. $(x)Bx$ 12, UG

(10) 1. $\sim(\exists x)(Ax \cdot \sim Bx)$
   2. $\sim(\exists x)(Bx \cdot \sim Cx)$ / $(x)(Ax \supset Cx)$
   3. $(x)\sim(Ax \cdot \sim Bx)$ 1, CQ
   4. $(x)\sim(Bx \cdot \sim Cx)$ 2, CQ
   5. $\sim(Ax \cdot \sim Bx)$ 3, UI
   6. $\sim(Bx \cdot \sim Cx)$ 4, UI
   7. $\sim Ax \lor Bx$ 5, DM, DN
   8. $\sim Bx \lor Cx$ 6, DM, DN
   9. $Ax \supset Bx$ 7, Impl
   10. $Bx \supset Cx$ 8, Impl
   11. $Ax \supset Cx$ 9, 10, HS
   12. $(x)(Ax \supset Cx)$ 11, UG

(15) 1. $\sim(\exists x)(Ax \vee Bx)$
     2. $(\exists x)Cx \supset (\exists x)Ax$
     3. $(\exists x)Dx \supset (\exists x)Bx$ / $\sim(\exists x)(Cx \vee Dx)$
     4. $(x)\sim(Ax \vee Bx)$ 1, CQ
     5. $\sim(Ax \vee Bx)$ 4, UI
     6. $\sim Ax \cdot \sim Bx$ 5, DM
     7. $\sim Ax$ 6, Simp
     8. $\sim Bx$ 6, Com, Simp
     9. $(x)\sim Ax$ 7, UG
   10. $(x)\sim Bx$ 8, UG
   11. $\sim(\exists x)Ax$ 9, CQ
   12. $\sim(\exists x)Bx$ 10, CQ
   13. $\sim(\exists x)Cx$ 2, 11, MT
   14. $\sim(\exists x)Dx$ 3, 12, MT
   15. $(x)\sim Cx$ 13, CQ
   16. $(x)\sim Dx$ 14, CQ
   17. $\sim Cx$ 15, UI
   18. $\sim Dx$ 16, UI
   19. $\sim Cx \cdot \sim Dx$ 17, 18, Conj
   20. $\sim(Cx \vee Dx)$ 19, DM
   21. $(x)\sim(Cx \vee Dx)$ 20, UG
   22. $\sim(\exists x)(Cx \vee Dx)$ 21, CQ

II.

(1) 1. $(x)[Px \supset (Hx \vee Nx)] \supset \sim(\exists x)Cx$
     2. Cf / $(\exists x)(Px \cdot \sim Nx)$
     3. $(\exists x)Cx$ 2, EG
     4. $\sim(x)[Px \supset (Hx \vee Nx)]$ 1, 3, DN, MT
     5. $(\exists x)\sim[Px \supset (Hx \vee Nx)]$ 4, CQ
     6. $\sim[Pm \supset (Hm \vee Nm)]$ 5, EI
     7. $\sim[\sim Pm \vee (Hm \vee Nm)]$ 6, Impl
     8. $Pm \cdot \sim(Hm \vee Nm)$ 7, DM, DN
     9. $Pm \cdot (\sim Hm \cdot \sim Nm)$ 8, DM
   10. Pm 9, Simp
   11. $\sim Hm \cdot \sim Nm$ 9, Com, Simp
   12. $\sim Nm$ 11, Com, Simp
   13. $Pm \cdot \sim Nm$ 10, 12, Conj
   14. $(\exists x)(Px \cdot \sim Nx)$ 13, EG

(5) 1. $(x)[(Px \cdot \sim Ax) \supset Ix]$
     2. $\sim(\exists x)(Px \cdot Ix)$ / $(x)(Px \supset Ax)$
     3. $(x)\sim(Px \cdot Ix)$ 2, CQ
     4. $\sim(Px \cdot Ix)$ 3, UI
     5. $\sim Px \vee \sim Ix)$ 4, DM
     6. $\sim Ix \vee \sim Px$ 5, Com
     7. $Ix \supset \sim Px$ 6, Impl
     8. $(Px \cdot \sim Ax) \supset Ix$ 1, UI
     9. $(Px \cdot \sim Ax) \supset \sim Px$ 7, 8, HS
   10. $(\sim Ax \cdot Px) \supset \sim Px$ 9, Com
   11. $\sim Ax \supset (Px \supset \sim Px)$ 10, Exp
   12. $\sim Ax \supset (\sim Px \vee \sim Px)$ 11, Impl
   13. $\sim Ax \supset \sim Px$ 12, Taut
   14. $Px \supset Ax$ 13, Trans
   15. $(x)(Px \supset Ax)$ 14, UG

(10) 1. $\sim(\exists x)[Px \cdot (Gx \vee Hx)]$
     2. $(x)[Nx \supset (Px \cdot Hx)]$
     3. $(\exists x)(Px \cdot Cx) \vee (\exists x)(Px \cdot Nx)$ / $(\exists x)(Cx \cdot \sim Gx)$
     4. $(x)\sim[Px \cdot (Gx \vee Hx)]$ 1, CQ
     5. $\sim[Px \cdot (Gx \vee Hx)]$ 4, UI
     6. $\sim Px \vee \sim(Gx \vee Hx)$ 5, DM
     7. $\sim Px \vee (\sim Gx \cdot \sim Hx)$ 6, DM
     8. $(\sim Px \vee \sim Gx) \cdot (\sim Px \vee \sim Hx)$ 7, Dist

9. $\sim Px \vee \sim Gx$	8, Simp
10. $\sim Px \vee \sim Hx$	8, Com, Simp
11. $\sim(Px \cdot Hx)$	10, DM
12. $Nx \supset (Px \cdot Hx)$	2, UI
13. $\sim Nx$	11, 12, MT
14. $\sim Nx \vee \sim Px$	13, Add
15. $\sim Px \vee \sim Nx$	14, Com
16. $\sim(Px \cdot Nx)$	15, DM
17. $(x) \sim(Px \cdot Nx)$	16, UG
18. $\sim(\exists x)(Px \cdot Nx)$	17, CQ
19. $(\exists x)(Px \cdot Cx)$	3, 18, Com, DS
20. $Pm \cdot Cm$	19, EI
21. $(x)(\sim Px \vee \sim Gx)$	9, UG
22. $\sim Pm \vee \sim Gm$	21, UI
23. Pm	20, Simp
24. $\sim Gm$	22, 23, DN, DS
25. Cm	20, Com, Simp
26. $Cm \cdot \sim Gm$	24, 25, Conj
27. $(\exists x)(Cx \cdot \sim Gx)$	26, EG

Exercise 8.4
I.

(1)
1. $(x)(Ax \supset Bx)$		
2. $(x)(Ax \supset Cx)$	/	$(x)[Ax \supset (Bx \cdot Cx)]$
3. Ax	CP	
4. $Ax \supset Bx$	1, UI	
5. $Ax \supset Cx$	2, UI	
6. Bx	3, 4, MP	
7. Cx	3, 5, MP	
8. $Bx \cdot Cx$	6, 7, Conj	
9. $Ax \supset (Bx \cdot Cx)$	3–8, CP	
10. $(x)[Ax \supset (Bx \cdot Cx)]$	9, UG	

(5)
1. $(x)(Ax \supset Bx)$		
2. $(x)[(Ax \cdot Bx) \supset Cx]$	/	$(x)(Ax \supset Cx)$
3. Ax	CP	
4. $Ax \supset Bx$	1, UI	
5. $(Ax \cdot Bx) \supset Cx$	2, UI	
6. Bx	3, 4, MP	
7. $Ax \cdot Bx$	3, 6, Conj	
8. Cx	5, 7, MP	
9. $Ax \supset Cx$	3–8, CP	
10. $(x)(Ax \supset Cx)$	9, UG	

(10)
1. $(x)(Ax \supset Bx)$		
2. $Am \vee An$	/	$(\exists x) Bx$
3. $\sim(\exists x) Bx$	IP	
4. $(x) \sim Bx$	3, CQ	
5. $Am \supset Bm$	1, UI	
6. $An \supset Bn$	1, UI	
7. $(Am \supset Bm) \cdot (An \supset Bn)$	5, 6, Conj	
8. $Bm \vee Bn$	2, 7, CD	
9. $\sim Bm$	4, UI	
10. Bn	8, 9, DS	
11. $\sim Bn$	4, UI	
12. $Bn \cdot \sim Bn$	10, 11, Conj	
13. $\sim\sim(\exists x) Bx$	3–12, IP	
14. $(\exists x) Bx$	13, DN	

(15) 1. $(\exists x)\, Ax \supset (\exists x)\, (Bx \cdot Cx)$
      2. $(\exists x)\, Cx \supset (x)\, (Dx \cdot Ex)$ / $(x)\, (Ax \supset Ex)$
         3. Ax CP
         4. $(\exists x)\, Ax$ 3, EG
         5. $(\exists x)\, (Bx \cdot Cx)$ 1, 4, MP
         6. $Bm \cdot Cm$ 5, EI
         7. Cm 6, Com, Simp
         8. $(\exists x)\, Cx$ 7, EG
         9. $(x)\, (Dx \cdot Ex)$ 2, 8, MP
        10. $Dx \cdot Ex$ 9, UI
        11. Ex 10, Com, Simp
     12. $Ax \supset Ex$ 3–11, CP
     13. $(x)\, (Ax \supset Ex)$ 12, UG
(20) 1. $(x)\, [Ax \supset (Bx \cdot Cx)]$
      2. $(x)\, [Dx \supset (Ex \cdot Fx)]$ / $(x)\, (Cx \supset Dx) \supset (x)\, (Ax \supset Fx)$
      3. $(x)\, (Cx \supset Dx)$ CP
         4. Ax CP
         5. $Ax \supset (Bx \cdot Cx)$ 1, UI
         6. $Bx \cdot Cx$ 4, 5, MP
         7. Cx 6, Com, Simp
         8. $Cx \supset Dx$ 3, UI
         9. Dx 7, 8, MP
        10. $Dx \supset (Ex \cdot Fx)$ 2, UI
        11. $Ex \cdot Fx$ 9, 10, MP
        12. Fx 11, Com, Simp
     13. $Ax \supset Fx$ 4–12, CP
     14. $(x)\, (Ax \supset Fx)$ 13, UG
     15. $(x)\, (Cx \supset Dx) \supset (x)\, (Ax \supset Fx)$ 3–14, CP

II.
 (1) 1. $(x)\, (Ax \supset Wx)$
      2. $(x)\, (Rx \supset Cx)$ / $(x)\, [(Rx \cdot Ax) \supset (Cx \cdot Wx)]$
         3. $Rx \cdot Ax$ Cp
         4. Rx 3, Simp
         5. Ax 3, Com, Simp
         6. $Ax \supset Wx$ 1, UI
         7. $Rx \supset Cx$ 2, UI
         8. Cx 4, 7, MP
         9. Wx 5, 6, MP
        10. $Cx \cdot Wx$ 8, 9, Conj
     11. $(Rx \cdot Ax) \supset (Cx \cdot Wx)$ 3–10, CP
     12. $(x)\, [(Rx \cdot Ax) \supset (Cx \cdot Wx)]$ 11, UG
 (5) 1. $(x)\, (Ax \supset Dx)$
      2. $(x)\, [(Ex \cdot Ax) \supset Cx] \cdot (x)\, [(Cx \cdot Dx) \supset Fx]$ / $(x)\, [(Ex \cdot Ax) \supset Fx]$
         3. $Ex \cdot Ax$ CP
         4. $(x)\, [(Ex \cdot Ax) \supset Cx]$ 2, Simp
         5. $(x)\, [(Cx \cdot Dx) \supset Fx]$ 2, Com, Simp
         6. $(Ex \cdot Ax) \supset Cx$ 4, UI
         7. $(Cx \cdot Dx) \supset Fx$ 5, UI
         8. Cx 3, 6, MP
         9. Ax 3, Com, Simp
        10. $Ax \supset Dx$ 1, UI
        11. Dx 9, 10, MP
        12. $Cx \cdot Dx$ 8, 11, Conj
        13. Fx 7, 12, MP
     14. $(Ex \cdot Ax) \supset Fx$ 3–13, CP
     15. $(x)\, (Ex \cdot Ax) \supset Fx$ 14, UG

(10) 1. $(\exists x)(Gx \cdot Px) \lor (\exists x)(Ax \cdot Px)$
      2. $(\exists x)Px \supset (\exists x)[Ax \cdot (Cx \cdot Dx)]$ / $(\exists x)(Dx \cdot Cx)$
           3. $\sim(\exists x)(Dx \cdot Cx)$ IP
           4. $(x) \sim(Dx \cdot Cx)$ 3, CQ
           5. $\sim(Dx \cdot Cx)$ 4, UI
           6. $\sim(Cx \cdot Dx)$ 5, Com
           7. $\sim(Cx \cdot Dx) \lor \sim Ax$ 6, Add
           8. $\sim Ax \lor \sim(Cx \cdot Dx)$ 7, Com
           9. $\sim[Ax \cdot (Cx \cdot Dx)]$ 8, DM
          10. $(x) \sim[Ax \cdot (Cx \cdot Dx)]$ 9, UG
          11. $\sim(\exists x)[Ax \cdot (Cx \cdot Dx)]$ 10, CQ
          12. $\sim(\exists x) Px$ 2, 11, MT
          13. $(x) \sim Px$ 12, CQ
          14. $\sim Px$ 13, UI
          15. $\sim Px \lor \sim Gx$ 14, Add
          16. $\sim Gx \lor \sim Px$ 15, Com
          17. $\sim(Gx \cdot Px)$ 16, DM
          18. $(x) \sim (Gx \cdot Px)$ 17, UG
          19. $\sim(\exists x)(Gx \cdot Px)$ 18, CQ
          20. $(\exists x)(Ax \cdot Px)$ 1, 19, DS
          21. $Am \cdot Pm$ 20, EI
          22. Pm 21, Com, Simp
          23. $\sim Pm$ 13, UI
          24. $Pm \cdot \sim Pm$ 22, 23, Conj
      25. $\sim\sim(\exists x)(Dx \cdot Cx)$ 3-24, IP
      26. $(\exists x)(Dx \cdot Cx)$ 25, DN

Alternate method:

       1. $(\exists x)(Gx \cdot Px) \lor (\exists x)(Ax \cdot Px)$
       2. $(\exists x) Px \supset (\exists x)[Ax \cdot (Cx \cdot Dx)]$ / $(\exists x)(Dx \cdot Cx)$
            3. $\sim(\exists x) Px$ IP
            4. $(x) \sim Px$ 3, CQ
            5. $\sim Px$ 4, UI
            6. $\sim Px \lor \sim Gx$ 5, Add
            7. $\sim Gx \lor \sim Px$ 6, Com
            8. $\sim(Gx \cdot Px)$ 7, DM
            9. $(x) \sim(Gx \cdot Px)$ 8, UG
           10. $\sim(\exists x)(Gx \cdot Px)$ 9, CQ
           11. $(\exists x)(Ax \cdot Px)$ 1, 10, DS
           12. $Am \cdot Pm$ 11, EI
           13. Pm 12, Com, Simp
           14. $\sim Pm$ 4, UI
           15. $Pm \cdot \sim Pm$ 13, 14, Conj
       16. $\sim\sim(\exists x) Px$ 3-15, IP
       17. $(\exists x) Px$ 16, DN
       18. $(\exists x)[Ax \cdot (Cx \cdot Dx)]$ 2, 17, MP
       19. $An \cdot (Cn \cdot Dn)$ 18, EI
       20. $Cn \cdot Dn$ 19, Com, Simp
       21. $Dn \cdot Cn$ 20, Com
       22. $(\exists x)(Dx \cdot Cx)$ 21, EG

Exercise 8.5

I.

(1) 1. $(x)(Ax \supset Bx)$
     2. $(x)(Ax \supset Cx)$ / $(x)(Bx \supset Cx)$

For a universe consisting of one member, we have

$$Aa \supset Ba \quad / \quad Aa \supset Ca \quad // \quad Ba \supset Ca$$
    F T T   F T F   T F F

(5) 1. $(x)[Ax \supset (Bx \lor Cx)]$
     2. $(\exists x) Ax$ / $(\exists x) Bx$

For a universe consisting of one member, we have

$$Aa \supset (Ba \lor Ca) \quad / \quad Aa \quad // \quad Ba$$
    T T F T T   T   F

(10) 1. $(\exists x)(Ax \cdot Bx)$
      2. $(\exists x)(\sim Ax \cdot \sim Bx)$ / $(x)(Ax \equiv Bx)$
      For a universe consisting of one member, we have
      $Aa \cdot Ba$ / $\sim Aa \cdot \sim Ba$ // $Aa \equiv Ba$
      T T   F T T̸   F

      For a universe consisting of two members, we have
      $(Aa \cdot Ba) \vee (Ab \cdot Bb)$ / $(\sim Aa \cdot \sim Ba) \vee (\sim Ab \cdot \sim Bb)$
      T T T T T F F   F T F F T T̸ F T F T F

      // $(Aa \equiv Ba) \cdot (Ab \equiv Bb)$
           T T T F T F F
      For a universe consisting of three members, we have
      $(Aa \cdot Ba) \vee [(Ac \cdot Bb) \vee [(Ac \cdot Bc)]$ /
      T T T T T F F T F F F

      $(\sim Aa \cdot \sim Ba) \vee [(\sim Ab \cdot \sim Bb) \vee (\sim Ac \cdot \sim Bc)]$
      F T F F T T F T F T F T T F T T F

      // $(Aa \equiv Ba) \cdot [(Ab \equiv Bb) \cdot (Ac \equiv Bc)]$
           T T T F T F F F F T F

II.
(1) 1. $(x)[(Vx \cdot Px) \supset (Ax \cdot Mx)]$
     2. $(\exists x)(Vx \cdot Ox)$ / $(\exists x)(Mx \cdot Ax)$
     For a universe consisting of one member, we have
     $(Va \cdot Pa) \supset (Aa \cdot Ma)$ / $Va \cdot Oa$ // $Ma \cdot Aa$
     T F F T F F F   T T T   F F F

Exercise 8.6
I.
  1. Rcp
  5. $(x)(Tjx \supset Gx)$
 10. $(\exists x)[Px \cdot (y) Sxy]$
 15. $(x)(Isx \supset Fxs)$
 20. $(\exists x)\{Px \cdot (y)[(Py \cdot Mxy) \supset Axy]\}$
 25. $(x)\{Lx \supset (y)[(Wy \cdot Cy) \supset Rxy]\}$
 30. $(\exists x)(Sx \cdot Dx) \supset (\exists x)[(Sx \cdot Dx) \cdot Hx]$
II.

(1) 1. $(x)[Ax \supset (y) Bxy]$
     2. Am / $(y) Bmy$
     3. $Am \supset (y) Bmy$ 1, UI
     4. $(y) Bmy$ 2, 3, MP

(5) 1. $(\exists x) Ax \supset (\exists y) By$ / $(\exists y)(x)(Ax \supset By)$
     2. Ax CP
     3. $(\exists x) Ax$ 2, EG
     4. $(\exists y) By$ 1, 3, MP
     5. Bm 4, EI
     6. $Ax \supset Bm$ 2–5, CP
     7. $(x)(Ax \supset Bm)$ 6, UG
     8. $(\exists y)(x)(Ax \supset By)$ 7, EG

(10) 1. $(x)(\exists y) Axy \supset (x)(\exists y) Bxy$
      2. $(\exists x)(y) \sim Bxy$ / $(\exists x)(y) \sim Axy$
      3. $(\exists x) \sim (\exists y) Bxy$ 2, CQ
      4. $\sim(x)(\exists y) Bxy$ 3, CQ
      5. $\sim(x)(\exists y) Axy$ 1, 4, MT
      6. $(\exists x) \sim (\exists y) Axy$ 5, CQ
      7. $(\exists x)(y) \sim Axy$ 6, CQ

(15) 1. $(\exists x)(y)(Ayx \supset \sim Axy)$ / $\sim(x) Axx$
      2. $(y)(Aym \supset \sim Amy)$ 1, EI
      3. $Amm \supset \sim Amm$ 2, UI
      4. $\sim Amm \vee \sim Amm$ 3, Impl
      5. $\sim Amm$ 4, Taut
      6. $(\exists x) \sim Axx$ 5, EG
      7. $\sim(x) Axx$ 6, CQ

(20)　1. $(x)(y)[Axy \supset (Bx \cdot Cy)]$
　　　2. $(x)(y)[(Bx \lor Dy) \supset \sim Axy]$　　　／　$\sim(\exists x)(\exists y)Axy$
　　　3. $(\exists x)(\exists y)Axy$　　　IP
　　　4. $(\exists y)Amy$　　　3, EI
　　　5. Amn　　　4, EI
　　　6. $(y)[Amy \supset (Bm \cdot Cy)]$　　　1, UI
　　　7. $Amn \supset (Bm \cdot Cn)$　　　6, UI
　　　8. $Bm \supset Cn$　　　5, 7, MP
　　　9. Bm　　　8, Simp
　　10. $(y)[(Bm \lor Dy) \supset \sim Amy]$　　　2, UI
　　11. $(Bm \lor Dn) \supset \sim Amn$　　　10, UI
　　12. $Bm \lor Dn$　　　9, Add
　　13. $\sim Amn$　　　11, 12, MP
　　14. $Amn \cdot \sim Amn$　　　5, 13, Conj
　　15. $\sim(\exists x)(\exists y)Axy$　　　3–14, IP

III.

(1)　1. $(x)[Px \supset (y)(Ay \supset Oxy)]$
　　　2. $Pj \cdot \sim Ojm$　　　／　$\sim Am$
　　　3. $Pj \supset (y)(Ay \supset Ojy)$　　　1, UI
　　　4. Pj　　　2, Simp
　　　5. $(y)(Ay \supset Ojy)$　　　3, 4, MP
　　　6. $Am \supset Ojm$　　　5, UI
　　　7. $\sim Ojm$　　　2, Com, Simp
　　　8. $\sim Am$　　　6, 7, MT

(5)　1. $(x)\{(Hx \cdot Px) \supset [(y)(By \supset Cy) \supset Rx]\}$
　　　2. $(\exists x)[(Hx \cdot Px) \cdot \sim Rx]$　　　／　$(\exists x)(Bx \cdot \sim Cx)$
　　　3. $(Hm \cdot Pm) \cdot \sim Rm$　　　2, EI
　　　4. $Hm \cdot Pm$　　　3, Simp
　　　5. $(Hm \cdot Pm) \supset [(y)(By \supset Cy) \supset Rm]$　　　1, UI
　　　6. $(y)(By \supset Cy) \supset Rm$　　　4, 5, MP
　　　7. $\sim Rm$　　　3, Com, Simp
　　　8. $\sim(y)(By \supset Cy)$　　　6, 7, MT
　　　9. $(\exists y) \sim(By \supset Cy)$　　　8, CQ
　　10. $\sim(Bn \supset Cn)$　　　9, EI
　　11. $\sim(\sim Bn \lor Cn)$　　　10, Impl
　　12. $Bn \cdot \sim Cn$　　　11, DM, DN
　　13. $(\exists x)(Bx \cdot \sim Cx)$　　　12, EG

(10)　1. $(x)(Ix \supset [(\exists y)(Cy \cdot Ay) \supset Ex]\}$
　　　2. $[(\exists x)Tx \lor (\exists x)Wx] \supset [(\exists x)Ix \cdot (\exists x)Cx]$
　　　3. $(x)(Cx \supset Ax)$　　　／　$(\exists x)Tx \supset (\exists x)(Ix \cdot Ex)$
　　　4. $(\exists x)Tx$　　　CP
　　　5. $(\exists x)Tx \lor (\exists x)Wx$　　　4, Add
　　　6. $(\exists x)Ix \cdot (\exists x)Cx$　　　2, 5, MP
　　　7. $(\exists x)Ix$　　　6, Simp
　　　8. Im　　　7, EI
　　　9. $Im \supset [(\exists y)(Cy \cdot Ay) \supset Em]$　　　1, UI
　　10. $(\exists y)(Cy \cdot Ay) \supset Em$　　　8, 9, MP
　　11. $(\exists x)Cx$　　　6, Com, Simp
　　12. Cn　　　11, EI
　　13. $Cn \supset An$　　　3, UI
　　14. An　　　12, 13, MP
　　15. $Cn \cdot An$　　　12, 14, Conj
　　16. $(\exists y)(Cy \cdot Ay)$　　　15, EG
　　17. Em　　　10, 16, MP
　　18. $Im \cdot Em$　　　8, 17, Conj
　　19. $(\exists x)(Ix \cdot Ex)$　　　18, EG
　　20. $(\exists x)Tx \supset (\exists x)(Ix \cdot Ex)$　　　4–19, CP

Exercise 9.1

I.
1. Sufficient condition.
5. Necessary condition—the gun must also be loaded.
10. Necessary condition—electricity must also be supplied from the main lines.

II.
1. Method of difference—sufficient condition.
5. Double method of agreement—sufficient and necessary condition.
10. Double method of agreement—sufficient and necessary condition.
15. Method of difference—sufficient condition.

III.
1. By the inverse method of agreement, A is the cause in the sense of a sufficient condition.
5. By the joint method of agreement and difference, A is the cause in the sense of a sufficient and necessary condition.

Exercise 9.2

I.
1. 1/6
5. $2/52 = 1/26$

II.
1. $P(6 \text{ or } 1) = P(6) + P(1) = 1/6 + 1/6 = 2/6 = 1/3$
5. $P(A_1 \text{ or } A_2) = P(A_1) + P(A_2) - P(A_1 \text{ and } A_2)$
$$= 4/52 + 4/52 - (4/52 \times 4/52)$$
$$= 25/169 = .148$$
10. a. $P(R_1 \text{ and } R_2) = P(R_1) \times P(R_2 \text{ given } R_1)$
$$= 3/12 \times 2/11$$
$$= 6/132 \times .045$$
  b. $P(Y \text{ and } G) = P(Y_1 \text{ and } G_2) + P(G_1 \text{ and } Y_2)$
$$= (5/12 \times 4/11) + (4/12 \times 5/11)$$
$$= 20/132 + 20/132$$
$$= 10/33 = .303$$
  c. $P(R \text{ or } G) = 1 - P(Y_1 \text{ and } Y_2)$
$$= 1 - (5/12 \times 4/11)$$
$$= 1 - 20/132$$
$$= 28/33 = .848$$
  d. $P(G_1 \text{ or } G_2) = 1 - P(\text{not } G)$
$$= 1 - [P(R_1 \text{ and } R_2) + P(R_1 \text{ and } Y_2) + P(Y_1 \text{ and } R_2)$$
$$+ P(Y_1 \text{ and } Y_2)]$$
$$= 1 - [(3/12 \times 2/11) + (3/12 \times 5/11) + (5/12 \times 3/11)$$
$$+ (5/12 \times 4/11)]$$
$$= 1 - [6/132 + 15/132 + 15/132 + 20/132]$$
$$= 1 - 56/132$$
$$= 19/33 = .57$$
  e. $P(\text{same color}) = P(R_1 \text{ and } R_2) + P(G_1 \text{ and } G_2) + P(Y_1 \text{ and } Y_2)$
$$= (3/12 \times 2/11) + (4/12 \times 3/11) + (5/12 \times 4/11)$$
$$= 6/132 + 12/132 + 20/132$$
$$= 19/66 = .288$$
15. $P(\text{two on same day}) = 1 - P(\text{separate days})$
$$= 1 - (7/7 \times 6/7 \times 5/7 \times 4/7)$$
$$= 1 - 840/2401$$
$$= 1561/2401 = .65$$

Exercise 9.3

I.

  1. Since the water in the lake may not be circulating, the algae content of the water at one end may not be representative of the whole lake. Thus, the sample might be biased.
  5. Since the calls were placed at a time when most people are working, and since most of the people with 9-to-5 jobs are not avid soap opera viewers, the sample is probably biased.
 10. The problem concerns the meaning of "average." If the average is a mean, most of the toys could be over $15, and a few very cheap toys could bring the average down to $15. If the average is a mode, there might be a few toys priced at $15, and all the other toys might have varying prices exceeding $15. Only if the average is a median can one be assured that half the toys are $15 or less.
 15. Since the axes are not scaled, there is no way of knowing how many bugs are killed with one application or how long the spray remains potent. Furthermore, no information is given on the conditions under which these results are supposed to be obtained.
 20. The goal was to increase the productivity 500 units per week. The actual increase was 200 units per week. Thus, the effort of the efficiency expert was only 40 percent successful.

GLOSSARY/INDEX

Biconditional sign: The symbol consisting of three short parallel lines that means "if and only if," 208, 212

Biconditional statements, 212, 220

Bimodal curves, 392–393

Boole, George, 152

Boolean standpoint (modern standpoint), 152–153, 155, 159, 175–176, 185–186, 190, 192–193; in predicate logic, 299–302

"Both . . . not," 213

Bound variable: A variable that is bound by a quantifier, 301

Braces, 212

Brackets, 212, 337

Broad definitions, 65

Campbell, Stephen K., 397n

Cantril, Albert H., 385n

Carroll, Lewis, 205

Categorical proposition: A proposition that relates two classes (or categories), 130–170; in class notation, 133; letter names of, 134; standard form, 131–132

Categorical syllogism: A syllogism in which all three statements are categorical propositions, 172–206; exceptive propositions, 198–199; figure of, 174–177; form of, 175; mood of, 174–177; in ordinary language, 197–199; reconstruction of, from mood and figure, 176–177; reducing number of terms in, 194–196; rules for, 189–193; standard form of, 173–174; Venn diagrams for, 179–186, 195–196

Causal inference: An inductive inference that proceeds from knowledge of a cause to a claim about the effect, or from knowledge of an effect to a claim about the cause, 23

Causality, 348–363

Change of quantifier rule: A rule of inference that allows one kind of quantifier to be replaced by another, provided that certain negation signs are deleted or introduced, 318–321; with overlapping quantifiers, 339, 342

Circular definitions, 65–66

Circular reasoning. *See* Begging the question

Classical theory of probability: The theory according to which probabilities are computed *a priori* by dividing the number of favorable outcomes by the number of possible outcomes, 368–370, 372

Class statement, 99–101

Cogent argument: An inductive argument that is strong and has true premises, 31–32

Coherence. *See* Internal coherence

Collective predication: An attribute is predicated collectively when it is assigned to a class as a whole, 99–101

Common names, 44

Commutativity: A valid rule of inference that provides for the rearrangement of conjunctions and disjunctions, 268–272

Complex question: A fallacy that occurs when a single question that is really two or more questions is asked, and a single answer is applied to both questions, 91–93

Composition: A fallacy that occurs when the conclusion of an argument depends on the erroneous transference of a characteristic from the parts of something onto the whole, 98–100

Compound statement: A statement that contains at least one atomic statement as a component, 208; truth values of, 220–222

Conclusion: The statement in an argument that is intended to follow from the evidence presented in the premises, 2; tautologous, 244, 290–291

Conclusion indicator: A word that provides a clue to identifying a conclusion, 3

Conditional proof, 283–286; incorrect use of, 286; indirect proof and, 290–292; in predicate logic, 323–325, 327, 340–341; to prove logical truths, 294–295

Conditional sign: The horseshoe symbol that means "if . . . then," 208, 210

Conditional statement: An "if . . . then" statement, 12–15; inferences and, 13–15; in propositional logic, 208–211, 218, 220; translating into categorical propositions, 166–168

Conjunct: A component in a conjunctive statement, 209

Conjunction: A valid rule of inference: "p / q // p and q," 260–263

Conjunction sign: The dot symbol that means "and," 208–209

Conjunctive statements, 209, 217, 220

Connectives: Symbols used to connect or negate atomic propositions in propositional logic, 207–208

Connotation: Intensional meaning or intension, 45–48

Connotative definition. *See* Intensional definition

Consequent: The component of a conditional statement immediately following the word "then"; the component of a conditional statement that is not the antecedent, 12–13, 209

Constant. *See* Individual constant

Constructive dilemma: A valid argument form / rule of inference: "If p then q, and if r then s / p or r // q or s," 235, 237–239, 260–262

Context, definitions and, 67

Contingent statement: A statement that is neither necessarily true nor necessarily false, 228–229

Contradictory premises, 244, 263

Contradictory statements: Statements that necessarily have opposite truth values, 138–140, 229–230

Contraposition: An operation that consists in switching and negating the subject and predicate terms in a standard form categorical proposition, 146–149; by limitation, 144n; proof of, 160–161; to reduce number of terms in syllogism, 195–196

Contrapositive, 146, 149

Contrary: The relation by which two statements are necessarily not both true, 138–140

Conventional connotation: The intensional meaning conventionally agreed upon by the members of the community that speak the language in question, 46

Converse, 143, 148

Converse accident. *See* Hasty generalization

Conversion: An operation that consists in switching the subject and predicate terms in a standard form categorical proposition, 143–144,

Exclusive disjunction, 209–210

Exclusive premises, 190

Exclusive propositions, 168–169, 303

Exhortation: A kind of nonargument composed of statements that urge the reader or listener to do a certain thing, 11

Existential fallacy: (1) A formal fallacy that occurs when the traditional square of opposition is used in conjunction with propositions that make assertions about nonexistent things, 153. (2) A formal fallacy that occurs when the premises of a categorical syllogism are universal and the conclusion is particular, 192–193

Existential generalization: A rule of inference that introduces existential quantifiers, 309–310, 313ff; invalid applications of, 315–316, 343

Existential instantiation: A rule of inference that removes existential quantifiers, 310ff; invalid applications of, 315–316; restrictions on, 311–313

Existential names, 311–313

Existential quantifier: The quantifier used to translate particular statements in predicate logic, 301ff

Existential standpoint, 175–176, 185–186, 193

Explanandum: The component of an explanation that describes the event or phenomenon to be explained, 15–16

Explanans: The component of an explanation that explains the event indicated by the explanandum, 15–16

Explanation: A statement or group of statements intended to shed light on some event, 15–17

Exportation: A valid rule of inference that allows conditional statements having conjunctive antecedents to be replaced with conditional statements having conditional consequents, and vice versa, 276–277

Extensional definition: A definition that assigns a meaning to a term by indicating the members of the class that the term denotes, 56–59

Extensional meaning (extension): The members of the class that a term denotes, 45–48

External consistency: The extent to which a hypothesis agrees with other, well-confirmed hypotheses, 416–417

Fallacies of ambiguity: A group of informal fallacies that occur because of an ambiguity in the premises or conclusion, 88–89, 93–98

Fallacies of grammatical analogy: A group of informal fallacies that occur because of a grammatical similarity to other arguments that are nonfallacious, 89, 98–102

Fallacies of presumption: A group of informal fallacies that occur when the premises of an argument presume what they purport to prove, 88–93, 108, 113–116

Fallacies of relevance: A group of informal fallacies that occur because the conclusion of an argument is irrelevant to the premises, 72–85, 108–113, 116–118

Fallacy: A defect in an argument arising from some source other than merely false premises, 70–71. *See also* Formal fallacy; Informal fallacy

False analogy: A fallacy that occurs when the conclusion of an argument depends on an analogy (or similarity) that is not strong enough to support the conclusion, 108–111

False cause: A fallacy that occurs when the conclusion of an argument depends on some imagined causal connection that does not really exist, 82–84

"Few," "a few," 166

Figurative definitions, 66

Figure: An attribute of a categorical syllogism that specifies the location of the middle term, 174–177

Formal fallacy: A fallacy that can be identified through mere inspection of the form or structure of an argument, 70–71. *See also* specific fallacies

Form of an argument, 36–42

Form of a categorical syllogism, 173–175

"For this reason," 4

Free variable: A variable that is not bound by a quantifier, 301

Fruitfulness: The extent to which a hypothesis suggests new ideas for future analysis and confirmation, 417

Galilei, Galileo, 409, 413

Galle, Johann, 408, 414

Gallup poll, 385

General conjunction rule: In probability theory, a rule for computing the probability of two events occurring together whether or not the events are independent, 373–374, 376–378

General disjunction rule: In probability theory, a rule for computing the probability of either of two events whether or not they are mutually exclusive, 375–377

General statement: A statement that makes a claim about all the members of a class, 24, 99–101

Generalization. *See* Existential generalization; Inductive generalization; Universal generalization

Genus, 61–62

Goclenian sorites, 202n

Graphs, 393–395

Grasping a dilemma by the horns, 237–238

Hasty generalization: A fallacy that occurs when a general conclusion is drawn from atypical specific cases, 81–82, 99–100

Helmont, Jan Baptista Van, 410

Horns of a dilemma, 237–238

Huff, Darrell, 392n

Hypotheses: Conjectures offered as possible solutions to a problem, 403–418; empirical, 413–414; proof of, 413–414; tentative acceptance of, 414–417; theoretical, 413–414

Hypothetical reasoning: The reasoning process used to produce hypotheses, 403–418

Hypothetical syllogism: A syllogism having a conditional statement for one or both of its premises, 232. *See also* Mixed hypothetical syllogism; Pure hypothetical syllogism

I proposition: A categorical proposition having the form "some S are P," 134ff

Ignoratio elenchi. See Missing the point

Illicit contraposition: A formal fallacy that occurs when the conclusion of an argument depends on the contraposition of an **E** or **I** statement, 147

Illicit conversion: A formal fallacy that occurs when the conclusion of an argument depends on the conversion of an **A** or **O** statement, 144

Modern square of opposition (*continued*)
contains only the contradictory relation, 151–153, 157–158

Modus ponens: A valid form/rule of inference: "If *p* then *q* / *p* // *q*," 233–234, 239, 251–256

Modus tollens: A valid argument form/rule of inference: "If *p* then *q* / not *q* // not *p*," 233–234, 239, 251–256

Molecular statement, 208; truth value of, 220–222

Mood: An attribute of a categorical syllogism that specifies the kind of statements (**A, E, I, O**) that make it up, 174–177

Names, 44; existential, 311–313

Narrow definitions, 65

Natural deduction: A procedure by which the conclusion of an argument is derived from the premises through the use of rules of inference, 251; in predicate logic, 307–347; in propositional logic, 251–296

Necessary condition: The condition represented by the consequent in a conditional statement, 211, 234–235, 349ff

Needham, John, 411, 413, 415

Negated statements, 209, 216–217, 220, 236

Negation rule: A rule for computing the probability of an event from the probability of the event *not* happening, 377–378

Negation sign: The tilde symbol that means "not," 208–209, 213

Negative definitions, 66

Negative statement: A statement that denies class membership, 133–134

"Neither . . . nor," 213–214

Neptune, discovery of, 407–408, 413–415

Newton, Isaac, 410, 415, 417

Newton's second law, 54

Nonarguments, typical kinds of, 11–17

Non causa pro causa, 83

"None but," 168, 303

Nonstandard quantifiers, 166

Nonstandard verbs, translation of, 163

Normal probability distribution: A distribution of random phenomena having the shape of a bell, 389–393

"Not both," 213

"Not either," 213–214

O proposition: A categorical proposition having the form "Some *S* are not *P*," 134ff

Obscure definitions, 66

Obverse, 145, 148

Obversion: An operation that consists in changing the quality and negating the predicate of a standard form categorical proposition, 144–149, 195; proof of, 160

"Only," 168–169, 303

Operational definition: A definition that assigns a meaning to a word by specifying experimental procedures that determine whether or not the word applies to a certain thing, 60–61

Ostensive definition. *See* Demonstrative definition

Overlapping quantifiers: Quantifiers that lie within the scope of one another, 335–343

Parameter: A phrase that, when introduced into a statement, affects the form but not the meaning, 164, 197–198

Parentheses, 212

Particular statement: A statement that makes a claim about one or more (but not all) members of a class, 24, 133–134; in predicate logic, 301ff; in a restricted universe, 330–331

Pascal, Blaise, 409–410

Pasteur, Louis, 411–413, 415–416

Percentages, 396–399

Perier, F., 409–410

Persuasive definition: A definition intended to engender a favorable or unfavorable attitude toward what is denoted by the definiendum, 54–55, 59, 62

Petitio principii. See Begging the question

Pictogram: A diagram that compares two situations through drawings that differ either in size or number, 395–396

Piece of advice: A kind of nonargument composed of statements that recommend something to the reader or listener, 11

Plato, 49

Post hoc ergo propter hoc, 83

Precising definition: A definition intended to reduce the vagueness of a word, 52–53, 62

Predicate logic: A kind of logic that combines the symbolism of propositional logic with symbols used to translate predicates, 297–347

Predicate symbol: An upper case letter used to translate a predicate, 298

Predicate term: In a standard form categorical proposition, the term that comes immediately after the copula, 130–132

Predication. *See* Collective predication; Distributive predication

Prediction: An inductive argument that proceeds from knowledge of some event in the relative past to a claim about some other event in the relative future, 22

Premise: A statement in an argument that sets forth evidence, 2; contradictory, 244, 263; exclusive, 190

Premise indicator: A word that provides a clue to identifying a premise, 3

Principle of indifference: In the classical theory of probability, the principle that the various possible outcomes are equally probable, 369

Probability calculus: A set of rules for computing the probability of compound events from the probabilities of simple events, 371–379

Probability of a necessary event, 371–372

Probability of an impossible event, 371–372

Pronouns, translation of, 164

Proper names, 44

Proposition: The information content of a statement, 5; exceptive, 198–199; exclusive, 168–169, 303; statements and, 5–6. *See also* Categorical proposition

Propositional logic: A kind of logic in which the fundamental components are whole statements or propositions, 207–296

Proving invalidity, 36–42; in predicate logic, 329–333

Psychological factors affecting a sample, 385–387

Ptolemy, 414

Pure hypothetical syllogism: A valid argument form/rule of inference: "If *p* then *q* / If *q* then *r* // If *p* then *r*," 232–233, 239, 251–256

Quality: The attribute of a categorical proposition by which it is either affirmative or negative, 132–134

Substitution instance: An argument or statement that has the same form as a given argument form or statement form; of an argument form, 38–42, 232–235; of a statement form, 217

Sufficient and necessary condition, 212, 349ff

Sufficient condition: The condition represented by the antecedent in a conditional statement, 211, 234–235, 349ff

Suppressed evidence: A fallacy that occurs when the arguer ignores relevant evidence that would tend to undermine the premises of an otherwise good argument, 113–116, 398

Suppressed premise, 41

Syllogism: A deductive argument consisting of two premises and one conclusion, 172. *See also* Categorical syllogism; Disjunctive syllogism; Mixed hypothetical syllogism; Pure hypothetical syllogism

Synonymous definition: A definition in which the definiens is a single word that connotes the same attributes as the definiendum, 59–60

Tautologous conclusion, 244, 290–291

Tautology: (1) A statement that is necessarily true, 228; proving 294–295. (2) A rule of inference that eliminates redundancy in conjunctions and disjunctions, 276–277, 341

Term: A word or group of words that can serve as the subject of a statement, 44

Terms without nouns, translation of, 163

"The only," 169

Theoretical definition: A definition that provides a theoretical picture or characterization of the entity or entities denoted by the definiendum, 53–54, 59, 62

Theoretical hypotheses: Hypotheses that concern how something should be conceptualized, 413–414

"Thus," 3, 12, 17

Torricelli, Evangelista, 409, 413–417

Traditional square of opposition: A diagram that exhibits the necessary relations that prevail between the four kinds of standard form categorical propositions, 137–140, 147–148, 151–152, 158–159

Transposition: A valid rule of inference that allows the antecedent and consequent of a conditional statement to switch places if and only if both are negated, 167, 276–278

Truth. *See* Logical truth

Truth function: A compound statement is a truth function of its components if its truth value is determined by the truth value of the components, 216–222

Truth functional equivalence: Having the same truth value, 212, 230

Truth table: An arrangement of truth values that shows how the truth value of a molecular proposition varies depending on the truth value of its atomic components, 225; for propositions, 225–230; for arguments, 242–244, 247–250

Truth value: The attribute by which a statement is either true or false, 32; of molecular statements, 220–222; undetermined, 139–140, 144, 147–149

Tu quoque: A variety of the argument against the person fallacy that occurs when an arguer shifts the burden of guilt onto a second arguer for the purpose of discrediting his or her argument, 76–77

"Two wrongs make a right" fallacy, 77

Undetermined truth value: A condition that exists when a certain statement is not necessarily either true or false, given the truth value of some related statement, 139–140, 144, 147–149

Undistributed middle, 189–190

Unexpressed quantifiers, 165

Universal generalization: A rule of inference that introduces universal quantifiers, 308–309, 313ff; invalid applications of, 315–316, 343; restrictions on, 324–327, 339–340

Universal instantiation: A valid rule of inference that removes universal quantifiers, 307–310, 313ff; invalid applications of, 315–316, 342

Universal quantifier: In predicate logic, the quantifier used to translate universal statements, 299–300

Universal statement: A statement that makes an assertion about every member of its subject class, 133–134; in predicate logic, 299–301, 303ff; in a restricted universe, 330–331

"Unless," 167–168, 210

Use of a word, 45

Vague definitions, 66–67

Vagueness: Lack of clarity or distinctness, 52–53

Valid argument forms, 231–235, 239. *See also* Rules of inference; Valid syllogistic forms

Valid deductive argument: An argument in which the conclusion follows necessarily from the premises, 28–29. *See also* Invalidity

Validity, form of an argument and, 36

Valid syllogistic forms, 175–176

Variable, bound, 301; free, 301; individual, 299ff; statement, 217

Variance: In statistics, a measure of how far the data vary from the mean value, 391

Venn, John, 154

Venn diagram: A diagram consisting of two or more circles used to represent the information content of categorical propositions, 154–161; for categorical syllogisms, 179–186, 195–196; for particular statements in predicate logic, 302; for sorites, 202; for universal statements in predicate logic, 300

Viviani, Vincenzo, 409

Warning: A kind of nonargument composed of statements that caution the reader or listener against the occurrence of a certain event, 11

Weak inductive argument: An argument in which the conclusion does not follow probably from the premises even though it is intended to, 30–31

CONDITIONAL AND INDIRECT PROOF

$$
\begin{array}{ll}
\text{—} & \\
\text{—} & \\
\text{—} & / \; q \supset r \\
q & \text{CP} \\
\underline{} & \\
\text{—} & \\
\text{—} & \\
r & \\
q \supset r & \text{CP}
\end{array}
\qquad
\begin{array}{ll}
\text{—} & \\
\text{—} & \\
\text{—} & / \; {\sim} q \\
q & \text{IP} \\
\underline{} & \\
\text{—} & \\
{\sim} q & \\
q \cdot {\sim} q & \\
{\sim} q & \text{IP}
\end{array}
$$

RULES FOR REMOVING AND INTRODUCING QUANTIFIERS

($a, b, c, \dots u, v, w$ = individual constants;
x, y, z = individual variables)

1. Universal instantiation (UI)

$$\frac{(x)\mathscr{F}x}{\mathscr{F}y} \qquad\qquad \frac{(x)\mathscr{F}x}{\mathscr{F}a}$$

2. Universal generalization (UG)

$$\frac{\mathscr{F}y}{(x)\mathscr{F}x} \qquad \begin{array}{c}not\\allowed:\end{array} \qquad \frac{\mathscr{F}a}{(x)\mathscr{F}x}$$

Restrictions:
(conditional and indirect proof)

(1) UG must not be used within the scope of an indented sequence if the instantial variable occurs free in the first line of that sequence.

(overlapping quantifiers)

(2) UG must not be used if $\mathscr{F}y$ contains an existential name and y is free in the line where that name is introduced.

3. Existential instantiation (EI)

$$\frac{(\exists x)\mathscr{F}x}{\mathscr{F}a} \qquad \begin{array}{c}not\\allowed:\end{array} \qquad \frac{(\exists x)\mathscr{F}x}{\mathscr{F}y}$$

Restriction: The existential name a must be a new name that has not occurred earlier in the proof.

4. Existential generalization (EG)

$$\frac{\mathscr{F}a}{(\exists x)\mathscr{F}x} \qquad\qquad \frac{\mathscr{F}y}{(\exists x)\mathscr{F}x}$$

CHANGE OF QUANTIFIER RULES

$$
\begin{array}{ll}
(x)\mathscr{F}x \equiv {\sim}(\exists x){\sim}\mathscr{F}x & \qquad (\exists x)\mathscr{F}x \equiv {\sim}(x){\sim}\mathscr{F}x \\
{\sim}(x)\mathscr{F}x \equiv (\exists x){\sim}\mathscr{F}x & \qquad {\sim}(\exists x)\mathscr{F}x \equiv (x){\sim}\mathscr{F}x
\end{array}
$$